To. Fiona & John
        With love on your ~~~~~~
        May you have many
        gourmet meals with this !!
            Xmas 1988.

CREATIVE COOKS' FAMILY COOKBOOK

CREATIVE COOKS' FAMILY COOKBOOK

OCTOPUS BOOKS

First published in this format 1987 by
Octopus Books Limited
59 Grosvenor Street
London W1

Under license from
Eaglemoss Publications Limited
7 Cromwell Road
London SW7

© Kluwerpers/Utrecht, Holland 1981,
1982, 1983, 1984
© Eaglemoss Limited 1985

ISBN 0 7064 2855 2

Printed in Hong Kong

CONTENTS

INTRODUCTION

The *Creative Cooks' Family Cookbook* will help you understand and practise new methods of cookery and show you how to combine flavours and textures in exciting ways. With clear and precise instructions it leads you through all the stages of recipe preparation to presenting the finished dish. You will also learn everything you need to know about different cooking techniques, interesting ingredients, well-balanced menus, kitchen tools and equipment.

The book is divided into six sections, the first of which concentrates on explaining the basic methods and techniques. If pastry-making is a weakness, then turn to this chapter for step-by-step guidance with many extra tips to ensure perfect results. Other sections, such as Main Meals and Snacks, make interesting use of ingredients to provide dishes suitable for family meals and every occasion. International Cuisine takes you on a wonderful trip around the world sampling the specialities of many nations.

Each recipe gives the times for preparation and cooking which are a guideline when planning menus. However, preparation times can only be approximate as different cooks work at different speeds.

Every recipe in the book has been tested, and both metric and imperial measures are given. It is important to follow one set or the other as they are not interchangeable within a recipe.

The notes below explain the symbols used throughout.

Hundreds of useful hints and tips from experienced cooks and chefs are given throughout, indicated by this symbol. Many of these 'tricks of the trade' will save you time, money and effort.

At-a-glance menu planner
To help you create well-balanced meals that are satisfying but not over-rich, every recipe has a star rating:

☆☆☆ indicates a rich dish

☆☆ indicates a moderate dish

☆ indicates a light dish

○ virtually fat-free

The richness of a dish is based on its fat content – be it butter, oil, cream or the fat content of meat. Often, this fat content is not obvious, as in a cake or a casserole.

❋ **To freeze:** Where appropriate, a recipe indicates whether the dish is suitable for freezing so, once again, you can plan ahead.

Measures The metric quantities are based in general on the 1oz:25g measure, but may vary with the recipe.
All spoon measures are level, unless otherwise stated. Where teaspoons are given, a British Standard 5 millimetre measure has been used. Where tablespoons are given, a British Standard 15 millimetre measure has been used.

TECHNIQUES

For successful cooking it is important to understand the technique of the cooking method used. Magical changes take place when heat is applied to food. The texture changes, the colour alters, bubbling and sizzling are heard and aromas fill the air. Cooking is a science and an art which makes our food more interesting, palatable and digestable.

It is important to choose the most appropriate cooking method for the ingredients being used. This section outlines some of the simpler methods, emphasising the basic principles and giving easy-to-follow instructions.

A part of the secret of success is knowing how to make the most of your kitchen equipment. For example, a steamer is very easy to use and gives an excellent result, as it allows the steam to circulate around the food. Steaming is a particularly suitable method to use for cooking fish, vegetables and rice, as well as the traditional favourite, steamed pudding.

A wok is an essential item of equipment for stir-frying, as the shape of the vessel keeps a minimum amount of oil hot and the sloping sides make it easier to keep the food moving. There is even an electric version which enables the food to be cooked at the table.

Poaching is a gentle, moist form of cooking, which can be done on the hob or in the oven. The liquid is kept under boiling point so that it just 'shivers'. This is an excellent method for delicate ingredients, such as whole fish, shellfish and fruit.

Stewing is a popular form of moist cooking, which can be used for basic everyday food or something really substantial. Casseroles and stews are particularly good for tougher cuts of meat which need long, slow cooking, or dishes where the flavours require time to be absorbed by the food.

Roasting is a dry method of cooking, which is a form of baking with a little added fat. It is ideal for larger pieces of meat and poultry. The success of the traditional British roast depends on timing and organisation.

Sauces are very important in good cooking as they can transform and extend foods such as meat, vegetables and plain puddings. Dressings, too, can make a salad come to life. Instructions and tips in this section will help you to master a range of sauces and dressings as well as other basic techniques.

● The following pages describe many different kinds of kitchen equipment – from the best knife for the job to handling a wok, food processor, fish kettle or steamer. Throughout, the *Techniques* Chapters show you how to use many of the basic items, and also less familiar ones.

● The simple techniques, such as poaching and steaming, have been given prominence: nowadays it is recognized that they help maintain the nutritional value of food – and lightly poached dishes go well with subtle sauces.

Poaching

Poaching is gentle simmering in a liquid, a cooking method that can be adapted to suit a surprising variety of foods. The temperature is sufficiently high to cook the food quickly yet gentle enough to conserve most of its flavour. This fact alone makes poaching a favourite technique with today's top chefs. It is easy to master, it preserves the nutrients in food and it is also economical: the poaching liquid itself—water, wine, milk or stock depending on the food being cooked—often forms the basis of a sauce to serve with the finished dish.

Apart from the need to choose good quality raw materials, the only essential step to success is to control the temperature of the poaching liquid. Always keep it below boiling point so that the food cooks indirectly, in heat transferred through the barely moving liquid. The protein in egg whites, for instance, actually begins to set at around 150F (70C). Boiling over-cooks it and turns it rubbery as well as distorting its shape. And this rule applies to anything you poach: fish, fruit, meat, fresh pasta and gnocchi, as well as eggs. The secret is to poach food just enough to make it tender but to ensure it still retains its shape.

Most foods are suitable for poaching. For fish, shellfish and delicate offal, such as sweetbreads, it is one of the most perfect cooking methods, for maximum moisture is retained and you can use the fish liquid as the basis of seafood soup. Fruits such as apples and pears or stone fruits, such as apricots, plums or peaches, will disintegrate if rapidly boiled, but when poached they will hold their shape and are deliciously tender. Foods such as poultry, meat and game are equally suitable for poaching, and well worthwhile for the extra succulence.

The poaching liquid

The simplest poaching liquid is water, lightly seasoned with a little salt. It is suitable for eggs, certain fish and shellfish, and discarded after use. Other poaching liquids are made by adding flavourings such as herbs and aromatic vegetables (onion, shallot, leek or carrot) to the basic liquid. These enhance the flavour of the food as it cooks. If the liquid is boiled to

reduce it it concentrates the flavour, and also provides a flavourful base for the final sauce. Choose appropriate herbs and vegetables, ones that complement rather than mask the natural flavour of the food: the following recipes have been chosen to give you a very good idea of combinations to use.

Court bouillon

The standard poaching liquid for fish is a delicately flavoured stock made by simmering vegetables in water to make what is called a court bouillon. Small whole fish such as trout or mackerel, or fish steaks and fillets are then lowered into the simmering, ready-flavoured liquid to poach for the required time. With larger, whole fish such as salmon, sea trout or turbot, it's best to start them off in a court bouillon that has been allowed to get cold, otherwise the surface flesh will be cooked before the inside is done.

Court bouillon is made from vegetables such as onion or shallot, carrot and herbs such as parsley and bay—all

The poaching liquid

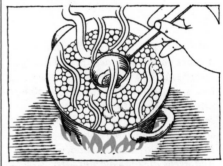

Boiling liquid is too hot for a gentle cooking method such as poaching; bubbling just breaks up the food.

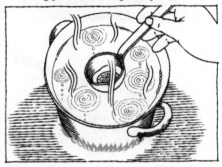

Turn down the heat to maintain a gentle simmer where the surface of the liquid barely moves. Only a few small bubbles should be visible, rising from the base of the pan to the surface of the liquid.

aromatic enough to lend flavour to any fish without overwhelming its delicacy. As the following recipes show, many subtle and delicious variations are possible, both in the vegetables used and in the liquid itself. Fish particularly benefit from the addition of an acidic liquid such as white wine, or a little lemon juice. Both these firm up the delicate flesh and help preserve its colour.

For meat and poultry

Meat and poultry are poached in liquid which has flavouring vegetables added at the start of cooking. By the time the food is tender, the liquid, too, will be permeated with flavour, making a light stock that can be strained and stored or used immediately to make a sauce.

Poaching in stock or syrup

Homemade stock makes a wonderful poaching medium. Fish stock is easily and rapidly made (page 106) from the trimmings left over from filleting, particularly the gelatinous bones from fish such as turbot, sole or plaice. Simply simmer the trimmings with a few vegetables and herbs then strain and freeze the cooled stock until you need it. You can then add some of this stock to make up some–or all–of the poaching liquid. For meat and poultry dishes, use meat or chicken stock. Offal can be poached in either chicken or veal stock. Fruits, such as peaches, are usually cooked in a light syrup. This is made by boiling water and sugar, and the fruit is added to it with flavourings such as lemon or orange peel, spices, wine or spirits.

The poaching pan

For foods that require little space such as eggs, scallops, oysters or whole fruits, or for small pieces of

Fish such as the salmon shown here in a court bouillon is ideal for poaching, either whole in a fish kettle, or as fillets or steaks. You can poach almost any food: shellfish such as oysters or scallops, delicate offal such as sweetbreads, or whole chicken, in a liquid flavoured with onion, carrot and herbs all take on a greater succulence with poaching. Fruits, ranging from the peaches shown here, to plums, apricots, cherries, apples or pears, are equally tasty poached.

food, use a saucepan or deep frying-pan for poaching. Small whole fish can also be cooked in a relatively small saucepan if you coil the fish around the inside of the pan.

To keep whole fish or fillets flat, or to poach larger fish, you must use a pan that will accommodate the fish comfortably. Either use a specially designed pan known as a fish kettle (shown below), or improvise by using a rectangular roasting tin and covering it with a lid of foil. True fish kettles have removable racks which fit into the bottom for the purpose of lifting whole fish in and out of the poaching liquid without breaking. If you don't have a fish kettle, you can make a 'rack' for an ordinary pan or roasting tin out of foil.

Fold 2 or 3 thicknesses of foil into a long rectangle and arrange this in the bottom of the pan with the ends projecting up and over the sides by a couple of inches (6cm). The two projecting ends can then be used to lift out the food when cooked.

The amount of liquid

Choose a pan that is big enough to accommodate the food comfortably. Apart from fruit where you can pack it loosely to come slightly more than halfway up the pan, arrange the food in a single layer. If you are going to reduce the liquid later to make a sauce, it makes sense to use as little as possible. You must, however, make sure there's enough to at least half-cover the food, then poach it covered with a lid so that it cooks partly in the steam. To keep large items like a whole chicken moist during longer cooking, add liquid to barely cover.

Keep the goodness in
Because poaching is a remarkably quick as well as a gentle cooking method, all the food's natural nutrients and flavour are preserved and it can be regarded as one of the healthiest cooking methods. The fact that the food cooks in liquid, flavoured appropriately, without any added fat, also adds to its healthy appeal. Any water-soluble vitamins that do leach out into the cooking liquid can be recaptured when you make the final sauce to accompany the dish.

The ideal pan

Whole small fish, steaks and fillets can be poached in any pan broad enough to hold them flat; a rectangular roasting pan is ideal. Use a rectangular sheet of foil as a lid.

Special pans such as fish kettles are only necessary if you intend to poach large fish whole.

Note: If the pan you are using is too long to fit on to a hotplate, you can poach in the oven instead. Simply cover the pan and place it in an oven preheated to 180C (350F) or Gas 4 for the same amount of time.

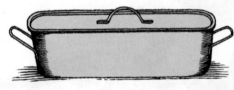

Two common forms of fish kettle, one long and narrow, the other an oval turbotière. Both shapes will accommodate large fish such as whole turbot or salmon. All fish kettles have removable racks so that the fish can be lifted in and out without breaking.

Poached Sole with White Wine Sauce

This simple fish dish produces tender sole fillets served with a delicious sauce made from the poaching liquid. Serve it with creamed potatoes or whole new potatoes and baby carrots or courgettes.

Serves 4
Preparation and cooking time:
   1 hour 10 minutes

---

2 sole (about 1lb (500g) each) cleaned

Poaching liquid:
¾ pint (450ml) white wine
¾ pint (450ml) water
3 carrots, sliced
1 tablespoon chopped onion
6 parsley stalks, chopped
small piece of lemon peel
6 white peppercorns, crushed

Sauce:
1oz (25g) butter
3 tablespoons flour
1 egg yolk
3 tablespoons single cream
salt

Bring the white wine and water to the boil in a pan that is large enough to hold the fish.

☐ Add the carrot, onion, parsley, lemon peel and the crushed peppercorns. Reduce the heat and simmer gently for 20 minutes. Strain the liquid, return to the pan and bring back to the boil.

☐ Gently lower both the sole into the boiling poaching liquid. Reduce the heat to a simmer. Cover and cook for 10 minutes until the fish are tender, then remove them with a fish slice. Drain on kitchen paper then transfer them to a heated plate and cover with foil to keep warm.

☐ Strain the poaching liquid, return it to the pan and boil rapidly until reduced to about half.

☐ In a saucepan, melt the butter over a medium heat. When the foam has subsided add the flour and stir it in well. Continue to cook, stirring continuously, for a minute or two without letting it brown.

☐ Remove it from the heat and stir in a little of the poaching liquid. Return to the heat, and cook, stirring, until all the liquid is added. Continue to cook the sauce for a further 2 to 3 minutes until smooth and glossy.

☐ In a small bowl mix together the egg yolk and cream. To prevent the egg yolk curdling, stir in 3 tablespoons of the hot sauce, then pour the egg yolk mixture (liaison) into the pan and stir. Immediately remove the pan from the heat and season the sauce to taste.

☐ To serve the dish, use a fish slice or a broad knife to lift off the upper fillets. Pull away and discard the backbone to release the two lower fillets.

☐ Arrange the fish on a warmed serving dish. Spoon a little sauce over each fillet and serve the rest separately in a warmed sauceboat.

☐ Garnish the dish with wedges of tomato or lemon, and sprigs of parsley and, if you like, a little chopped parsley or chives as a topping for the sauce.

Poached Turbot with Caper Sauce

You can serve this dish either with a Velouté Sauce garnished with capers, or with the 5-Minute Caper Sauce given on the next page.

Serves 4
Preparation: 10 minutes
Cooking time: about 50 minutes
   (Velouté), or about 40 minutes
   (5-Minute Caper Sauce)

---

4 turbot steaks each weighing about 6oz
   (175g)
salt

Poaching liquid:
¾ pint (450ml) dry white wine
¾ pint (450ml) water
6 parsley stalks, roughly chopped
1 tablespoon onion, finely chopped
6 white peppercorns, crushed

Rub the turbot steaks lightly with salt.

☐ Bring the wine and water to the boil in a pan or fish kettle. Add the parsley, onion and peppercorns.

Lower the turbot steaks into the hot liquid, reduce the heat to a simmer. Cover and cook the steaks until tender:
10-12 minutes for thin steaks,
12-14 minutes for thicker ones.
Follow the shorter time if serving the fish with Velouté Sauce.
☐ Lift the fish steaks from the poaching liquid and allow them to drain slightly over the pan. Remove the skin and as many bones as possible, being careful not to break up the steak. Place the fish on a heated serving plate. Cover and keep hot while you make the sauce.

Velouté Sauce with Capers

poaching liquid, strained and
    reduced to ¾ pint (450ml)
2oz (50g) butter
3 tablespoons flour
3 tablespoons single cream
1 egg yolk
3 tablespoons drained capers
1 tablespoon chives or parsley, finely
    chopped
salt and pepper

Use the reduced poaching liquid to make a Velouté Sauce (see page 50 for method). Add capers and herbs and season to taste.

☐ Spoon a little of the sauce on to each steak and serve the rest in a warmed sauceboat.

5-minute Caper Sauce

3 egg yolks
2 tablespoons poaching liquid
2 tablespoons white wine
1 tablespoon liquid from caper jar
3oz (75g) softened butter
1 tablespoon capers
1 tablespoon chives or parsley, finely
    chopped
salt and pepper

Whisk together the egg yolks, poaching liquid, white wine and caper liquid. Add the butter and continue whisking; the butter will separate into small pieces.
☐ Set the bowl over a pan of hot, but not boiling water. Over a low heat, whisk until the sauce begins to thicken.
☐ Remove from the heat. Stir in the capers and herbs. Season to taste.
☐ Either pour the sauce over the fish or serve it separately in a warmed sauceboat.

Varying the poaching liquid
If you like, omit the wine from any of these recipes and make up the amount of liquid with water. Add some extra flavourings to compensate: a handful of parsley stalks, a sliced carrot or two, a bay leaf and perhaps a squeeze of lemon juice.

Remember that if you have fish stock in the freezer you can use it to give a richer, fuller flavour to both fish and final sauce. Substitute the stock for some of the water and proceed as usual.

Carrots, onion and parsley are the usual flavourings to add to a court bouillon for delicate fish like sole. But you can include more strongly aromatic additions like leek or celery for other fish.

Poached turbot steaks served with a sharply contrasting caper sauce. You can garnish the dish with sprigs of parsley as here, and serve it with potatoes and courgettes mixed with dill pickles, or with a vegetable such as broccoli.

Stuffed Chicken with Grape Sauce

Chicken stays juicy and succulent when cooked by this method. A sauce made from the poaching liquid, garnished with grapes, complements the finished dish.

Serves 4
Preparation: 15 minutes
Cooking time: 1 hour
Sauce: 15 minutes

☆☆☆

---

3 rashers streaky bacon
2 chicken livers
7oz (200g) veal or pork, minced
1 tablespoon parsley, chopped
1 oz (25g) fresh breadcrumbs
1 egg
salt and white pepper
½ teaspoon paprika
1 oven-ready chicken
    weighing about 2lb (1kg)
1¾ pints (1 litre) chicken stock
¾ pint (450ml) Velouté Sauce
    (page 50)
3 tablespoons sherry
7oz (200g) white grapes

Mince or finely chop the bacon and chicken livers.

☐ Combine minced meats, parsley, breadcrumbs, egg and seasonings and knead well together. Stuff the chicken with the mixture.

Stuffed Chicken with Grape Sauce.

☐ Using kitchen string and a needle, sew up the vent as shown, then truss the bird.

☐ Choose a pan large enough to hold the chicken comfortably.

☐ Pour in the chicken stock and bring to the boil. Lower the chicken into the stock, reduce the heat to a simmer, and poach until tender; about an hour, depending on size.

☐ To test for doneness, pierce the thickest part of the flesh on the inside of the leg with a skewer.

☐ Transfer the cooked chicken to a warmed serving dish, closely cover with foil to keep warm.

☐ Strain the poaching liquid into a saucepan and boil vigorously to reduce it by about half.

☐ Peel the grapes and remove the pips with the eye of a large needle.

☐ Using the reduced poaching liquid, prepare the sauce as described on page 50. Stir the sherry, grapes and grape juice into the sauce.

☐ Remove the trussing strings, spoon some of the sauce over the chicken and serve the rest separately.

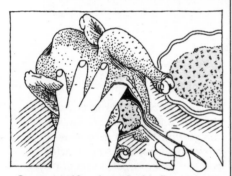

Spoon stuffing into the bird's cavity.

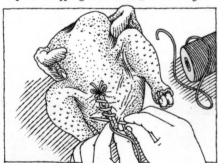

Use a needle and fine string to stitch up the vent.

Stuffing birds for poaching
Buy an untrussed chicken so that you can stuff it. To keep the bird in a compact shape for poaching, stuff it according to the method shown above. Poussin, duck, quail and pigeon can be stuffed and poached in the same way.

Chicken Breasts with Prawn Sauce

Chicken breast fillets, bought separately, make a quick and delicious supper dish. Try them with other sauces from the Sauce section.

Once cooked, prawns may toughen and lose their flavour if kept hot for too long. Stir them into the sauce just before serving and do not bring the sauce back to the boil.

Serves 4 ☆☆☆
Preparation: 5 minutes
Cooking time: 14 minutes
Sauce: 15 minutes

---

1 pint (600ml) chicken stock
12 parsley stalks, chopped
piece of leek, finely chopped
4 chicken breast fillets, together
weighing about 1½lb (700g)
¾ pint (450ml) Velouté Sauce,
thickened with egg yolk and cream
(pages 50 and 51)
4oz (100g) shrimps or prawns, peeled
salt and white pepper
2 large tomatoes, skinned
1 tablespoon chives, finely chopped

Bring the stock to the boil in the poaching pan.

☐ Add the parsley and leek and simmer for 5 minutes. Reduce the heat to a simmer, add the fillets and poach for 6-8 minutes, or until tender.

☐ Using a fish slice or a slotted spoon, remove them from the pan. Cover and keep warm.

☐ Strain the poaching liquid and use to prepare the Velouté Sauce. Stir in the peeled prawns or shrimps.

☐ Lightly season the chicken fillets with salt and pepper. Coat them with a little of the sauce and serve the rest separately in a sauce boat. If you like, garnish the dish with tomato wedges or a few chopped chives.

Variation: you can prepare a turkey breast, sliced in half lengthways, in the same way. If you like, leave out the prawns and add a little curry powder to the final sauce.

Pigeons in Mushroom Sauce

Pigeons are available all year. As they are so small they cook quickly so long as you choose young birds, known as squabs. Young birds have a fat breast with a supple breastbone, and a flexible beak.

Serves 4 ☆☆☆
Preparation time: 3 minutes
Cooking time: 15 minutes
Sauce: 20 minutes

---

4 pigeons each weighing about 8oz (225g)
1 pint (600ml) brown stock
¼ pint (150ml) red wine
3oz (75g) cold butter
2oz (50g) button mushrooms, sliced
3 tablespoons flour
2 tablespoons sherry
salt and pepper
squeeze of lemon juice

Choose a pan that accommodates the pigeons comfortably.

☐ Pour in the stock and wine and bring to the boil.

☐ Lower the pigeons into the hot liquid and reduce the heat to a simmer.

☐ Cover the pan and cook for 15-20 minutes or until the pigeons are tender.

☐ Transfer them to a warmed serving dish, cover and keep warm.

☐ Boil the stock to reduce it to about ¾ pint (450ml). Over a moderate heat melt a third of the butter in a sauté pan.

☐ Add the mushrooms to the pan just as the butter begins to change colour. Cook, stirring, until lightly coloured.

☐ Stir in the flour, then gradually stir in the reduced stock. Cook the sauce for 5-7 minutes until it thickens.

☐ Add sherry, seasoning and lemon juice to taste.

☐ Cut the remaining butter into small cubes. Whisk it piece by piece, into the sauce. Remove the pan from the heat and thoroughly whisk in the last addition. Spoon the sauce over the pigeons and serve.

Last steps in preparing the mushroom sauce

Whisk in the butter piece by piece.

Off the heat, thoroughly whisk in the last of the butter.

Poached Veal Medaillons

Poaching is quick and delicate, so it is only suitable for tender meat such as these boneless loin slices, called medaillons.

Serves 4 ☆☆

Preparation: 10 minutes
Cooking: 14 minutes
Sauce: 5 minutes

---

4 veal medaillons, each about 4oz (125g)

The poaching liquid:
1 pint (600ml) veal or chicken stock
12 parsley stalks, chopped
small piece of lemon peel
6 peppercorns, crushed

2 tablespoons chives, finely chopped
2 tablespoons parsley, finely chopped
½ teaspoon lemon peel, finely grated
white pepper
2oz (50g) cold butter cut into 4 pieces

Bring the stock to the boil in the poaching pan and add the parsley stalks, lemon peel, and peppercorns.
☐ Lower the pieces of veal into the pan. Bring the liquid to the boil, reduce the heat to a simmer. Poach until tender, about 8 minutes.
☐ Remove and drain the veal, blotting it dry with kitchen paper. Arrange the pieces on a warmed serving dish; cover and keep warm.
☐ Strain the stock into a small saucepan and boil vigorously until reduced to about ½ pint (300ml). Season to taste with salt and pepper.
☐ To make the sauce, remove the pan from the heat; whisk in butter one piece at a time. Whisk for a few minutes to make a smooth, thickened sauce. Stir in the chives, parsley and grated lemon peel, spoon the sauce over the veal slices and serve.

Sweetbreads, poached in stock, served with a herby Velouté Sauce.

Poached Sweetbreads with Herb Sauce

Blanched sweetbreads have a firmness and delicacy that makes them ideal for poaching. Serve with boiled rice and any seasonal vegetable.

Serves 4 ☆☆☆

Preparation: 10 minutes
Cooking time: 30 minutes
Sauce: 15 minutes

1lb (500g) calves' sweetbreads

The poaching liquid:
1½ pints (900ml) veal or
    chicken stock
4 parsley stalks, chopped
small sprig of fresh thyme, or a
    pinch of dried thyme
1 celery stick, chopped
2 small carrots, sliced
piece of leek, chopped
small piece of lemon peel

The sauce:
¾ pint (450ml) Velouté Sauce (page 50)
salt
1 tablespoon finely chopped chives
1 tablespoon finely chopped parsley
2 teaspoons finely chopped chervil

Soak the sweetbreads in several changes of cold water until the water is clear.
☐ Blanch them by bringing to the boil in a large pan of cold water with a squeeze of lemon juice. Simmer for 2-3 minutes, then plunge into cold water. Peel off membrane.
☐ Bring the stock to the boil in the poaching pan. Add the parsley stalks, thyme, celery, carrots, leek, and lemon peel.
☐ Lower the prepared sweetbreads into the stock, reduce the heat to a simmer and poach until tender.
☐ Transfer them to a warmed serving dish, cover and keep warm.
☐ Using some strained poaching liquid, make a Velouté Sauce.
☐ Remove the sweetbreads from the pan when the sauce is ready. Slice and arrange them on the serving dish. Stir the chopped fresh herbs (chives, parsley and chervil), into the sauce and spoon some over the sweetbreads. Serve rest separately.

Steaming

This is one of the most simple of cooking methods. Food is cooked not in water, but in the steam created by boiling water. Because the food remains clear of the water's agitation it is an excellent means of cooking delicate food, such as fish. Again because the food is not immersed, there is less leaching out of nutrients, flavour and colour – a distinct advantage for cooking vegetables, in particular. Granular foods such as rice and couscous benefit especially from steaming as the grains remain separate and dry, and the flavour is brought out fully.

Steaming is also an immensely practical cooking method in that more than one tier of ingredients can be handled by one hotplate or burner, giving not only a saving of fuel, but the facility for producing more food in a limited space.

Since food is not in direct contact with the water, steaming is usually a slower method of cooking, and prolonged steaming allows development of good full flavours – as in steamed puddings.

Suitable equipment

There are various types of pans designed for steaming but it is also easy to improvise your own.

Collapsible steaming baskets can be adjusted to stand in any medium-to-large saucepan and there are steamers with perforated bases which can be set one on top of another inside saucepans. Stacking bamboo baskets and other exotic equipment can be bought from specialist kitchen shops for cooking items such as rice, Chinese dumplings and couscous. For cooking fish, elongated pans with trivets are readily available.

In the absence of a steamer, try any of these easy make-do alternatives:

For rice or couscous: cook in a wire sieve or an ordinary colander lined with a piece of muslin. Use foil to cover it if without a suitable lid.

For vegetables: use a sieve, colander, or chip basket, without any muslin. For small vegetables like peas, line with muslin or foil and pierce with a skewer in several places.

For fish: use a deep, covered roasting tin. In the absence of a trivet, use the rack from a meat tin or grill pan, and stand it on empty enamel mugs, or cans, to keep it above the water.

For puddings: use any of suggested 'steamers', or simply crumple a large piece of foil in the bottom of the pan and set the pudding basin on that.

How to steam

Have on the burner or hot-plate a deep pan containing the required amount of water, or a stock flavoured with herbs and seasonings – which may be used later to make a sauce – at a good, rolling boil. Set the food on its trivet or in its container in the pan. Cover tightly and cook for the stated time. Remember to:

● keep the steamer tightly covered
● keep the water boiling rapidly
● keep the food clear of the water
● make sure the pan doesn't boil dry during long cooking, and top up with boiling water at intervals.

Modified steaming

Some vegetables, such as peas, which cook quickly can be wrapped in a foil parcel and dropped straight into boiling water. This method preserves most of the flavour and nutrients, and more than one vegetable can be cooked in one pan at a time.

Small cutlets or fillets of fish can be placed between two plates, or on a plate covered with foil and set over a pan of boiling water.

Steaming equipment

Collapsible steaming basket: place the closed basket on the bottom of the pan, feet down. Add water to come just up to the bottom of the basket – but not through it. Open the basket out and add the food. Cover the pan tightly to steam.

Tiered Steamers may be oval but are more commonly round. They are usually made of aluminium and designed to fit over standard saucepans.
Each tier can be used to cook a different item, perhaps several, each wrapped in a foil parcel, with potatoes boiling in the water below.

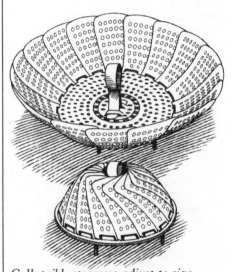

Collapsible steamers adjust to size.

Oval tiered steamers work well for fish.

Halibut is quite similar in texture and taste to turbot or, more economical, brill. Any one of these may easily be substituted in recipes for the others.

Halibut in a rich tarragon sauce: Duchesse potatoes and steamed broccoli florets make a perfect accompaniment.

Tarragon Halibut

Serves 4 ☆☆
Preparation and cooking: 35 minutes

---

4 halibut fillets, together about 1½lb (700g) skinned
7 fl oz (200ml) dry white wine
7 fl oz (200ml) water
a few parsley stalks, roughly chopped
3 lemon slices
a sprig of fresh tarragon
1 bay leaf, crumbled
1 teaspoon sea salt
6 black peppercorns
3oz (75g) butter
3 tablespoons flour
lemon wedges and parsley sprigs, to garnish

Rinse fillets and pat dry.
☐ Put the wine, water, parsley, lemon slices, tarragon, bay leaf, sea salt and peppercorns into a steamer. Bring to boil, then set the fish over.
☐ Cover pan tightly and steam for 7-10 minutes, or until the fish is opaque and firm. Transfer the fish to a serving dish and keep hot. Strain the cooking liquid and reserve.
☐ Melt 2oz (50g) of the butter in a heavy-based saucepan until it begins to bubble. Stir in the flour and cook, stirring, until foaming. Whisk in cooking liquid and boil. Cook, whisking constantly, until thick. Reduce heat and whisk in remaining butter.
☐ Garnish with lemon and parsley and serve.

Mackerel with Fennel

The mild aniseed flavour of fennel blends particularly well with the richness of mackerel. Serve with baked potatoes and mangetout peas.

Serves 4 ☆☆☆
Preparation and cooking: 40 minutes

8 mackerel fillets, together about 1½lb (700g)
7 fl oz (200ml) dry white wine
7 fl oz (200ml) water
1 lemon, sliced
1 teaspoon sea salt
6 black peppercorns

The sauce:
1 fennel bulb
salt and freshly ground black pepper
4 tablespoons double cream
4oz (125g) ice-cold butter, cubed

Rinse the fillets under cold running water and pat dry.

☐ Put the wine, water, lemon, salt and peppercorns into a steamer. Bring to the boil, then simmer gently for 5 minutes. Put the fish in a steamer basket and set it over the cooking liquid.

☐ Cover the pan tightly and steam the fish for 7-8 minutes or until the flesh is opaque and flakes easily. Remove the steamer from the heat and leave the fish in it to keep hot.

☐ Trim the fennel, reserving the tender fronds. Finely chop the bulb and cook it for 5 minutes in boiling, salted water until just tender.

☐ Purée it in a liquidizer or food processor and return it to the rinsed-out pan with the cream and 2 tablespoons of the cooking liquid. Bring it to the boil.

☐ Gradually whisk in the butter, one piece at a time, removing the pan from the heat for the final addition. Season to taste.

☐ Remove the skin from the fish and arrange on a hot serving dish. Spoon the sauce over, garnish with the fennel fronds and serve.

Variation: Give the fennel sauce an intriguing extra strength by adding 1 or 2 tablespoons of pernod with the cream.

Tuna in Red Butter Sauce

When you are lucky enough to find fresh tuna, try cooking it with this unusual red butter sauce.

Serves 4 ☆☆☆
Preparation: 15 minutes
Cooking: 30 minutes

4 tuna steaks or fillets, together about 1½lb (700g)
14 fl oz (400ml) water
6 bay leaves, crumbled
1 lemon, sliced
1 teaspoon sea salt
12 black peppercorns

The sauce:
2 tomatoes, skinned
1 teaspoon tomato purée
a pinch of dried thyme
2 tablespoons red wine
5oz (150g) unsalted butter
a squeeze of lemon juice
salt and freshly ground black pepper

Rinse the fish under cold running water and pat dry.

☐ Put the water, bay leaves, lemon, salt and peppercorns into a steamer. Bring it to the boil, then let it simmer for 5 minutes.

☐ Place the fish in a steamer basket and set it over the cooking liquid. Cover the pan tightly and steam the fish for about 12 minutes or until the fish is opaque and flakes easily. Remove the pan from the heat and leave the fish in it to keep hot.

☐ Halve the tomatoes, scoop out the seeds and squeeze out the juice. Chop the flesh and put it into a small saucepan with the tomato purée, thyme, and wine. Bring to the boil then simmer for 5 minutes, stirring constantly.

☐ Purée the tomatoes and liquid in a liquidizer or food processor. Beat the butter until it is soft then gradually mix in the tomatoes.

☐ In a small saucepan, heat the sauce until hot, but not boiling, and season to taste with lemon juice, salt and pepper. Arrange the tuna on a warmed serving dish and serve the sauce separately.

Try using slices or wedges of orange, instead of lemon, as a garnish for fish. Not only does it make an interesting change and look more exciting, but the flavour of the juice goes well with most sauces—particularly those containing peppers or tomatoes.

Enriching sauces with butter

Add the butter to the sauce a piece at a time and beat to incorporate.

Tuna in Red Butter Sauce
Red vermouth in place of the wine gives an interesting spicy flavour.
This recipe works equally well with salmon or salmon trout.

Monkfish with Sweet Pepper Sauce
The purée for the sauce can be made in advance, ready to use when required. Keep in the refrigerator for 2-3 days or freeze in small containers and store for up to 2 months. Add the stock and boil up just before serving.

Orange and Lemon Plaice
Serve with boiled rice with some sultanas forked through it and fresh garden peas for a tasty family supper.
For an interesting variation, rub the fish with a little curry powder or ground ginger before cooking. Add the lemon and orange halves, after juicing, to the steaming liquid for extra flavour.

White pepper is recommended for pale sauces with fish dishes as black pepper gives a speckled appearance.

Skinning sweet red peppers

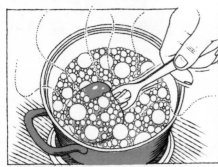

Boil whole peppers for 15 minutes, then run cold water over them and peel.

Or, scorch over a low flame until black. Wash away charred skin under cold water.

Monkfish with Sweet Pepper Sauce

Serve with plain boiled rice and steamed courgettes.

Serves 4 ☆☆
Preparation: 20 minutes
Cooking: 25 minutes

4 monkfish fillets, together about 1½lb (700g)
7 fl oz (200ml) dry white wine
7 fl oz (200ml) water
1 small onion, chopped
6 parsley stalks, roughly chopped
1 teaspoon sea salt
6 black peppercorns

The sauce:
2oz (50g) butter
3oz (75g) onion, chopped
2 large garlic cloves, chopped
2 large red peppers, skinned and chopped
a pinch of dried basil
2 tablespoons white wine vinegar
salt and freshly ground black pepper

Start by making the sauce. Put the butter into a saucepan over a moderate heat until melted.
☐ Fry the onion, garlic and peppers very gently, for 20 minutes, stirring occasionally, until very soft but not browned. Add basil and vinegar and bring to the boil.
☐ Purée in a liquidizer or processor. Return to the rinsed-out pan and set aside while cooking the fish.
☐ Rinse the monkfish under cold running water and pat dry with kitchen paper. Put the wine, water, onion, parsley, salt and peppercorns into the base of a steamer. Bring to the boil and simmer for 5 minutes.
☐ Put the fish in a steamer basket and set it over the water. Cover tightly and steam for about 10 minutes, or until the flesh is opaque.
☐ Transfer the fish to a warmed serving dish and keep hot.
☐ Strain off ¼ pint (150ml) of the steaming liquid and add to the sauce. Bring to the boil and cook vigorously, stirring frequently, for 2-3 minutes until thick and smooth.
☐ Adjust the seasoning to taste. Spoon the sauce around the monkfish fillets and serve.

Orange and Lemon Plaice

Serves 4 ☆☆☆
Preparation and cooking: 35 minutes

2lb (1kg) plaice fillets, skinned
9 fl oz (275ml) Fish Stock or equal parts Fish Stock and dry white wine
pared rind of ½ orange
pared rind of ½ lemon
1 teaspoon sea salt
6 black peppercorns

The sauce:
2oz (50g) butter
2 tablespoons flour
juice of ½ lemon
juice of ½ orange
1 teaspoon of finely grated orange rind
salt and freshly ground black pepper
3 tablespoons single cream
1 egg yolk

Rinse the fillets under cold running water and pat dry with kitchen paper. Fold them in half, skinned-side inwards and secure with cocktail sticks.
☐ Pour the fish stock or stock and wine in a steamer. Add the citrus rinds, salt and peppercorns.
☐ Bring liquid to the boil, then simmer gently for 5 minutes. Put fish in a basket and set over liquid.
☐ Cover the pan tightly; steam fish for 5-6 minutes, or until firm and opaque. Remove from the heat and leave fish in the pan to keep warm.
☐ Melt the butter until it begins to bubble, then add the flour. Cook, stirring, for 1-2 minutes until foaming but not browned.
☐ Gradually add strained cooking liquid, citrus juices, orange rind, and season with salt and pepper. Bring to the boil, whisking constantly. Reduce heat and let simmer, stirring occasionally.
☐ Mix together the cream and egg yolk. Stir a little sauce into the egg mixture, then return it to the pan.
☐ Remove from the heat and stir until the egg cooks and the mixture thickens. If necessary, adjust taste with more orange rind, salt or pepper. Remove the cocktail sticks, pour the sauce over and serve.

Lobster with Butter Sauce

Serves 4 ☆☆☆
Preparation and cooking: 35 minutes

2 bunches of fresh dill, roughly chopped,
    or 2 teaspoons dill seeds
1 lemon, sliced
1 teaspoon sea salt
6 black peppercorns
2 fresh lobsters, each about 2lb (1kg)

The Old-fashioned Butter Sauce (page 51)
5oz (150g) chilled butter
3 tablespoons flour
salt and freshly ground white pepper
lemon wedges and dill to garnish

In a steamer put about 1 inch (2cm) water. Add the dill, lemon, salt and peppercorns. Bring to the boil and simmer for 5 minutes.

☐ Put the lobsters in a steaming basket and set over liquid. Cover tightly and steam for 18-20 minutes. The shell should be bright red when fully cooked. To check, twist off a little leg close to the body and break open. The flesh should be opaque and easy to detach.

☐ Remove lobsters from pan. Break off claws and crack them. Cut each lobster in half down the back, discard intestinal sacs and stomachs and keep lobsters hot.

☐ Make Old-fashioned Butter Sauce using the steaming liquid. Serve in a sauceboat and garnish lobsters with lemon and dill.

Lobster with Butter Sauce
For thorough and even cooking arrange the lobsters only one layer deep.
Hollandaise and other butter emulsion sauces also go well with steamed lobster.
Crayfish, crab, and king prawns can be steamed in the same way as lobster.
Allow 6-7 minutes for king prawns
        10-12 minutes for crab
        15-20 minutes for crayfish

Buying lobster
Try to buy lobster live on the day you intend to cook them. Ask the fishmonger to kill them for you quickly and humanely.

Lobster with Butter Sauce makes a magnificent dish for a special occasion, accompanied, quite simply, by boiled rice and a green salad.

Cucumbers Stuffed with Peas

Try fresh dill instead of mint for a more subtle flavour.

If you have a proper asparagus steamer, stand the stems with their heads up in the basket. Steam in the same way then make the sauce in the base of the pan.

Steamed Chicory

Serve to accompany roast chicken or veal dishes, or with mashed potatoes and a good cheese sauce for supper.

Serves 4 ○
Preparation: 5 minutes
Cooking: about 5 minutes

---

8 heads of chicory, weighing about 2lb (1kg)
½ pint (300ml) Chicken Stock or water
chopped chives to garnish (optional)

Remove any blemished outside leaves and hollow out the centre core from the base of chicory. Place in a steaming basket.

☐ Set over a pan of boiling stock or water and cover tightly. Steam for about 5 minutes until tender. Garnish with the chives, if using, and serve.

Cucumbers Stuffed with Peas

These make an excellent accompaniment to fine fish dishes.

Serves 4 ☆
Preparation: 10 minutes
Cooking: about 10 minutes

---

1 cucumber, weighing about 1lb (500g)
8oz (225g) frozen peas
a sprig of fresh mint
salt and freshly ground black pepper
2 tablespoons double cream
1 tablespoon chopped parsley

Trim the ends from the cucumber, then peel it thinly. Cut into 4 equal lengths then cut each piece in half lengthways. Scoop out the seeds with a pointed spoon or sharp knife and discard.

☐ Place in a single layer in a steaming basket. Set over a pan of boiling water, cover tightly and steam for 7 minutes. Remove from the basket and keep warm.

☐ Meanwhile, cook the peas with the mint in boiling salted water for about 4 minutes, or until tender.

☐ Drain, remove the mint and

purée the peas in a liquidizer or processor. Mix in the cream and season to taste.

☐ Spread the purée in the cooked cucumber, sprinkle with parsley and serve immediately.

Variation: Steamed cucumber can be stuffed with several other purées to great effect. Try substituting any of the following:

watercress and celery;spinach with a dash of nutmeg;carrot and fresh dill.

Asparagus with Cream and Butter Sauce

Serve on its own as a splendid first course, or to accompany roast poultry and grilled fish.

Serves 4 ☆☆☆
Preparation: 5 minutes
Cooking: about 30 minutes

1½lb (700g) asparagus
16 fl oz (450ml) Chicken Stock
¼ pint (150ml) double cream
3oz (75g) ice-cold unsalted butter
salt and freshly ground black pepper

Wash the asparagus and trim off the woody stem bases.

☐ Lay the prepared asparagus flat on the bottom of a steaming basket. Put the stock in the base of a steamer and bring it to the boil.

☐ Set the basket in place over the liquid, cover tightly and steam for 12-15 minutes, until tender when tested with a fork. Transfer the asparagus to a serving plate and keep hot.

☐ Boil the stock in the pan vigorously to reduce to about ¼ pint (150ml). Stir in the cream and boil again for about 5 minutes to reduce by about a half.

☐ Cut the butter into 4 pieces and beat these into the sauce one at a time using a wooden spoon, removing the sauce from the heat for the final addition and beating in process.

☐ Adjust seasoning, pour the sauce over the asparagus and serve immediately.

Roasting

The intense dry heat of the oven is perfect for the cooking of large cuts of meat and game, whole fish and birds. The dishes produced by oven-cooking not only make more spectacular presentations than individual portions, but the combination of crisp exterior and juicy interior makes them universal favourites. Once called 'baking', oven-cooking is now usually referred to as 'roasting', with the exception perhaps of gammon and fish. Roasting also provides an excellent way of coping with uneven or irregularly shaped pieces, and of feeding many people at once.

Joints of meat, game, whole poultry and fish are all well suited to oven-cooking, retaining most of their natural taste and a juicy texture. Fatty meats and poultry, such as duck, are set on racks to let the fat drain off, while lean 'dry' meats such as game are barded with strips of pork belly fat. Whole fish are usually given a coating of melted fat or butter to prevent drying out.

Degrees of roasting

Traditional cooking demanded that joints of meat be briefly fried on all sides on top of the stove, to brown the outside evenly and seal in the juices. For convenience, this has been replaced by initial 'searing' in the oven at a higher temperature for 5-10 minutes. However, everyone likes their meat cooked to different degrees of 'doneness'. Some like it brown outside and pink in the centre. Others prefer it less brown, but evenly cooked all the way through. Used correctly, the oven can give you meat just the way you want it.

Brown exterior

Start with a very high setting until the outside of the meat has browned. Reduce the setting and cook until as well-done inside as you like.

Less brown exterior

Cook the meat all the way at a moderate setting for as long as necessary to cook through as you like it—depending on the weight of the meat or game.

Today's ovens heat up so speedily, it is possible to put in the meat before heating to the required temperature. In this case, the meat heats up as the oven heats. This method is better if you want a less well-browned outside. Bear in mind that this is how it will cook if the oven is set to cook while you're out.

If you are cooking meat or poultry with a lot of fat in or around it, sprinkle well with salt near the end of the cooking time to add crispness to the outside.

Do not season meat before cooking, or the salt will draw juices out to the surface of the meat.

Roasting times

In an oven pre-heated to 350F (180C) Gas 4, rule-of-thumb cooking times to achieve the necessary internal temperatures are:

Beef (medium-done): 15 min per lb (450g) plus 15 min over
Beef (well-done): 20 min per lb (450g) plus 20 min over
Lamb: 25 min per lb (450g) plus 25 min over
Pork and poultry: 30 min per lb (450g) plus 30 min over

Why roasting?

First, it's a simple way of cooking anything that is suitable. Apart from the occasional basting, roast dishes require relatively little attention during cooking. If you have an oven with an automatic timer, it can be set to turn itself on in your absence, so roasts can be planned well in advance.

Second, it's more economical, for more than one dish can be cooked in the oven at the same time and at the same temperature. Vegetables, which benefit from cooking in the juices from the main roast dish, and baked sweet dishes—such as custards and fruits—can fill every corner of the oven while it is hot.

Today's entire meal and tomorrow's casserole can all be bubbling away in the oven while you work, or enjoy a Sunday lunchtime drink.

What to roast

Like grilling, roasting produces best results when used for the more tender cuts of meat, poultry and game. However, some tougher foods, like brisket, benefit from slower roasting at lower temperatures.

Whole birds are particularly suited to roasting as it ensures thorough cooking of all parts of their irregular form.

Roasting temperatures

Many factors are involved in the success of a roast: shape, thickness, and the presence or absence of bone all play a part. The best measure of 'doneness' is internal temperature. (Meat thermometers are invaluable kitchen aids, especially for larger joints.)

Beef is considered to be medium-done when it reaches an internal temperature of 160F (71C) and is well done at 174F (79C); lamb should reach an internal temperature of 180F (82C), and pork and poultry 190F (88C).

How to roast

Meats such as beef, which 'bleed' their juices, benefit from preliminary sealing by rapid browning on the hob, or from brief initial cooking at the oven's highest setting.

● Foods with a lot of natural fat like ducks and geese are pricked all over before cooking to allow the excess fat to run off. These and the fattier cuts of meat should be set on racks or trivets, or a bed of vegetables, to ensure that the bottom of the food doesn't simply fry.

● Drier meats, like veal and game birds, need to be given added fat by barding or larding. Most foods benefit from basting with their own cooking juices, or some added butter or oil. To preserve moisture, some foods such as fish or turkey are often wrapped in foil.

● Stuffings provide fish, poultry and rolled joints of meat with added flavour and extra fat for succulence. Seasoned or herbed coatings, or slivers of garlic and sprigs of herbs inserted into the flesh, also infuse roasts with flavours as they cook.

● Juices from the roasting pan make excellent sauces and gravies. Generally the pan is deglazed with a little stock or wine and thickened with flour, cornflour, cream, or vegetable purées.

Oven-baked fish

Round fish such as herring, mackerel, trout, cod, grey mullet and, of course, salmon are all particularly good for oven-cooking. Indeed, because they are round they benefit from the all-round heat of the oven, without any liquid cooking medium to leach out the flavour.

To cook even large fish is very simple: if you don't have a pan large enough, improvise with a sheet of foil to extend a baking tray or meat tin.

Cooking time is relatively short so whole fish can easily be prepared and served with little planning.

Baked fish looks and tastes excellent, and requires very little attention. It benefits from a favourite stuffing if you have time, but good fresh fish is almost better plain. Add a few herbs or a pat of a flavoured butter for a real treat.

Baked Herrings with Shallot Butter

Serves 8   ★★☆

Preparation and cooking: about 20 minutes

---

8 fresh herrings, cleaned
salt and freshly ground black pepper
2oz (50g) butter, melted
2 tablespoons finely chopped shallot
2 tablespoons finely chopped chives
1 tablespoon finely chopped parsley
2oz (50g) butter, softened

Set the oven to 400F (200C) gas 6.
☐ Rinse the herrings inside and out under cold running water. Pat dry with kitchen paper. Sprinkle the insides with salt and pepper. Brush the fish all over with melted butter and lay them flat in a large shallow roasting tin or deep baking tray.
☐ Cook for about 10 minutes, brushing with more melted butter.
☐ Meanwhile beat the shallot and herbs with the softened butter.
☐ Carefully transfer the herrings to a warmed serving dish. Dot with flavoured butter and serve.

Fennel-baked Trout

Serves 4   ★★★

Preparation and cooking: about 15 minutes

---

2 teaspoons oil
3 tablespoons pumpkin seeds
salt
4 trout, each about 10oz (275g)
4 sprigs of fresh fennel leaves
1oz (25g) butter, melted
¼ pint (150ml) crème fraîche

Set the oven to 400F (200C) gas 6.
☐ Heat the oil in a small frying-pan over a moderate heat. Stir-fry the seeds for 2-3 minutes to brown lightly. Sprinkle lightly with salt and drain on kitchen paper.
☐ Rinse the trout and pat dry. Put a sprig of fennel inside each, and brush the outsides with butter.
☐ Arrange the fish flat on a shallow roasting tin, or deep baking tray. Bake for about 10 minutes, brushing with the rest of the butter.
☐ Carefully transfer to a warmed serving dish. Spoon the cream over and sprinkle with the seeds.

Herrings are rich in fat so therefore don't need much added during cooking – but butter does enhance their flavour.
Trout are much leaner fish. Add butter and cream for a better flavour and to add succulence. To lessen the calories, however, use only enough butter or oil to prevent sticking during baking and replace the cream with natural yogurt.

Crème Fraîche

To make crème fraîche, add 1 tablespoon soured cream to ½ pint (300ml) double cream. Heat to lukewarm, pour into a container and let it stand at room temperature for about 8 hours or until thickened. Stir, then cover and refrigerate until required.

Serve Baked Herrings with Shallot Butter accompanied by a sharply dressed onion, celeriac and beetroot salad topped with chopped gherkins.

Baked Salmon

Serves 6-8   ☆☆☆

Preparation and cooking: about 20 minutes

---

1 fresh salmon about 2lb (900g), cleaned and gutted
4oz (100g) butter, melted
salt and freshly ground black pepper
a few sprigs of fresh dill
Lemon Baskets (see sidelines)
Lemon Butter (see sidelines)
a few sprigs of parsley for garnish

Rinse the salmon under cold running water and pat dry with kitchen paper. Brush the inside with butter, then sprinkle with salt and pepper. Place the dill in the cavity.

☐ Set oven to 400F (200C) gas 6.

☐ Line a roasting tin with foil and brush it with butter.

☐ Brush the salmon all over with butter and place in the lined tin.

☐ Cook in the pre-heated oven for 5 minutes, brush with butter then cook for a further 5 minutes.

☐ Turn the fish by lifting the foil and rolling it over. Brush with butter and cook for 5 minutes more.

☐ Pierce the fish at its thickest part with a thin sharp knife. When cooked the flesh will flake and look opaque.

☐ With two large fish slices, transfer salmon to a serving plate.

☐ Serve garnished with lemon baskets filled with lemon butter, and parsley.

To serve: With a sharp knife, cut the salmon lengthways along the spine. Slide the knife between the bones and the flesh on either side of the backbone. Cut the whole top fillet lengthways along the dividing ridge. Cut each of these pieces across into two.

Clip the spine across at top and tail with scissors. Lift it out. Cut the bottom fillet in the same way.

Lemon Baskets

With a sharp knife, slice across a lemon about half-way up, stopping just short of the centre. Turn the lemon and cut in from the other side in the same way. Cut down from one end to meet a crossways cut, and repeat with the second side. Lift out the thick wedges of lemon to leave the 'handle'. Cut carefully around the flesh of the half lemon, release and scoop it out. With scissors, cut free the flesh still attached to the 'handle'.

Lemon Butter

Beat 1 tablespoon lemon juice and the grated rind of ½ a lemon into 3oz (75g) softened butter. Beat in 2 tablespoons finely chopped chervil. Pipe into the baskets with a forcing bag fitted with a ½in (1cm) rose pipe. Alternatively just pile it in with a teaspoon and create decorative swirls with the tines of a fork.

Spinach-stuffed Grey Mullet

Serve with warmed potato crisps and fresh garden peas.

Serves 6-8   ☆☆☆
Preparation: 20 minutes
Cooking: 35-40 minutes

2lb (1kg) grey mullet, after cleaning
Lemon Butter (see sidelines)

The stuffing:
2oz (50g) fresh spinach, chopped
3oz (75g) onion, finely chopped
4oz (125g) fresh breadcrumbs
1 tablespoon lemon juice
salt and freshly ground black pepper
3oz (75g) butter, melted

Rinse the fish inside and out under cold running water. Pat dry. Scrape off any remaining loose scales with the back of a knife.

☐ Set oven to 400F (200C) gas 6.

☐ Mix together the stuffing ingredients, using only half the butter. Pack stuffing firmly into the cavity of the fish. Secure closed with wooden cocktail sticks.

☐ On either side, make 3 diagonal slashes along the fish at the thickest part. Brush the fish all over with the remaining melted butter.

☐ Line a baking tray or roasting tin with foil and set the fish in it.

☐ Cook in the oven for 30-35 minutes. Test with the tip of a sharp knife at the thickest part, pushing through into the stuffing. The knife will feel hot on the wrist when the fish is cooked through.

☐ With two large fish slices, transfer the fish to a warmed serving plate. Remove the cocktail sticks. Spoon the stuffing into a hot serving dish. Meanwhile, put the Lemon Butter into a sauceboat and place in the turned off oven, to melt.

To serve: Fillet the fish in the same way as the Baked Salmon. Accompany with the melted Lemon Butter and the stuffing.

Tip: Small whole cod, or large whiting may be cooked in the same way.

Baked Salmon surrounded by attractive Lemon Baskets piped full of Lemon Butter makes a spectacular dinner-party main course served with sautéed whole new potatoes and baby carrots.

Cooking times for whole fish
Estimate the time by the thickness of the fish at the thickest part. Allow about 10 minutes per 1in (2.5cm). For stuffed fish, measure after stuffing.

Suitable pots for cooking large fish
If your roasting tin isn't quite long enough to take the whole fish and you don't have a fish kettle, place it diagonally across the tin. Or line a baking tray with foil and extend the foil beyond the end of the tray. But remember not to try to cook a fish which is too large for your oven as it will impede the air flow and the fish will not cook evenly.

Shapes and cooking times

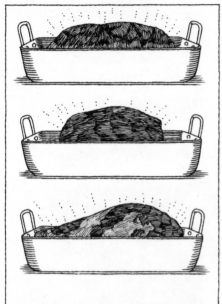

Joints of different shapes, and with different distributions of fat and meat, cook at different rates.
The accurate roasting time of large pieces will depend almost as much on the shape as on the actual weight. A long even roll like the one illustrated at the top will cook more quickly than one which is shorter but thicker, like the second one shown.
An irregularly shaped piece, like the third illustration (such as a leg of lamb) also takes longer – to ensure that the thickest part is also cooked through.

Roast forerib

This cut cooks nicely at a higher setting, to give a brown exterior and good gravy. This higher temperature is also good for cooking crisp Yorkshire pudding and roast potatoes.

Roasting meat on the bone is less easy to carve, but the price per lb (kg) is lower, they cook through more quickly and some find them more tasty.

Roasting meat

For home-cooking choose the joint of meat to suit the size of the family and the capacity of the oven. The average 'Sunday joint' will usually not be more than about 3lb (1.5kg) but it makes sense to buy a bigger piece of meat and eat 'cold roast' for at least the following day.

Cooking times for small pieces of meat seem long when compared to those for larger joints because the 'start-up time' is about the same for both. Cooking times are not as predictable as for large joints, so times are given for individual recipes.

The smaller the joint of meat, the better it is to choose one with a low fat content. However, fat does brown well and gives a better, fuller 'roast' flavour. This is why it is usual to have some fat on roasting joints. If there is no natural fat, it should be added before or during the cooking by barding, larding or basting with oil or dripping.

Roasting beef

Some less tender cuts, and some of the very lean cuts, such as those listed below, are better cooked at a lower temperature.

Rolled topside is a very popular cut, with a barding layer of fat simply wrapped around and tied in place. Eye of silverside is sometimes sold as a long thin piece with almost no fat at all, and fillet, too, can be trimmed to give a very lean joint of a similar shape.

Sirloin and other rib cuts may be sold on or off the bone.

Leaner pieces of economical brisket make very good roasts if cooked slowly. This meat has a coarser texture, but the flavour is good and the higher fat content makes it brown well and gives a very good rich gravy.

The density, fat content and the shape all vary with the cut and need to be taken into account when calculating cooking times. Some cuts are better cooked until well-done, while others look and taste better when rare.

Roast Rib of Beef, Yorkshire Pudding, Roast Potatoes and Gravy

Serves 6-8   ☆☆☆
Preparation: 20 minutes
Cooking: about 1¼ hours

5½lb (2.5kg) (2-bone) forerib of beef
2lb (1kg) potatoes
½ pint (300ml) Meat Stock (optional)

The Yorkshire Pudding:
4oz (100g) plain flour
a pinch of salt
1 egg
¼ pint (150ml) milk
¼ pint (150ml) water
2oz (50g) dripping

Pat the meat dry with kitchen paper. Place in a roasting tin.
☐ Set oven to 425F (220C) gas 7.
☐ Sift the flour and salt into a mixing bowl. Make a well in the centre and add the egg. Beat into the flour, gradually adding the milk and water.
☐ Using a wire whisk, whisk to a smooth batter with the consistency of single cream. Set the batter aside.
☐ Divide the dripping among 12 small deep bun tins.
☐ Cook the potatoes in boiling salted water for 4 minutes, rinse under cold running water and drain.
☐ Put the meat in the oven and roast for 30 minutes, basting two or three times with the juices which collect in the pan.
☐ Add the potatoes to the pan. Turn in the juices to coat. Cook for 15 minutes, basting the meat once. Put the bun tins into the oven for 5 minutes to heat the fat.
☐ Whisk the batter well. Pour into the hot fat in the bun tins. Return to the oven. Cook for about 25 minutes until well puffed and crisp.
☐ Reduce the oven to its lowest setting. Transfer the meat, potatoes and Yorkshire puddings to hot serving dishes and keep warm in the oven while you make the gravy.
☐ Pour off any excess fat from the pan. Set over a moderate heat. Stir

in the stock, or some of the water used to boil the potatoes. Boil briskly for 2-3 minutes, stirring to cook up all the meat residue.

☐ Strain the gravy into a warmed sauceboat. Serve immediately, with the meat, puddings and the roast potatoes.

Roast Sirloin with Soured Cream Sauce

Serve with creamed potatoes and crisp Brussels sprouts.

Serves 6-8   ☆☆☆
Preparation: 5 minutes
Cooking: 1¾-2 hours

3lb (1.5kg) rolled, boned sirloin
2 tomatoes, chopped
1 tablespoon flour
7 fl oz (200ml) Meat Stock
¼ pint (150ml) soured cream
2 small gherkins, chopped
1 tablespoon capers, chopped
1 tablespoon parsley, chopped
1 tablespoon chives, chopped
salt and freshly ground black pepper

Set the oven to 350F (180C) gas 4.
☐ Pat the meat dry with kitchen paper. Place in a roasting tin and put in the oven. Cook for about 1½ hours, to required degree, basting 3 or 4 times during cooking.

☐ Reduce the oven to its lowest setting. Transfer the meat to a serving plate and keep warm in the oven while making the sauce.

☐ Set the roasting tin over a moderate heat. Add the tomatoes and simmer for 5-7 minutes to soften, stirring frequently. Stir in the flour and gradually stir in the stock and cook for 2-3 minutes until thickened, stirring constantly.

☐ Sieve the sauce. Return to the rinsed-out pan. Stir in the soured cream, chopped gherkins, capers and herbs. Season to taste with salt and pepper and heat through.

☐ Pour into a warmed sauceboat. Serve with thick slices of the meat.
Tip: topside of beef can be cooked in the same way. To test rolled meats: pierce with the tip of a sharp thin knife right to the centre, and press meat to see if juices run clear.

Serve Rolled Sirloin with Soured Cream Sauce sliced thickly and garnished with extra chopped tomatoes, and gherkin fans.

Carving meat
The traditional wisdom dictates that joints of meat be allowed to 'rest' for a few minutes after they are removed from the oven before they are carved, to make carving easier. This allows time for the fibres to relax from the rigidity produced by the intense heat of the oven, and for the juices to distribute themselves more evenly through the meat. These effects, however, are barely noticeable in today's small-sized joints, and these will certainly be ready for carving in the few minutes taken to make gravy.

Roast boned and rolled meat
A lower setting causes less shrinkage of the meat. If cooked to the well-done stage, the outside of the meat will be browned. If you want the meat rare, the outside will obviously be a little less well-browned.

With boned, rolled joints, remember always to remove any string or elastic mesh before carving.

A lower oven setting is better suited to eye of silverside as the meat has very little fat to protect it from drying out. The soft, fine grain of this cut is very tender if cooked slowly and it is at its best cooked rare and served in thick slices.

Roast Silverside with Madeira Sauce

Serves 5-6 ☆☆
Preparation: 3 minutes
Cooking: about 50 minutes

2lb (1kg) trimmed eye of silverside
1oz (25g) dripping, melted
2 teaspoons flour
7 fl oz (200ml) water
3 tablespoons Madeira
salt and freshly ground black pepper

Set the oven to 300F (150C) gas 2.
☐ Pat the meat dry with kitchen paper, brush all over with dripping and place in a shallow roasting tin. Roast for 20 minutes; turn the joint over, and brush with dripping.
☐ Cook for a further 20 minutes, then turn and brush again.
☐ Cook for 10-15 minutes, to the required degree. (For rare meat, the juices will be very pink if you pierce the joint with a fork, and the meat will 'give' when pressed.)
☐ Transfer to a carving board.

Cover with foil and leave for 5-10 minutes while you make the gravy.
☐ Put the roasting tin over a moderate heat. Stir in the flour. Gradually stir in the water until the gravy has thickened.
☐ Stir in the Madeira and salt and pepper to taste. Cook, stirring constantly, for 2-3 minutes. Pour into a warmed sauceboat.
☐ Serve the meat cut in thick slices, garnished with vegetables as shown and serve the gravy separately.
Tip: garnish the beef with fresh vegetables *à la jardinière*: chopped turnips, tomato baskets filled with petits pois, mangetout peas, baby carrots, young green beans and broccoli tips. Cook each vegetable lightly, arrange in separate piles and alternate the colours for greater effect.

Roast Silverside with Madeira Sauce dressed with a striking jardinière of freshly cooked vegetables makes an impressive, but economical, dinner-party main course.

Roast Entrecôte with Oven Chips and Brandywine Sauce

Serves 4
★★★
Preparation: 3 minutes
Cooking: about 1¼ hours

1¾lb (800g) entrecôte in the piece
1oz (25g) butter, melted
salt and freshly ground black pepper
1lb (500g) frozen oven chips
¼ pint (150ml) Meat Stock
¼ pint (150ml) red wine
2 tablespoons brandy
tomato lilies and parsley sprigs to garnish

Set the oven to 350F (180C) gas 4.

☐ Pat the meat dry with kitchen paper. Brush all over with butter. Set on a rack in a roasting tin.

☐ Roast for 10 minutes. Turn the meat on the rack and brush again with butter.

☐ Roast for another 10 minutes. Turn, brush again and continue roasting for 20 minutes. Turn the oven up to 425F (220C) gas 7.

☐ After about 5 minutes, season the meat with salt and pepper. Put the chips in a single layer in a shallow pan and place in the oven on the shelf above the meat. Cook for about 15 minutes to brown the chips and the meat.

☐ Turn the oven to its lowest setting. Remove the meat to a warmed serving plate and the chips to a dish. Keep hot in the oven while you make the gravy.

☐ Put the roasting tin over a moderate heat and let the contents bubble until all the moisture evaporates and the fat stops sizzling. Gradually stir in the stock and the wine.

☐ Boil vigorously for about 5 minutes, stirring to cook up the sediment from the pan. Add the brandy and strain into a hot sauceboat.

☐ Garnish the meat with tomato lilies and parsley and serve the chips and gravy separately.

Tip: to serve the meat cold, remove to a carving board when cooked. Leave to cool. Carve thinly and wrap in cling film. Store in the refrigerator for up to 24 hours. Deglaze the pan juices with the wine and brandy only, let cool and then mix this into ¼ pint (150ml) mayonnaise to make a superb cold dressing.

✱ This meat also freezes very well. Wrap the slices singly, first in cling film then in foil. Store in the freezer for up to 2 months. Thaw in the wrapping in the refrigerator overnight, or for 2 hours at room temperature.

Roast Entrecôte

Like all the most tender cuts of beef, entrecôte is at its best rare. If you prefer it well done, allow about 15 minutes longer at the lower oven temperature.

Roast Entrecôte with Oven Chips and Brandywine Sauce needs only a fresh green salad to make a superb family meal.

Scoring fatty joints

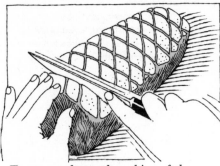

To ensure thorough cooking of the meat, cut through any skin and fat in a series of diagonal slashes to make a diamond pattern as shown.

Loin of Pork

If you ask the butcher to chop—not chine as for a rack—the joint, it will be easier to cut it into thin slices.

Loin is often sold with the skin and some of the fat removed. If you like to have crackling, buy a piece with the skin on.

To test pork

It is important to cook pork thoroughly. Pierce right through at the thickest part with a skewer or a sharp knife, when you think it will be ready. Ease the meat back so you can see that the meat inside is free of any hint of pink. Test again every 5 minutes or so until cooked through.

Roast Loin of Pork

Serve accompanied by apple sauce, roast potatoes and celeriac purée.

Roast leg of lamb

If the meat is well covered with fat, it will require no basting so can be cooked on a rack. If it is very young 'spring' lamb, it may have very little fat. In such a case, set the lamb in the tin and keep basting it.

Roast Loin of Pork

Serves 4   ★★☆
Preparation and cooking: 1¾ hours

2¼lb (1.25kg) loin of pork, skin removed
1 tablespoon melted lard

Set the oven to 350F (180C) gas 4 and pat the meat dry.

☐ If there is a thick layer of fat on the outside curve of the meat, slash into a diamond pattern with a sharp knife as shown. Brush any uncovered part of the meat with lard.

☐ Place in a roasting tin, fat-side up and cook for about 1½-1¾ hours, or until well browned and cooked through, brushing with the pan juices two or three times.

Roast Pork with a Cheese Crust

Serves 4   ★★☆
Preparation and cooking: 1¾ hours

2¼lb (1.25kg) loin of pork, skin removed
1 tablespoon melted lard

The crust:
2 slices of crispbread, crushed
2 tablespoons grated Parmesan cheese
1oz (25g) butter, melted

Cook meat as Roast Loin of Pork.

☐ Mix together the ingredients for the crust. Pack this on the outer curve of the meat 15 minutes before the end of cooking and roast until crust is browned and crunchy.

Roast Rack of Lamb

Serves 6   ★★☆
Preparation: 2 minutes
Cooking: 1½-1¾ hours

1 rack of lamb, about 3½lb (1.5kg)
7 fl oz (200ml) Brown Stock
1 oz (25g) butter, softened
salt and freshly ground black pepper

Set the oven to 350F (180C) gas 4 and pat the meat dry with kitchen paper.

☐ Place it in a roasting tin, bone-side down. Pour half the stock over. Roast for 30 minutes. Turn the meat with the ribs up, spread half the butter over the ribs and baste with juices. Cook for 30 minutes.

☐ Turn the meat again and spread the rest of the butter over the meat. Roast for about 30 minutes or until cooked to taste.

☐ To test the meat: Cut down beside the centre bone with a sharp knife and ease the meat back so you can see the degree of pink. Test every 5 minutes until cooked as you like it.

☐ Transfer the meat to a carving board. Cover with foil to keep it hot while you make the gravy.

☐ Pour off any excess fat from the tin. Set over a moderate heat and add the rest of the stock. Boil for 3-4 minutes, stirring to cook up the meat residue from the pan.

☐ Strain the gravy into a warmed sauceboat and serve with the lamb cut into chops.

Tip: It is advisable to order a rack of lamb or crown roast by the number of cutlets, according to how many people you plan to serve. It is usual to allow 2 cutlets per person, although for small spring lamb you may wish to serve 3.

● It is easier to cook the whole rack in a piece in the oven when you have 6 people, than to cook the separate cutlets. They don't require very much attention when cooking in the oven. This cut of meat may also be referred to as a loin or 'carré' and consists of all the rib bones on one side with the meat on the upper part.

● If you ask the butcher to trim off the fat at the bone ends, or do it yourself, you get the more characteristic 'rack' look which is so attractive when presented at the table – particularly with cutlet frills on each bone.

● Accompany with small new potatoes, broccoli and carrots.

Roasting poultry

Roast domestic fowl with their well-browned skin and moist, juicy flesh are among the nation's most popular dishes. Roasting is the easiest way to cook poultry, makes the most of its natural taste and texture and is the best way to deal with birds which have a naturally irregular size and shape. It also gives the opportunity of varying the dish with a delicious array of different stuffings.

To tell when poultry is cooked: Pierce the thickest part of the flesh inside the leg. The juices should run clear. Another test is to move one of the legs: It should move easily in its socket. Most poultry should be well cooked but tender ducks are very good if slightly under done.

Cashew-stuffed Roast Chicken

Serve with potato croquettes and crisp broccoli florets.

Serves 5   ☆☆☆
Preparation: 25 minutes
Cooking: about 1½ hours

4lb (1.8g) oven-ready chicken
2oz (50g) clarified butter
2 teaspoons flour
9 fl oz (275ml) Chicken or Giblet Stock
salt and freshly ground black pepper

The stuffing:
3 tablespoons oil
1 large stick celery, sliced
1 medium onion, sliced
3oz (75g) fresh breadcrumbs
2oz (50g) salted cashew nuts, chopped
1 teaspoon dried thyme

Set the oven to 350F (180C) gas 4 and pat the chicken dry with kitchen paper.

☐ Put the oil in a 8in (20cm) frying-pan over a moderate heat. Add the celery and onion. Cook, stirring occasionally, for 5 minutes to soften the vegetables.

☐ Mix with breadcrumbs and nuts, then season to taste with thyme and salt and pepper.

☐ Spoon the stuffing into the body cavity of the chicken. Pin or sew the skin together to hold the stuffing in place. Truss the bird with string to hold the wings and legs close to the body.

☐ Place in a shallow oven dish or roasting tin. Brush all over with the clarified butter.

☐ Roast for 1¼-1½ hours until well browned and cooked, brushing every 15 minutes with butter or pan juices.

☐ Transfer the chicken to a warmed serving dish. Discard the pins or string and keep hot.

☐ Set the roasting tin over a moderate heat.

☐ Stir in the flour until well mixed in. Gradually stir in the stock. Cook for 3 minutes, stirring constantly until thick and smooth.

☐ Season the gravy to taste. Strain into a warmed sauceboat and serve with the chicken.

Variation: For another superb flavour, use butter instead of oil and substitute finely chopped fresh tarragon for the thyme.

Cashew-stuffed Roast Chicken looks good when garnished with a ring of freshly steamed broccoli florets.

To give a richer, deeper colour and heightened flavour to the chicken skin, add 2 teaspoons soy sauce to the butter for brushing.

Giblet Stock
Cook the giblets in water to cover with a little chopped celery, onion and carrot. Add a sprig of parsley, thyme and a bay leaf, to make an excellent stock for the gravy. For an even richer flavour, add 2 tablespoons sherry to the stock at the end of cooking.

When using nuts in a stuffing mixture such as this one, do not prepare too far in advance of use, or the nuts will lose their crisp texture.

If cooking large frozen birds, such as turkeys, ensure that they are totally defrosted before roasting. Check that the legs move freely and feel for ice inside the cavity. It is inadvisable to stuff recently thawed frozen turkeys as the cooking of both stuffing and interior of the bird is retarded. Cook the stuffing separately.

Roasting game birds

Game birds are much smaller than domestic fowls, each usually serving from one to three people. They are generally much drier and require the addition of fat, and sometimes stock, during cooking to keep them moist and tender. They may be brushed with butter, or the breasts can be covered with bacon or strips of pork fat to protect them.

Lemon jelly glaze for roast duck, goose or game birds

Melt 2 tablespoons lemon jelly marmalade and spread over the cooked bird. Heat 3 tablespoons brandy or whisky in a small saucepan until it steams. Set alight and pour, flaming over the bird.

For an alternative glaze, use 2 tablespoons clear honey and 2 tablespoons orange juice (as in Chinese-style Wild Duck) per bird. Garnish with orange or grapefruit segments.

Chinese-style Wild Duck

Serve on a bed of egg-fried rice or pilaff, accompanied by sweetcorn kernels.

Roast Grouse

Serve with gaufrette potatoes, garden peas and carrots. Another excellent accompaniment to these is fried breadcrumbs: Melt 2oz (50g) butter in a 9in (23cm) frying-pan over a moderate heat. Stir in 4oz (100g) fresh white breadcrumbs. Cook, stirring constantly, until golden brown.

Roast Pheasant

Serve with game chips, Brussels sprouts and braised celery.

It is traditional to serve pheasants with the tail feathers on as a garnish.

Frothing

To give game birds a crisp brown skin, they are often 'frothed' at the end of roasting. First, they are sprinkled with flour or salt and then generously basted with stock, cider or wine.

Chinese-style Wild Duck

Serves 4 ☆☆☆
Preparation and cooking: 1¾ hours

2 wild ducks, each about 1½lb (700g) dressed weight
4 fl oz (100ml) clear honey
4 tablespoons orange juice

The stuffing:
1 large orange, segmented
3oz (75g) fresh breadcrumbs
1 medium onion, finely chopped
½ teaspoon salt
½ teaspoon dried thyme
3 celery sticks, chopped

Set the oven to 350F (180C) gas 4. Rinse and pat dry inside and out.
☐ Mix together all the stuffing ingredients and pack into the ducks. Secure closed with poultry pins.
☐ Put the ducks in a roasting tin. Mix together the honey and orange juice and spoon over the ducks.
☐ Cover the tin loosely with foil and roast for 20 minutes.
☐ Brush the ducks well with the pan juices, re-cover and cook for a further 20 minutes. Repeat process and cook for another 20 minutes.
☐ Remove the foil and continue roasting for 25-30 minutes, brushing 3 or 4 times with the pan juices, until browned and cooked through.

Roast Grouse

Serves 4 ☆☆
Preparation and cooking: 1 hour

2 grouse, each about 1lb (500g) dressed weight
6 rashers streaky bacon, rinds removed
¼ pint (150ml) Chicken Stock
2 tablespoons raspberry jelly
¼ pint (150ml) port
2oz (50g) raspberries

Set the oven to 375F (190C) gas 5. Rinse the grouse inside and out and pat dry. Trim off neck flap.
☐ Lay 3 rashers of bacon lengthways along the breast of each grouse. Secure the bacon in place by tying around with string in 2 places. Wrap each leg in crumpled foil.
☐ Place the grouse in a shallow roasting tin (large enough to leave about 1in (2.5cm) between them).
☐ Roast for 45-50 minutes, until the legs can be easily moved.
☐ Cut the strings and remove the bacon. Discard the foil. Cut the grouse lengthways with poultry shears. Keep hot on a serving plate.
☐ Set the roasting tin over a moderate heat. Add the stock and boil vigorously for 5 minutes. Add the jelly and the port and boil, stirring constantly, for 3 minutes.
☐ Strain the gravy into a warmed sauceboat and stir in raspberries.

Roast Pheasant

Serves 4 ☆☆☆
Preparation and cooking: 1¼ hours

2 pheasants, each about 2lb (900g) dressed weight
2oz (50g) butter, melted
juice of 1 lemon
½ pint (300ml) Chicken Stock

The stuffing:
6oz (175g) fresh breadcrumbs
1 medium onion, finely chopped
2 tablespoons finely chopped parsley
grated rind of 1 lemon
1 teaspoon dried basil
2oz (50g) butter, softened
salt and freshly ground black pepper

Set the oven to 375F (190C) gas 5. Rinse the pheasants and pat dry.
☐ Mix together all the stuffing ingredients, season well and use to stuff both pheasants. Tie the legs of each together with string.
☐ Place them in a roasting tin. Mix together the butter, lemon juice and stock and pour over birds.
☐ Roast for about 1 hour, basting several times with the juices, until tender when tested with a skewer on the inside of the legs.
☐ Transfer pheasants to a carving board and cover with foil.
☐ Place the roasting tin over a moderate heat and bring the juices to the boil. Season and serve.

Stir-frying

This age-old Chinese method of cooking is enjoying a well-deserved vogue in the West. Food cut into small pieces is fried very quickly in a flavoured oil over a high heat. The natural textures and colours are well preserved, and the fullest flavour developed. Also, little of the nutritional value is lost as the cooking is so brief and no cooking medium is discarded. Stir-frying is also done in a minimum of oil or fat, making it a valuable method for the health-conscious.

Cut meat into equal-sized pieces.

The traditional vessel for stir-frying is the wok. The deep, rounded sides pool the oil at the bottom, distribute the heat and allow the food to be stirred and tossed vigorously for rapid and thorough cooking.

The cooking oil is generally flavoured at an early stage in the process by stir-frying ingredients such as garlic, spring onions and ginger in it to 'awaken' the wok. These may or may not be incorporated in the finished dish. The Chinese then pour a little rice wine around the wok which evaporates quickly but leaves an extra, subtle flavour.

The cooking itself is done at the highest of heats. The wok should be heated until it is smoking before the oil is added and then cooking proceeds when that oil is visibly hot and its surface trembling. The food is then 'surprised' by the wok and cooked so rapidly that any juices leaking from it quickly evaporate and form a surface seal. The food may or may not be browned. One of the joys of stir-frying is the ability to preserve natural coloration, like the white of cooked chicken flesh and the pale pinks and reds of seafood, and combine that with the vivid colours of leaf and root vegetables and vegetable fruits.

Food is cooked in successive batches normally starting with the meats, or any item requiring lengthier cooking, and finishing with any tender vegetable and fragile or volatile flavouring element. After all the batches are cooked, the ingredients are all returned to the wok and tossed to mix and re-heat.

Experienced wok-wielders can cook in this way without ever actually taking anything out of the pan – they merely push cooked batches up the sides. This is really only practicable at home when cooking small amounts. Otherwise keep a large, deep, covered serving dish warm in the oven to receive cooked food.

The process can also be continued with some gentle stewing in added stock or wine to ensure that the food is cooked through. This can then be thickened into a sauce.

Alternatively, tougher cuts of meat and denser vegetables may be par-cooked in advance.

Meats and poultry are often also prepared for stir-frying by marinating them in rice wine, soy sauce or even lemon juice.

Stir-frying is an excellent way of using up leftover food – both raw and cooked – and entire meals may be quickly cooked in the one pan.

However, the true satisfaction of stir-frying lies in bringing out the full flavours of fresh meat, poultry, fish, seafood and vegetables and marrying them together in arresting and unusual combinations of texture, type, colour and taste. Apart from being aesthetically satisfying, stir-frying can also be a lot of fun.

Finally stir-frying is a perfect method of cooking for entertaining. Most of the lengthy preparation can be done in advance and guests left only briefly for the few minutes it takes to toss up a memorable meal.

Foods for stir-frying
It is important to choose foods which are tender enough to cook quickly, but which have enough resilience to withstand constant stirring. White fish and some starchy vegetables tend to break up. Shellfish, monkfish, squid and carrots, for example, are all good.

Flavouring ingredients
Garlic and onions, particularly spring onions, make an important addition of flavour to stir-fried dishes. To extract as much flavour as possible, put them into the oil on a low heat at the beginning. Let them stew away for a few minutes then push aside before turning up the heat (they burn easily).
Fresh root ginger, sliced and then cut into fine strips gives an unusual, and distinctly oriental flavour to any stir-fry.

Monosodium glutamate, the 'taste catalyst', and soy sauce are the traditional seasonings in Chinese cuisine. Use salt very sparingly (and remember that soy sauce is very salty in itself) and freshly ground black pepper, of course. For variety, however, try a shake of cayenne, ground ginger, a little curry paste or chilli paste – sometimes even a little sugar or honey.

To use the wok
Place the wok straight over the heat source, and use a high heat. The wok can be supported on an accompanying 'converter' or stand. The cooking takes place at the very bottom of the bowl, so the fact that it doesn't sit flat on the cooker is not important. Stir-frying is not always easy on an electric cooker. Try using a sauté pan or high-sided, heavy-based frying-pan.

Lamb with Spring Vegetables

If you wish to add a more oriental flavour put in 2 or 3 slices of fresh root ginger, cut into fine strips, with the garlic. Alternatively, try marinating the lamb beforehand in equal parts soy sauce and rice wine–or leftover red wine. Season the finished dish with soy sauce rather than salt.

For an easier, quicker version, omit the baby onions and use about a dozen coarsely chopped spring onions.

Chicken with Crab and Broccoli

Use seafish sticks if crab sticks are not available, or try a small tin of crab meat, drained.

Step-by-step to Lamb with Spring Vegetables.

Lamb with Spring Vegetables

Serve on a bed of rice or noodles or with a buttery potato and celeriac purée.

───────────────────────────

Serves 4   ☆☆☆
Preparation: 30 minutes
Cooking: about 20 minutes

───────────────────────────

1¼lb (600g) boned leg of lamb
6oz (175g) mangetout peas, trimmed
6oz (175g) French beans, trimmed
6oz (175g) baby carrots, trimmed
12 small onions, about 6oz (175g)
salt and freshly ground black pepper
3 tablespoons oil
2 garlic cloves, finely sliced
3 spring onions, finely chopped
3 fl oz (100ml) Meat Stock

───────────────────────────

Cut the meat into slices about ½in (1cm) thick and pat dry with kitchen paper. Cut into cubes and spread them out on a plate.

☐ Cook the peas, beans, carrots and onions for 1 minute in boiling salted water, then rinse under cold running water. Drain them and peel the onions.

☐ Put 1 tablespoon of the oil in a wok set over a high heat until the oil is hot.

☐ Stir-fry the garlic for about 1 minute to flavour the oil, then remove and discard.

☐ Stir-fry the meat in 5 batches for about 3 minutes each, using more oil as necessary, removing each cooked batch with a slotted spoon and keeping warm. Let the oil re-heat between each addition until it stops sputtering.

☐ Add the peeled onions to the wok and cook for about 5 minutes until lightly browned.

☐ Return all the meat to the wok. Stir in the rest of the vegetables and the spring onions. Pour the stock over. Bring to the boil, lower the heat, cover and simmer for 5 minutes. Season to taste and serve immediately.

Chicken with Crab and Broccoli

Serves 4-6 ☆☆
Preparation: 20 minutes
Cooking: 10 minutes

8oz (225g) broccoli
salt and freshly ground black pepper
¾lb (350g) chicken breast fillet
8oz (225g) crab sticks, thawed if frozen
1oz (25g) butter
2 tablespoons oil
2 teaspoons cornflour
9 fl oz (275ml) Chicken Stock
soy sauce

Trim the florets from the broccoli, then cut the stems into ¼in (5mm) pieces. Discard any leaves. Wash the broccoli and drain.

□ Cook the sliced stems for 3 minutes in boiling salted water. Drain and quickly rinse under running water. Drain again and pat dry.

□ Pat the chicken and crab sticks dry and cut into thin fingers.

□ Put the butter and oil in a wok set over a high heat. When the mixture browns slightly, stir-fry the chicken in 3 batches for 2-3 minutes each until lightly browned. Remove each batch when cooked and keep warm until all the chicken is cooked.

□ Stir-fry the broccoli stems for 2 minutes. Remove and keep warm.

□ Stir-fry the crab sticks in 3 batches for about 1 minute each. Remove each as it is cooked and keep warm.

□ Put all the ingredients back in the wok together with the broccoli heads and cook for about 1 minute.

□ Mix the cornflour with 1 tablespoon of the stock. Pour the rest of the stock into the wok. Bring to the boil, lower the heat, cover and simmer gently for 2 minutes.

□ Add 2 tablespoons of hot stock to the cornflour mixture. Stir this mix well into the wok. Simmer gently for 2-3 minutes to thicken. Season with soy sauce and pepper, serve.

Chicken with Crab and Broccoli

For a subtler but strong ginger flavour use thinly shredded fresh root ginger instead of ground and cook it with the garlic and onion.

Pork with Rice and Mushrooms

Turn this into a dinner-party dish by substituting Chinese rice wine for the stock and letting the pork marinate in it overnight before cooking. Garnish the dish with some cooked peeled prawns and a spoonful or two of cream mixed with chives.

To clarify butter

Melt the butter in a small pan over a low heat. When foam subsides remove from heat and skim off any remaining foam with kitchen paper. Then carefully pour off the liquid butter, leaving white solid residue in the pan.

Pork with Rice and Mushrooms

Serves 4   ☆☆
Preparation: 20 minutes
Cooking: 30 minutes

¾lb (350g) pork escalope or fillet, thinly
    sliced
½ teaspoon ground ginger
salt and freshly ground black pepper
1½oz (40g) butter, clarified
2 large garlic cloves, finely chopped
4oz (125g) spring onions, trimmed and sliced
4oz (125g) button mushrooms, wiped,
    trimmed and sliced
4oz (125g) cooked long-grain rice
6 tablespoons Chicken Stock
2 tablespoons finely chopped chives

Pat the meat dry with kitchen paper. Cut into 1½in (4cm) squares. Dust well with ginger, salt and pepper.
☐ Put the butter in a wok over a low heat along with the garlic and onion. Stir-fry for about 5 minutes to soften – but not brown! Remove with a slotted spoon and keep warm.
☐ Turn up the heat. When the butter is beginning to brown, stir-fry the meat in 3 batches for 3 minutes each until lightly browned. Remove each batch and keep warm. Re-heat the butter between each addition.
☐ Add the mushrooms. Stir for 1 minute to coat with butter. Add and stir in the cooked vegetables and pork.
☐ Stir in the rice and the stock and mix well. Bring to the boil then turn down the heat and cover the pan. Cook gently for about 25 minutes, stirring occasionally, until the pork is tender.
☐ Adjust the seasoning and serve, sprinkled with chopped chives.

Pork with Rice and Mushrooms makes a satisfying family 'one-pot' meal.

Veal with Peppers and Noodles.

Veal with Peppers and Noodles

Serves 4 ☆☆
Preparation and cooking: 30 minutes

¾lb (350g) fillet of veal, cut into strips
4oz (125g) Chinese noodles
3 tablespoons oil
1 garlic clove, finely chopped
4 spring onions, sliced
2 small green peppers, deseeded and sliced
2 small pieces of preserved ginger, chopped
¼ pint (150ml) Chicken or Veal stock
salt and freshly ground black pepper

Pat the meat dry with kitchen paper.
☐ Prepare the noodles, following package instructions, and drain well.
☐ Meanwhile, put the oil, garlic and onion in a wok over a low heat. Stir-fry for 5 minutes until soft, but not brown. Remove and keep warm.
☐ Turn up the heat. Stir-fry the meat in 3 batches for 1½-2 minutes each. Remove each cooked batch and keep warm.
☐ Stir-fry the peppers for 2 minutes. Return everything to wok.
☐ Stir in the ginger, cooked noodles and stock. Bring to the boil, lower heat, cover and simmer for 2 minutes.
☐ Season to taste and serve.

Veal with Leeks

Serves 4 ☆☆☆
Preparation and cooking: 20 minutes

¾lb (350g) veal, cut in 1in (2.5cm) cubes
salt and freshly ground black pepper
6oz (175g) trimmed leeks
1½oz (40g) clarified butter
3 tablespoons dry sherry
¼ pint (150ml) double cream

Pat the veal dry with kitchen paper and sprinkle with salt and pepper.
☐ Wash the leeks well under cold running water. Drain, pat dry and cut into fingers. Cut these in half lengthways and then into thin strips.
☐ Put ½oz (15g) of the butter in a wok over a high heat until it begins to brown. Stir-fry the meat in 3 batches for 1½-2 minutes each. Remove the veal as it is cooked and keep warm. Add more butter as necessary and re-heat between additions.
☐ Add the leeks and stir-fry for 2-3 minutes, until tender but not browned. Stir the cooked veal back into the leeks.
☐ Add the sherry and stir well. Stir in the cream and heat through for 1 minute before serving.

Veal with Peppers and Noodles
This dish makes a complete meal – cooked in only one pan.

Buying veal for stir-frying
For both of the recipes, use either veal escalope or the 'flash-fry' veal sold in some supermarkets. Both come ready-cut in thin slices. All you then have to do is to cut them across into strips or squares.

Chinese-style noodles are often sold partially cooked. All they may require is soaking in boiling water very briefly. Follow the instructions on the pack.

Stir-fried Carrots with Herbs

To thicken the sauce, mix 1 teaspoon cornflour to a smooth paste with 1 teaspoon of the stock. Stir this into the pan at the end of the cooking. Cook, stirring constantly, for 2-3 minutes. Add the herbs when the sauce is thickened. Use the rest of the carrots in soups, stews or puréed to thicken sauces.

Any green leafy vegetable is good stir-fried. Just cook long enough to wilt the leaves but retain the full colour. Season with grated nutmeg or mace, and stir in a few toasted slivered almonds for an extra touch of taste, texture and colour-contrast.

Step-by-step to Stir-fried Carrots with Herbs.

Stir-fried Carrots with Herbs

An unusual accompaniment to roast or grilled meats or poultry.

Serves 4 ☆

Preparation and cooking: 20 minutes

1½lb (700g) carrots
1oz (25g) clarified butter
3 tablespoons Chicken Stock
2 tablespoons dry sherry
1 tablespoon finely chopped parsley
1 tablespoon finely chopped chives

Wash and pare the carrots thinly. Scoop out balls with a melon baller.

☐ Cook the carrots in a large pan of boiling salted water for 6 minutes. Drain well and pat dry.

☐ Melt the butter in a wok over a high heat until it begins to brown. Stir-fry the carrots for 2-3 minutes.

☐ Add the stock and sherry and bring to the boil. Lower the heat, cover and simmer for 2 minutes.

☐ Stir in the chopped herbs and serve immediately.

Sesame Spinach

Serves 4 ☆☆

Preparation and cooking: 10 minutes

1½lb (700g) leaf spinach
1oz (25g) sesame seeds
2oz (50g) poultry fat or clarified butter
a pinch of salt
a pinch of cayenne pepper
a pinch of sugar

Wash the spinach thoroughly under cold running water. Trim off and discard the coarse stems. Drain the leaves well and pat dry. Cut across into ½in (1cm) slices.

☐ Stir-fry the sesame seeds in a wok over a moderate heat without any fat for 3-4 minutes until lightly browned, then remove and set aside.

☐ Melt the fat in the wok over a high heat until it starts to brown. Add spinach and stir-fry for 1-2 minutes until wilted but still bright green.

☐ Sprinkle with the sesame seeds, salt, cayenne and sugar to taste.

Casseroles & Stews

Slow stewing in the oven can be among the most rewarding of techniques for the creative cook. Like braising, it is better for tougher cuts of meat, poultry and game, and some fish and vegetables also benefit from prolonged cooking at a fairly low temperature. However, more liquid is used and the principal ingredients are often almost totally immersed. This allows the cook to add secondary flavouring ingredients such as vegetables, herbs, spices – or even fruit. The cooking medium itself plays a part in the final flavour and stock, wine, cider, beer, milk or cream can all be used. In some recipes the food may be browned first for added colour and taste and most stews can also be cooked entirely on top of the stove, though the oven does provide the best means of ensuring the steady low temperatures required.

Many regard 'stews' as humble cooking, and the term for the French oven dish, 'casserole', has increasingly been adopted in its stead to give greater respectability. Whether a 'stew' or a 'casserole', such dishes provide an unequalled means of blending different foods and flavours in an economical way, to produce results that are not just elegant but impressive. They are also perfect for entertaining, as most of the cooking proceeds unattended in the oven. Similarly, a casserole or stew makes the perfect one-pot meal for the busy household.

Stewing: the composite technique.

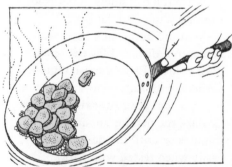

First, coat any meat or poultry in seasoned flour and sauté lightly.

Put in ingredients that take longer to cook. Add liquid. Cover closely.

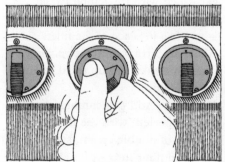

Long, slow cooking at low temperatures is always best.

Cook fish in a shallow roasting tin. Cover with foil.

Stewing step by step:
● Choose a deep ovenproof dish large enough to take all the ingredients comfortably. Too large, and the food may dry out; too small and the food will not cook evenly.
● Choose a deep flameproof dish if you are browning any ingredient first on top of the stove, or cooking the whole stew on top of the stove.
● Put out the ingredients in cooking order: those that take the longest, first.
● For meat or poultry stews, there will be time to prepare vegetables while the meat is cooking. For fish stews, prepare and almost cook the vegetables before adding the fish.
● If necessary, brown the principal ingredients by sautéing them briefly first. Coating them in seasoned flour helps to thicken the finished dish.
● Place the main ingredients in the dish. Pour over cooking liquid to cover. Add herbs and seasonings and cover tightly.
● Later, when the tougher ingredients are partially cooked, add any vegetables and adjust seasoning.
● 15 minutes before the end of cooking, add any ingredients, such as mushrooms or spinach, which would lose texture if slightly overcooked.
● At this stage, check if any fat needs to be skimmed off, then add any thickening agent required, such as cornflour mixed with water, beurre manié (kneaded butter) or an egg and cream liaison.

Choosing the dish
Most deep ovenproof dishes will do, but the traditional casserole, made of cast iron or earthenware, takes up and distributes the heat to its contents in the most effective way. It is also better if the dish has a close-fitting lid to seal in all moisture and encourage the circulation of condensed cooking juices back into the dish.

Re-heating casseroles and stews
Many stews, particularly those containing alcohol of some kind, are even better if allowed to cool and then re-heated. Stewing is a perfect means of 'réchauffage', that is the French term for making the most of leftovers or pre-cooked meats. A turkey fricassée made from cold roast turkey is a perfect example.

Thickening fish stews

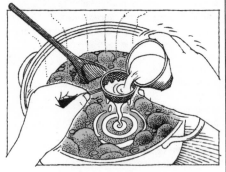

Mix flour and water into a smooth paste, add some of the hot cooking liquid and then stir this back into the dish.

Smoked Fish Casserole

A simple supper dish to serve with creamed potatoes and a green vegetable or salad. Two or three tomatoes, skinned, halved and added with the fish give a good extra flavour.

Sweetcorn kernels make a natural flavour partner for smoked fish and provide a good texture contrast.

Provençal Fish Stew

Serve with slices from a crusty French loaf. This can also be made with salt cod, soaked in several changes of water, then added as for white fish. Adjust the seasonings accordingly (no salt) and omit the wine.
Variation: Add a handful of black or green stoned olives 5 minutes before the end of cooking time to either dish.

Paprika Fish Casserole

Serve with plain boiled potatoes or rice and, if cucumber is not included in the recipe, a lettuce and cucumber salad. It is also good with sauerkraut, or cabbage cooked with dill seeds.

Smoked Fish Casserole

Serves 4   ☆☆
Preparation and cooking: 30 minutes

1lb (500g) smoked haddock or cod fillets
½ pint (300ml) milk
¼ pint (150ml) water
1oz (25g) butter
1 small onion, finely chopped
2 bacon rashers, cooked and finely chopped
4oz (100g) canned sweetcorn kernels, drained
freshly ground pepper
2 tablespoons flour

Heat the oven to 350F (180C) gas 4.
☐ Rinse the fish under cold running water. Remove skin, then pat dry and cut into bite-sized pieces.
☐ Put all but 2 tablespoons of the milk, the water, butter, onion, bacon, sweetcorn and pepper to taste in a deep ovenproof casserole. Cover and cook in the oven for about 15 minutes, until the onion begins to soften.
☐ Add the fish and cook for another 5 minutes.
☐ Mix the flour to a smooth paste with the reserved milk. Stir in a little of the casserole juices and return to the dish. Cook for a further 5 minutes, or until the fish flakes easily when forked.

Provençal Fish Stew

Serves 4   ☆☆☆
Preparation: 15 minutes
Cooking: about 1 hour

1lb (500g) white fish fillets such as cod, haddock or hake, skinned
4oz (100g) shallots, peeled and finely chopped
2 garlic cloves, finely chopped
5 or 6 large sprigs of fresh parsley, finely chopped
1 large onion, cut in rings
2 lemons, peeled and sliced
salt and freshly ground pepper
3 tablespoons olive oil
¼ pint (150ml) dry white wine
4 tablespoons dry breadcrumbs
2oz (50g) butter

Set the oven to 325F (160C) gas 3.
☐ Rinse the fish fillets, pat dry and cut into bite-sized pieces. Layer the bottom of a small ovenproof dish with half of the shallots, garlic, parsley, onion and lemon slices, and season well.
☐ Place the fish on top and add another layer of flavourings.
☐ Pour over the olive oil and wine, sprinkle with breadcrumbs, dot with butter and cook for about 1 hour, until the fish flakes easily.

Paprika Fish Casserole

Serves 6   ☆☆☆
Preparation and cooking: 50 minutes

3lb (1.5kg) freshwater fish fillets, such as carp, perch or bream
1½oz (40g) butter
1 large onion, finely chopped
salt and freshly ground black pepper
1 tablespoon paprika
½ pint (300ml) double cream
lemon twists to garnish

Set the oven to 350F (180C) gas 4.
☐ Wash the fish fillets under cold running water and pat dry.
☐ Melt the butter in a large shallow flameproof dish and fry the onion until golden. Place the fish on top, sprinkle with salt, pepper, and paprika, and pour over the cream.
☐ Bake the fish for about 20 minutes or until the flesh flakes easily when tested with a fork.
☐ Carefully lift the fish on to a warmed serving plate. Spoon the sauce over the fish and serve garnished with the lemon twists.
Tip: If you prefer, use fish steaks or whole fish in place of the fillets. Allow an extra 5 minutes cooking time for steaks and up to 20 minutes for whole fish.
Variation: Add ½ cucumber, diced but not peeled, with the fish. Instead of double cream, stir 1 teaspoon flour into ¼ pint (150ml) natural yogurt and ¼ pint (150ml) single cream, and pour over fish.

Cod with Mushrooms in Lemon Sauce

Serves 4 ☆☆
Preparation: 15 minutes
Cooking: 25 minutes

1¾lb (700g) cod fillet in thick pieces, skinned
salt and freshly ground pepper
2 tablespoons flour
2oz (50g) butter
1 large garlic clove, peeled and crushed or
    finely chopped
½ pint (300ml) milk
8oz (225g) button mushrooms, wiped and
    trimmed
2 egg yolks
1 teaspoon grated lemon rind
a squeeze of lemon juice, or to taste
1 hard-boiled egg, sliced

Set the oven to 350F (180C) gas 4.
Rinse the fish and pat dry with
kitchen paper. Dust both sides with
salt, pepper and a little of the flour.
☐ Grease the inside of a shallow
oval ovenproof dish with some of
the butter. Sprinkle the garlic in the
dish and arrange the fish on top.
☐ Pour the milk over the fish.
Cover the dish with foil and cook

for 15-20 minutes, until the flesh
flakes easily.
☐ Drain off and reserve as much of
the cooking liquid as possible. Keep
the fish hot in its dish.
☐ While the fish is cooking, melt
the remaining butter in a small
saucepan over a moderate heat. Add
the mushrooms and sauté for about
3 minutes, or until lightly browned.
Lift out with a slotted spoon and set
aside.
☐ Add the remaining flour to the
butter remaining in the pan and mix
well. Gradually stir in the cooking
liquid from the fish. Boil for 2
minutes, stirring constantly.
☐ Mix the egg yolks in a bowl. Stir
in a little of the hot sauce. Return it
to the pan and stir in lemon rind
and juice to taste.
☐ Pour the sauce over the fish,
return it to the oven for 5 minutes
just to 'set'. Spoon the mushrooms
over the fish and garnish with the
egg slices. Leave to heat for 2-3
minutes in the oven before serving.
Variation: For a party version,
replace ¼ pint (150ml) milk with ¼
pint (150ml) single or double cream.

*Cod with Mushrooms in Lemon Sauce
makes a good family supper dish,
served with fluffy white rice and a
green salad.*

**Cod with Mushrooms in Lemon
Sauce**
In this delicate-tasting fish dish the 'stewing'
juices are used to make the sauce.

Cooking cod in the oven
If the fillets are thick, they will take about 20
minutes to 'stew' in a covered dish.
Thinner fillets should be checked earlier to
ensure they don't over-cook. Always serve
cooked fish at once, unless freezing the dish.

Rich Beef Stew with Dumplings

Serve with chunky bread and butter and boiled cabbage.

Serves 8-10 ☆☆☆
Preparation: 30 minutes
Cooking: about 2¼ hours

3lb (1.5kg) chuck steak
3oz (75g) flour
salt and freshly ground black pepper
3oz (75g) beef dripping
3 medium onions, sliced
2 large celery sticks, sliced
1½ pints (900ml) water
½ pint (300ml) dry cider
juice and grated rind of 2 large oranges
8 black peppercorns, crushed
2 bay leaves
large sprig of parsley
1½lb (700g) carrots
a knob of butter
2oz (50g) walnut halves

The dumplings:
1oz (25g) lard
4oz (100g) self-raising flour
about 4 tablespoons milk

Set the oven to 300F (150C) gas 2.
☐ Pat the meat dry with kitchen paper and cut it into 1in (2.5cm) cubes, discarding any fat and connective tissue.
☐ Season the flour generously with salt and pepper and put it in a large plastic bag. Add one-third of the meat at a time to the bag and shake well to coat with the flour.
☐ Put one-third of the dripping into an 8in (20cm) frying-pan over a moderate heat. When a faint haze shows, add the onion. Stir-fry for about 3 minutes to glaze. Transfer to a 6-pint (3.5 litre) ovenproof casserole.
☐ Add more dripping, heat and fry the celery for about 3 minutes. Transfer to the casserole.
☐ Brown the meat in three batches, adding more dripping as required.
☐ Pour the water, cider and orange juice over the meat and vegetables. Stir in the orange rind, peppercorns, bay leaves and parsley.
☐ Cover the casserole and cook in the oven for 1 hour.
☐ Meanwhile, peel the carrots and cut them into finger-sized sticks. Stir into the stew. Remove the bay leaves, and cook for a further hour.
☐ To make the dumplings: Rub the lard into the flour. Gradually stir in the milk to make a firm dough. Cut into 10 equal-sized pieces and roll into balls.
☐ About 20 minutes before the end of cooking time, place the dumplings on top of the stew. Cover and return to the oven until they are well risen.
☐ Meanwhile, heat the butter in a small frying-pan over a moderate heat. Brown the walnuts for a minute or so, sprinkle with a little salt and dot over the finished stew.
✱ Put into shallow foil containers. Cool, cover, label and freeze for up to 2 months.

To re-heat: Put the covered containers into the oven pre-heated to 350F (180C) gas 4 for about 40 minutes, or until very hot. Turn out into a casserole dish. If dumplings are being included, add them at this stage and return casserole to the oven for about 15 minutes.

Belgian Waes Stew

Serves 4 ☆☆☆
Preparation: 30 minutes
Cooking: 2-2¼ hours

1¼-1½lb (575-700g) chuck steak
2oz (50g) beef dripping
3 medium onions, coarsely chopped
1 large carrot, coarsely chopped
salt and freshly ground black pepper
¼ pint (150ml) Meat Stock
7 fl oz (200ml) dark beer or stout
1 tablespoon tomato purée
1 tablespoon herb vinegar
1 tablespoon crushed coriander seeds
1oz (25g) breadcrumbs

The topping:
6 tablespoons dry brown breadcrumbs
2 tablespoons grated Parmesan cheese
1oz (25g) butter

Set the oven to 300F (150C) gas 2.
☐ Pat the meat dry with kitchen paper and cut into 1¼in (3cm) cubes.
☐ Put half the dripping into a frying-pan or wok over a high heat. Stir-fry the meat in three batches for about 3 minutes each until lightly browned. Remove each batch with a slotted spoon and set aside.
☐ Cook the onion and carrot in the same way with the rest of the dripping.
☐ Return all the meat and vegetables to the pan or wok. Season well and stir-fry together for a minute or so.
☐ Transfer to a shallow 4-pint (2.25 litre) ovenproof dish.
☐ To make the sauce: Mix the rest of the ingredients together in a 7in (18cm) saucepan. Bring to the boil, then simmer for 3 minutes, stirring.
☐ Pour the sauce over the meat and vegetables, cover the dish and cook in the oven for about 2¼ hours, until the meat is tender. Turn up the heat to 400F (200C) gas 6.
☐ To make the topping: Mix together the crumbs and cheese, then rub in the butter. Sprinkle over the centre of the cooked casserole dish.
☐ Return to the hotter oven for about 10 minutes to brown.

Belgian Waes Stew
This is just one of many delicious casserole dishes which incorporate beer – Carbonnade of Beef being perhaps the best known.

❋ To freeze
Turn the cooked mixture into shallow foil dishes. Cool. Cover, label and freeze for up to 2 months.
To thaw and re-heat: Put the covered dishes into the oven pre-heated to 350F (180C) gas 4 for about 50 minutes. Turn out into a shallow ovenproof dish, cover with the crumb mixture and brown under the grill or in the oven as above.

The crumb topping can be made 2-3 weeks in advance and stored in the fridge.

The various stages in preparing, cooking and serving Belgian Waes Stew. Accompany with buttered noodles and braised chicory.

Preparing cabbage

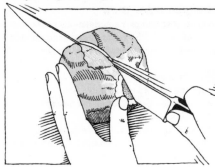

Cut across in half.

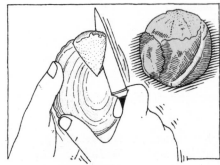

Trim out the hard base core.

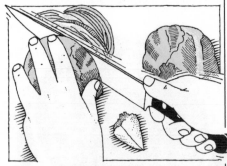

Slice or shred as shown.

To test lentils
The instructions given are for lentils which hold their shape and feel slightly crisp when bitten. If you prefer them to be mushy, add 2-3 more tablespoons of stock and cook for about 30 minutes longer. In that case, add the parsnips, etc, after 1½ hours.

To test beans
The instructions given will produce beans which will be tender but still hold their shape. For softer beans cook longer, testing every 15 minutes until cooked as required.

3-Bean Casserole

Serves 4-6   ☆☆☆
Preparation: 10 minutes plus soaking
Cooking: 2¾-3 hours

4oz (100g) dried green beans
4oz (100g) dried red beans
4oz (100g) dried white beans
1¼lb (575g) belly pork
2 medium onions, sliced
3 sprigs of fresh sage
2 tablespoons mustard oil or 1 teaspoon made mustard mixed with 2 tablespoons oil
1½ teaspoons salt
18 fl oz (500ml) Meat Stock

Soak all the beans in cold water overnight. Discard water.
☐ Set oven to 300F (150C) gas 2. Remove the skin from the pork. Cut the meat into 1in (2.5cm) cubes, removing as much meat as possible from the bones.
☐ Put alternate layers of beans, onion, pork, including the bones, and sage into a deep 4-pint (2.25-litre) casserole. Stir in the mustard oil, salt and stock.
☐ Cover the casserole and cook in the oven for 2¾-3 hours.

Lentil Stew

Serves 4   ☆
Preparation: 30 minutes plus soaking
Cooking: about 1¾ hours

8oz (225g) red lentils
1 large carrot, sliced
a large garlic clove, pressed
1 large onion, sliced
½ teaspoon curry paste
about 14 fl oz (400ml) Meat Stock
1 medium parsnip, sliced
1 celery stick, sliced
1 large leek, sliced
1 tablespoon chopped parsley
2oz (50g) salted cashew nuts
3 tablespoons natural yogurt
salt and freshly ground black pepper
1 tablespoon chopped chives

Soak the lentils in cold water to cover overnight. Discard the water.
☐ Set oven to 300F (150C) gas 2.

Put the lentils in a 4-pint (2.25-litre) casserole.
☐ Stir in the carrot, garlic, onion, curry paste, and 8 fl oz (250 ml) stock.
☐ Cover the casserole and cook in the oven for 45 minutes.
☐ Stir, add ¼ pint (150ml) more stock and cook for a further 20 minutes.
☐ Stir in the parsnip, celery, leek, parsley and nuts. If the lentils appear dry, add 1-2 tablespoons more stock.
☐ Cook for about 45 minutes or until the lentils are fully cooked. Stir in yogurt and salt and pepper to taste and sprinkle with chopped chives.

Creamy Cabbage

Serves 4   ☆☆
Preparation and cooking: 1-1¼ hours

1½lb (700g) cabbage
2oz (50g) butter
1 small onion, finely chopped
2 tablespoons flour
14 fl oz (400ml) milk
½ teaspoon celery seeds
salt and pepper
1½ teaspoons caraway seeds

Set the oven to 300F (150C) gas 2.
☐ Trim the cabbage, discard the outer leaves and the core and cut into thin slices as shown. Wash in cold water and drain thoroughly.
☐ Put the butter in a 7in (18cm) saucepan over a moderate heat. Add the onion and cook, stirring, for 5 minutes to soften but not brown.
☐ Add the flour and mix well. Gradually stir in the milk and simmer for 2 minutes. Season to taste with celery seeds, salt and pepper.
☐ Put a layer of cabbage into a 3½-pint (2-litre) shallow casserole. Sprinkle with some caraway seeds and spoon over half the sauce.
☐ Finish with another layer of the cabbage, caraway and sauce. Cover tightly and cook for about 50 minutes until just tender.

Savoury Sauces

There's something special about a sauce, whether it's a light, flavoursome vinaigrette or a thick and glossy mayonnaise. Both add life and texture to crisp salad ingredients. A creamy sauce with a sprinkling of fresh herbs or a dash of liqueur gives a touch of luxury to a chicken joint. A quick brown sauce—with onions, tomatoes and cloves—will lift a chop into the gourmet class, while the merest hint of a whipped butter sauce transforms a poached fish into something spectacular.

Learning to make beautiful sauces is the best, most effective way of giving your whole style of cooking a new and immediate appeal. Even if you're a complete novice at sauce-making, there's no quicker way of transforming the familiar ingredients into exciting and satisfying dishes.

Start with something simple—a salad dressing made with yogurt or soft cheese, a delicious mint sauce for tender roast lamb or a basic white sauce to serve with fresh vegetables.

And when you've discovered just how easy it can be, go on and try something new. Experiment with different tastes and flavours, different textures and techniques. Soon, you'll be able to make the most of whatever is to hand and start creating sauces of your own.

All you need at the beginning are a few simple tools, so don't think that to make a good sauce you have to spend hours and hours in simmering and stirring. Today's electric whisks, blenders and non-stick pans all make light work of blending sauces.

Follow the few basic rules and you'll discover the secrets of the great classics, many of which have been modified in keeping with today's tastes and trends in cooking. Even if you are already an expert sauce-maker, there are new flavour combinations for you to try.

The rôle of a sauce

A sauce should add piquancy, heighten flavour and give a good contrast of colour and texture. It should enhance rather than dominate the food it accompanies.

Many satisfying dishes include elements of the four basic tastes—sweet, sour, salty and bitter—as well as appealing aromatically to the sense of smell. It is the cook's skill in balancing these elements which often makes a dish and its sauce seem right and complete. So when you are next test-tasting a sauce as you make it, ask yourself which of the four elements needs adding to or balancing up.

Salad dressings

A salad dressing is, quite simply, what makes a 'salad' out of lettuce. Leafy green vegetables, apples and grapes, peppers, onions and cold cooked vegetables–these are just some of the ingredients that are given a new lease of life when tossed, stirred or marinated in a well-flavoured dressing.

Vinaigrette

The chief of the cold dressings is the one called 'French' or 'Vinaigrette'. Made with **one part vinegar to three or four parts oil**, it can be flavoured, as you wish, with herbs, herb-flavoured vinegars, or the finely grated rind of lemon, orange or lime. Lemon juice or dry white wine can be used instead of vinegar–especially for salads using fruits as well as vegetables, though the dressing may not keep so long if stored.
Vinaigrette dressing is simple to make, and is based on the principle that shaking or stirring the oil into the vinegar mixes them together into a temporary emulsion, which soon re-separates if left to itself. This is why it is important to shake up and re-emulsify the dressing if it is not all used up at once.
Serve with sliced avocado, a simple green salad, or cold, cooked green beans, or with cold boiled rice or cold boiled potatoes.

Vinaigrette with Garlic and Herbs

Serve with cold cooked leeks or chicory. Also good with well-drained canned cannellini.

Vinaigrette

It's a good idea to keep a small screw-top jar of this in the fridge ready to use. It will keep for several days. Store it in an instant coffee jar with a plastic top which won't be corroded by the salt in the dressing.

Try different oils and vinegars until you find your favourite flavour combinations in different foods.

---

2 tablespoons vinegar
salt
white pepper
½ teaspoon made English or French mustard
pinch of white sugar
6 tablespoons oil

Put the vinegar, a good pinch of salt, a dash of pepper, the mustard, and the sugar into a basin. Stir until the salt and sugar have dissolved. Gradually beat in the oil until the mixture turns cloudy.
☐ Taste the dressing before using and adjust the flavouring: add more oil if it's too acidic; more vinegar or salt if it lacks flavour.
Tip: You can also make this sauce in the screw-top jar. Just make sure the top is on tight, then shake all the ingredients together.

Making Vinaigrette. From left to right: Seasoning the vinegar, whisking in the oil and flavouring with herbs. Far right: Alternative or additional flavourings.

Vinaigrette with Garlic and Herbs

Try this as an alternative to a plain Vinaigrette. Finely chopped spring onion may be used instead of garlic.

Vinaigrette as recipe   ☆☆
1 tablespoon finely chopped parsley
1 tablespoon finely chopped chives
1 teaspoon very finely chopped celery leaves
1 clove garlic

Shake or stir the herbs and celery leaves into the dressing along with the garlic.
Tip: If you're storing the dressing for a time, leave the garlic whole, but if you want to serve it immediately, put the garlic through a garlic press or chop it finely.

Mint Sauce

So easy to make, this popular sweet-sour dressing is excellent with salads as well as the traditional roast lamb. The sauce itself is made just like tea—by steeping leaves in boiling water.

---

a handful of fresh mint leaves   ☆
4 teaspoons sugar
3 tablespoons boiling water
3 tablespoons vinegar

Finely chop the mint and put into a small heatproof dish or sauceboat with the sugar. Pour on the boiling water and stir until the sugar dissolves. Leave to cool to allow the flavour to develop.
☐ Stir in the vinegar just before serving.

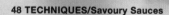

Honey-Yogurt Dressing

For a very simple sweet-sour dressing, there's nothing better than yogurt and honey. Be sure to mix it just before serving because yogurt quickly separates once stirred.

5oz (142ml) carton natural yogurt ☆
1 tablespoon strained lemon juice
1 tablespoon clear honey
salt and white pepper

Stir all the ingredients together in a small basin. Spoon immediately over the salad of your choice.

Soured Cream Dressing

Soured cream is another excellent foundation for salad dressings as an alternative to yogurt. Use whatever fresh leafy herbs are available—particularly dill, parsley, basil or chives.

---

2 tablespoons chopped, mixed fresh ☆
   herbs
5oz (142ml) carton soured cream
salt and pepper to taste

Stir the herbs into the soured cream, season, then serve immediately.

Roquefort Dressing

Of course, this dressing is named after the famous French blue cheese but other blue cheeses are also good: try Bleu de Bresse, Bleu d'Auvergne, Danish Blue, or Stilton. Taste the dressing before adding salt—all blue cheeses are fairly salty.

5oz (142ml) carton soured cream ☆☆
1 teaspoon strained lemon juice
2oz (50g) Roquefort or other blue cheese

Stir together the cream and lemon juice. Rub the cheese through a sieve into the cream and mix until smooth. Adjust the flavour with more lemon juice if liked.
Tip: A little coarsely grated dessert apple makes a good addition to this dressing, especially if you've overdone the salt after all.

Fresh Cream Dressing

A lovely dressing for fruits and other mild-flavoured foods; store up to 3 days in the fridge. Use finely grated orange or lime rind instead of lemon.

5oz (142ml) carton double cream ☆☆
1 egg yolk
1 tablespoon lemon juice
salt
a few drops liquor from bottled green
   peppercorns
a little finely grated lemon rind

Put all the ingredients into a small bowl and whisk until the mixture just holds its shape. Taste and adjust the seasoning if necessary.

Creamy dressings
Other marvellous dressings are quickly and simply made with plain yogurt, soured cream, soft cheeses or double cream as the base. They can be as tangy or as rich as you like; you can also experiment with the non-fat soft cheeses eg. the German quark and the French fromage blanc—now much more widely available. Quicker to whip up than either a mayonnaise or a salad cream, they can be flavoured with any of the suggestions already given for Vinaigrette, or try a light sprinkling of curry powder or spice.

Honey-Yogurt Dressing
Particularly good with iceberg lettuce, orange slices and salted peanuts; or with chicory, grapefruit and bananas.

Soured Cream Dressing
To make your own lightly soured cream, stir 1 tablespoon lemon juice or a few drops of vinegar into ¼ pint (150ml) double cream. This dressing is good with cucumbers, or with any variety of canned beans: use a mixture of red, green, yellow, and white as available. Always drain the beans thoroughly first.

Roquefort Dressing
Serve with a salad of sliced oranges, onions, and black olives for a delicious first course; try it with unskinned diced dessert apple, roughly chopped walnuts and sliced celery, or serve with grilled steak or rare roast beef.

Fresh Cream Dressing
Serve with grapefruit segments on a bed of crisp lettuce, or with cold poached white fish.

A ROUX (pronounced 'roo')

A roux is a kind of paste made by cooking together almost equal quantities of fat and flour. The sauce is usually easier to make if a little more fat than flour is used. The paste it forms is the foundation of a large family of sauces—usually savoury—which can be served with meat, fish, poultry and vegetables.

Roux-based white sauces

Different liquids and flavourings are added to the roux base to give a marvellous variety of sauces, like those on the following pages.

For a white sauce Add the liquid as soon as the paste is formed and before it colours. Continue cooking for a few minutes, stirring constantly. The resulting sauce is a pale creamy colour. This roux is used for most of the basic white sauces. including béchamel.

For a blond sauce Cook the roux for slightly longer, until it turns a light straw colour. A crust of bubbles will form over the surface as the liquid from the butter evaporates. When you add the liquid—milk or stock—continue cooking, stirring constantly. The resulting sauce is slightly darker in colour. This roux is used for the family of velouté (velvety) sauces.

Velouté Sauce

For a finer, more delicate sauce, add an egg and cream liaison (see sidelines, opposite).

Basic White Sauce

To serve with boiled or steamed vegetables.

Serves 4
Preparation and cooking time:
15 minutes

¾ pint (450ml) milk
2oz (50g) butter
3 tablespoons flour
salt and pepper

Heat the milk to lukewarm in a small saucepan set over low heat.
☐ Meanwhile, melt the butter slowly in a medium-size heavy-based saucepan. When the foam begins to subside, add the flour. Mix well with a wooden spoon.
☐ Continue to cook, stirring constantly, for a minute or two.
☐ Remove the pan from the heat and stir a little of the warm milk into the roux.
☐ Return to the heat and cook, stirring constantly, until the mixture thickens. Continue to add the milk gradually, taking the pan off the heat each time and still stirring, until all the milk has been added.
☐ Continue simmering and stirring the mixture for about 5 minutes to make sure all the flour is cooked into the sauce. By now, it should be well thickened and smooth.
☐ Season to taste with salt and pepper and serve, or allow to cool, then pack and freeze.
Variations: Add 2 tablespoons chopped fresh herbs or 2 tablespoons lightly sautéed mushrooms.

Velouté Sauce

Serve with chicken or veal cooked in stock, or poached fish.

Serves 4
Preparation and cooking time:
15 minutes

2oz (50g) butter
3 tablespoons flour
¾ pint (450ml) fat-free chicken stock
salt and pepper

Heat the stock gently to lukewarm. Melt the butter in a pan, add the flour and cook, stirring, to a blond roux. Gradually add the stock and, stirring, cook without boiling, until the sauce thickens. Season to taste.

Mornay Sauce

The egg and cream mixture added to this sauce is called a liaison.

Serves 4
Preparation and cooking time:
20 minutes

1oz (25g) butter
1oz (25g) flour
12 floz (350ml) lukewarm milk
5oz (150g) grated Cheddar or Gruyère cheese
1 egg yolk
4 tablespoons single cream
salt and pepper
a few drops of Worcestershire Sauce

Make the sauce in the same way as for Basic White Sauce.
☐ Mix in the cheese thoroughly, whisking or beating until the sauce is smooth and glossy. Do not allow to overheat otherwise the cheese will turn stringy and tough.

Making a roux

Sift the flour into the butter.

Beat until it holds together in a ball.

Slowly add warm milk, stirring well.

□ In a small basin, mix together the egg yolk and cream and stir 4-5 spoonfuls of the hot liquid into it. Return this mixture to the saucepan and stir in well.

□ Remove the pan from the heat and continue whisking to mix well and just cook the egg. Do not allow the mixture to boil or the egg yolk will cook too well and 'curdle' (scramble) in the sauce.

□ Season to taste with salt, pepper and Worcestershire sauce.

Béchamel Sauce

This is made in exactly the same way as the Basic White Sauce, but the milk is first flavoured with vegetables and herbs. It takes a little longer to make. Serve with either boiled or poached vegetables.

Serves 4   ☆☆
Preparation and cooking time:
  20 minutes

1 small bay leaf
1 blade of mace
4-5 peppercorns
1 small onion, stuck with 4-5 whole cloves
1 small carrot, peeled and cut in chunks
¾ pint (450ml) milk
2oz (50g) butter
3 tablespoons flour
salt and pepper

Put the flavourings into the milk. Set the milk over low heat and leave to heat up very slowly for about 10 minutes. It should *not* be allowed to boil.

□ Take the pan off the heat, strain off the vegetables and flavourings and proceed as for Basic White Sauce.

Gourmet Mustard Sauce

This is another variation of either the Basic White or Béchamel Sauce. Serve with grilled herrings or poached white fish.

Serves 4   ☆☆
Preparation and cooking time:
  20 minutes

Basic White or Béchamel Sauce as recipe
1 tablespoon French mustard
a squeeze of lemon juice

Make the Basic White, or Béchamel, Sauce.

□ Beat in the mustard and season to taste with a little extra salt and pepper. Add a little lemon juice.
Tip: Don't cook the sauce for long after the mustard is added as it will make the sauce bitter. If serving with poached fish, replace some of the milk with poaching liquid.

Adding a liaison
A liaison is a mixture of egg yolk and cream—single or double—which is added to a white or a velouté sauce towards the end of the cooking time to enrich the basic sauce and make it creamy in texture. It has a thickening effect and also makes a good addition to cream soups.

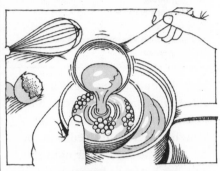

Put the egg yolk in a small basin with the cream. Add a little hot sauce.

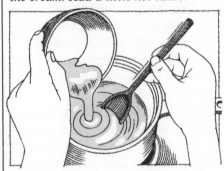

Pour the egg and cream liaison back into the hot sauce in the pan, stirring well. Then remove the pan from the heat and continue stirring or whisking. If the heat is too high, the egg yolk will curdle and spoil the sauce.

Old-fashioned Butter Sauce
Make a Velouté Sauce, remove from the heat and gradually beat in 3½oz (100g) *ice cold* butter (cut into small pieces). Serve warm. Do not re-heat.

Top: Mornay Sauce.
Bottom: Gourmet Mustard Sauce.

Basic Brown Sauce

Serve with casseroles or any browned meats, or use as a foundation for other sauces. The sugar aids browning and gives a richer flavour.

Cooking time: about 10-12 minutes
Makes about ¾ pint (450ml)

2oz (50g) butter
3 tablespoons flour
pinch of sugar
¾ pint (450ml) lukewarm brown stock
salt and pepper

Melt the butter slowly in a heavy-based, medium-sized saucepan over a moderate heat. As soon as the foam has nearly subsided, add the flour and the sugar. Stir until the roux has begun to brown but *do not let it scorch.*

☐ Remove from the heat and stir in a little of the stock. Return to the heat and cook, stirring, until thick. Continue to add more stock off the heat and to stir continuously on the heat until it is all added.

☐ Cook for a further 5-7 minutes, stirring all the time, until the sauce is completely cooked and thickened. Season to taste with salt and pepper.

Simple Tomato Sauce

Serve this sauce with grilled, fried or barbecued meat or poultry.

Preparation and
   cooking time: 15 minutes
Makes about ¾ pint (450ml)

Basic Brown Sauce made with ¼ pint (150ml)
   red wine in place of ¼ pint (150ml) of the stock
2oz (50g) tomato purée
pinch of sugar

Prepare the basic brown sauce, then stir the tomato purée into the sauce at the end of the cooking time.

☐ Add a little sugar to soften the acidity of the tomato.

Variation: Stir in chopped parsley and/or chives to taste. Also stir in a little cream to taste. Check the seasoning and adjust if necessary before serving.

Fresh Tomato Sauce

The success of this sauce lies in using ripe, juicy, red tomatoes.

If the tomatoes are not red and ripe enough, add a teaspoon or two of tomato purée for colour and flavour. Serve with minced meat, meat rissoles or croquettes, or on pasta dishes.

Preparation: 20 minutes
Cooking time: 30 minutes
Makes about 1 pint (600ml)

1¾lb (700g) ripe tomatoes
2 tablespoons olive oil
1oz (25g) onion, coarsely chopped
1 clove garlic, finely chopped
large sprig of parsley
1 stick celery, coarsely chopped
½ teaspoon dried oregano
½ teaspoon dried thyme
2oz (50g) butter
3 tablespoons flour
9 floz (275ml) lukewarm stock
1 teaspoon sugar
salt and freshly ground black pepper
1 tablespoon finely chopped chives

Chop the tomatoes coarsely. Put the oil into a large saucepan over a moderate heat. Add the onion and garlic and cook until just beginning to brown. Add the tomatoes, parsley, celery and herbs, cover and cook gently for 20-25 minutes until the tomatoes and celery are well softened. Rub through a sieve.

☐ Heat the butter slowly in a medium-sized saucepan over a low heat. When the foam begins to subside, add all the flour and mix in well with a wooden spoon. Continue to cook, stirring constantly, for a minute or two. Remove from the heat and mix in a little of the warm stock. Return to the heat and cook until beginning to thicken.

☐ Continue the gradual cooking of the stock. Add the sieved tomato mixture and cook for a further 5 minutes. Season to taste with sugar, salt, and black pepper. Add the chives just before serving.

Tip: Freshly ground black pepper is particularly good with tomatoes.

Variation: Add 1-2 tablespoons ruby port and serve with fried fish.

Rich Red Wine Sauce

Preparation: 5 minutes
Cooking time: about 1 hour
Makes ¾ pint (450ml)

The stock:
1¼ pints (750ml) brown stock
¾ pint (450ml) red wine
small bay leaf, crumbled
sprig each of fresh thyme and parsley
1 shallot or small onion, chopped
1 stick of celery, chopped

The sauce:
2oz (50g) butter
3 tablespoons flour
1 teaspoon sugar
salt and pepper

Put all the stock ingredients into a saucepan and simmer gently until reduced to about ¾ pint (450ml).

☐ Strain and use with the butter, flour and seasonings to make a sauce as for Basic Brown Sauce.

Simple Game Sauce

Serve with roast or grilled game.

Preparation: 35 minutes
Cooking time: 40 minutes
Makes about ¾ pint (450ml)

The stock:
2 tablespoons oil
about 1lb (400-500g) duck or game bones
1 large onion and 1 clove garlic, chopped
1 large carrot and 1 stick celery, sliced
7 floz (200ml) red wine
1 pint (600ml) water
1 bay leaf, crumbled
4 juniper berries, crushed
4 black peppercorns
sprig each of parsley and rosemary

The sauce:
2oz (50g) butter
3 tablespoons flour
salt and pepper
2oz (50g) redcurrant jelly, melted

Heat the oil in a saucepan and brown the bones and vegetables.

☐ Add the other stock ingredients, cover and simmer for 30 minutes. Strain, return the liquid to the pan, and simmer uncovered until reduced to about ¾ pint (450ml). Use with the butter and flour to make the sauce as for Basic Brown Sauce. Season and stir in the jelly.

Ingredients for Espagnole Sauce.

Espagnole Sauce

This is the most elaborate of the brown sauces, and forms the base for other rich sauces. Make it when you have time in hand, and remember that it freezes well until needed. Serve with grilled steaks, cutlets, or with game.

Preparation: enriched stock   ☆☆
     about 1 hour
Cooking time: 45 minutes
Makes about ¾ pint (450ml)

The enriched stock:
1¾ pints (1 litre) brown stock
6 black peppercorns
sprig of fresh thyme
1 bay leaf, crumbled
1 shallot or small onion studded with 4 whole
     cloves

The sauce:
2oz (50g) butter
2oz (50g) streaky bacon, chopped
1oz (25g) onion, chopped
1 large carrot, sliced
3 tablespoons flour
4 large ripe tomatoes
1 teaspoon vinegar
1 teaspoon sugar
salt and freshly ground black pepper
2 tablespoons ruby port (optional)

First make a rich-flavoured stock by simmering together all the stock ingredients until reduced to about half the original volume. When the enriched stock is sufficiently concentrated, strain off and use to make the sauce.

☐ To make the sauce, melt the butter in a medium-sized saucepan and cook the bacon to extract the fat and slightly brown the bacon. Add the onion and carrot before the bacon is too dark, and continue to stir over a low heat until the onion has begun to brown. Sprinkle the flour over and stir in well, cooking until it is lightly browned.

☐ Remove from the heat and gradually stir in the reduced stock. Return to the heat and cook, stirring constantly, until the sauce boils and thickens. Reduce the heat and leave to simmer.

☐ Chop the tomatoes, add them to the sauce, and cook very gently for a further 20 minutes, stirring occasionally to prevent sticking. Strain the sauce and adjust the flavour with vinegar, sugar, and salt and pepper. Add a little ruby port to make this one of the finest sauces of all.

✳ It is worth making this sauce in quantity when you have enough stock, as it can be frozen in portions. *Tip:* Add Madeira instead of port. Serve with boiled ham or tongue.

Mushroom Sauce

Preparation: enriched stock about
     1 hour   ☆☆
Cooking time: 50 minutes
Makes about 1 pint (600ml)

Espagnole Sauce as recipe
dash of cayenne pepper
4oz (100g) mushrooms, finely chopped
2 tablespoons finely chopped chives

Prepare the Espagnole Sauce but season it with cayenne instead of black pepper and omit the vinegar. Add the mushrooms to the sauce. Cook for 5 minutes, stirring constantly.

☐ Add the chives just before serving.

Basic Mayonnaise

Serves 6-8
Preparation: about 30 minutes

2 egg yolks
a little salt
dash of white pepper
pinch of dry or made mustard
about 2 tablespoons vinegar or lemon juice
½ pint (300ml) oil

Put the egg yolks into a clean bowl with the seasonings and a tablespoon of the vinegar or lemon juice. Whisk the mixture until creamy and smooth.

☐ Start adding the oil, drop by drop, as you continue whisking, until the sauce begins to form and thicken. You will feel this happening as you whisk.

☐ Once the sauce begins to thicken, start adding the oil more quickly in a series of thin trickles. Add each new trickle of oil *only* after the previous one has been fully absorbed into the sauce. The consistency of the mayonnaise should be like thick cream which has been whipped until it just holds its shape.

☐ If the sauce is too thick, whisk in a few extra drops of vinegar, *or* a few drops of warm water.

Tip: Adjust seasoning to taste with a few drops of Worcestershire sauce, a little lemon juice or a pinch of sugar, depending on the strength of flavour of the oil you have used.

Note: If substituting lemon juice for vinegar, it is wiser to use the mayonnaise on the day it is made. If stored, the lemon juice can make the mayonnaise clot.

Blender Mayonnaise

Preparation: 10-15 minutes

You can make mayonnaise quickly and successfully in a blender or food processor. Follow the basic recipe, but if you are using a blender you can use one whole egg instead of the two egg yolks. Mayonnaise made with a whole egg is lighter in texture and paler in colour and saves you having to use up leftover egg whites. Put all the ingredients except the oil into the goblet or bowl and start the machine. Pour in the oil in a thin, steady trickle, which can turn into a stream as the eggs begin to absorb the oil and thicken. Stop when the required volume has been reached.

Herb Mayonnaise

Use lemon juice instead of vinegar when making the Basic Mayonnaise for this recipe; it gives a pleasantly fresh taste.

Serves 6-8
Preparation: 40 minutes,
    plus 30 minutes chilling

Basic Mayonnaise as recipe
2 tablespoons finely chopped parsley
2 tablespoons finely chopped chives
1 teaspoon very finely chopped celery
½ teaspoon finely chopped tarragon or dill

Right: Three stages in the making of mayonnaise: the egg yolks are put in a clean bowl with vinegar or lemon juice, then whisked lightly. Lastly, the emulsion forms and the sauce thickens as oil is added.

Prepare the mayonnaise.

☐ Stir the chopped herbs into the mayonnaise. Leave in a cool place (not the refrigerator) for 30 minutes so the flavours can develop.

☐ Stir again before serving.

Tomato Mayonnaise

Serve with poached or fried white fish, shellfish or hard-boiled eggs. A tablespoon of finely chopped chives makes a good addition.

Serves 6-8   ☆☆☆
Preparation: 30 minutes

Basic Mayonnaise as recipe
3 tablespoons tomato purée
pinch of sugar

Prepare the mayonnaise.

☐ Mix the tomato purée with the sugar, then gradually stir into the mayonnaise. Add just enough to suit your taste.

Variations: Just before serving, whip $\frac{1}{4}$ pint (150ml) whipping or double cream to the same consistency as the mayonnaise. Stir lightly into the mayonnaise and adjust the seasoning with salt and pepper. This also works well with leftover mayonnaise if you adjust the quantity of cream: use in the ratio of 1 part cream to 2 parts mayonnaise.

You can also add 1 or 2 tablespoons of chopped fresh tomato to the mayonnaise and 2-3 tablespoons of ruby port.

Storing mayonnaise

Mayonnaise is at its very best when completely fresh, but it can be stored in a covered container in the refrigerator for a few days. If a deeper yellow skin forms on the surface, just whisk it in before serving. **The timings** are based on making the mayonnaise and its variations by hand. It will be much quicker to prepare in a blender or processor.

Rescuing mayonnaise

Even if you know the way, accidents can sometimes happen. If you find you have added too much oil too quickly in the early stages and the mixture has separated or 'curdled', do not despair. There are two ways of rescuing the sauce at this point:

● Put a fresh egg yolk in a bowl and gradually stir in the curdled mayonnaise drop by drop until a true, smooth emulsion forms again. Then continue to add oil to the mayonnaise, following the basic recipe.

● Put a teaspoon of made mustard and a tablespoon of the curdled sauce into a warmed bowl and whisk the two together. Add the curdled sauce a teaspoon at a time and the mayonnaise will thicken again. This is also a useful way to 'bring back' mayonnaise that has separated or thinned out while stored in the refrigerator.

1. Basic Mayonnaise 2. Tartare Sauce 3. Tomato Mayonnaise 4. Herb Mayonnaise.

Ravigôte Sauce

Mayonnaise with soured cream and herbs is delicious with a plate of cold meats. Served with a green salad and game chips, this makes a lovely summer supper.

Rémoulade Sauce

This colourful version of mayonnaise is made with several herbs, capers, pickled onions and gherkins. Use whichever green herbs are available in varying quantities to suit your taste. Since the sauce is flavoured with mustard, it is particularly good with grilled fish, pork and beef.

Tartare Sauce

The best possible accompaniment to fried, grilled or baked fish, especially if the sauce is home-made. If you are serving a dry white wine with the fish, omit the hard-boiled eggs. They give a metallic tang to the wine.

Rub cooked egg yolks through a fine-meshed sieve for Tartare Sauce.

Use a cradle knife (a double-handled herb chopper) with a rocking motion to chop egg whites finely for the Tartare Sauce.

Ravigôte Sauce

Serves 6-8 ☆☆☆
Preparation: 35 minutes,
   plus 30 minutes standing

Basic Mayonnaise as recipe
5floz (142ml) carton soured cream
2 tablespoons finely chopped parsley
2 tablespoons finely chopped stuffed olives
1 tablespoon finely chopped chervil, tarragon, or celery leaves
1 tablespoon onion or shallot, cut into fine strips
salt and white pepper

Prepare the mayonnaise.

☐ Gradually stir in the soured cream, then add the herbs and onions. Stir lightly just to mix. Adjust the seasoning. Leave in a cool place (not the refrigerator) for 30 minutes for the flavour to develop fully.

☐ Stir again before serving.

Rémoulade Sauce

Serves 6-8 ☆☆☆
Preparation: 40 minutes,
   plus 30 minutes standing

Basic Mayonnaise as recipe
1 teaspoon made English or French mustard
3 tablespoons finely chopped gherkins
3 tablespoons finely chopped cocktail onions
2 tablespoons finely chopped parsley or chervil
1 tablespoon finely chopped celery leaves, tarragon or dill
2 tablespoons capers, drained and chopped
a little juice from the capers
a little anchovy paste

Mix the mayonnaise with the other ingredients and leave in a cool place (not the refrigerator) to stand for 30 minutes for the flavours to develop.

☐ Stir again before serving.

Right: Rémoulade Sauce.

Tartare Sauce

Serves 6-8 ☆☆☆
Preparation: 45 minutes,
   plus 30 minutes standing

Basic Mayonnaise as recipe
1 teaspoon made mustard
2 hard-boiled eggs
3 tablespoons finely chopped gherkins
1 tablespoon finely chopped parsley
1 tablespoon finely chopped chives
1 tablespoon finely chopped onion
1 tablespoon capers, drained and chopped
salt and white pepper

Mix together the mayonnaise and the mustard. Shell the eggs, cut them in half and remove the yolks. Rub the yolks through a sieve and finely chop the whites.

☐ Mix the egg yolks thoroughly into the sauce, then lightly stir in the remaining ingredients, including the chopped egg whites. Adjust the seasoning to taste.

☐ If the sauce is too thick, thin it down with a little juice from the capers, or a little cream if it is already sufficiently well-flavoured. Leave to stand in a cool place (not the refrigerator) for 30 minutes for the flavours to develop.

☐ Stir again before serving.

Cocktail Sauce with Whisky

This goes especially well with chicken or shellfish.

Serves 8   ★★☆
Preparation: 35 minutes

Basic Mayonnaise as recipe
2-3 tablespoons tomato purée
2 tablespoons whisky
salt
pinch of cayenne pepper
¼ pint (150ml) double or whipping cream

Prepare the mayonnaise, then stir in the tomato purée followed by the whisky, salt, and a very little cayenne (but remember it is *hot*).

☐ Just before serving, lightly whip the cream to the same consistency as the mayonnaise and fold it in lightly.

Cocktail Sauce with Brandy and Port:

Substitute 1 tablespoon brandy and 2 tablespoons ruby port for the whisky. Season with salt and pepper and you have a delicious sauce for prawns, crab or lobster.

Green Cocktail Sauce with Vermouth

This sauce is excellent with mussels, or with any poached fish.

Serves 6-8   ★★☆
Preparation: 1 hour

Tartare Sauce as recipe
3 fl oz (100ml) double cream
2 tablespoons dry vermouth

Prepare the Tartare Sauce.

☐ Whip the cream and the vermouth together until they have reached the same consistency as the sauce. Lightly fold into the sauce.

Anchovy Cocktail Sauce

Serve with hard-boiled eggs.

Serves 6-8   ★★☆
Preparation: 35 minutes

Basic Mayonnaise as recipe
6 anchovy fillets, finely chopped
grated rind of ½ lemon
squeeze of lemon juice

Prepare the mayonnaise.

☐ Add anchovies and lemon rind. Adjust the flavour with lemon juice.

COCKTAIL SAUCES

Mayonnaise makes the perfect base on which to create a cocktail sauce to serve with shrimps, prawns, mussels, crab and other types of seafood. These cocktail sauces also complement canned fish and, with a sprinkling of parsley or a fine chopping of egg white to garnish, you have a quickly made and popular first course. A little alcohol lifts a sauce like this into the 'special' class.

Cocktail sauces need not be limited to serving with seafood. Hand one of these round with cold roast chicken, turkey or poached or fried white fish.

Remember not to overwhelm the food with the sauce, or the sauce with the flavouring.

Serving tips

● Pieces of leftover cooked poultry mix well with prawns, shrimps or other seafood.
● You can 'stretch' crab and lobster by mixing it with pieces of cooked white fish such as plaice, whiting or monkfish, or even cooked diced vegetables such as celery, carrot or fennel.

Left to right:
Cocktail Sauce with Whisky, Green Cocktail Sauce with Vermouth, Cocktail Sauce with Brandy and Port.

Unsalted butter
It is best to use unsalted butter for the Hollandaise family of sauces as it gives a better flavour. Seasoning—including salt—is added at the end of cooking.

Rescuing Hollandaise
If you are unlucky and do slightly overheat the sauce so that it separates, here is a simple remedy. Drop in an ice cube; you will find you can then beat the sauce back to smoothness again.

Peeling tomatoes for Tomato Hollandaise
Pour boiling water into a bowl. Nick the skins of the tomatoes to be peeled by cutting a small cross on the base opposite the stalk end, then immerse them in the boiling water. After 1-2 minutes, lift out with a slotted spoon, or drain the tomatoes. Their skins should now peel off easily using a knife or your fingers. (If peeling them by hand, let them cool a little first, or keep them under running cold water for a minute or two.)

Hollandaise Sauce

Serve with asparagus, broccoli or salmon.

Preparation and ☆☆☆
    cooking time: about 45 minutes
Makes ¾ pint (450ml) to serve 6-8

The stock:
3 tablespoons white wine vinegar
2 tablespoons water
4 coarsely ground black peppercorns
1oz (25g) finely chopped shallot
    or onion
small bay leaf
sprig of parsley, roughly chopped

The sauce:
3 egg yolks, size 2
5-7oz (150-200g) unsalted butter,
    softened
salt and white pepper
few drops lemon juice

Put the ingredients for the stock into a small saucepan over a low heat. Simmer gently, stirring occasionally, until the liquid has been reduced by at least half. The more slowly the stock cooks and the longer it takes to reduce, the better will be the flavour.

☐ Strain the liquid through a piece of muslin (as shown) or cheesecloth, or through a coffee filter paper.

☐ Put the egg yolks into a small pan or basin (or in the top compartment of a double-boiler) over a pan of water on a low heat. Gradually stir in the strained liquid and cook until it is just beginning to thicken. Keep the water below boiling point to prevent the sauce curdling.

☐ Gradually whisk in 2 rounded teaspoons of the butter. Remove from the heat and continue to whisk in the rest of the butter, a little at a time. The finished sauce will be smooth and glossy and fairly stiff.

☐ Season to taste with salt, pepper and lemon juice. Serve in an unheated sauceboat.

Tip: This sauce is always served lukewarm because if over-heated it separates; hence the unheated sauceboat.

Right: Ingredients and equipment for making the perfect Hollandaise. Straining the reduced stock through muslin or cheesecloth and cooking the sauce in a double saucepan.

Tomato Hollandaise Sauce

This rich, apricot-coloured sauce is one of the loveliest of the Hollandaise family. Making the tomato stock takes a little patience but it gives the sauce the most subtle, delicate flavour. Serve with poached white fish.

Preparation and   ☆ ☆ ☆
     cooking time: about 1 hour
Makes ¾ pint (450ml) to serve 6-8

The stock:
6oz (175g) ripe tomatoes
1 tablespoon unsalted butter
pinch of sugar
few drops Worcestershire sauce
salt and white pepper

The sauce:
3 egg yolks, size 2
5-7oz (150-200g) unsalted butter,
    softened
a few drops lemon juice
salt and white pepper

Below: Adding concentrated orange juice to make Maltese Sauce, and a sauceboat of Mousseline Sauce (Hollandaise with whipped cream added). Both these recipes are on the next page.

Peel the tomatoes (see the sidelines on the opposite page), cut them in half and scoop out the seeds. With your hand, press the tomatoes flat on kitchen paper to remove as much liquid as possible. Liquidize or process the tomatoes to a purée.

☐ Melt the butter in a small saucepan over a low heat. Add the tomato purée and simmer for 2 minutes, stirring all the time. Season with sugar, Worcestershire sauce, salt and pepper.

☐ Use this stock to make a sauce with the egg yolks and butter in the same way as for the basic Hollandaise Sauce.

☐ Adjust the flavour with lemon juice and seasoning.

Tip: Ready-made concentrated tomato purée is too strong in flavour for this sauce.

Variation: Add some chopped chives to the sauce before serving.

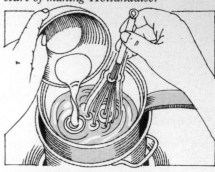

Whisking egg yolks in a bowl at the start of making Hollandaise.

Adding the stock to the egg yolks over gently simmering water.

Mousseline Sauce

Serve with poached trout, grilled sole, broccoli, sea kale and asparagus. Serve as soon as possible as it is very light and delicate.

Preparation and ☆☆☆
  cooking time: about 1 hour
Makes ¾ pint (450ml) to serve 6-8

Hollandaise Sauce as recipe
4 tablespoons double cream
salt and white pepper

Prepare the Hollandaise Sauce and leave to cool.
☐ Whip the cream to soft peaks. Whisk the Hollandaise until it is completely cool.
☐ Fold in the whipped cream and season to taste.

Maltese Sauce

The juice of blood oranges is used as a 'stock' (or flavouring liquid) and a little orange peel is added as a garnish. Serve with salmon, trout, asparagus or calabrese.

Preparation and ☆☆☆
  cooking time: about 45 minutes
Makes ¾ pint (450ml) to serve 6-8

3 egg yolks, size 2
3 tablespoons blood orange juice
5-7oz (150-200g) unsalted butter,
  softened
salt to taste
squeeze of lemon juice
a few strips of orange peel, to garnish

Heat the egg yolks with the orange juice and whisk in the butter in the same way as for Hollandaise Sauce. Add salt and lemon juice to taste.
☐ To prepare the orange peel garnish, thinly pare an orange, taking care not to remove any white pith with the peel. Cut the peel into thin strips and blanch in boiling water for 2-3 minutes. Drain and rinse in cold water. Sprinkle the strips over the sauce.
Tip: When blood oranges are not available, any type of orange may be used.

Béarnaise Sauce

Tarragon is the characteristic flavour of this great sauce so it is best to make it with the fresh herb. Serve with steak and other grilled meats.

Preparation and ☆☆☆
  cooking time: about 45 minutes
Makes ¾ pint (450ml) to serve 6-8

The stock:
4 tablespoons white wine vinegar
4 white peppercorns
1 tablespoon finely chopped shallot
  or onion
1 tablespoon finely chopped leek,
  white part only
small bay leaf, crumbled
sprig of parsley, roughly chopped
sprig of fresh tarragon

The sauce:
3 egg yolks, size 2
5-7oz (150-200g) softened butter
2 teaspoons finely chopped fresh
  tarragon
salt
squeeze of lemon juice

Combine the stock ingredients, cook to reduce by half and use to make the sauce as for Hollandaise Sauce.

Salad Cream

Preparation and ☆☆☆
  cooking time: 20 minutes
Makes ¾ pint (450ml) to serve 6-8

3 egg yolks, size 2
1 teaspoon made mustard
4 tablespoons oil
4 tablespoons double cream
2 tablespoons white wine vinegar
salt and white pepper
dash of Worcestershire sauce
1 teaspoon sugar (optional)

Put the egg yolks, mustard, oil, cream and vinegar into a large basin and set over a pan of water on a low heat. Keep the water just below boiling point, and whisk at intervals until the sauce begins to thicken. Continue whisking until it resembles a thick, smooth custard.
☐ Remove from the heat and add salt, pepper and Worcestershire sauce. Add the sugar, if liked.

Mousseline Sauce

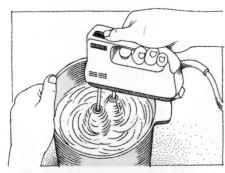

Whisk double cream to soft peaks with an electric whisk.

Stir the whipped cream into the Hollandaise sauce.

Salad Cream
We have become so accustomed to having salad cream from a bottle that we forget how easy it is to make at home. It can be served hot with poached fish dishes but is best if left to get cold. Serve with cold cooked vegetables, salads, cold chicken and fish. If serving with shellfish, add a little tomato purée.

Sweet Sauces

Sweet sauces are simple and quick, and with this set of basic sauces you can create a host of others to complement the puddings and desserts you most enjoy. Learn to whip up a speedy Butterscotch Sauce or a Celebration Strawberry Sauce, and you'll never be at a loss when unexpected guests arrive. Some, like the Sabayon and the Chocolate Sauce, can be turned into desserts on their own. Most can be served hot or cold, and keep well for several days in the fridge, ready to transform a winter pudding, summer ice or creamy rice pudding into something special.

Sweet sauces, such as the basic Vanilla Sauce, are usually thickened with cornflour (or arrowroot) and often eggs as well, because these give a finer, more glossy finish to a sauce. However, the hard butter sauces, many of the fruit purée sauces, and those based on jam or syrup need no thickening.

Master the basic technique, then experiment as you like with essences and spices, or a subtle drop of spirit or liqueur, to create your own variations of flavour and texture. Always remember to start with a little, then gradually add the chosen flavouring until you have achieved the required strength.

Vanilla Sauce

Serves 4   ☆☆
Preparation and cooking time:
   10-15 minutes

½ vanilla pod (split lengthways)
18 fl oz (500ml) milk
2 teaspoons cornflour
2 tablespoons caster sugar
3 egg yolks, size 2

Place the vanilla pod in a heavy-based saucepan with the milk. Set the pan over a low heat and bring very slowly to just below boiling point. Take the pan off the heat and remove the vanilla pod.

☐ In a small basin, mix together the cornflour, sugar and egg yolks until smooth. Stir in a little of the hot milk, then pour this mixture back into the milk in the pan.

☐ Return the pan to the heat and cook gently, stirring all the time, until thickened and smooth. For a slightly thinner sauce, stir in a little extra milk.

Tip: It is natural for a skin to form as the sauce cools. Either skim it off before serving or, if keeping the sauce hot, cut out a piece of greaseproof paper or foil and press it lightly over the surface. This should prevent a skin from forming.

Rules for sweet sauces

1 When making milk-based sauces such as Vanilla Sauce, always keep the heat moderate to avoid the milk 'catching' on the base of the pan.
2 Stir constantly when making milk-based sauces, to avoid scorching and uneven thickening.
3 With egg-based sauces, keep to a moderate heat, otherwise the egg will separate out before the sauce is cooked.
4 Sauces made with cornflour can be cooked quickly in a saucepan, but they're even better if you cook them more slowly in a double boiler. This way you should only need to stir them occasionally.
5 Arrowroot is often used in sauces instead of cornflour. It gives a softer 'set' and a greater translucency. It is most commonly used as a glaze for fruit tarts and cakes.
6 Richer sauces can be made by replacing part of the milk with single cream.

To tell when a pouring custard is cooked: Dip a metal tablespoon into the sauce, then invert it over the pan. The custard should form a rim around the edge of the spoon when it's ready.

Vanilla Sauce

Hot vanilla sauce is good with steamed puddings, light fruit sponges and hot fruit pies. Cold, it makes a delicious accompaniment to fresh fruit salad, compotes, and jellies.

Variations

Mix instant coffee, ground cinnamon, ginger or nutmeg into the cornflour when making the sauce. Try 1 level teaspoon first, until you decide the strength of flavour.
● Coffee goes well with steamed puddings.
● Cinnamon goes well with poached apples.
● Ginger goes well with poached pears.
● Nutmeg goes well with prunes.
For a rich Vanilla Sauce, if cold, fold in 3 fl oz (100ml) whipped cream just before serving.

Instead of using a vanilla pod, use vanilla sugar, made by storing a split vanilla pod in a jar of sugar.
You can use a vanilla pod over and over again until the flavour gradually goes. Just wipe it dry after use and store it in its jar until the next time it's needed.

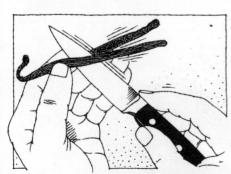

Split the vanilla pod lengthways for maximum flavour.

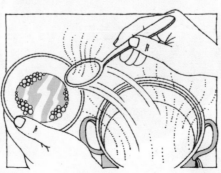

Add a little hot milk to the yolks before stirring them in.

Chocolate Sauce

One of the simplest of all the sweet sauces is thickened just with cornflour. To this basic sauce, you can add whatever flavour you like. This chocolate sauce is just one example; another is the Raspberry Sauce.

You'll notice there are no eggs to act as additional thickeners, so the amount of cornflour has to be increased. Some recipes tell you to mix the sugar with the cornflour and cocoa; if you stir it in at the end there is less chance of the mixture sticking to the pan.

Chocolate Dessert

Leave the Chocolate Sauce to get cold, then quickly turn it into a light dessert. Remove any skin from the top and fold in 3 fl oz (100ml) lightly whipped double cream.

Sabayon Sauce

If you have no Madeira or Marsala, use sherry instead (dry or sweet according to taste). If serving on its own as a dessert, serve with small, crisp biscuits such as langues de chat.'

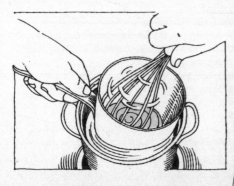

A Sabayon pan: deep for immersing in water, rounded for whisking.

Chocolate Sauce

Serve hot with chocolate sponge pudding, steamed lemon pudding, vanilla blancmange, or hot or cold with ice cream or ice cream desserts.

Serves 4   ☆
Preparation and cooking time:
  5 minutes

---

18 fl oz (500ml) milk
2 tablespoons cornflour
2 tablespoons cocoa
a few drops vanilla essence
2oz (50g) sugar

Mix a little of the cold milk in a basin with the cornflour and cocoa to form a smooth paste. Put the rest of the milk on to heat until nearly bubbling, then stir it into the cornflour mixture.

☐ Return the flavoured milk to the saucepan and cook, stirring constantly, over a moderate heat until the sauce is thickened and smooth. Stirring in a little vanilla essence helps to heighten the chocolate flavour. Add the sugar.

Tip: For a thinner sauce, stir in more milk before serving.

Note: This sauce can be boiled (because it contains no egg), but cooking it more slowly improves the flavour and less is wasted by being cooked on to the pan.

Sabayon Sauce

Although this is similar to one of the most famous of Italian desserts (Zabaglione), it can also be made as a sauce. Try it with poached pears, ice cream, or a light sponge pudding. It should be served warm because it separates out as it cools.

Serves 4 as a dessert, 8 as a sauce ☆
Preparation and cooking time:
  15 minutes

---

5 eggs, size 2, separated
2oz (50g) sugar
5 tablespoons Madeira or Marsala
grated rind of ½ lemon

Place all the ingredients except the egg whites into a basin, or the top of a double boiler, and set this over a pan of hot water on a low heat. Whisk until very thick and foamy, then remove from the heat.

☐ Whisk the egg whites until they form soft peaks, then fold into the cooked mixture. Serve immediately.

Sweet White Wine Sauce

Serves 4   ☆

Preparation and cooking time:
  10-15 minutes

2 eggs, size 2, separated
2oz (50g) sugar
7 fl oz (200ml) sweet white wine
2-3 tablespoons orange juice

Put the egg yolks, sugar and wine
into a basin and set it over a pan of
hot water on a low heat. Whisk
occasionally until the mixture cooks
to a light custard.
☐ Stir in orange juice to taste.
☐ Whisk the egg whites until they
form soft peaks and fold them into
the custard. Serve immediately.
Variation: Substitute the juice of 1
lemon for the orange juice, adding
extra sugar if necessary.

*From left to right: Chocolate
Sauce, Sabayon Sauce,
Sweet White Wine Sauce and
Cumberland Rum Butter.*

Cumberland Rum Butter

Serves 4   ☆☆☆

Preparation: 8-10 minutes

4oz (100g) unsalted butter, softened
4oz (100g) soft brown sugar
grated rind of ½ orange or ⅓ lemon
about 3 fl oz (100ml) light or dark rum

Beat the butter and sugar together
until very soft, pale and fluffy.
☐ Beat in the grated orange or
lemon rind, then gradually beat in
the rum, until the sauce is the
consistency of thickly whipped
cream.
Variation: If you prefer a smoother
texture, use icing sugar instead of
the soft brown sugar. The sauce will
be paler, but still delicious.

Butterscotch Sauce
Golden syrup makes an excellent quick
butterscotch sauce to serve with hot puddings
or ice cream. Simply heat together 8oz (225g)
golden syrup, 2oz (50g) butter and ½ teaspoon
vanilla essence until melted. Remove from
heat, stir, and serve hot or cold.

Cumberland Rum Butter
Christmas pudding just isn't complete without
this traditional sauce. It can be made a few
days in advance and stored in a cool place. If
stored in the fridge it will keep at least a
week, but the chilling makes it hard again.

Brandy Butter
Use brandy instead of rum.

Sauces with liqueurs
Most sweet sauces benefit from a little spirit
or liqueur. Add a drop or two, taste it, then
add more until the necessary depth of flavour
is reached. Remember that the aim is to
improve the flavour, not overwhelm it.
As a guide, use about 3 tablespoons spirit or
liqueur for any of these recipes:
● Try crème de cacao in chocolate sauce to
serve with chocolate or lemon ices.
● Try orange-flavoured liqueurs in vanilla
sauces (omit the vanilla). Serve with
chocolate mousse or poached pears.
● Amaretto is delicious in either chocolate or
vanilla sauce. Serve with poached or baked
apples, or with pancakes or waffles.
● Try maraschino or kirsch with raspberry,
pineapple, or cherry sauce. Serve with
mousses, ices or rice puddings.

Soft Fruit Sauce

Canned fruits are particularly good for making sauces because they are already cooked and therefore easy to purée. Use your blender or processor to do this for you, or rub the fruit with its juice through a mouli-mill or a sieve using the back of a wooden spoon. With fresh fruit, cook it with a little water and sugar to taste then use in the same way.

Celebration Strawberry Sauce

Some of the best fruit sauces are made without either cooking or thickening. This one is for special occasions and superb to serve with ice cream, sorbets and mousses. Try it, too, with one of the low-fat soft cheeses (such as quark), or with Petit Suisse cheeses.

Soft Fruit Sauce

Serve hot with a light sponge pudding, ice cream, or cold with cream-filled meringue shells.

Serves 4

Preparation and cooking time:
  10 minutes

15½oz (430g) can of fruit—peaches,
  pineapples, apricots, gooseberries or
  plums
1 tablespoon cornflour
sugar to taste
a few drops of lemon juice

Purée the fruit with its juice.
☐ Mix a little of the cold purée with the cornflour in a large basin and put the rest in a pan to heat.
☐ Stir the hot purée into the cornflour mixture, return this to the saucepan and continue cooking over a moderate heat. Stir frequently until thickened.
☐ Add sugar to taste, then add a little lemon juice to heighten the flavour.

Celebration Strawberry Sauce

Serves 4-5
Preparation: 10 minutes

12oz (350g) fresh strawberries
3 tablespoons port
2-3oz (50-75g) caster sugar

Hull the strawberries, then cut them into small pieces. Rub through a sieve or mouli-mill, or blend or process to a purée. Stir in the port and sugar to taste. Serve immediately.
☐ When serving, set a jug of the chilled sauce in a dish of crushed ice and garnish with whole fresh strawberries.
Tip: If making this ahead, whisk lightly before serving, as some of the juice separates out on standing.
Note: You can also use frozen strawberries, or thawed strawberry purée for this sauce.

From left to right: Soft Fruit Sauce made with canned peaches, Celebration Strawberry Sauce, Orange Sauce and Foamy Raspberry Sauce.

Orange Sauce

Serve hot with puddings, or cold with sorbets and water ices such as lemon, orange, or apricot.

Serves 4-6
Preparation and cooking time:
   5-10 minutes

grated rind of ½ orange
14 fl oz (400ml) orange juice
3 tablespoons cold water
1 tablespoon cornflour
squeeze of lemon juice
about 1 tablespoon sugar

Heat the orange rind and juice in a saucepan until just beginning to bubble.
☐ Mix the water and cornflour to a smooth paste in a large bowl, then stir in the hot liquid. Return this to the saucepan and cook, stirring constantly, for 2-3 minutes until lightly thickened.
☐ Add lemon juice and sugar to taste. If served cold, stir before serving.

Foamy Raspberry Sauce

☆

Serves 4-6
Preparation and cooking time:
   15 minutes

4 eggs, size 2
½ pint (300ml) raspberry juice
caster sugar to taste

Whisk the eggs in a basin. Heat the juice in a saucepan, then gradually whisk the juice into the eggs. Pour the juice back into the saucepan or into the top of a double boiler. Set the pan over another filled with hot water, over a low heat.
☐ Cook, whisking frequently, until the sauce begins to cling to the whisk and only falls from it if the whisk is shaken lightly. Remove from the heat and stir in a little sugar if liked. Serve hot or cold.
Tip: If the sauce is to be served cold, lightly whisk it again just before serving.

Orange Sauce
Many fruit juices are now available in cans or cartons, or sometimes in bottles, and these are very good to use for sauces like this. Serve it with hot desserts such as chocolate or ginger sponge, or, with a plain Madeira or almond sponge cake which has been wrapped in foil and warmed in the oven.

As with many of the sauces, this one can be made special with the addition of a liqueur such as curaçao, Grand Marnier, or even whisky.

Foamy Raspberry Sauce
In this sauce, whole eggs are used for the thickening. In fact, this is really a raspberry-flavoured egg custard, and it's just the right texture to serve with desserts such as upside-down peach pudding, hot waffles, ice cream or a cool, creamy rice pudding.

Dried Apricot Sauce

Serves 6 ☆

Preparation and cooking time:
  20 minutes poaching, plus
  15 minutes

4oz (100g) dried apricots
18 fl oz (500ml) white wine
juice of ½ lemon
6oz (175g) sugar
4 egg yolks, size 2
1 whole egg, size 2

If necessary, soak the apricots overnight in the wine. (Some dried fruit does not need soaking. Be guided by the instructions on the pack.)

☐ Poach the fruit in the wine until tender, then liquidize, process, rub through a mouli-mill or sieve. Stir in lemon juice to taste with half the sugar.

☐ Whisk the egg yolks with the whole egg and the rest of the sugar.

☐ Place in a basin over a saucepan of hot water on a low heat, or in the top of a double boiler, and gradually whisk in the apricot purée, continuing until the sauce is the consistency of a light custard. Serve hot or cold.

Gooseberry Sauce

Serve hot or cold with steamed puddings, ices or mousses.

Serves 4 ◯

Cooking time: 15 minutes

12oz (350g) fresh or frozen gooseberries
3oz (75g) caster sugar
sprig of mint
4 fl oz (125ml) sweet white vermouth
a few drops green food colouring (optional)

Put all the ingredients, except the food colouring, into a saucepan.

☐ Simmer gently over moderate heat for 6-10 minutes until the fruit is mushy. Discard the mint. Liquidize or process the fruit to a smooth purée. Add colouring.

☐ Sieve and serve hot or cold.

Tip: For this sauce, you can use frozen gooseberries without thawing them first. Cook a little longer.

Redcurrant Sauce

Serves 4 ◯

Cooking time: 10 minutes

8oz (225g) redcurrant jelly
6 tablespoons red wine

Put jelly and wine in a small, heavy-based saucepan. Heat gently until the mixture bubbles, stirring constantly.

☐ Reduce the heat and continue stirring until the sauce thickens enough to give a little resistance when stirred. Serve immediately.

Dried Apricot Sauce

Dried apricots have a unique flavour quite unlike that of either fresh or canned. This sauce is very good to serve with spicy desserts, or with light fluffy cold sweets such as mousses. Try it, too, with such everyday things as blancmange or 'instant' whipped desserts.

Redcurrant Sauce

Serve hot or cold with ice cream and pears or rice pudding.

Marmalade Sauce

Follow the instructions for Redcurrant Sauce, using 8oz (225g) jelly marmalade and 6 tablespoons white wine. Serve with winter puddings such as Spotted Dick.

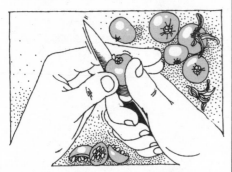

Before cooking berried fruit (eg. gooseberries), top and tail them.

As an alternative to a blender, use a mouli-mill.

Pastry

Many traditional and continental recipes require some form of pastry to be made, yet pastry-making is an art which many people find difficult to master. A few general rules, plus the recipes, tips and advice in this section will ensure good results.

Always work in cool conditions and handle the pastry as little as possible. (Hands can be cooled by running the wrists under a cold tap.) Do not be tempted to add too much water to the dough – it requires kneading to pull it together, not just liquid! If possible, allow time to chill the dough before rolling out, especially the richer pastries which have a high fat content. While rolling out, never turn the rolled pastry over as it will take up too much flour.

Plain flour should be used as it is stronger than self-raising. To vary the texture of the pastry and to add extra fibre, some of the flour can be replaced with oatmeal, wholemeal or buckwheat flour. Pastry made entirely with wholemeal flour requires a little more skill in handling, so it is best to start by only using a proportion of wholemeal. Oatmeal and buckwheat flour do not contain much gluten: use them in the proportion of one part to four parts plain or wholemeal flour.

Always use hard fats for pastry-making as they contain less water and are easier to rub into the flour. A food processor can be a great help with 'rubbing in' as it prevents too much handling. It is important to chill the fats well to avoid over-processing. A pastry blender is useful if a food processor is not available. All pastry dough can be frozen in handy portions, so it is worth making large quantities when you have the time.

Specific pastry quantities are given in the recipes but you may like to vary the sizes. Generally, 12oz (350g) of dough will make either two 8in (20cm) shallow flan cases or one 8in (20cm) double-crust tart.

Shortcrust is the most widely used pastry and the best one to perfect before attempting the flaky pastries. A basic shortcrust pastry is always based on half fat to flour with 1 tablespoon water to each 4oz (125g) flour. The fats are usually half butter or margarine and half lard. Butter gives colour and flavour, while lard has better shortening properties. The aim is to make very fine breadcrumbs – the finer the crumbs, the better the pastry. The crumbs are then mixed to a dough with a very little cold water.

Flaky pastries are enriched with a much higher proportion of fat and this is incorporated into the pastry in an entirely different manner. Puff pastry has many crisp layers and a light texture. It is considered to be one of the highest achievements in the whole of the cookery repertoire. In this pastry, the fat, usually butter, is left in a block and the dough is wrapped around it. Repeated foldings, turnings and rollings create the many layers. At each stage the pastry must be wrapped and chilled to prevent it becoming difficult to handle.

Choux pastry has its own set of rules as it does not require lengthy handling or chilling. It is more like a paste and is cooked during preparation. Plain or wholemeal flour can be used and the liquid can be milk or water, or a mixture of the two. The fat used is usually butter or margarine. It is a very versatile pastry as it is suitable for both sweet and savoury dishes.

The following chapter will help you rediscover or develop hidden talents for making satisfying sweet and savoury tarts and flans. With practice, pastry-making will become easier and more enjoyable, with successful results every time.

Freezing shortcrust pastry: You can also freeze the pastry ready-shaped in flan or tart cases. Wrap the made cases in foil and freeze quickly. To thaw, unwrap and leave at room temperature for at least 30 minutes before filling or baking.

Making pastry with food processors: Modern food processors make pastry-making an easy one-step operation. Process the dry ingredients and fat until the mixture has the right texture then add the liquid and process briefly using the pastry attachment until the dough forms into a ball.

Pastry tartlet cases

It is easier to line a tin with pastry if you have a little extra. Use the trimmings to make little individual flan cases. Store them in the freezer ready to fill with savoury mixtures for hors d'oeuvres, first courses or to make decorative containers for vegetable accompaniments.

Flavouring pastry for savoury flans

Try adding a dash of cayenne, a pinch of celery seeds, or a teaspoon of dried herbs to the flour before you rub in the butter.

Adding the water

Sprinkle 1 tablespoon of water over the surface and mix in. Then add more water, just 1 teaspoon at a time, mixing continually until you can form the dough into a ball. Even a teaspoon too much water can make your pastry less tender.

Making Plain Flan Pastry.

If you are making a large batch of dough, you can measure out the water and dribble it in gradually. For the given recipe, it is better to use a spoon so you add only a very little at a time.

Savoury Flans

There are many mixtures of savoury foods which make delicious and economical lunch or supper dishes when baked in a flan.

Cooked meats, poultry, fish, seafood and vegetables with a cheese sauce or a savoury custard can be used, and the pastry may be cooked in advance or made fresh – or even bought from the supermarket freezer. For savoury flans, the pastry is made with only flour and butter – and just enough water to mix. It is quick to make, but if you make a large batch at a time you can store it for later use. Freeze the dough in the piece or as shaped unbaked cases of various sizes – or even as baked cases.

When making pastry for savoury flans, remember that the more you rub the butter into the flour, the less water you will need for mixing – and the more tender your pastry will be. It will also hold its shape better in baking.

If you don't have a spring-form tin, use a cake tin with a loose bottom or a deep flan ring set on a greased baking tray.

Plain Flan Pastry

Makes about 12oz (350g)
Preparation: 15 minutes

7oz (200g) plain flour
4oz (125g) cold butter
1-2 tablespoons cold water

Put the flour and butter into a mixing bowl. Cut the butter into as small pieces as possible. With the fingertips, rub in the butter thoroughly to make a mixture with the consistency of coarse moist crumbs.

☐ Gradually stir in cold water until you can form the mixture into a ball of dough.

☐ Turn out on a floured surface and work lightly into a smooth dough. Sprinkle the dough with a little flour to prevent sticking.

☐ Roll the dough out to about ¾-in (1.5-cm) thickness. Fold over one-third of it, then fold the remaining third over the top of that.

☐ Wrap the dough in film or foil and chill for half an hour before rolling. Or, freeze for up to 2 months.

With two knives, cut butter into flour, then rub in with the fingertips.

Stir in enough water to bind, mixing constantly.

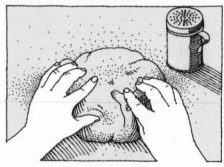

On a sparingly floured surface, lightly work to a smooth dough.

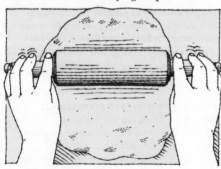

Roll out to an even rectangle.

Fold the pastry in three as shown.

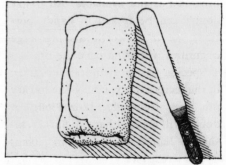

Wrap in foil or film and chill.

Leek and Ham Flan

Serves 6 ☆☆☆
Preparation: 20 minutes
Cooking: 40 minutes

about 12oz (350g) Plain Flan Pastry
1oz (25g) butter
8oz (225g) leeks, trimmed and sliced
4oz (125g) sliced cooked ham

The sauce:
1oz (25g) butter
2 tablespoons flour
9fl oz (250ml) milk
4oz (125g) grated cheese
1 egg, size 2
salt and freshly ground black pepper
½ teaspoon dried thyme

Set the oven to 425F (220C) gas 7.
☐ On a lightly floured board, roll the pastry into a circle about 12 in (30 cm) across. Fold in half then in half again into a fan shape.
☐ Lift into a 9½-in (24-cm) diameter spring-form tin and place the tip of the fan in the centre. Unfold the pastry and smooth carefully back across the bottom and up the sides of the tin. Press gently but firmly against the tin.
☐ With a knife, trim the pastry to a depth of about 1¼ in (3 cm) around the sides. Prick the base with a fork. Line the pastry with foil 12 in (30 cm) square, pressing the foil into the pastry.
☐ Bake 'blind' for 10 minutes in the oven. Lift away the foil and bake for about another 10 minutes until the bottom of the pastry is set.
☐ While the pastry is baking, prepare the filling: Put the butter into a medium frying-pan over a moderate heat. Cook the leeks gently, turning frequently, for about 10 minutes to soften without browning.
☐ To make the sauce: Melt the butter in a medium saucepan over a moderate heat. Stir in the flour then gradually stir in the milk until the mixture is thick and smooth. Mix in the cheese and egg and season to taste with salt, pepper and thyme.
☐ Arrange the ham over the bottom of the baked pastry. Spread the leeks over the ham and cover with the sauce.
☐ Bake for about 20 minutes to brown the top of the filling.
☐ Serve hot or cold, cut into wedges.

The various stages in preparing and cooking Leek and Ham Flan.

The pastry mixtures for the little savoury balls and for the shortbread are very rich in butter. It is easier to cut the butter in well to such a mixture with a pastry blender.

Chopping hazelnuts
Put the nuts in a plastic bag. Hold the end closed, then crush the nuts with a rolling pin. Transfer to a chopping board and chop with a sharp knife (otherwise, without initial flattening, the nuts roll around and are difficult to chop).

Cheese Snacks, Cheese Shortbread and Savoury Nut Balls all make excellent cocktail snacks.

Cheese Snacks

Makes about 48 ☆☆
Preparation and cooking: about 25 minutes

4oz (100g) plain flour
5oz (125g) finely grated Cheddar cheese
cayenne
3oz (75g) cold butter, cubed small

Set the oven to 400F (200C) gas 6.
☐ Mix the flour and cheese in a bowl and add cayenne to taste.
☐ Add the butter to the dry ingredients and rub in finely with the fingertips. Knead together into a dough.
☐ Pinch off pieces of dough about the size of a small walnut. Roll under the hand on a work surface to form smooth little balls.
☐ Place on greased baking trays and bake in the oven for about 10 minutes until lightly browned.
☐ Transfer to a wire rack to cool. Store in an airtight container in a cool place for not more than a day, or in the freezer for up to 1 month.
☐ To serve hot: Re-heat in the oven pre-heated to 325F (160C) gas 3 for 5-7 minutes.

Cheese Shortbread

Serves 8-10 ☆☆☆
Preparation and cooking: 1 hour

11oz (300g) plain flour
4oz (125g) Dutch cheese, finely grated
10oz (275g) cold butter, cubed small
1 tablespoon finely chopped parsley
1 tablespoon finely chopped celery leaves
2-3 tablespoons milk for glazing

Set the oven to 350F (180C) gas 4.
☐ Mix the flour and cheese together in a bowl and add the butter.
☐ With 2 knives or a pastry blender, cut the butter up until it is about the size of small peas.
☐ Stir in the herbs. Knead into a dough. Put in a 9½-in (24-cm) loose-bottomed flan tin. Press it firmly and evenly into the tin.
☐ Brush the top of the shortbread with milk and bake for 30 minutes. Re-glaze then bake for a further 5-10 minutes until a good brown.
☐ Press flat then cool in the tin.

Savoury Nut Balls

Makes about 24 ☆☆
Preparation and cooking: 40 minutes

4oz (100g) self-raising flour
2oz (50g) hazelnuts, skinned and finely chopped
3oz (75g) cold butter, cubed small

Set the oven to 350F (180C) gas 4.
☐ Put the flour and nuts in a mixing bowl and add the butter. With 2 knives or a pastry blender, cut the butter in until the mixture resembles coarse dry crumbs.
☐ Work the mixture well with the hand to form it into a ball of dough. Pinch off walnut-sized pieces and roll to make little balls.
☐ Place on baking trays with about 1in (2.5cm) between them. Bake for 20-25 minutes, until lightly browned.
☐ Serve while hot, or cool on a wire rack and store in an airtight tin in a cool place for up to 2 days.

Basic sweet pastry

Sweet pastry is made in the same way as many biscuits, but usually with less sugar. Cold butter is finely rubbed into the flour and sugar, then the crumbs are bound with beaten egg.

Sweet Flan Case

☆☆

Preparation and cooking: 35 minutes

8oz (225g) plain flour
3oz (75g) caster sugar
4oz (125g) cold butter
grated rind of ½ an orange or lemon
    (optional)
1 egg, size 2, lightly beaten

Set the oven to 350F (180C) gas 4.
□ Sieve the flour and sugar into a bowl. Add butter and rind, if using.
□ With 2 knives cut the butter into the dry ingredients as finely as possible, then rub it in with the fingertips to make fine crumbs.
□ Gradually stir in the egg. Turn out on a lightly floured surface and knead to a smooth dough.
□ Place in a 9½-in (24-cm) buttered flan tin. Press with knuckles to fit.
□ Trim off the spare pastry, then prick the pastry case with a fork.
□ Press a 12-in (30-cm) square of foil into the pastry-lined tin.
□ Bake 'blind' for 10 minutes. Lift out the foil then bake for about 10 minutes until lightly browned.
□ Cool on a rack. Remove from tin.

Step-by-step to a Sweet Flan Case. You can roll this type of sweet pastry very thinly to make all sizes of flan case, or simply shape it into the tin as shown with your hands. If using sandwich tins, such as these, butter them well beforehand so that the baked cases can be removed easily.

*From left to right: unglazed and
glazed versions of Strawberry Flan,
Blackcurrant Tart, Tarte à l'Orange
and Kiwi and Banana Flan.*

Making fruit flans

Sweet pastry flans are all made in much the
same way except for the type of glaze used
to cover the filling. With a baked pastry case
in the freezer, you can very quickly produce
a beautiful and delicious dessert using
seasonal or frozen fruits.

The glazes given with the different recipes
are interchangeable. Just vary the flavour to
suit the fruit.

You can bake sweet pastry cases in flan
dishes then serve from the dish. Or you can
use loose-bottomed or spring-form tins, or
flan rings set on baking trays. Use the
trimmings from large flans to make
individual tart cases. Store them in the
freezer for later use.

Rolling sweet pastry

For a thinner, crisper pastry, roll it with a
rolling pin on a lightly floured surface to an
⅛in (3mm) thickness. Loosen from the surface
with a palette knife. Roll around the rolling
pin then unroll over the tin. Press neatly into
place with the fingers. Trim off excess dough.

Fruit-filled flans should be served soon
after making, otherwise moisture from the
fruit makes the pastry soggy. A thin layer of
jam or whipped cream between the two
helps but does add calories! The flans
should not be frozen after filling!

Strawberry Flan

Serves 6   ☆☆
Preparation: 10-15 minutes
plus chilling

9½-in (24-cm) baked Sweet Flan Case
2 tablespoons strawberry jelly or jam
12oz (350g) fresh strawberries

The glaze:
2 teaspoons arrowroot
¼ pint (150ml) dry white wine
2 tablespoons strawberry jelly or
sieved strawberry jam
a few drops of red colouring

Spread the 2 tablespoons jelly or
jam over the bottom of the flan case
and arrange the fruit on top.
☐ To make the glaze: Mix the
arrowroot smoothly with 1
tablespoon of the wine. Put the rest
of the wine in a small saucepan over
a low heat with jelly or sieved jam.
☐ Stir this into the mixed arrowroot
and return it to the saucepan.
Simmer, stirring constantly, for 2-3
minutes until thick and smooth.
☐ Remove from the heat. Stir in a
few drops of red colouring and cool.
☐ Spoon the glaze over and chill to
set – but serve within 2 hours!
☐ Alternatively, omit the glaze and
decorate the flan with whipped cream.

Blackcurrant Tart

Serves 6   ☆☆
Preparation: 10-15 minutes
plus chilling

9½-in (24-cm) baked Sweet Flan Case
12oz (350g) frozen blackcurrants
3oz (75g) caster sugar
about 4 tablespoons red wine
2 teaspoons arrowroot
whipped cream to decorate (optional)

Put the currants, sugar and 3
tablespoons of wine into a saucepan
over a moderate heat and bring to
the boil.
☐ With a slotted spoon, lift out and
drain the blackcurrants and set aside
to cool.
☐ Mix the arrowroot with 1
tablespoon of red wine. Stir in the
hot liquid and return it to the
saucepan. Cook, stirring constantly,
for 2-3 minutes until thick and
smooth. Add a little more wine if a
thinner glaze is desired.
☐ Remove from the heat and cool.
☐ Arrange the blackcurrants in the
pastry case and spread the glaze
over. Chill to set, but serve within 2
hours. If liked, decorate with piped
whipped cream, or serve with a bowl
of lightly whipped cream.

Tarte à l'Orange

Serves 6 ☆☆
Preparation: 20 minutes
plus 30 minutes chilling

9½-in (24-cm) baked Sweet Flan Case
4 large oranges

The glaze:
¼ pint (150ml) sweet white wine
2 tablespoons orange liqueur
1 teaspoon powdered gelatine

Peel the oranges and remove all the white pith. Cut neatly into segments and pat dry.

☐ Put the wine and liqueur into a small saucepan. Sprinkle the gelatine over the surface.

☐ Place on a low heat and stir until the gelatine is dissolved and the mixture is completely clear.

☐ Remove from the heat and set the saucepan in a large pan of cold water. Stir occasionally, until the mixture begins to thicken.

☐ Arrange the orange in the case and spoon the jelly over.

☐ Chill for about 30 minutes.

Variation: Use dessert apple slices. Poach in a little water and sugar and use cooking liquid in place of wine, and brandy instead of liqueur.

Kiwi and Banana Flan

Serves 6 ☆☆
Preparation: 10 minutes

9½-in (24-cm) baked Sweet Flan Case
2 large bananas
2 large kiwi fruit

The glaze:
5 teaspoons liquid glucose
4 teaspoons banana liqueur or white rum

Peel and slice the bananas and kiwi fruit. Arrange in the baked pastry case.

☐ Heat the measuring spoon under hot running water then use to measure out the liquid glucose into a small saucepan. Add the liqueur or rum.

☐ Place over a low heat and stir until well mixed and of a good pouring consistency.

☐ Remove from the heat, cool and spoon over the fruit. Serve immediately.

Tip: Liquid glucose is available in jars from chemists and makes a good instant glaze. It is like a very thick syrup and is crystal clear. It is easier to measure accurately if you use a hot spoon, so that it doesn't stick to it.

Raspberry Tartlets

Makes 9 ☆☆☆
Preparation: 20 minutes

---

9 baked deep sweet pastry tartlets, about 3-in (7.5-cm) diameter

The glaze:
2 tablespoons raspberry or redcurrant jelly
1-2 tablespoons water

The filling:
¼ pint (150ml) double cream
2 tablespoons kirsch
8oz (225g) raspberries

First make the glaze: Put the jelly and 1 tablespoon water into a small saucepan over a low heat. Stir occasionally until melted to a thick syrup. If required to give a pouring consistency, add a little more water. Cool.

☐ Make the filling: Whip the cream and liqueur together until stiff. Pile, or pipe, into the baked cases.

☐ Arrange the fruit over the cream then carefully spoon the glaze over.

☐ Serve within an hour or so.

Tip: It is easy to make these delicious little tartlets – with any fresh fruits – if, whenever you make a flan, you use the pastry trimmings to make cases and freeze them.

Deep Apple Lattice Tart

If you don't have ground almonds, finely chopped almonds are good instead.

It is better to use dessert apples for this dish as cooking apples are a bit too juicy and this spoils the pastry.

Small cubes of butter dotted over the surface of the apples before covering gives an even more delicious flavour.

The various stages in making, decorating and cooking Deep Apple Lattice Tart.

Deep Apple Lattice Tart

Serves 6   ★★☆
Preparation: 20 minutes
Cooking: 40-50 minutes

The pastry:
9oz (250g) plain flour
4oz (125g) caster sugar
5oz (150g) cold butter
1 egg, size 2, lightly beaten

The filling:
2¼lb (1kg) dessert apples
4oz (125g) ground almonds
4oz (125g) caster sugar
a little beaten egg to glaze

Make the Sweet Flan Pastry as directed on page 71. Roll thinly on a lightly floured surface and fold into 4 to form a fan shape.

☐ Place the pastry in a 9½-in (24-cm) spring-form tin or loose-bottomed cake tin with the tip of the fan in the centre. Unfold the pastry.

☐ Press firmly and neatly across the bottom and up the sides. Trim off the top with the back of a knife.

☐ Set oven to 350F (180C) gas 4.

☐ Make the filling: Peel and core the apples. Cut into cubes and mix with the ground almonds and sugar. Place in the pastry-lined tin.

☐ Roll the pastry trimmings into thin ropes. Moisten the edges of the pastry with water, and arrange the ropes across in a lattice.

☐ Trim and press the edges firmly. If there is enough dough left, shape it into another rope to press around the edge to finish neatly.

☐ Brush the lattice all over with a little beaten egg.

☐ Bake in the centre of the oven for 35-40 minutes, or until well browned.

☐ Move the tin to the floor of the oven and bake for a further 5-8 minutes to ensure that the underside of the pastry is cooked.

☐ Set the tin on a wire rack and leave to cool. Remove the sides of the tin and transfer the tart to a serving plate.

☐ Serve immediately, cut in wedges.

Shortcrust pastry

English shortcrust is one of the most versatile of all pastries. It finds its best use in classic small and large pies, tarts or flans – with both sweet and savoury fillings. Good shortcrust pastry should' be light with a crisp crumbly texture.

The traditional method of making this pastry is to rub the fat finely into plain flour and then bind it together using as little water as is necessary to form a dough. Too much will result in a pastry that is tough. During cooking the water evaporates and the pastry's texture is created by the fat and flour binding together. Usually the fat ingredient used is a mixture of butter and lard but there are many recipes which require a single fat. For a less rich pastry, margarine can be used instead. Butter and margarine both contain a certain amount of water, so if using one or other on their own you will require more fat. White fats like lard have no water content and will produce a shorter pastry, so less is needed if it is used alone.

Baking times and temperatures

These vary depending on the recipe. As a rough guide, 400F (200C) gas 6 is the usual setting. A lower temperature is used for items which take longer to cook, such as tarts and flan cases baked in ceramic or glass.

Baking blind

To prepare a flan case or tart for a liquid, or ready-cooked filling, it is 'baked blind'.

This is done by placing a piece of aluminium foil or greaseproof paper in the uncooked tart or flan case. (It is sometimes weighted by filling it with dried beans, uncooked pasta shapes or rice kept especially for the purpose). This prevents the pastry from rising and supports the sides. The base of the pastry is usually also pricked well with a fork to release any trapped air.

Cook the pastry for between 10-20 minutes, depending on whether or not the filled case is to be returned to the oven.

Secrets of success with shortcrust

● Use chilled fats and cold water and try to make pastry in a cool kitchen.
● It is important to handle the pastry as little as possible to prevent it from becoming oily.
● Rub the fat in thoroughly so that all the flour particles are well coated with fat. Shake the bowl occasionally to make unmixed fat come to the surface.
● Add the water a little at a time. Too much generally results in tough and unevenly baked pastry.
● When cooking in glass or ceramic dishes, put them on pre-heated baking trays to ensure thorough cooking of the base.
● Roll the pastry thinly on a lightly floured surface, taking care not to include too much added flour at this stage which will alter the balance of ingredients.
● Roll pastry lightly in 2 directions. This prevents it from becoming over-stretched and shrinking when baked.

English Shortcrust Pastry

Makes about 1½lb (700g) ☆ ☆ ☆

1lb (400g) plain flour
4oz (100g) firm butter, cubed
4oz (100g) firm lard, cubed
4-5 tablespoons cold water

Put the flour into a large bowl and add the fats. With the tips of the fingers, rub the fat into the flour until mixture resembles fine crumbs.
☐ Dribble the water over the surface, one tablespoon at a time, mixing in with a palette knife. Continue adding water, carefully, until you form a firm ball of dough.
☐ Turn out on a lightly floured surface and knead lightly until the dough is smooth and evenly mixed.
☐ Use at once or wrap and freeze.

Storing shortcrust pastry

Shortcrust pastry stores well in several forms. A jar of the flour-fat mixture will keep in the fridge for up to 2 weeks or in the freezer for up to 2 months. Made-up pastry, uncooked, can be stored, well wrapped, in the freezer for up to 2 months – but, if kept in the fridge, it must be used within 2 days. If you have space in your freezer, you may find it convenient to line plates or tins with pastry ready for baking. Many baked dishes made with shortcrust, such as small pastries, tarts with fairly dry fillings, or top-crust-only pies also store well in the freezer.

Making shortcrust pastry

Rub the fat into the flour until it resembles fine dry crumbs.

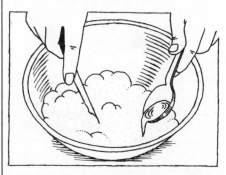

Stir the water in a little at a time until you can form a firm ball of dough.

Decorating pie edges

The simplest way to finish off the edge is to squeeze the pastry gently between the thumb and finger of one hand and, using the forefinger of the other, push the pastry in between the other two fingers. Repeat all round.

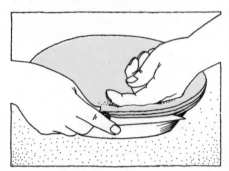

A more professional way to finish off your pie is to 'knock up' the pastry by pressing gently with one finger and lightly cutting the edge with a knife to create a raised edge.

Then 'scallop' the knocked-up edge by pressing down with the thumb and drawing the pastry back to one side with the knife.

Using leftover shortcrust pastry

Gather together into a ball and roll thinly. Make barquettes (tiny boats) or tartlet cases. Store in plastic bags in the freezer ready to fill with a quiche mixture, pizza filling, jam or fruit.

Tricorns

Cut out 3in (7.5cm) rounds of pastry. Place a rounded teaspoon of mincemeat, jam or other filling in the centre. Brush the edges of the circle with water. Draw up the pastry from 3 equidistant points around the edge. Press together in the centre to seal. Bake in the oven pre-heated to 400F (200C) gas 6 for 10-12 minutes.

Steak and Stuffing Pie

Serves 4-5   ☆☆☆
Preparation and cooking: 1¾ hours

---

about 1lb (450g) English Shortcrust Pastry (page 75)

The filling:
12 pitted prunes, soaked overnight in ¼ pint (150ml) port or sweet sherry
1¾lb (675g) chuck steak, trimmed and cubed
1oz (25g) butter
2 tablespoons oil
1 medium onion, chopped
2 celery sticks, sliced
2 teaspoons dried mixed herbs
2 tablespoons flour
¼ pint (150ml) Brown Stock
salt and pepper

The forcemeat stuffing:
4oz (125g) fresh white breadcrumbs
2oz (50g) shredded suet
1 tablespoon chopped parsley
1 teaspoon dried mixed herbs
grated rind of ½ lemon
2oz (50g) bacon, rinded and chopped
1 egg, size 2, beaten

Heat the butter with 1 tablespoon of oil in a large saucepan over a moderate heat and add one-third of the meat. Fry for 5 minutes, stirring frequently, to brown lightly. Remove the meat and cook the remainder in the same way in 2 batches, adding extra oil.

☐ Add the onions and the celery and cook for 5 minutes to soften without colouring. Return all the meat to the pan and add the herbs and the flour. Drain the prunes and add the port to the pan, stirring constantly. Gradually add the stock and cook for 2-3 minutes until thick. Cover and simmer gently for 45 minutes.

☐ Season the meat to taste and transfer to a 1½ pint (900ml) pie dish and allow to cool slightly.

☐ Make the forcemeat stuffing balls: In a large bowl mix the breadcrumbs, suet, parsley, dried mixed herbs, lemon rind, bacon and nearly all the beaten egg, reserving some for brushing the top of the pastry. Season the mixture with salt

and pepper and divide into 12 small balls.

☐ Set oven to 400F (200C) gas 6. On a lightly floured surface roll the pastry out to a thickness of ⅛in (3mm). Cut a piece of pastry to fit the top of the dish and re-roll the trimmings. Cut a strip about ½in (1cm) wide and long enough to go round the edge of the dish.

☐ Add the drained prunes and the forcemeat balls to the meat in the dish and mix in. Brush the edge of the dish with water and place the pastry strip around. Brush the strip with water and cover with the pastry top. Seal the edges and decorate the top with pastry trimmings. Make a small steam hole in the centre.

☐ Place dish on a baking tray and bake for 30-40 minutes. Serve hot.

Fruit Lace Tart

Serves 4   ☆☆☆
Preparation and cooking: 55 minutes

12oz (350g) English Shortcrust Pastry (page 75)
¼ pint (142ml) carton double cream, whipped
8oz (225g) raspberries or redcurrants
2 tablespoons redcurrant jelly
1 tablespoon water
icing sugar to dust

Set the oven to 400F (200C) gas 6.

☐ To make the top: roll one-third of the pastry on greaseproof paper to a thickness of ⅛in (3mm). Use an inverted 7in (18cm) fluted flan tin to cut out a circle of pastry. Use aspic cutters to punch out a lace pattern over the pastry. Slide paper on to a baking tray. Bake for 12-15 minutes until lightly browned. Cool.

☐ Roll out remaining pastry and use to line flan tin. Bake blind for 15-20 minutes (see page 75). Cool.

☐ Spread cream over pastry and cover with the fruit.

☐ Heat jelly and water in a small pan until syrupy. Cool and spoon over fruit.

☐ Slide pastry top on to fruit. Dust with icing sugar and serve at once.

Bakewell Tart

Serves 6   ★★☆
Preparation: 20 minutes
Cooking: 50 minutes

10oz (300g) English Shortcrust Pastry
   (page 75)
3oz (75g) butter
3oz (75g) caster sugar
3 eggs, size 2
4oz (125g) ground almonds
2oz (50g) self-raising flour
8oz (225g) raspberry jam
icing sugar to dust

Set oven to 375F (190C) gas 5 and grease a 1¾ pint (1 litre) flan dish.

☐ Roll the pastry out to a thickness of ⅛in (3mm) and use to line the dish. Bake blind for 10 minutes.

☐ Beat the butter and sugar together until very light and creamy. Beat in the eggs one at a time. Add the ground almonds and the flour. Fold them in lightly.

☐ Spread the jam in the bottom of the pastry case. Spoon the filling on top of the jam and spread level.

☐ Bake in the oven for 25 minutes. Reduce the heat to 300F (150C) gas 2 and bake for about 15 minutes until set in the centre.

☐ Dust with icing sugar and serve hot or cold.

Apple Custard Tart

Serve, heaped with ice cream, for a special family dessert.

Serves 4-6   ★☆☆
Preparation: 15 minutes
Cooking: about 1¼ hours

12oz (350g) English Shortcrust Pastry
   (page 75)
8oz (225g) cooking apples
1 teaspoon ground cinnamon
2 eggs, size 2
½ pint (284ml) carton soured cream
2oz (50g) caster, or soft brown, sugar
1 tablespoon demerara sugar

Set the oven to 350F (180C) gas 4 and grease a deep 7½in (19cm) loose-bottomed flan tin. Roll the pastry

out to a thickness of ⅛in (3mm) and use to line the tin. Bake blind (page 75) for 10 minutes.

☐ Peel, core and thinly slice the apples and spread into the baked pastry case. Bake in the oven for 15 minutes. Remove from the oven and sprinkle with the cinnamon.

☐ Mix together the eggs and soured cream. Strain and stir in the caster, or soft brown, sugar. Carefully spoon the mixture over the apples.

☐ Bake for about ¾ hour until the custard is set. Sprinkle with the demerara sugar and bake for a further 5 minutes.

☐ Serve warm.

Lemon Chiffon Pie

Serves 4-6   ★★☆
Preparation: 20 minutes
Cooking: 30 minutes

10oz (300g) English Shortcrust Pastry
   (page 75)
3 eggs, size 2, separated
6oz (175g) caster sugar
grated rind and juice of 1 large lemon
3 tablespoons water

Set the oven to 325F (160C) gas 3. Grease a 1¾ pint (1 litre) flan dish.

☐ Roll the pastry to a thickness of ⅛in (3mm) and use to line the dish. Bake blind for 10 minutes.

☐ Put the egg yolks and 4oz (100g) of the sugar into a bowl with the lemon juice and rind and the water. Set over a pan of hot water on a low heat.

☐ Whisk until the mixture is very thick and pale and a trail is left after the whisk is removed. Remove from the heat.

☐ Whisk the egg whites to soft peaks. Gradually whisk in the remaining sugar to form a meringue which holds stiff peaks.

☐ Lightly fold the meringue into the lemon mixture. Turn into the baked pastry case. Bake in the oven for about 20 minutes until well risen and golden brown.

☐ Serve immediately.

The traditional Bakewell Tart, which the locals insist must be called 'Bakewell Pudding' did not contain ground almonds, and was more like the custardy 'mirlitons' of France than the rich moist tarts nowadays so popular.

Pineapple Tartlets
Line 18 small tartlet tins with pastry. Bake blind and cool. Drain an 8½oz (250g) can of crushed pineapple and put the juice in a small pan with 2 tablespoons of pineapple jam. Simmer for 4-5 minutes until syrupy. Sieve and cool. Brush tartlets with a little syrup. Spoon drained fruit on top. Whip ¼ pint (142ml) carton of double cream with 1 tablespoon of kirsch. Spoon on top and drizzle over the remaining syrup.

Ways to perfect puff pastry

● It is easier if you work with a small amount of pastry. Too large a piece of dough is difficult to roll easily and neatly.

● Temperature control is very important. Wrap the dough and chill as often as necessary. The fridge is just as important as the oven in the making of puff pastry.

● Rolling butter between 2 sheets of greaseproof paper prevents it sticking to either the board or the pin. You can also use the paper to lift the butter on to the dough.

● Roll the dough large enough to completely encase the butter. No butter should come through the edges of the envelope at any stage. Allow a thumb's width between butter and the edge of the dough.

● It isn't necessary to continue with all the stages at one session. If necessary, you can spread the rolling and folding out over 24 hours. Be sure to wrap the dough well before putting in the refrigerator and allow it to 'come to', after refrigeration, before working with it.

● To keep the dough edges straight, bat them into line with a ruler held perpendicular to the board.

Rolling flaky pastries

Work on a lightly floured board and add as little flour as possible when it is needed to prevent the dough sticking as this causes distortion and produces uneven layers. Use a rolling pin which is at least as long as the width you want the pastry to be. It is difficult to roll pastry evenly with a pin which is too short.

Roll with short strokes and a firm action rather than stretching or pulling the pastry. For puff pastry, it is important to roll the dough to the same thickness each time to ensure good, even rising when cooked.

Glazing and baking puff pastry

Egg gives a rich, deep colour to puff pastry, but it's important not to let it run down the edges – it makes the edges stick together and sticks the pastry to the tray.

When the pastry is baked on the underside, it will move easily on the tray.

Puff Pastry

Makes about 1lb (450g)

8oz (225g) strong white flour
8oz (225g) butter
7-8 tablespoons iced water
1 teaspoon lemon juice

Sift the flour into a large bowl. Cut off a small piece of the butter and add it to the flour. Rub it in finely with the fingertips.

☐ Mix together the water and lemon juice. Gradually stir in enough to bind to a dough.

☐ Turn on to a lightly floured board and knead gently to a smooth elastic ball.

☐ Shake a little flour into a plastic bag. Add the ball of dough, seal the bag and put in a cool place for half an hour.

☐ Place the block of butter between 2 sheets of greaseproof paper. Tap and roll with a rolling pin to a square about ¾in (1.75cm) thick.

☐ On a lightly floured surface roll the dough to a rectangle about ½in (1cm) thick. Set the flattened butter in the centre of it.

☐ Fold the long ends of the dough in over the butter, overlapping them to form a sealed 'envelope'. Tap the seams closed.

☐ Give the dough parcel a quarter turn so that the folded ends are at the sides. With a short firm action roll to a rectangle three times as long as it is wide, keeping the edges straight. Fold over in three again as before. Chill for 15 minutes.

☐ Repeat the rolling, folding, and chilling 6 times in all, giving the dough a quarter turn in the same direction each time and always rolling to the same thickness.

☐ Use the pastry while fresh or wrap and store in the fridge for up to 3 days. You can freeze puff pastry for up to 2 months. Thaw it in its wrapping in the fridge overnight or for 2 hours at room temperature.

Tip: If you make a great deal of pastry, a marble slab will help as it keeps the dough cool.

Folding and rolling Puff Pastry

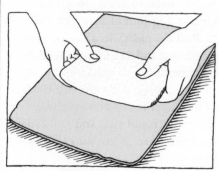

Roll to a rectangle ½in (1cm) thick and place butter in centre.

Fold the bottom third up and top third down to form an envelope.

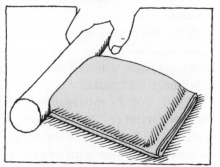

Press the pastry edges closed with the rolling pin.

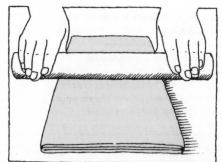

Give a quarter turn so that folds are at the sides. Roll as before.

Pigeon Croustade

Serves 6 ☆☆☆

Preparation, cooking and chilling: 1¼ hours

---

about 1lb (450g) Puff Pastry
beaten egg to glaze

The filling:
two 8oz (225g) pigeons, roasted
4oz (100g) minced veal
4oz (100g) minced pork
4oz (100g) mushrooms, finely chopped
1 tablespoon chopped fresh rosemary
grated rind of ½ lemon
3 tablespoons Madeira
salt and pepper

Roll out the pastry on a sheet of greaseproof paper to a thickness of ⅛in (3mm).

☐ Cut out 2 circles: one 6½in (16cm) in diameter the other 8in (20cm). Chill.

☐ Make the filling: Remove the breasts whole from the pigeon. Remove any remaining meat and mix with the veal, pork, mushrooms, rosemary, lemon rind and Madeira. Season to taste.

☐ Set oven to 425F (220C) gas 7.

☐ Spread half the filling over the smaller circle, leaving a thumb's width clear around the edges. Place the breasts on top and cover with the remaining mixture.

☐ Brush around the clear edge with egg. Carefully place larger circle over filling. Press around the top with the hands so the edges of the two circles are even and the croustade is a neat shape.

☐ Press firmly to seal. 'Knock-up' the sides with a sharp knife and flute the edge as shown on page 76.

☐ Glaze with beaten egg. With the back of a knife, score the top very lightly like wheel spokes. Pierce a steam vent and chill for 15 minutes.

☐ Bake for about 10 minutes, then reduce the oven temperature to 375F (190C) gas 5 and bake for a further 30 minutes until golden.

☐ Serve hot with freshly cooked vegetables, or cold with salads.

Chicken Jalousie

Serves 6 ☆☆☆

Preparation and cooking: 1¼ hours

¾lb (350g) Puff Pastry
beaten egg to glaze

The filling:
2oz (50g) butter
1 small onion, finely chopped
2oz (50g) mushrooms, finely chopped
3 tablespoons flour
9 fl oz (250ml) Chicken Stock
8oz (225g) cooked boneless chicken, chopped
about 3 tablespoons single cream
¼ teaspoon ground mace
salt and pepper

Roll the pastry on 2 sheets of greaseproof paper to a rectangle 12 × 11in (30 × 28cm).

☐ Cut in two lengthways to give one piece 12 × 5in (30 × 13cm) and one 12 × 6in (30 × 15cm). Slide the narrower piece of pastry and one sheet of paper on to a baking tray.

☐ Fold the second piece of pastry in half lengthways.

☐ With a sharp knife, make slashes about 1in (2.5cm) apart along the folded side, cutting to within 1in (2.5cm) of the other side. Chill.

☐ Make the filling: Melt the butter in a medium-sized saucepan over a low heat. Cook the onions and mushrooms for 5-7 minutes, stirring, until soft but not browned.

☐ Sprinkle in the flour, gradually stir in the stock and cook 3-4 minutes, stirring constantly, until thick. Stir in the chicken and the cream. Remove from the heat and season with mace, salt and pepper.

☐ Set oven to 425F (220C) gas 7.

☐ Spoon filling on the pastry base to within 1in (2.5cm) of the edges. Brush the border with egg. Open out the other piece of pastry and carefully place on top.

☐ Press the edges firmly to seal. 'Knock up' edges with a knife (page 76) and brush top with egg.

☐ Bake for 35-40 minutes until well browned.

☐ Serve hot or cold.

Cutting puff pastry

Use a sharp knife so you can make a clean cut and not drag the pastry. Saucers or small saucepan lids make good guides.

Chicken Jalousie

This way of making a puff pastry top takes its name from the French for 'slatted blinds'. Try serving it with a mixed cream salad.

Preparing puff pastry for a Jalousie

Roll the pastry to a 12 × 11in (30 × 28cm) rectangle.

Fold one piece in half lengthways.

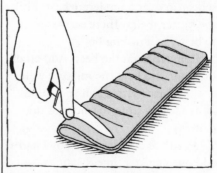

Slash at 1in (2.5cm) intervals to within 1in (2.5cm) of the other side.

Step-by-step to Choux Buns.

Basic Choux Pastry

Makes about 18oz (500g) ☆☆
Preparation: 10 minutes

3oz (75 g) butter
¼ pint (150ml) water
4oz (125g) plain flour, sifted
3 eggs, size 2

Put the butter and water in a
saucepan over a moderate heat until
the butter melts. Increase the heat
to bring to a rolling boil.
☐ Remove from the heat. Add all of
the flour and beat the mixture well
until it forms into a ball and comes
away cleanly from the sides of the
pan.
☐ Turn the dough into a bowl and
add one egg at a time, beating
vigorously after each addition, to
make a stiff glossy paste.

Choux Buns

Makes 12 ☆☆☆
Preparation: 10 minutes
Cooking: 15-18 minutes

Basic Choux Pastry (as left)
½ pint (300ml) double cream
a few drops of vanilla essence
oil for greasing
icing sugar for dusting

Set the oven to 425F (220C) gas 7
and grease two large baking trays.
☐ Put a ½in (1cm) plain pipe into a
forcing bag and fill with pastry.
☐ Squeeze to shape into 12 mounds
on the baking trays. Bake for 15-18
minutes until crisp and firm.
☐ With the tip of a sharp knife,
immediately cut a small slit in the
side of each bun to allow excess
moisture to escape. Leave the buns
to cool on a wire rack.
☐ Whip the cream with the vanilla
to soft peaks. Slice the buns across
horizontally, sandwich back together
with the cream and dust with icing
sugar. Serve fresh.
Variation: You can simply drop the
choux mixture on to greased trays
using a spoon instead of piping it.

Chocolate Profiteroles

Serves 6-8 ☆☆☆
Preparation and cooking: 25
minutes

12 Choux Buns (as left)
½ pint (300ml) double cream
2 tablespoons rum or brandy

The chocolate sauce:
7oz (200g) golden syrup
3-4 oz (75-100g) plain chocolate

Cut the buns open at one side. Whip
the cream and spirit to soft peaks
and spoon into the buns. Pile in a
pyramid on a serving dish.
☐ Put the syrup into a small
saucepan over a low heat. Break the
chocolate into small pieces and add
it to the syrup. Heat gently to melt,
stirring well to mix.
☐ Serve the sauce in a warmed
sauceboat to accompany the buns.
Variation: Make the buns half the
size. Bake in the same way, cool, and
fill with the whipped cream. Divide
among 6 or 8 serving glasses and
serve with the sauce dribbled over.

Fish Gougère

Serves 4-6 ☆☆☆
Preparation: 45 minutes
Cooking: 25 minutes

Basic Choux Pastry (opposite)
melted butter for greasing

The filling:
8oz (225g) salmon steaks
8oz (225g) thick haddock fillets
4 large scallops, deveined
½ pint (300ml) milk
a sprig of fresh tarragon
1 small onion, chopped
a few green peppercorns
4oz (100g) button mushrooms, sliced
4oz (100g) peeled cooked prawns

The sauce:
2oz (50g) butter
3 tablespoons flour
3 tablespoons double cream
5 tablespoons dry white wine
2oz (50g) grated Gruyère cheese
a squeeze of lemon juice
salt and pepper

Set oven to 350F (180C) gas 4.
☐ Rinse the fish and scallops and pat dry. Place in a shallow oven dish about 7in (18cm) square.
☐ Add the milk, tarragon, onion and peppercorns. Cover and cook in the oven for about 15 minutes until all the fish is just firm and opaque.
☐ Strain the cooking liquid from the fish and reserve.
☐ Remove any skin and bones, from the fish and flake the flesh into bite-sized chunks. Cut the scallops to about the same size.
☐ Return the cooked fish to the rinsed oven dish with the mushrooms and prawns.
☐ Make the sauce: Put the butter into a medium saucepan over a moderate heat. When melted, stir in the flour. Gradually add the strained fish cooking liquid and cook, stirring constantly, for about 5 minutes until thick and smooth.
☐ Add the cream, wine, cheese and lemon juice. Season to taste and pour sauce over the filling.
☐ Cover with a piece of foil the exact size of the dish and, with a brush, grease the top with butter.

☐ Set oven to 425F (220C) gas 7.
☐ Make the choux pastry as directed (opposite). Fit a forcing bag with a rose pipe about ¾in (1.75cm) and fill the bag with the choux pastry. Pipe around the edges of the dish.
☐ Bake in the oven for about 25 minutes until well risen and browned then carefully remove the foil by pulling from the centre.
☐ Serve immediately.

Savoury Bouchées

Makes about 48

Make the Basic Choux Pastry. Put small teaspoonfuls of the mixture on greased baking trays. Bake at 425F (220C) gas 7 for about 15 minutes until crisp and brown. Pierce tops with a skewer.

Cocktail Éclairs

Makes about 24

Put the Basic Choux Pastry mixture into a forcing bag fitted with a ½in (1cm) plain pipe. Shape into fingers or crescents about 4in (10cm) long on greased trays. Bake as above.

Shrimp Filling

Fills 48 bouchées or 24 éclairs

1oz (25g) butter
2 tablespoons flour
¼ pint (150ml) single cream
salt and pepper
a pinch of grated nutmeg
1 tablespoon brandy or sherry
4oz (125g) peeled or cooked shrimps

☐ Melt the butter with the flour in a saucepan on a low heat. Gradually stir in the cream. Cook, stirring constantly, for 4-5 minutes until thick and smooth.
☐ Season to taste with salt and pepper, nutmeg and the brandy or sherry. Stir in the shrimps.
☐ Use hot or cold.

Tips to success with choux
● Be sure to use plain flour. Choux pastry made with self-raising flour collapses when baked.
● It is important to form a ball of dough before the eggs are added. If necessary, return the pan to the heat for a minute or so, mixing continuously.
● Use a strong whisk or a wooden spoon for beating in the eggs, or put the mixture into a food processor.

Choux pastry is very good with savoury fillings, as well as sweet, and can be made into small buns or finger shapes for use as hot savouries to serve with drinks. It also makes an excellent top for fish or chicken pies. Keep a supply of baked choux pastries in the freezer for use when required.

Choux pastry pies
You can make the choux mixture and keep it in a forcing bag in the fridge for an hour or two. About half an hour before required, pipe it on top of your favourite savoury filling. Chicken or turkey, or cheese and hard-boiled egg, mixed with the sauce used for Fish Gougère all make delicious pies.

Small choux-topped pies
Put a suitable filling into individual shell dishes and pipe the choux pastry around the edges. Or, if you prefer, spoon a small mound of pastry in the centre.

Savoury choux buns
Fill Choux Buns with a suitable savoury mixture and serve with a hot cheese sauce poured over them.

Fish Gougère
The greased aluminium foil prevents the choux mixture from becoming soggy on contact with the filling.

Chocolate Éclairs
Pipe 8 éclairs in the same way as Cocktail Éclairs. Cut, fill with whipped cream and coat the tops with chocolate icing as shown on page 82.

Chocolate Icing

Use a small heavy pan and keep the heat very low. For extra flavour, use Crème de Cacao in place of water.

Coating buns with icing

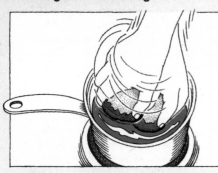

Using a twisting action, dip the bun into the warm icing.

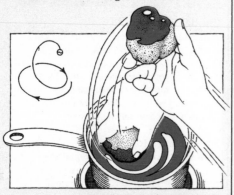

Lift out the bun and quickly turn it upright; this will hold the icing in place and prevent dribbling down the sides.

Peach Cream Buns

Makes 12 ☆☆☆
Preparation: 30 minutes

---

12 Choux Buns (page 80)
7 fl oz (200ml) milk
3 tablespoons flour
2 egg yolks from size 2 eggs
2oz (50g) sugar
3 tablespoons brandy
8oz (225g) cold butter, diced
4 fresh peaches
icing sugar for dusting

Mix a little of the cold milk with the flour, egg yolks and sugar to make a smooth paste. Put the rest of the milk in a small saucepan over a low heat.

☐ When the milk begins to bubble around the edges, stir it into the flour mixture. Return this to the saucepan and cook, stirring constantly, for 3-4 minutes until very thick and smooth.

☐ Remove from the heat and stir in the brandy. Gradually whisk in the cubes of butter then let the sauce cool.

☐ Peel the peaches (page 93) and cut in thin slices.

☐ Cut the buns across in half. Place a spoonful of filling on each base. Put some peach slices on top.

☐ Cover with the rest of the filling. Set the tops of the buns in place, dust with icing sugar and serve immediately.

Mandarin Whirls

Makes 12 ☆☆☆
Preparation: 30 minutes plus 30 minutes setting

---

12 Choux Buns (page 80)

The chocolate icing:
3oz (75g) plain chocolate
2 tablespoons water
about 8oz (225g) icing sugar

To fill and decorate:
¾ pint (450ml) double cream
11oz (300g) canned mandarin oranges, drained

Cut the Choux Buns across in half.

☐ Make the icing: Break the chocolate into small pieces and put with the water in a small saucepan set over a low heat. Stir until the chocolate melts.

☐ Gradually stir in sufficient icing sugar to give the consistency of thick cream.

☐ Dip the tops of the buns into the chocolate icing as shown. Set upright on a wire rack and leave to cool for about half an hour until set.

☐ Whip the cream to soft peaks. Put a ½in (1cm) rose pipe into a forcing bag.

☐ Pipe a whirl of cream into each bun. Setting aside 12 mandarin segments for decoration, divide the remaining fruit between the buns. Set the iced bun tops in place.

☐ Pipe the rest of the cream on top and decorate with the reserved mandarin segments.

Cakes & Gâteaux

Baking cakes is the perfect opportunity to direct your creative skills towards cooking for compliments. Imaginative cake-making not only provides delicious tea-time treats but can create decorative desserts to impress dinner-party guests.

Methods of making cakes

One of the main objectives when preparing cakes for baking is to make the finished product as light as possible. The three techniques commonly used are: 'rubbing-in' which relies mainly on raising agents, 'creaming' where eggs are included and air is beaten in and, finally, 'whisking' where the mixture relies almost entirely on whisked-in air for its light texture.

Rubbing-in The fat is rubbed into the flour with the fingertips to form a breadcrumb-like consistency. Sugar and eggs are added and perhaps a little liquid. This type of cake is quick and easy to make and is at its best fresh.

Creaming With 'creamed' cakes, the fat and sugar are beaten together until very light. The secret lies in very thorough beating at this stage to incorporate a lot of air. This process is made easier if you start with softened (*not* melted) fat. The eggs are then beaten in and flour folded in lightly.

Whisking Eggs and sugar are whisked until the mixture is very thick, airy and pale. The flour is lightly folded in and, sometimes, melted fat is added at the end to enrich.

Cake Ingredients

Flour is available in several forms and it is important to use the one called for in the recipe. Plain flour is used when it is necessary to adjust the amount of raising agent used. Self-raising flour is very convenient, but it contains a fixed quantity of raising agent. 'Sponge flour' should only be used with recipes provided by the manufacturer as it requires a special balance of ingredients.

● **Fats** used in baking are mainly butter or margarine. Butter gives the best flavour in cakes, but many people prefer to use margarine. When substituting margarine for butter, be sure to use the brands sold in block form. The soft types need specially devised recipes.

● **Sugars** differ widely but, among the white sugars, caster sugar gives the best results. Cakes can be made with icing sugar if a denser consistency is required. Larger-grained sugars do not beat in quite so well and can produce coarse cake. Soft brown sugar should only be used in specially devised recipes. It is not only very fine but it also has a degree of acidity which can affect the cake's structure.

Cake tins

If you are baking a large cake, it will bake a little more quickly in aluminium or tin than in ovenglass containers.

● A cake baked in an 8-in (20-cm) round tin will take approximately the same time as one baked in a 10-in (25cm) loaf pan.

Turning out cakes

For best results, use non-stick pans or tins with loose bottoms. There are also tins available which are made with a spring-form or a moving scraper which loosens the cake.

● When using ordinary tins or pans, after greasing the pan, line the centre bottom with a small square of greaseproof paper.

● If you have difficulty in releasing a baked cake from its tin, loosen round the edges with a palette knife then invert the tin on to a cooling rack. If the cake is domed on top, quickly reverse it on to a second rack.

Apart from the heavier fruit cakes, most cakes taste better when they are eaten within a day of baking. If you need to store a cake for longer, wrap it in foil or place it in an airtight tin. Keep cakes in a cool, dry place but not in the refrigerator as low temperatures make them rather solid.

❄ Freezing

Cakes which have a high fat content will generally freeze well while plainer cakes are better served when fresh. It is better to freeze cakes before decorating or filling. You can freeze either a whole cake, well wrapped in foil or freezerwrap, or individual slices wrapped separately. These individual portions are very convenient and any appropriate number can be thawed quickly. To retain the best flavour, do not store a cake in the freezer for more than about 2 months. To thaw, leave the cake in its wrappings to defrost at room temperature. A whole 4-egg cake will need about 5 hours to thaw while you only need to allow about 1½ hours to defrost individual slices.

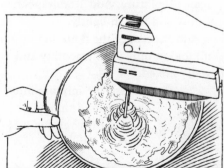

For 'creamed' cakes, beat the butter and sugar until very soft and light.

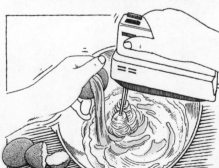

Add one egg at a time and beat each in well.

Add the flour in two or three batches and mix in lightly with a spatula.

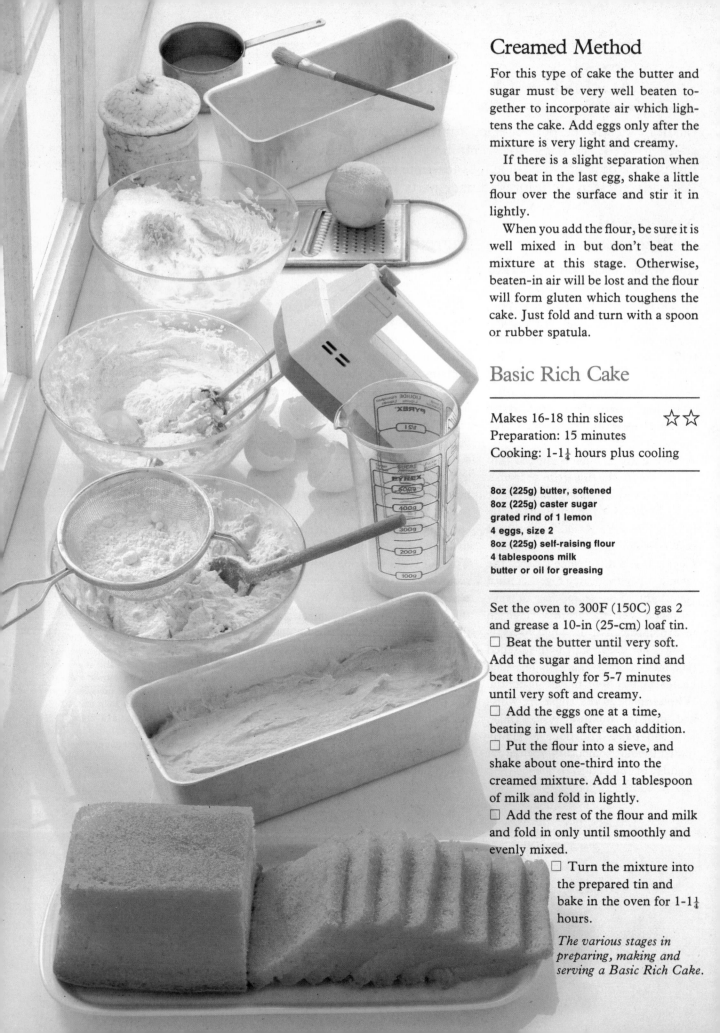

Creamed Method

For this type of cake the butter and sugar must be very well beaten together to incorporate air which lightens the cake. Add eggs only after the mixture is very light and creamy.

If there is a slight separation when you beat in the last egg, shake a little flour over the surface and stir it in lightly.

When you add the flour, be sure it is well mixed in but don't beat the mixture at this stage. Otherwise, beaten-in air will be lost and the flour will form gluten which toughens the cake. Just fold and turn with a spoon or rubber spatula.

Basic Rich Cake

Makes 16-18 thin slices ☆☆
Preparation: 15 minutes
Cooking: 1-1¼ hours plus cooling

8oz (225g) butter, softened
8oz (225g) caster sugar
grated rind of 1 lemon
4 eggs, size 2
8oz (225g) self-raising flour
4 tablespoons milk
butter or oil for greasing

Set the oven to 300F (150C) gas 2 and grease a 10-in (25-cm) loaf tin.
☐ Beat the butter until very soft. Add the sugar and lemon rind and beat thoroughly for 5-7 minutes until very soft and creamy.
☐ Add the eggs one at a time, beating in well after each addition.
☐ Put the flour into a sieve, and shake about one-third into the creamed mixture. Add 1 tablespoon of milk and fold in lightly.
☐ Add the rest of the flour and milk and fold in only until smoothly and evenly mixed.
☐ Turn the mixture into the prepared tin and bake in the oven for 1-1¼ hours.

The various stages in preparing, making and serving a Basic Rich Cake.

□ When baked, the cake will be well-browned and a skewer inserted into the centre will come out clean. As a final check, listen to the cake – it should not sizzle.

□ Leave in the tin to cool for 10 minutes then loosen around the sides with a knife and turn out and leave to cool on a wire rack.

Tip: Use only 1 tablespoon of milk if using a round 8-in (20-cm) tin.

Feather-iced Chocolate Cake

Makes 8 slices ☆☆
Preparation and finishing: 30 minutes
Cooking: about 25 minutes plus cooling and setting

4oz (100g) butter, softened
3oz (75g) soft brown sugar
3oz (75g) golden syrup
½ teaspoon vanilla essence
2 eggs, size 2
5oz (125g) plain flour
1½ teaspoons baking powder
3 tablespoons cocoa
1 tablespoon warm water
4oz (100g) apricot jam, warmed
1oz (25g) walnuts, finely chopped
butter or oil for greasing

The icing:
5oz (125g) icing sugar
about 4 teaspoons cold water
1 teaspoon cocoa
2 teaspoons hot water

Set the oven to 350F (180C) gas 4 and grease two 7-in (18-cm) sandwich tins.

□ Beat the butter until very soft. Add the sugar, syrup and vanilla and beat until very light and creamy.

□ Add the eggs one at a time, beating thoroughly after each.

□ Put the flour, baking powder, and cocoa into a sieve. Sift about half into the mixture. Fold in lightly. Repeat with remaining flour. Add water.

□ Turn into the prepared tins and bake for about 25 minutes until well risen, and springy to the touch.

□ Turn out on to a rack to cool.

□ Sandwich the cakes with some of the jam and spread the rest around the sides. Press the nuts firmly on the sides and wrap with a band of greaseproof paper.

□ Mix the icing sugar with enough water to give a stiff spreading consistency. Transfer a generous tablespoon to a separate bowl.

□ Mix the cocoa smoothly with hot water then mix that with the 1 tablespoon of white icing. Put into a small paper forcing bag.

□ Ice the top of the cake with white icing. Feather with the chocolate icing (see sidelines) and leave to set.

□ Serve fresh, cut into wedges.

Streusel-topped Spice Cake

Makes 24 pieces ☆
Preparation and cooking: 1 hour

10oz (275g) plain flour
6oz (175g) caster sugar
6oz (175g) butter, cubed
2 teaspoons baking powder
2 teaspoons mixed spice
4oz (100g) raisins
2 eggs, size 2
5 tablespoons milk
butter or oil for greasing

Set the oven to 350F (180C) gas 4.

□ Grease a 6½ × 10½in (16 × 26cm) shallow tin. Lay a strip of foil 3in (7.5cm) wide and 14in (35cm) long across the bottom and up the sides.

□ Sift the flour and sugar into a bowl. Add the butter and rub in well to make fine crumbs.

□ Set aside 5oz (125g) of mixture.

□ Sift the baking powder and spice into the rest and stir to mix well. Stir in the raisins, eggs and milk.

□ Spread the cake mixture evenly into tin. Sprinkle with crumb mixture.

□ Bake in the oven for about 40 minutes until a skewer inserted into the centre comes out clean.

□ Leave to cool in the tin for 15 minutes. Loosen along the sides and corners with a palette knife. Use the foil strip to lift it out carefully. Cool.

□ Serve fresh, cut in squares.

Coating a cake with chopped nuts
Put the nuts in a line across the centre of a piece of greaseproof paper. With one hand underneath and the other one on top, lift the cake. Roll the sides of the jam-coated cake in the nuts then press them on firmly with a palette knife.

Converting recipes for cakes from loaf to round, and vice versa, is a tricky business because of the complexities of varying heat transference due to differing pan and cake surface areas. In general, more liquid is used in loaf type cakes to keep the surface from 'doming' too much and splitting. Wherever possible, stick to instructions – we give alternatives in some recipes.

To feather-ice a cake
Wrap a double thickness of greaseproof paper, as broad as the depth of the cake, around the sides like a bandage. Secure with 2 or 3 pins. Spread the top of the cake with icing.

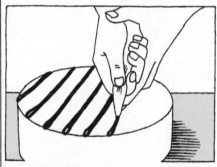

While still wet, draw parallel lines across the cake with the chocolate icing, at about 1in (2.5cm) intervals.

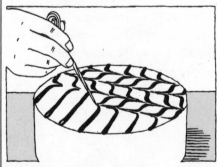

Immediately, draw the tip of a skewer at right angles across the chocolate lines at regular intervals in alternating directions.
When set, remove the pins and carefully pull away the paper collar.

Don't try making sponge cakes in non-stick pans—the mixture can't grip the sides during cooking, so the cakes don't rise properly and cave in on themselves.

Making Genoese Sponge

Like Basic Whisked Sponge but with melted butter stirred in.

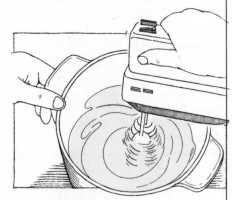

Whisk the eggs and sugar until very thick and fluffy.

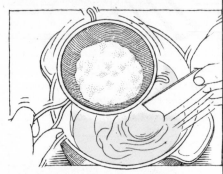

Lightly fold in the sifted flour.

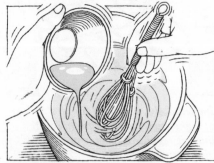

Stir in the melted butter lightly but thoroughly.

Whisked sponges

The lightest and most delicate types of cake are those made by whisking the eggs and sugar together until they are light and creamy and then gently folding in the flour. Plain flour or flour with only a small amount of raising agent is used.

These sponges are tender and moist but have a slight elasticity which makes them less crumbly and therefore easier to ice.

Genoese sponges

If a richer sponge cake is required, melted butter is lightly stirred into the mixture. This type is called Genoese and, although as tender and moist as those made without fat, it tends to be firmer.

Baking tins

The easiest way to bake both basic whisked sponges and the Genoese type is to use sandwich tins. If you are making a cake with several layers and have insufficient sandwich tins, use large, round, loose-bottomed or springform tins.

If the cake is to be rolled or sandwiched in strips, use a shallow Swiss Roll tin. If you want to serve a sponge cake whole, it is a good idea to use a tin which has a centre tube so that the cake cooks evenly. Loaf tins are unsatisfactory for baking sponges because the cake cooks unevenly with the outer edges cooking quicker than the centre.

Testing for thorough baking

The cakes should be well-risen with a good golden-brown colour. They should feel springy and there should be no sound of sizzling.

Removing baked cakes from tins

Sponge cakes baked in sandwich or other shallow tins can be turned out immediately after baking. Loosen each cake around the sides with a warmed knife. Invert on to a wire rack, then flip over on to a second rack.

Rules for success:

● Whisk the egg-and-sugar mixture very thoroughly. This is to ensure that the sugar is dissolved and the mixture is as elastic as possible. Setting the bowl over warm water helps to make the whisking time shorter but do not let the water get hot enough to cook the egg. Continue whisking until the mixture has increased in volume about threefold. It should appear to have the consistency of soft whipped cream.

● A wide mixing bowl rather than a deep one makes it easier to fold in the flour without breaking down too much of the foam.

● Sprinkle the flour over the whole surface. Continue to cut and turn gently to ensure that all the flour is evenly mixed in. Be certain that there are no lumps or pockets of flour left in the mixture.

Basic Whisked Sponge

Serves 6-8 ☆
Preparation: 20 minutes
Cooking: 20-25 minutes

---

3 eggs, size 2
2 egg yolks from size 2 eggs
6oz (175g) caster sugar
6oz (175g) plain flour
butter or oil for greasing

Set the oven to 375F (190C) gas 5 and grease two 9in (23cm) sandwich tins.

☐ Put the eggs, yolks and sugar into a bowl and set over a pan of hot water on a low heat.

☐ Whisk the mixture for about 10 minutes until it is very thick and the whisk leaves a trail on the surface. Remove from the heat.

☐ Sift half the flour over the surface and fold it in lightly. Repeat with the rest of the flour.

☐ Turn into prepared sandwich tins and bake for 20-25 minutes.

☐ Turn out on a wire rack and cool. Use while fresh, or freeze.

Variation: Alternatively, put the mixture into a greased 9in (23cm) deep springform or loose-bottomed cake tin and bake at 350F (180C) gas 4 for about 40 minutes.

Banana and Kiwi Cake

Serves 8   ☆☆☆
Preparation: 45-50 minutes

**Basic Whisked Sponge baked in a
9in (23cm) round cake tin
(see opposite)**

The filling and topping:
12 fl oz (350ml) sweet white wine
2 tablespoons brandy
2 teaspoons powdered gelatine
3 large bananas
2 large kiwi fruit

To decorate:
3 fl oz (100ml) double cream
3oz (75g) flaked or chopped almonds

Put the wine, brandy and gelatine into a small saucepan. Set over a low heat and stir until the gelatine is dissolved and the liquid is clear.
☐ Remove from the heat and set the pan into cold water until cool. Chill for a few minutes in the fridge until it is beginning to set.
☐ Cut the cake across into 3 equal layers. Peel and slice the fruit. Arrange banana slices over two pieces of cake, and a mixture of kiwi and banana on the third piece.
☐ Carefully spoon about one-third of the jelly over each of the banana layers and stack them one on top of the other.
☐ Set the top layer in place and spoon remaining glaze over. Leave in a cool place for a few minutes.
☐ Whip the cream to spreading consistency. Put the nuts into the bottom of the grill pan and place under a pre-heated moderate grill for 2-3 minutes, stirring until lightly browned, then allow to cool.
☐ Spread the sides of the cake with the whipped cream. With a palette knife, press the nuts on to the cream to make a neat finish. Cool but do not refrigerate.
☐ Serve within 2 or 3 hours.
Variations: Raspberries, strawberries or fresh peaches are equally good for this cake.
● In place of nuts, try grated chocolate or coconut for decoration.

Praline Cream Cake

Serves 6   ☆☆☆
Preparation: about 25 minutes
Cooking: about 45 minutes

3 eggs, size 2, separated
4oz (125g) caster sugar
3oz (100g) plain flour
½ teaspoon baking powder
butter or oil for greasing

The Praline:
2oz (50g) caster sugar
2oz (50g) chopped almonds

To finish:
¼ pint (150ml) double cream

Set the oven to 350F (180C) gas 4 and grease an 8½-in (21-cm) fluted ring mould.
☐ Put the egg whites into a large bowl and whisk to soft peaks.
☐ Whisk in half the sugar until the mixture resembles soft meringue.
☐ Put yolks and remaining sugar into a bowl. Whisk until pale and fluffy, then fold lightly into whisked whites.
☐ Put the flour and baking powder into a sieve. Sift about half over the surface of the whisked eggs and fold it in lightly. Repeat with remainder.
☐ Turn into the prepared mould and bake for about 45 minutes.
☐ Invert on a wire rack and leave to cool. Release from the tin by easing it out with the tip of a sharp knife. Use fresh, or freeze.
☐ To make the Praline: put the sugar into a heavy frying-pan set over a moderate heat. Keep turning the pan to heat evenly – but do not stir – until sugar melts. Add almonds.
☐ As soon as sugar is golden brown, turn out on a piece of greased greaseproof paper.
☐ Tap with a rolling pin to break into pieces then put in a plastic bag and crush with the rolling pin to the size of coarse breadcrumbs.
☐ Whip the cream to spreading consistency and lightly fold in praline.
☐ Spread all over the top and sides of the cake and serve within 2 hours.

Banana and Kiwi Cake
It is better not to refrigerate a cake with bananas as they tend to darken when very cold.

It is a good idea to make a quantity of praline in advance and store it in an airtight jar in a cool dry place. It will keep well for 3 to 4 weeks.

Praline Cream Cake
This method of making a whisked sponge is preferred by some to that given for the Basic Whisked Sponge, as it is a little quicker.

Slices of Banana and Kiwi Cake make a refreshing and unusual dessert.

Grated chocolate
Hold a block of chocolate with a piece of paper wrapped around to prevent it melting due to the warmth of the hand. Use the coarse side of a grater and grate on to a sheet of greaseproof paper. You can store the grated chocolate in an airtight jar in the fridge for several weeks.

As an alternative to the praline, fold coarsely-grated chocolate into the cream. Also try flavouring the cream with rum, brandy or an orange liqueur.

Rolling a Swiss Roll

If a Swiss Roll is to be filled with jam only, you can spread it on before its first rolling. For other fillings, it is important to cool the cake before filling it.

Turn the baked cake out on a piece of greaseproof paper lightly sprinkled with caster sugar. Trim off the crisp edges and straighten the sides. About 1in (2.5cm) in from the nearer short end, slice a groove across the sponge about halfway through its depth. To facilitate folding, fold this grooved end over to start the rolling.

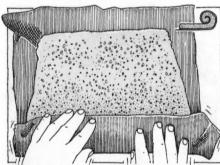

Roll the cake up with the paper and leave to cool on a wire rack.

Unroll the cooled cake and spread with filling. Re-roll.

Chocolate Roulade

A roulade is not a true cake, but it is made by the same method of whisking eggs and sugar. It makes a rich and delicious dessert. During the 'setting' inside the foil covering, the crust softens so the roulade can be rolled. If cracks form, smooth them together using the paper and dust over with sugar.

Swiss Roll

Makes 12 slices ☆
Preparation: 10 minutes
Cooking: 15 minutes

3 eggs, size 2, separated
4oz (125g) caster sugar
3oz (100g) plain flour
½ teaspoon baking powder
butter for greasing
caster sugar for sprinkling

The filling:
¼ pint (150ml) double cream
about 3oz (75g) plum (or other red) jam

Set the oven to 350F (180C) gas 4 and generously grease a 9 × 13in (23 × 33cm) Swiss Roll tin with butter.

☐ Make the sponge mixture in the same way as for Praline Cream Cake (page 87).

☐ Spread into the prepared tin and bake in the oven for 12-15 minutes until golden and coming away from the sides of the tin.

☐ Turn out on greaseproof paper lightly sprinkled with caster sugar. Trim and roll (see sidelines). Allow cake to cool still rolled around the paper.

☐ Whip the cream to spreading consistency and warm the jam in a small saucepan until it will spread easily.

☐ Unroll the cake, spread it well with jam, then cream − keeping the cream to within about a thumb's width of the edges. Re-roll.

☐ Serve while fresh, cut in slices, for tea.

Sponge Slices

Make and bake the sponge mixture in the same way as for Swiss Roll. Turn out and leave flat until cool.

☐ Cut into strips about 4 × 3in (10 × 7cm). Sandwich together in pairs with jam. Spread the tops with whipped cream and dust with grated chocolate, praline or chopped nuts and mixed glacé fruits. Serve fresh, cut into slices.

Chocolate Roulade

Serves 6 ☆☆☆
Preparation: 20 minutes, plus 8-10 hours setting
Cooking: about 15 minutes

about 1½oz (40g) plain chocolate
2 tablespoons cocoa
2 tablespoons warm water
3 eggs, size 2, separated
4oz (100g) caster sugar
a little oil for greasing

The filling:
2oz (50g) plain chocolate
1 tablespoon water
¼ pint (150ml) double cream

To serve:
¼ pint (150ml) double cream
3 tablespoons brandy

Set the oven to 350F (180C) gas 4. Liberally oil a 12 × 8in (30 × 20cm) Swiss Roll tin, line it with greaseproof paper and oil again.

☐ Put the chocolate, cocoa and water in a bowl set over a pan of hot water on a low heat. Stir until melted but not hot. Remove.

☐ Whisk the egg yolks and sugar until very pale and thick. Add the chocolate. Whisk until well mixed.

☐ Whisk the egg whites until they form soft peaks. Fold lightly but thoroughly into the chocolate.

☐ Turn into the prepared tin and bake for about 15 minutes until a firm crust forms on the surface.

☐ Remove and immediately wrap the cake and tin together in foil. Leave for 8-10 hours then unwrap.

☐ Invert on to a piece of greaseproof paper dusted with caster sugar. Carefully scrape the lining paper away and trim off the sides.

☐ To make filling: Melt chocolate in a bowl with the water as before.

☐ Whip the cream to soft peaks. Add the melted chocolate and whip to a thick spreading consistency.

☐ Spread over the chocolate to within a thumb's width of the edges. Roll up like Swiss Roll. Slice.

☐ Whip the cream and brandy to soft peaks and top slices.

Fruit cakes

All traditional fruit cakes are better left to mature for a few days and many keep for a long time, but Dundee Cake is best served within 4 to 6 weeks. To store, wrap in foil and keep in a cool dry place.

Dundee Cake has a traditional pattern of almonds on top and is one of the most popular of fruit cakes. Like most fruit cakes it is usually made by the creaming method, but the recipe here is much easier: just rubbing the butter into the dry ingredients then stirring in the fruit and eggs.

Dundee Cake

Makes 12-14 slices   ☆☆
Preparation: 20 minutes
Cooking: about 1½ hours

5oz (150g) raisins, cleaned
5oz (150g) currants, cleaned
3 fl oz (100ml) dark rum
8oz (225g) self-raising flour
5oz (150g) soft brown sugar
grated rind of ½ orange
5oz (150g) cold butter
2oz (50g) glacé cherries, quartered
2oz (50g) candied peel, chopped
2oz (50g) blanched almonds, chopped
3 eggs, size 2
butter, for greasing

To decorate:
2oz (50g) blanched almonds, split

Set the oven to 300F (150C) gas 2 and grease and line an 8-in (20-cm) round cake tin (see sidelines).

☐ Put the raisins and currants into a bowl, pour the rum over and leave to soak while you prepare the rest of the cake.

☐ Sieve the flour and sugar into a bowl. Add the orange rind and butter. With the fingertips, rub the butter in, to form a mixture with a crumb-like consistency.

☐ Add fruit, cherries, peel, chopped almonds and 1 egg and mix together. Add the 2 remaining eggs and stir together well.

☐ Turn into the prepared tin. Arrange the split almonds over the top and bake in the oven for about 1½ hours until a warmed skewer inserted into the centre comes out clean.

☐ Leave in the tin to cool, carefully turn out and remove the paper. Wrap in foil to store. Serve cut in wedges.

Variation: If you like a darker cake, add 2 teaspoons of mixed spice to the flour, and use dark brown sugar.

Tip: If the top of your baked fruit cake is a little too crusty for your taste, put a layer of sliced raw apple over it just before you wrap the cake in foil. In a day the cake will become soft and moist.

Lining cake tins
Fruit cakes bake better in tins which have been lined with a double thickness of greaseproof paper. Butter the paper between the thicknesses and on the side which is placed next to the tin, to hold it in place.

Splitting almonds
Bring the whole skinned almonds to the boil. Strain off the water. Insert the tip of a sharp knife into the tip of the almond and prise apart at the dividing mark.

Dundee Cake

Making Strawberry Gâteau

It is more convenient if you make both the cake and the Crème Pâtissière the day before required. Finishing the gâteau is then very easy. The cake also tastes better if left to mature for a day.

Crème Pâtissière

If the cream is too thick to spread easily, whisk again until creamy. Use immediately, or store in a covered container in a cool place—not in the fridge—for up to 24 hours.

Jelly glaze

Gelatine mixtures in small quantities set very quickly so it is better not to chill the glaze. But if you are in a hurry, put one or two ice cubes into the pan of cold water to make the glaze set more quickly.

Strawberry Gâteau

Serves 8   ☆☆☆
Preparation: 1 hour, plus chilling
Cooking: 30-35 minutes

The Genoese Sponge:
4 eggs, size 2
4oz (125g) caster sugar
4oz (125g) less 1 tablespoon plain flour
2oz (50g) butter, melted and cooled

The Crème Pâtissière:
2 tablespoons flour
2oz (50g) caster sugar
1 egg yolk from a size 2 egg
4 fl oz (125ml plus 1 tablespoon) milk
4 tablespoons kirsch
6oz (175g) unsalted butter, cubed small

To decorate:
3-4oz (75-125g) flaked almonds
3 fl oz (100ml) sweet white wine
½ teaspoon powdered gelatine
¾lb (350g) small strawberries

Set the oven to 350F (180C) gas 4 and grease and flour a 9in (23cm) springform or loose-bottomed cake tin.

☐ Put the eggs and sugar into a large bowl. Set over a pan of hot water on a moderate heat.

☐ Whisk for about 10 minutes, scraping the mixture down the sides of the bowl during whisking, until the centre of the mixture feels tepid, and the mixture has increased to about three times its original volume.

☐ Sieve one-third of the flour over the mixture. Add one-third of the butter at the side of the bowl. With a balloon whisk or rubber spatula, mix very lightly but thoroughly.

☐ Repeat with remaining flour and butter.

☐ Turn into the prepared cake tin and bake for 30-35 minutes.

☐ Invert on a wire rack. Cool, then

remove from the tin. Use immediately, or wrap and store in a cool place for not more than a day, or freeze for up to 2 months.

☐ To make the Crème Pâtissière: Mix the flour, sugar, and egg yolk smoothly with a little of the cold milk. Put the rest of the milk into a small saucepan over a moderate heat.

☐ When the milk bubbles around the edge, stir it into the flour mixture. Return this to the saucepan and cook, stirring constantly, for 3-4 minutes until thick and smooth.

☐ Remove from the heat and stir in the liqueur. Gradually whisk in the cubes of butter until it has the look of a rich mayonnaise. Cool.

☐ To decorate: Put the almonds into a dry frying-pan over a

moderate heat and stir for a few minutes to brown lightly.

☐ Put the wine and the gelatine into a small measuring jug. Set in a saucepan of hot water over a low heat. Stir until the liquid is clear.

☐ Remove the jug and set in a pan of cold water.

☐ Cut the cake across into 3 equal slices. Sandwich with Crème Pâtissière and spread a little around the sides of the cake.

☐ Press the nuts on the sides and spread remaining Crème Pâtissière on top.

☐ Arrange the berries on top. When the jelly begins to thicken, spoon it carefully over the fruit.

☐ Chill for ½ hour before serving.

It is important to have the butter melted so it will mix into the cake, but it must not be hot or it may set some of the egg.

Whisking the cake
Whisking over hot water helps shorten the process. Do not let the bowl become warmer than is comfortable to hold against the hand. Otherwise, if the bottom of the bowl becomes hot it will begin to cook the cake mixture.

The various stages in making, assembling and decorating a Strawberry Gâteau made with Genoese Sponge.

Coffee Caramel Crystal Gâteau

Makes 8-10 slices ☆☆☆
Preparation: 30 minutes
Cooking: 30-35 minutes

4 eggs, size 2
4oz (125g) caster sugar
4oz (125g) minus 1 tablespoon plain flour
2oz (50g) butter, melted and cooled
oil or butter for greasing

The filling and coating:
10oz (275g) butter, softened
12oz (350g) icing sugar
2 tablespoons instant coffee
2-3 tablespoons boiling water
5 tablespoons Tia Maria

The Caramel Crystal:
5oz (150g) caster sugar
4 tablespoons water
oil for greasing

To decorate:
1-2oz (25-50g) chocolate coffee beans

Make, bake, and cool the cake as for Strawberry Gâteau (page 90). Cut across into 3 layers.

☐ Make the filling and coating: Mix the coffee in sufficient boiling water to dissolve, and add the Tia Maria.

☐ Beat the butter until very soft. Gradually whisk in the icing sugar, then whisk in the coffee liquid.

☐ Make the Caramel Crystal: Put the sugar and water into a small saucepan. Place over a low heat and stir until the sugar dissolves. Do not boil until the syrup is quite clear. Wash any sugar down the sides of the pan with a wet pastry brush.

☐ Boil the syrup rapidly until it turns a light brown. Immediately pour into a greased shallow cake tin.

☐ Leave until the caramel has set and cooled. Invert the tin over a sheet of greaseproof paper on a flat surface and tap the tin to release the caramel. Break it into large pieces.

☐ Put the pieces into a large plastic bag and pound or roll with a rolling pin to break into pea-sized pieces.

☐ Put into a sieve and shake to remove the fine 'dust'. Reserve this

Coffee Caramel Crystal Gâteau.

for use in other cakes. Put the caramel pieces in a line along the centre of a piece of greaseproof paper.

☐ To finish the gâteau: Sandwich the layers and coat the sides with the buttercream. Roll the sides in the Caramel Crystal to coat well and press on the shards with a palette knife.

☐ Set the gâteau on a serving plate and spread the top lightly with more buttercream. Put the rest of the buttercream into a forcing bag fitted with a ½in (1cm) rose pipe. Decorate the top of the cake as shown.

Tips: Make the cake, the filling and the crystal in advance. The last-minute finishing will then only take a few minutes.

● The size of tin on which you pour the cooked caramel is not important.

● Caramel Crystal is a useful ingredient to make and store for use when required. As long as it is kept completely dry, it will last for several weeks.

● The buttercream should not be made more than about a day ahead, and it must be stored in a cool place – not in the refrigerator!

Peach and Kiwi Gâteau

Makes 8-10 slices   ☆☆☆
Preparation: 30 minutes
Cooking: 30-35 minutes

---

4 eggs, size 2
4oz (125g) caster sugar
4oz (125g) minus 1 tablespoon plain flour
2oz (50g) butter, melted and cooled
oil or butter for greasing

To fill and decorate:
4oz (125g) peach jam
juice of ½ an orange
2 tablespoons orange liqueur
about 9 fl oz (250ml) double cream
2 large kiwi fruit
4 peaches

Make, bake, and cool the cake as for Strawberry Gâteau (page 90). Cut across into 3 layers.

☐ Put the jam into a small saucepan with orange juice and liqueur. Place over a moderate heat until jam melts. Simmer briefly until it develops a spreading consistency. Remove and let cool.

☐ Whip the cream until it just holds soft peaks. (Don't over-whip as it may separate during piping, as the action works the cream even more). Put into a forcing bag fitted with a ½in (1cm) rose pipe.

☐ Sandwich the 3 layers of cake with some of the jam.

☐ Set the cake on an icing turntable. Hold the forcing bag nearly upright so the pipe is almost parallel to the sides. Pipe fingers of cream all the way around the sides of the gâteau. Carefully transfer to a serving plate.

☐ Peel and slice the kiwi fruit. Peel the peaches and cut inwards towards the stones to shape wedges.

☐ Sieve the remaining jam. Arrange the peaches and kiwis over top of the gâteau as shown. Carefully spoon the jam glaze over the fruit. Finish off with a whirl of cream if liked.

☐ Serve fresh, cut into wedges.

Tip: When peaches are not in season, use a good brand of canned peach.

Variation: Fresh oranges are also good in this recipe. Either peach jam or orange marmalade can be used as the filling and glaze.

Peach and Kiwi Gâteau makes an elegant dessert to follow a rich meal.

Peach and Kiwi Gâteau

To remove the skins from peaches more easily and neatly, first blanch them in hot water. Dip one peach at a time into a pan of boiling water. Take them out as soon as you can rub the skin off with the back of a fork. Immediately refresh under cold running water to prevent the fruit going soft.

If you want to prepare the peaches a little in advance, put them into a basin with a little lemon juice after you have cut them into slices, to prevent discoloration.

To make it easier to move the cake on and off the icing turntable, leave it on its base when cooling.

FIRST COURSES

A first course is more likely to be served with a special occasion meal than an everyday one. Its purpose is to stimulate the appetite in preparation for the courses to come and the aim should be to make them nutritious, colourful and not too filling.

Salad or vegetable dishes are an ideal choice as they are usually quick and easy to prepare. Good fresh ingredients are essential and all salads should be made on the day of serving, although the dressings and sauces can be made in advance. Careful thought should be given to the selection of salad vegetables and for this you need a reliable greengrocer or supermarket. Although it is possible to buy salad ingredients all year round, they are more expensive in the winter months, and it is worth watching out for reasonably priced vegetables, such as beetroot, carrots and cauliflower.

Pâtés are a traditional first course, but they can also be served as a snack meal or as part of a buffet. There are many types, the texture varying as much as the ingredients. With a rich meat pâté, a lighter main course should be considered. Lighter pâtés can be made with fish, which can be fresh, frozen or canned. These often contain butter or cream but, if you wish to reduce the fat content, it is often possible to replace some of the ingredients with low fat soft cheese or yogurt.

Soups make a very popular first course, and they are always a safe choice if you do not know the guests well. In this chapter you will find a wide variety of flavours and textures to suit all tastes. They range from a clear vegetable soup to a creamy chicken chowder and Mediterranean-style fish 'stew'.

If you make soup in large quantities, a blender or food processor can cut preparation time quite drastically. They are a good investment if you require a machine that is also efficient at chopping, grating, slicing and mixing; and many now have whisking attachments. Liquidizers and sieves are cheaper alternatives, although sieving ingredients can be very time-consuming.

Entertaining always requires a certain amount of forward planning: pâtés and soups are particularly suitable for freezing, so it is sensible to make extra portions, especially in the summer months when the ingredients are plentiful. To avoid overloading the freezer, make soups more concentrated and add the extra liquid after defrosting.

Soaking: Leaving dried vegetables, pulses and fruits in liquid to cover, for varying periods – up to 24 hours – to re-constitute, soften and sometimes flavour, before cooking. The more up-to-date the initial drying process, the shorter the soaking time. Fruits are then often simmered in the soaking liquid.

Blanching: This is done by plunging the food into a pan of boiling water for a very short time, then draining and rinsing under cold running water to stop the cooking and set the colour. Blanching helps tenderize tough textures (for example, peppers), tones down strong flavours (onions), removes excess saltiness (ham), and whitens (sweetbreads). Tomatoes are blanched to help remove their skins, vegetables to prepare them for freezing.
Fried foods such as chipped potatoes are blanched (pre-fried) in hot fat for a short time to part-cook and seal before a second frying.

Sweating: An important process which brings out the flavours of vegetables better than any other. You heat a very little fat in a frying or sauté pan over very low heat, then add finely chopped vegetables such as onions, garlic, carrots – and cook them very gently for several minutes without browning. The flavours and juices are extracted from the vegetables as they soften, often in a covered pan. Used as the first stage of braising or soup-making.

Salads

Salads make versatile and imaginative starters. They can be varied with vegetables in season and provide a perfect contrast to a rich main course.

Crudités avec Anchoïade

Raw vegetables with anchovy dip

Serves 4 ☆ ☆ ☆
Preparation: 50 minutes

The vegetables:
1 head celery, trimmed, with sticks halved and cut into even lengths
1 small cauliflower, divided into florets
4 carrots, peeled and cut into thin sticks
½ cucumber, cut into sticks, with seeds removed
1 large red or green pepper, cored, seeded and sliced into rings
1 bunch radishes, topped and tailed

The dip:
2 × 1¾oz (50g) cans anchovies in oil, drained and soaked in milk for 20 minutes
2 tomatoes, skinned, seeded and chopped
2 cloves garlic, crushed
1 tablespoon tomato purée
2 tablespoons wine vinegar
about ½ pint (300ml) olive oil

To prepare the anchovy dip, drain the anchovies and pat dry with kitchen paper.

☐ Put the anchovies in an electric blender or food processor with the tomatoes, garlic, tomato purée and wine vinegar. Work to a smooth purée, then add the oil a drop at a time until the mixture begins to thicken, as when making mayonnaise.

☐ Continue adding the oil in a thin, steady stream until a thick, smooth paste is formed. Transfer to a serving bowl. Cover and leave to stand at room temperature until serving time.

☐ Arrange the prepared vegetables in groups in a large salad bowl or basket, with the dip placed in separate bowls. Or place a bowl of the dip in the centre of a large tray or platter and arrange the groups of vegetables around the outside.

Crudités avec Anchoïade
Serve these crudités and the anchoïade dip for a dinner-party starter, either handing them round with drinks before guests sit down at the table, or serving them as a first course with everything arranged as a colourful centrepiece on the table. Guests help themselves to the vegetables and a spoonful or two of dip and eat with their fingers. The selection of vegetables can vary according to personal taste and seasonal availability, as long as they are fresh and crisp. If you like, serve the dip suggested here together with a thick homemade mayonnaise for contrast. If you enjoy a stronger flavoured anchoïade, use 3 × 1¾oz (50g) cans anchovies.

Crudités avec Anchoïade

Cheese with Prawns and Asparagus

Serves 4   ☆
Preparation: 10 minutes

1lb (450g) cottage cheese
8oz (225g) peeled prawns
salt and freshly ground black pepper
1 cucumber, peeled and diced
1 × 8oz (225g) can asparagus spears,
    drained and chopped
lettuce leaves

Place the cottage cheese and prawns in a bowl and mix together. Add salt and pepper to taste. Stir in the diced cucumber and chopped asparagus.
☐ Make a bed of lettuce leaves on four plates.
☐ Divide the cheese and prawn mixture into four and spoon on to the lettuce.
☐ Serve immediately.

Kidney Bean Salad

Serves 4   ☆☆☆
Preparation: 15 minutes

1 × 15oz (425g) can red kidney beans,
    drained
6oz (175g) Brie or Camembert cheese, cut
    into small pieces
4oz (125g) onions, peeled and chopped

The lemon vinaigrette:
¼ pint (150ml) olive oil
1 tablespoon wine vinegar
2 tablespoons lemon juice
the grated rind of 1 lemon
1 teaspoon French mustard
salt and freshly ground black pepper

First make the lemon vinaigrette: Place all the ingredients in a screw-top jar and shake vigorously until well mixed.
☐ Rinse the kidney beans thoroughly.
☐ Mix the salad ingredients together and serve with lemon vinaigrette.
☐ Serve immediately.
Tip: Orange juice can be used instead of lemon juice in the vinaigrette, but omit the rind.

Cheese-stuffed Pears

Serves 4   ☆☆
Preparation: 10 minutes plus chilling

10oz (275g) curd cheese
1oz (25g) walnuts, chopped
1 teaspoon ground ginger or ground mixed
    spice
salt and freshly ground black pepper
4 ripe medium pears, halved and cored
lettuce leaves, shredded

Mix the curd cheese, walnuts and spice together. Add salt and pepper to taste. Pile into the pear cavities.
☐ Divide the lettuce between four plates, place the pear halves on top and chill before serving.

Spinach, Avocado and Walnut Salad

Serves 4   ☆☆☆
Preparation: 15 minutes

1lb (450g) young spinach leaves
4oz (100g) lean ham
1 small avocado
1 small orange
2oz (50g) walnut halves
Lemon Vinaigrette

Wash and trim the spinach. Pat dry with kitchen paper. Roughly tear into pieces and place in a salad bowl.
☐ Cut the ham into strips. Peel and slice the avocado. Peel and slice the orange.
☐ Arrange the ham, avocado slices and walnuts over the spinach and top with the orange slices.
☐ Serve with Lemon Vinaigrette as in Kidney Bean Salad.

Melon and Prawn Salad

Serves 4   ☆☆☆
Preparation: 15 minutes

1 honeydew melon
6oz (175g) peeled prawns
½ pint (300ml) mayonnaise
2 tablespoons tomato purée

1 tablespoon grated lemon rind
1 teaspoon caster sugar
salt and freshly ground black pepper
lettuce leaves
watercress sprigs and whole
    peeled prawns to garnish

Halve the melon and scoop out the seeds. Cut the flesh into cubes or use a melon scoop.
☐ Put the melon and peeled prawns into a bowl.
☐ Mix the mayonnaise, tomato purée, lemon rind and caster sugar together. Season to taste with salt and pepper.
☐ Pour tomato mayonnaise over the melon and prawns. Mix together lightly to coat.
☐ Place lettuce leaves on four plates and divide the mixture between them. Garnish with watercress sprigs and peeled prawns and serve.

Pasta Salad

Serves 4
Preparation and cooking: about 20 minutes

½ pint (300ml) Chicken Stock
4oz (100g) small pasta shapes
4 sticks celery
1 small red pepper, cored and seeded
4 tomatoes, quartered
1 clove garlic, crushed
1 tablespoon fresh chopped basil
4oz (100g) Mozzarella cheese, grated
Lemon Vinaigrette

Put the stock into a pan and bring to the boil. Add the pasta shapes and cook for about 10 minutes until tender. Drain and allow to cool.
☐ Meanwhile cut the celery and pepper into strips and put into a bowl with the tomatoes. Add the garlic, basil and grated cheese. Stir well.
☐ Add the pasta and toss lightly with a little Lemon Vinaigrette.

Wurst Salat

Serves 4 ☆☆☆
Preparation: 15 minutes plus chilling

1lb (450g) mixed cooked German wurst,
   sliced
1 medium green pepper, cored, seeded and
   sliced
1 medium red pepper, cored, seeded and
   sliced
1 onion, peeled and sliced into rings
2 small pickled gherkins, halved, to garnish

The French dressing:
2 tablespoons wine vinegar
1 teaspoon salt
1 teaspoon freshly ground black pepper
6 tablespoons olive oil

To make the French dressing: Put
the vinegar, salt, pepper and oil in a
screw-top jar. Shake vigorously
until well mixed.
☐ Arrange the different types of
wurst and green and red peppers
decoratively on a serving plate.
Scatter over the onion rings.
☐ Pour over the French dressing
and garnish with the gherkin halves.
☐ Chill for about 30 minutes before
serving.
Tip: There are a wide variety of
smoked sausage and salami-type
meats to choose from and you can
buy a lot of them, ready sliced in
vacuum packs.

*Midsummer Salad, Russian Salad
and Wurst Salat.*

Shellfish Salad

Take this opportunity to try new types of shellfish or to use favourite but rather expensive fish such as lobster.

Serves 2
Preparation: 15 minutes

---

a mixture of salad leaves, such as endive or
    escarole, radicchio, iceberg lettuce,
    lambs' lettuce, watercress
2oz (50g) button mushrooms, finely sliced
1 firm tomato, skinned and diced
2 quails' eggs, hard-boiled and shelled
3oz (75g) cooked shellfish, such as scampi,
    prawns, crayfish tails, mussels

The dressing:
3 teaspoons lemon juice
2 tablespoons olive oil
salt and freshly gound pepper

Rinse the salad leaves, drain and dry well. Tear into bite-sized pieces and arrange on 2 serving plates.
☐ Put the mushroom slices in the centre of the salad and sprinkle the diced tomato over.
☐ Halve the eggs. Arrange the shellfish and egg around the mushrooms. Cover and chill.
☐ Shake the dressing ingredients in a screw-top jar until blended and spoon over the salad just before serving.
Variation: Marinate the mushrooms and shellfish in the dressing for 1 hour before serving, then pour the remainder over the salad.

Greek Rice Ring

Serves 6 ☆
Preparation and cooking: about 25 minutes plus 1 hour chilling

---

8oz (225g) long-grain rice
salt
lemon juice
2 large ripe tomatoes, skinned and chopped
4 teaspoons finely chopped fresh chives
4 teaspoons finely chopped fresh parsley
8 green olives, stoned and finely chopped
½ teaspoon dried marjoram
½ teaspoon dried basil
1 red pepper

The dressing:
4 tablespoons olive oil
2 tablespoons tarragon vinegar
salt and freshly ground black pepper
black olives to garnish

First make the dressing: Put the oil, vinegar and salt and black pepper to taste in a screw-top jar and shake vigorously until well mixed.
☐ Cook the rice in boiling salted water with 1 teaspoon lemon juice, for about 15 minutes or until just tender. Drain in a colander.
☐ Meanwhile, put the tomatoes in a large bowl with the chives, parsley, green olives, marjoram and basil.
☐ Blanch the pepper in boiling water for 5 minutes, then drain and remove the core and seeds. Cut into narrow strips. Add to the tomato mixture with the warm rice.
☐ Add enough of the dressing to moisten the rice mixture. Adjust the seasoning and sharpen with lemon juice.
☐ Press the mixture firmly into a small ring mould and chill for 1 hour.
☐ Invert on to a serving dish and garnish with black olives.
Variation: Serve the rice ring hot. Cover the mould with buttered foil and place it in a roasting tin containing ½in (1cm) boiling water. Heat on the top of the stove for 15 to 20 minutes. Remove the foil, invert the rice ring on to a serving dish and garnish with black olives.

Russian Salad

Serves 4 ☆☆☆
Preparation: 30 minutes

---

3 large potatoes, peeled
4 medium carrots, peeled
salt
4oz (100g) French beans, trimmed
4oz (100g) peas, shelled
1 small onion, peeled and very finely
    chopped
2oz (50g) cooked tongue, diced
4oz (100g) cooked chicken, diced
2oz (50g) garlic sausage, diced
a large pinch of cayenne pepper
8 fl oz (250ml) mayonnaise
2 hard-boiled eggs, sliced, to garnish

Cut the potatoes into even-sized pieces.
☐ Cook with the carrots in boiling salted water for 15 minutes until tender. Add the French beans and peas to the pan after 10 minutes.
☐ Drain the vegetables and allow to cool.
☐ Cut the potatoes and carrots into small dice. Cut the French beans in half.
☐ Put the cooked vegetables in a bowl with the onion, diced tongue, chicken and sausage.
☐ Sprinkle over the cayenne pepper and fold in the mayonnaise to coat.
☐ Garnish with egg and serve immediately.

Midsummer Salad

This salad is an ideal way of using up small quantities of ingredients. Add other sliced meats and vegetables that you may have.

Serves 4 ☆☆☆
Preparation: 20 minutes plus chilling

---

8 fl oz (250ml) double cream
1 teaspoon lemon juice
2oz button mushrooms, thinly sliced
4 small carrots, peeled and grated
salt and freshly ground black pepper
a large pinch of grated nutmeg
1 bunch of watercress
½ cucumber, thinly sliced
12oz (350g) salami, cold cooked meat or
    poultry, thinly sliced
1 small lettuce, shredded

Mix the cream with the lemon juice, and fold in the mushrooms and grated carrots.
☐ Season with the salt, pepper and nutmeg.
☐ Pile this mixture into the centre of a shallow serving dish and surround it with rings of cucumber and salami, meat or poultry garnished with watercress. Finish with a ring of shredded lettuce.
☐ Chill for 20 minutes before serving.

Pâtés

Pâtés start a meal off with style. Made from a variety of ingredients, they can be coarse-textured and laced with garlic or subtly-flavoured and of a spreading consistency. Not all recipes require lengthy preparation and some can be quickly blended just before serving. Some pâtés improve in flavour if made ahead and can therefore help considerably in the advance planning of your menu. Serve accompanied by toast, crusty bread or, for a really special occasion, encase the pâté in mouthwatering puff pastry.

Beef and Sausage Terrine en Croûte

Serves 4 ☆☆☆
Preparation: 35 minutes
Cooking: about 1¼ hours, plus cooling

8oz (225g) minced steak
4oz (100g) pork sausagemeat
2oz (50g) fresh brown breadcrumbs
1 small cooking apple, peeled, cored and chopped
1 small onion, peeled and chopped
1 tablespoon chopped fresh parsley
½ teaspoon dried savory
salt and freshly ground black pepper
4 tablespoons Meat Stock
1 egg, size 2, beaten
8oz (225g) Rough Puff Pastry
oil for greasing
flour for dusting
beaten egg to glaze

Set the oven to 350F (180C) gas 4. Grease and line the base of a 1lb (500g) loaf tin.
☐ Mix the minced steak, sausagemeat, breadcrumbs, apple and onion together. Add the parsley, savory, salt and black pepper to taste. Add stock and egg and stir.
☐ Turn into the prepared tin and level the top. Bake for 40 minutes and allow to cool in tin. Re-set oven to 425F (220C) gas 7.
☐ Roll out the pastry on a lightly floured surface to a 11in × 12in (28cm × 30cm) rectangle.
☐ Remove the loaf from the tin and place in the centre of the pastry. Brush the edges with water and fold the pastry round the meat loaf sealing the joins well.
☐ Use the trimmings to make decorations. Glaze with the beaten egg. Cut slits across the top for steam to escape. Place on a baking sheet.
☐ Bake for 30 minutes until pastry is golden brown. Reduce the heat to 375F (190C) gas 5 and continue cooking for 10 minutes.

Beef and Sausage Terrine en Croûte.

Smoked Mackerel Pâté; Sardine Pâté; Cod Brandade; Creamy Chicken Liver Pâté.

Cod Brandade

Serves 2 ☆☆
Preparation: 10 minutes plus chilling
Cooking: about 10 minutes

6oz (175g) cod fillet
milk
4 teaspoons lemon juice
salt and freshly ground black pepper
1oz (25g) slice of crustless white bread
2 tablespoons olive oil
1 clove garlic, crushed
capers and gherkins to garnish

Put the fish in a small pan with about 2 tablespoons of milk or sufficient to cover the base of the pan. Add 3 teaspoons of the lemon juice and salt and pepper.

☐ Cover fish and poach over a gentle heat until cooked. Cool in the liquor.

☐ Drain the fish, discard the skin and bones and flake finely.

☐ Soak the bread in 2 tablespoons milk, then squeeze as dry as possible. Mash the bread thoroughly, then beat in the flaked fish until smooth.

☐ Gradually beat in the oil, garlic, remaining lemon juice and salt and pepper to taste. Spoon into a serving dish. Cover and chill thoroughly.

☐ Serve garnished with capers and gherkins, with hot toast and butter.

Creamy Chicken Liver Pâté

Serves 2   ★★☆
Preparation and cooking: 20 minutes

6oz (175g) chicken livers
1 tablespoon finely chopped onion
1 clove garlic, crushed
1oz (25g) butter
1 tablespoon brandy
salt and freshly ground black pepper
2 tablespoons double cream
lemon twists and fresh parsley sprigs
    to garnish

Wash and drain livers. Blot dry.
☐ Melt butter in a frying-pan. Add onion and garlic and fry until soft.
☐ Add chicken livers, cover pan and cook gently for 5 minutes, stirring frequently.
☐ Add the brandy and cook for a further 5 minutes. Remove from the heat. Stir in seasoning and cream.
☐ Sieve, process or liquidize pâté.
☐ Put in dishes. Chill until set.
☐ Serve garnished.

Sardine Pâté

Serves 2   ★★☆
Preparation: 5 minutes plus chilling

---

1 × 4oz (125g) can sardines, drained
3oz (75g) cream cheese, softened
a pinch of finely grated lemon rind
1 tablespoon lemon juice
1 clove garlic, crushed
salt and freshly ground black pepper
about 1oz (25g) butter, melted
stuffed olive slices and parsley sprigs
    to garnish

Mash the sardines thoroughly, then beat in the cream cheese until smooth.
☐ Add the lemon rind and juice, garlic and salt and pepper to taste. Beat mixture well.
☐ Spoon mixture into a small serving dish. Level the top and cover with the melted butter. Chill the mixture until the melted butter has completely set.
☐ Garnish with sliced olives and parsley sprigs and serve with hot toast fingers or crispbread.

Smoked Mackerel Pâté

Serves 2   ★★★
Preparation: 10 minutes plus chilling
Cooking: 5 minutes

4oz (100g) smoked mackerel fillet, about 1
    small fillet
1oz (25g) butter
1 tablespoon finely chopped onion
1 clove garlic, crushed
1 hard-boiled egg, finely chopped
salt and freshly ground black pepper
3-4 tablespoons soured cream
tomato and cucumber slices to garnish

Remove the skin and bones from the mackerel and mash thoroughly.
☐ Melt the butter in a saucepan and fry the onion and garlic for 3-4 minutes until soft. Add to the mackerel with the egg, salt and pepper to taste. Stir in the cream and beat well.
☐ Put into 2 small dishes, fork up the top and chill until required.
☐ Garnish with tomato and cucumber slices and serve with hot toast or crusty bread.

Chicken and Lamb Terrine

Serves 6   ★★☆
Preparation: 35 minutes plus overnight chilling
Cooking: about 1¾ hours

---

2 large boneless chicken breasts, skinned
2 tablespoons sherry
12oz (350g) sausagemeat
12oz (350g) lambs' liver, minced
3 onions, peeled and finely chopped
1 teaspoon dried thyme
2 tablespoons double cream
1 egg, size 2
salt and freshly ground black pepper
10 rashers streaky bacon, rind removed
4 bay leaves
3 juniper berries
oil for greasing

Put the chicken breasts in a bowl, pour in the sherry and cover.
☐ Meanwhile, beat together the sausagemeat, liver, onion, thyme, cream, egg and salt and pepper.

☐ Stretch the bacon rashers on a board, using the back of a knife.
☐ Decorate the base of a 2lb (1kg) loaf tin with the bay leaves and juniper berries. Place the rashers of flattened bacon over base and sides, draping them over the rims of the tin to enable you to fold them over the pâté later.
☐ Drain the chicken breasts and mix the liquid with the minced mixture.
☐ Spoon half the mixture into the prepared tin and cover with the chicken breasts. Spoon the remaining mixture over the chicken and wrap the bacon rashers over.
☐ Set oven to 275F (140C) gas 1.
☐ Cover the pâté with a piece of greased foil and place in a roasting tin half filled with water.
☐ Cook in oven for about 1¾ hours until the pâté has shrunk from the sides of the tin and juices run clear when pierced with a knife. Cool.
☐ Place a 4½lb (2kg) weight on top and chill pâté overnight.
☐ To serve: Turn out and slice.

Smoked Salmon and Cream Cheese Pâté

Serves 6   ★★☆
Preparation: 30 minutes plus chilling

8oz (225g) full-fat soft cheese
1 large avocado pear, skinned and chopped
3 tablespoons lemon juice
6oz (175g) smoked salmon
salt and freshly ground black pepper
a pinch of cayenne pepper
a pinch of ground nutmeg
2 tablespoons double cream
2 tablespoons finely chopped watercress

Blend the cheese, avocado, lemon juice and 4oz (100g) of smoked salmon to a smooth purée.
☐ Add the salt, pepper, cayenne and nutmeg.
☐ Dice the remaining smoked salmon, and stir it into the mixture with the cream and chopped watercress. Adjust the seasoning and spoon into a pot. Chill for 1 hour.
☐ Serve with hot toast or bread.

Duckling Pâté

Duckling Pâté
To obtain the cooked duckling meat, roast a 3-4lb (1.5-1.8kg) bird at 400F (200C) gas 6 for 1¼ hours.
It is important to stand the bird on a trivet and prick the skin all over. This allows the fat, of which there is a great deal, to escape.

Duckling Pâté

Serves 4   ☆☆☆
Preparation: 15 minutes plus overnight chilling
Cooking: 10 minutes

8oz (225g) butter
1 duckling's liver
2 shallots, peeled and chopped
1 × 3lb (1.5kg) cold roast duckling, boned
the grated rind and juice of 1 orange
4 tablespoons port wine
a pinch of powdered bay
a pinch of dried rosemary
salt and freshly ground black pepper
bay leaves

To serve:
sliced gherkins and toast fingers

Melt ½oz (15g) of the butter in a saucepan. Add the liver and fry quickly until lightly browned on both sides. Remove from the pan and allow to cool.

☐ Melt a further ½oz (15g) butter in the pan. Add the shallots and cook gently until soft but not brown.

☐ Process or liquidize the liver, shallots, duckling and 3oz (75g) of the remaining butter until smooth.

☐ Stir in the orange rind and juice, port, herbs and salt and pepper to taste. Put into a terrine and smooth over.

☐ Melt the remaining butter in a pan over a gentle heat and pour over the pâté to seal.

☐ Leave in the refrigerator overnight to set. Serve with quarter slices of gherkin and toast fingers.

Tip: Use the duck carcass for stock.

Kipper Pâté

Serves 8 ☆☆☆
Preparation: 10 minutes plus 1 hour
chilling

8oz (225g) kipper fillets, cooked
8oz (225g) unsalted butter, softened
1 egg white from size 2 egg
1 clove garlic, peeled and chopped
grated rind of ½ lime
juice of 1 lime
1 teaspoon finely chopped tarragon
1 tablespoon finely chopped chives
salt and freshly ground black pepper
tarragon leaves and lime peel strips
    to garnish

Remove any skin and bones from
kippers. Process kippers with other
ingredients to a smooth paste.
☐ Pile into small dishes or one large
serving dish. Chill for 1 hour.
☐ Garnish with tarragon leaves and
strips of lime peel. Serve with
pumpernickel bread.

Duck Confit

Serves 6-8 ☆☆
Preparation: 30 minutes plus
6 hours chilling
Cooking: 2½ hours

---

1 duck, about 4½lb (2kg)
1 onion, peeled and coarsely chopped
1 large sprig fresh rosemary
2 teaspoons salt
strip of thinly pared lemon rind
7 fl oz (200ml) red wine
4 tablespoons raspberry vinegar
1oz (25g) seedless raspberry jelly

Set the oven to 300F (150C) gas 2.
☐ Quarter the duck. Put in an
ovenproof pan with all the other
ingredients except the jelly. Cover.
Cook in the oven for about 2½ hours
until very tender.
☐ Strain off juices and fat and set
aside. Discard skin and bones.
Shred flesh with 2 forks or chop
with a knife.
☐ Pack into 6-8 ramekins. Pour the
juices into a saucepan with the jelly.
Bring to the boil, stirring.

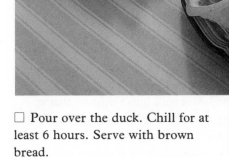

☐ Pour over the duck. Chill for at
least 6 hours. Serve with brown
bread.

Potted Beef

Serves 4 ☆☆☆
Preparation: 20 minutes plus 1 hour
chilling

8oz (225g) fillet steak in one piece
4oz (125g) butter, softened
2oz (50g) onion, peeled and chopped
1 teaspoon green peppercorns
1oz (25g) stoned green olives, chopped
1 teaspoon anchovy paste
2oz (50g) clarified butter, melted
oil for brushing

Brush steak with oil and brown both
sides under a hot grill, then cube.
☐ Process or liquidize to a smooth
paste with all but the melted butter.
Divide between small pots.
☐ Pour the melted butter on top.
Chill for 1 hour. Serve with hot
toast. (If preferred, refrigerate for 2-
3 days.)

Potted Beef:

Duck Confit
During chilling, some of the fat rises to the
top and forms a coating which helps
preserve the pâté. This fat can be eaten by
those who like rich food or it can be scraped
off.
For a less rich pâté, chill the juices so the fat
can be separated off before simmering the
juices with the jelly.
The confit will keep in the fridge for several
days as long as the fat is left on.

Potted Beef
Use rare roast beef in place of fillet if
available. Garnish with lemon twists
and parsley.

Sardine-stuffed Lemons and Kipper Pâté

Smoked mackerel and smoked eel are good instead of sardines or kippers in these recipes.

Stilton Pâté

Stilton Pâté will keep for several days in the fridge. Packed in attractive jars or pots it makes a pretty gift.

Sardine-stuffed Lemons

Serves 6   ★★☆

Preparation: 30 minutes plus 1 hour chilling

---

3 large lemons
2 × 4½oz (2 × 120g) cans sardines
salt and freshly ground black pepper
2 teaspoons grated horseradish
5 tablespoons white wine
2 teaspoons powdered gelatine
5 tablespoons double cream
lettuce leaves, parsley or chervil to
    decorate

Cut lemons in half lengthways. Cut out flesh. Reserve a few segments and squeeze remainder.

☐ Drain sardines. Mash well with seasoning and horseradish to taste. Add lemon juice.

☐ Put wine and gelatine in a small basin. Set in a saucepan of hot water. Whisk to dissolve the gelatine. Cool.

☐ Mix well into sardines. Stir in cream. Pile into lemon shells. Chill for 1 hour.

☐ Garnish with reserved lemon segments, lettuce leaves and sprigs of fresh parsley or chervil. Serve with brown bread and butter.

Sardine-stuffed Lemons.

Stilton Pâté

Serves 8   ★★★

Preparation: 10 minutes plus 1 hour chilling

8oz (225g) blue Stilton cheese
8oz (225g) cream cheese
2oz (50g) crème fraîche
2oz (50g) butter, softened
½ teaspoon ground nutmeg
4-5 tablespoons dry white vermouth
watercress to garnish

Process or liquidize the cheeses, crème and butter together to a smooth paste. Add the nutmeg and vermouth to taste. Mix in to combine the ingredients well.

☐ Spoon into small pots. Chill for 1 hour. Garnish with watercress and serve with rye or other coarse brown bread cut in chunks.

Variation: Instead of the Stilton use Roquefort or Gorgonzola.

Turkey Liver Pâté

Serves 8   ★★☆

Preparation: 30 minutes plus 1 hour chilling

1oz (25g) butter
2oz (50g) onion, chopped
1 large clove garlic, chopped
1lb (450g) turkey livers
4oz (125g) cream cheese
3 tablespoons whisky
salt and freshly ground black pepper
pinch ground allspice

Put the butter, onions and garlic in a frying pan on a low heat. Cook with occasional stirring for 10 minutes to soften the onions.

☐ Wash the livers in cold water. Blot dry. Chop roughly and add to the pan. Cook, stirring, for 5-7 minutes. Do not overcook.

☐ Liquidize or process to a smooth paste. Add the cheese and whisky and work until well mixed. Season to taste and add allspice.

☐ Turn into 8 small dishes. Chill for 1 hour. Serve with crisp biscuits or toast.

Soups

Homemade soups are one of the best beginnings to any meal. Almost any ingredient can be used – they invite experimentation! – and the results can be smooth textured, chunky, delicately flavoured or highly spiced, sweet or savoury. Many can be served hot or cold. Once made, soups keep for 2-3 days in the refrigerator and much longer in the freezer.

Cock-a-Leekie

Serve this full-bodied 'soup' with crusty bread and a light main meal.

Serves 6 ☆☆
Preparation: 15 minutes plus overnight soaking
Cooking: about 1½ hours

8oz (225g) dried prunes
1 × 3lb (1.5kg) chicken
2 pints (1.2 litres) Chicken Stock
bouquet garni
1 teaspoon dried thyme
1 bay leaf
3 parsley stalks
2oz (50g) pearl barley
1¼lb (700g) leeks, sliced

8oz (225g) dried prunes
¼ pint (150ml) double cream
salt and freshly ground black pepper

Put the prunes in a bowl with sufficient water to cover. Allow to stand overnight.
☐ Put the chicken, stock, bouquet garni, thyme, bay leaf, parsley and barley into a saucepan. Bring to the boil and cover. Simmer for 45 minutes.
☐ Add the leeks and continue cooking until the barley is cooked and the chicken is tender.
☐ Remove the chicken and cool. Strain stock and return to pan.

☐ Skin the bird and take the meat from the bones. Chop finely and return the chicken meat to the soup.
☐ Add drained prunes and simmer until tender. Stir in the cream and season with salt and pepper.
Variation: Chicken Broth with Barley. Put the chicken in a saucepan with sufficient water to cover. Bring to the boil and skim. Season with salt and pepper and cover. Cook for 1½ hours. Add 2 peeled and chopped onions, 2 cloves garlic, crushed, 2 carrots, peeled and chopped, 2 leeks, sliced, 3 sticks celery, sliced, 1 tablespoon of dried tarragon and 3oz (75g) pearl barley. Cook for a further 45 minutes. To serve: Remove the chicken and cut off the breasts. Skin and dice neatly and return to the broth. Allow the remaining chicken to become cold. Serve at another meal.

Cock-a-Leekie Soup.

Fish stock with fresh herbs

By adding fresh herbs such as parsley to your stock, you will get a spicier, stronger taste that will enhance the flavour of the fish. Fish stock made with fresh herbs will be even tastier if you double the quantity of parsley and add a coarsely chopped piece of the parsley root while the stock is cooking.

Keeping to the cooking time

Do not cook fish, or indeed any other stock for too long. The ingredients will have released all their flavours in the time given and longer cooking will only make the stock taste bitter.

Fish Soup with Crab

When you add the rice, stir 2 or 3 tablespoons of tomato purée into the soup to give it a good colour and flavour. You can add 3 tablespoons of port as well to enrich the soup.

Break large fish carcasses into pieces so they fit into the pan.

Fish Stock

Made from bones and trimmings with wine and herbs, this simple fish stock, when strained, makes a delicious basic broth as well as a poaching liquid. If you double the quantity of fish given below, the flavour will be more concentrated.

Makes about 1½ pints (900ml) ○
Preparation and cooking: 25 minutes

12oz (350g) fish bones and trimmings
1 tablespoon chopped parsley
3 white peppercorns, crushed
2 lemon slices
¾ pint (450ml) dry white wine
about 1 pint (600ml) water
½ bay leaf
1 teaspoon salt

Put the fish into a pan with the rest of the ingredients and bring to the boil. Remove the scum that rises to the surface.

☐ Lower the heat and simmer the stock gently for 15-20 minutes, skimming from time to time, if necessary.

☐ Strain through a sieve lined with muslin or kitchen paper.

Tip: Dampen the muslin, if used, so the fibres swell and help to trap tiny particles.

Fish Soup with Crab

Serves 4 ☆
Preparation and cooking:
15-20 minutes

5-7oz (150-200g) cooked crabmeat
1½ pints (900ml) Fish Stock
2 tablespoons finely chopped parsley
4 tablespoons boiled rice
4-6 tablespoons cooked peas
salt and white pepper
a few drops of Tabasco sauce
a few drops of lemon juice

Cut the crabmeat into small pieces, removing any pieces of shell.

☐ Bring the fish stock to the boil. Add the parsley and rice and bring it back to the boil.

☐ Add the peas, simmer for about a minute, then add the crabmeat and remove from the heat at once.

☐ Season the soup with salt, pepper and a few drops of Tabasco and lemon juice.

Fish Soup with Prawns and Tomatoes

Serves 4 ○
Preparation and cooking: 15 minutes

1½ pints (900ml) Fish Stock
salt and white pepper
3-4 large tomatoes, peeled
4-5oz (125-150g) peeled prawns, chopped if large
2 tablespoons finely chopped parsley
1 tablespoon finely chopped chives
a few drops of lemon juice

Bring the stock to the boil, reduce the heat to a simmer, then season with salt and pepper. Halve the tomatoes, remove the seeds and juice, then chop the flesh. Add to the fish stock and cook gently for 2 minutes.

☐ Stir in the prawns and the chopped parsley, remove the pan from the heat and ladle the soup into warmed bowls or plates. Sprinkle with chives. Sharpen the taste with lemon juice for serving.

Fish Soup with Herbs

Serves 4 ○
Preparation and cooking:
10-15 minutes

1½ pints (900ml) Fish Stock made with double the quantity of fish
salt and white pepper
1½ tablespoons finely chopped parsley
1½ tablespoons finely chopped chervil
1 tablespoon finely chopped chives
a few drops of lemon juice

Bring the strained stock to the boil. Season to taste.

☐ Stir in the parsley and chervil and sprinkle with chives to serve. Sharpen the taste with lemon juice.

North Sea Fish Soup

Serves 6 ☆
Preparation and cooking:
about 40 minutes

---

3 pints (1.75 litres) Fish Stock–double the
  basic recipe
12oz (350g) cod fillet, or other firm-fleshed
  white fish
juice of 1 lemon
1 small leek or 3 spring onions, trimmed
  and sliced into thin rings
2-3 sticks of celery, thinly sliced
2 large tomatoes, skinned, deseeded and
  diced
4 thick slices white bread, crusts removed
2oz (50g) butter
1 tablespoon oil
4oz (125g) peeled prawns
salt and white pepper
grated Parmesan cheese to serve

Bring the stock to the boil.

☐ Meanwhile, sprinkle the fish with
a little lemon juice and allow it to
stand for several minutes, then pat it
dry and cut it into small strips or
cubes.

☐ Add the leek or onion and the
celery to the boiling stock, reduce
the heat and simmer gently for 5
minutes.

☐ Add the fish and cook for a
further 3 minutes. Add the diced
tomatoes and continue cooking until
they are warmed through, then
remove the soup from the heat.

☐ Cut the bread into cubes. Heat
the butter and oil in a frying pan
and when foaming, add the bread
cubes and fry on all sides until
brown. Drain the croûtons on
kitchen paper and keep hot.

☐ Reheat the soup. Stir in the
prawns and season with salt and
pepper. Serve sprinkled with a little
lemon juice, the croûtons and hand
the Parmesan cheese separately.

*Serve North Sea Fish Soup for an
informal lunch or supper.*

Fish soups with cheese
Serve fish soups with a garnish of grated
cheese such as Gruyère, Cheddar or
Parmesan.

Mushroom Soup

Serves 4　☆
Preparation: 10 minutes
Cooking: about 35 minutes

1oz (25g) butter
1 small onion, peeled and sliced
8oz (225g) button mushrooms, washed and
　sliced
1oz (25g) flour
1 pint (600ml) Chicken Stock
¼ pint (150ml) milk
salt and freshly ground black pepper
finely chopped parsley to finish

Heat the butter and fry the onion
until soft.
☐ Add the mushrooms and sauté
for about 5 minutes.
☐ Stir in the flour and cook for 2
minutes.
☐ Allow to cool slightly, then add
the stock and milk gradually.
☐ Bring to the boil, stirring all the
time. Season well, cover and simmer
gently for about 20 minutes.
☐ Serve hot, sprinkled with
chopped parsley if liked.

Thick Vegetable Soup

Serves 4　☆
Preparation: 10 minutes
Cooking: 40 minutes

1oz (25g) butter
1lb (450g) leeks, cleaned and sliced
1 small onion, peeled and sliced
2 medium-sized potatoes, peeled and sliced
2 small carrots, peeled and sliced
1¾ pints (1 litre) Chicken Stock
salt and freshly ground black pepper

Heat the butter in a large saucepan
and fry the vegetables for about 5
minutes until the leeks are soft.
☐ Add the stock and seasoning,
bring to the boil and simmer,
covered, for 30 minutes until the
potatoes are soft.
☐ Sieve the soup or purée in a
blender. Return to the pan.
☐ Reheat, taste and adjust
seasoning. If wished, serve sprinkled
with chopped herbs.

Cream of Artichoke Soup

This is a deliciously flavoured soup
and is well worth making when
Jerusalem artichokes are in season
from November to June.

Serves 4　☆☆
Preparation: 15 minutes
Cooking: 15 minutes

1½oz (40g) butter
1 large onion, peeled and sliced
1½lb (700g) Jerusalem artichokes, peeled
　and sliced
½ pint (300ml) milk
1 pint (600ml) Chicken Stock
salt and freshly ground black pepper
sprigs of watercress to finish

Heat butter in a pan and cook onion
until soft but not coloured.
☐ Add the artichokes to the pan,
pour over the milk and stock, and
and cook slowly for about 7 minutes.
☐ Allow to cool, then sieve the soup
or purée to a cream in an electric
blender.
☐ Return to the pan, adjust
seasoning, reheat and serve with
sprigs of watercress.

Fresh Tomato Soup

Serves 4　☆☆
Preparation: 20 minutes
Cooking: 45 minutes

1½oz (40g) butter
1 small onion, peeled and sliced
1 rasher streaky bacon, rinded and chopped
1 stick celery, scrubbed and chopped
1½lb (700g) tomatoes, skinned and roughly
　chopped
2 tablespoons flour
1 pint (600ml) Chicken Stock
1 teaspoon dried basil
salt and freshly ground black pepper
4 teaspoons tomato purée (optional)
1 tablespoon medium dry sherry
finely chopped parsley to finish

Heat the butter in a pan and fry the
onion, bacon and celery until soft
but not coloured.
☐ Add the tomatoes and cook for a
few minutes.

☐ Stir in the flour, add the stock,
basil, seasoning and tomato purée
and bring slowly to the boil.
☐ Simmer for 30 minutes.
☐ Sieve the soup or purée to a
cream in an electric blender.
☐ Return to the pan, add sherry,
reheat, taste and adjust seasoning.
Serve sprinkled with chopped
parsley.

Avocado Soup

Serves 4　☆☆☆
Preparation: 10 minutes
Cooking: 15 minutes

1oz (25g) butter
1 tablespoon finely chopped onion
1 tablespoon flour
½ pint (300ml) Chicken Stock
1 ripe avocado, peeled, stoned and chopped
1–2 teaspoons lemon juice
a pinch of finely grated lemon rind
salt and freshly ground black pepper
¼ pint (150ml) creamy milk

To finish:
4 tablespoons cream
1 tablespoon finely chopped chives

Melt the butter in a saucepan. Add
the onion and fry until soft. Do not
allow to colour.
☐ Stir in the flour and cook for 1
minute. Gradually stir in the stock
and bring to the boil. Simmer for 3-
4 minutes.
☐ Add the avocado, with the lemon
juice, lemon rind and seasoning to
taste. Simmer for 5 minutes then
sieve or purée the soup. Rinse the
pan.
☐ Return the soup to the rinsed-out
pan. Stir in the milk. Reheat
without boiling.
☐ Adjust the seasoning and pour
into heated soup bowls. Swirl in the
cream and sprinkle with the
chopped chives.
Variation: The soup can also be
served chilled. After sieving or
puréeing add the milk and cream
and chill.
Tip: Sprinkle the prepared avocado
with the lemon juice to prevent
discoloration.

Cream of Spinach Soup

Serves 4 ☆☆
Preparation and cooking: 25 minutes

1lb (500g) spinach
1oz (25g) butter
1oz (25g) flour
1¾ pints (1 litre) White or Vegetable Stock
5 fl oz (150ml) cream
salt and freshly ground pepper
freshly grated nutmeg
2 tablespoons finely chopped parsley
2 hard-boiled eggs, sliced

Pick over the spinach and wash it thoroughly. Remove the tough stalks and chop the leaves roughly.

☐ Melt the butter in a large pan and add the spinach. Cover the pan and cook for about 5 minutes, stirring frequently or shaking the pan to ensure even cooking.

☐ Remove from heat, sprinkle the flour over the spinach and stir it in.

☐ Return to a moderate heat and gradually add the stock, stirring constantly until the soup begins to thicken. Simmer for 3 minutes.

☐ Blend or process until smooth, or pass it through a food mill.

☐ Add the cream and reheat. Do not allow it to boil. Season with salt, pepper and nutmeg and serve garnished with parsley and egg slices.

Cream of Broccoli Soup

Serves 4 ☆☆
Preparation and cooking: 25 minutes

12oz (350g) broccoli, washed
1¾ pints (1 litre) White or Vegetable Stock
1oz (25g) butter
1oz (25g) flour
5 fl oz (150ml) cream
salt and freshly ground pepper

Cut the florets off the stalks and divide them into small pieces. Chop the stalks roughly.

☐ Bring the stock to the boil and cook the broccoli stalks for 10 minutes, or until tender. Purée in a blender or food processor or pass through a food mill and set aside.

☐ Make a roux with the butter and flour in the rinsed-out pan, then gradually add the stock, stirring constantly. Bring to the boil, season to taste and add the broccoli florets. Simmer for 3-5 minutes, until the broccoli is cooked.

☐ Remove from the heat, stir in the cream and, if necessary, reheat gently before serving. Do not allow to re-boil.

Spinach Soup variation
Replace a quarter of the spinach with sorrel. This leafy plant, which has a distinctive acidic flavour, is becoming more available, and is easily homegrown.

Other vegetable soups
Use the same method as for Spinach and Broccoli Soups to make other vegetable soups—try carrot with orange, celery, or mushroom.

Cream of Spinach Soup and Cream of Broccoli Soup.

Clear Vegetable Soup.

French Onion Soup
The flavour can be enhanced by replacing a
little of the stock with wine or beer.

Clear Vegetable Soup

A perfect soup for slimmers, which
can be made more substantial by
adding cooked rice or small pasta
shapes to the soup with the vegetables.

Serves 4   ○
Preparation and cooking: 20 minutes

1¾ pints (1 litre) White or Vegetable Stock
8oz (225g) carrots, sliced
1 head of fennel, sliced
3 sprigs of thyme
8oz (225g) French beans, trimmed and cut
　　into short lengths
4 sticks of celery, sliced
1 leek, sliced
4oz (100g) mangetout, topped and tailed
salt and pepper

Bring the stock to the boil in a large
pan. Add the carrots, fennel and
thyme and cook for 5 minutes before
adding the remaining vegetables.
　□ Simmer for about 3 more
minutes, or until the vegetables are
cooked but still crisp.
　□ Remove the sprigs of thyme,
season and serve with grated cheese.

French Onion Soup

Serves 4   ☆ ☆
Preparation and cooking: 40 minutes

1oz (25g) butter
1 tablespoon oil
1lb (500g) onions, finely sliced
1¾ pints (1 litre) Meat or Brown Stock
salt and freshly ground black pepper
8 slices crusty French bread
4oz (100g) Gruyère cheese, grated

Melt the butter and oil in a large,
heavy-based pan. Fry the onions
gently for about 20 minutes, or until
they are golden and very soft.
　□ Add the stock and bring to the
boil. Reduce the heat, cover the pan
and simmer for 10 minutes. Season
to taste.
　□ Toast the bread on both sides,
divide the cheese between the slices
and grill until browned.
　□ Serve the soup with the slices of
toast floating on top, cheese-side
uppermost.

Vichyssoise

Serves 4   ☆ ☆ ☆
Preparation and cooking: 45 minutes
Cooling and chilling: 1½-2 hours

1oz (25g) butter
white part of 2lb (1kg) leeks, finely sliced
3 medium potatoes, diced
1¾ pints (1 litre) Chicken Stock
salt and freshly ground pepper
freshly grated nutmeg
½ pint (300ml) cream
1 tablespoon finely chopped chives

Melt the butter in a large pan, add the leeks and cook them very gently for about 15 minutes.
☐ Add the potatoes, stock, salt, pepper and nutmeg and simmer for 20 minutes.
☐ Purée the soup in a blender or processor or rub through a sieve with a wooden spoon.
☐ Cool, then chill the soup. When ice cold stir in the cream and sprinkle with the chives.

Cauliflower Cheese Soup

Serves 4   ☆ ☆ ☆
Preparation and cooking: 30 minutes

1 small cauliflower
scant pint (500ml) Chicken Stock
2oz (50g) butter
2oz (50g) flour
1 pint (600ml) milk
4oz (100g) Cheddar cheese
salt and freshly ground black pepper
a sprinkling of grated nutmeg

Divide the cauliflower into florets and rinse well. Bring the stock to the boil and cook the cauliflower until tender.
☐ Purée the cauliflower with some of the stock, using a blender or food mill.
☐ In a second pan mix together the butter and flour to make a roux. Gradually add the milk, stirring constantly until it comes to the boil and thickens. Cook for 5 minutes,

then remove from the heat and beat in the cheese.
☐ Gradually whisk in the cauliflower purée and the remaining stock and bring the soup to the boil.
☐ Season to taste, sprinkle with nutmeg and serve.
Variation: Replace the Cheddar cheese with 3oz (75g) of Stilton to give a distinctive flavour.
Variation: Instead of cauliflower cook 1lb (500g) courgettes in the stock and continue as above.

Chicken and Sweetcorn Chowder

Originating from Newfoundland and in the north-eastern coast of the United States, creamy, thick chowders can form a complete meal.

Serves 4   ☆ ☆ ☆
Preparation and cooking: 20 minutes

1¾ pints (1 litre) Chicken Stock
1 onion, finely diced
1 large potato, finely diced
1lb (500g) sweetcorn kernels
1lb (500g) cooked chicken, diced
2 hard-boiled eggs, finely chopped
salt and freshly ground black pepper
1 tablespoon finely chopped parsley
5 fl oz (150ml) double cream

Bring the stock to the boil, add the diced onion, potato and the sweetcorn and simmer for 5 minutes.
☐ Add the chicken and the egg, and season to taste. Stir in the parsley.
☐ Lightly whip the cream until it forms soft peaks.
☐ Serve the soup in individual bowls, topped with a spoonful of cream.
Variation: Replace the chicken stock and chicken with fish stock and shellfish such as prawns, mussels or scallops, or chunks of white fish. If raw, cook the shellfish or fish in the stock with the onion, potato and sweetcorn, together with some fried diced unsmoked bacon for a classic New England chowder.

Canned consommé
If there is no time to make stock use canned ready-made consommé as a basis for soups. The simplest way to present it is with a vegetable garnish such as finely diced leeks, which can be cooked very quickly in the soup as it is heated.

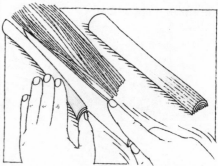

Clean the leeks and trim away the green part. Slice lengthways.

Cut across the strips to make very small dice.

Preparing cucumber

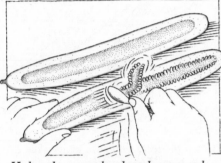

Halve the cucumber lengthways and scoop out the seeds with a teaspoon.

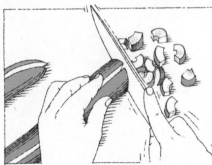

Cut into quarters and slice across into chunks.

Cream of Chicken Soup

Serves 4-6   ☆☆☆
Preparation and cooking:
15-20 minutes

1¾ pints (1 litre) Chicken Stock
5 fl oz (150ml) dry white wine
1oz (25g) butter
1oz (25g) flour
2 cooked chicken joints, or meat from a
     boiling fowl if used to make the stock, cut
     into bite-size pieces
salt and freshly ground pepper
2 egg yolks
5 fl oz (150ml) cream
2 tablespoons finely chopped mixed herbs

Bring the stock to the boil with the wine.

☐ Make a roux with the butter and flour in a separate pan, remove from the heat and gradually stir in the hot stock. Return to the heat and bring to the boil, stirring constantly.

☐ Add the chicken and season to taste with salt and pepper. Reduce the heat and simmer gently for 5 minutes.

☐ Beat the egg yolks and cream together. Take the soup from the heat and stir in the egg and cream liaison. Add the herbs and serve.

Chicken Liver and Tomato Soup

Serves 4   ☆☆
Preparation and cooking: 40 minutes

4oz (100g) chicken livers
2oz (50g) butter
2 tablespoons brandy
1oz (25g) flour
14oz (396g) can of tomatoes
1¾ pints (1 litre) Chicken Stock
salt and freshly ground pepper
1 tablespoon finely chopped chives

Rinse the chicken livers in cold water and pat dry with kitchen paper. Trim off any skin, fat or greenish parts.

☐ Melt half of the butter in a large saucepan and cook the livers gently, without browning.

☐ Remove the livers, slice them and sprinkle with the brandy. Leave to absorb the flavour while making the soup.

☐ Wipe out the pan with kitchen paper, then make a roux with the remaining butter and the flour.

☐ Press tomatoes through a sieve with juice, then stir the purée into the roux. Simmer for 10-15 minutes until thick, then add the stock.

☐ Bring to the boil and season to taste.

☐ Serve garnished with the chicken livers and the chives.

Clear Chicken Soup with Cucumber

Based on a well-flavoured chicken stock, which complements the subtle flavour of the cucumber, this clear soup would make a perfect first course to precede a substantial meal.

Serves 4   ◯
Preparation and cooking: 15 minutes

---

1 small cucumber
1¾ pints (1 litre) Chicken Stock
4 tablespoons Madeira or dry sherry
salt and freshly ground pepper
1 tablespoon finely chopped parsley
1 tablespoon finely chopped chives

Peel the cucumber, if preferred. Otherwise cut it in half lengthways. Scoop out the seeds and slice as shown.

☐ Pour the stock into a pan and bring it to the boil. Add the cucumber and simmer for 5 minutes. Stir in the Madeira or sherry and season to taste.

☐ Just before serving, stir in the parsley and chives.

Clockwise from the top: Cream of Chicken Soup, Chicken Liver and Tomato Soup and Clear Chicken Soup with Cucumber.

MAIN COURSES

Traditionally, main courses are based on poultry or meat, and for the dish to be successful it is essential that you buy the best quality you can afford. For this you need a reliable butcher and it is helpful if you can use a local firm on a regular basis and get to know the staff. It is likely that they will be more helpful when you require a special cut of meat or need poultry or joints boned and rolled. Remember to give them plenty of notice, especially if the meat is required for a weekend. You may find it more convenient to buy meat and poultry in a supermarket or freezer centre where you can find a good variety of cuts, portions and sizes.

Chicken is one of the most versatile meats and contains less fat than most. It can be cooked whole, boned and stuffed, in portions or sliced. It lends itself to many flavours, from hot curry spices and citrus fruits to herbs such as tarragon and basil.

Turkey has always been popular. As it is a large bird, there is often meat left over, and this is ideal for making up into quick supper or lunch dishes. Cuts of turkey are now widely available, breast being particularly useful, as well as other turkey products, such as joints, burgers and rissoles.

Duck is also available all year round in larger supermarkets. It has more fat than chicken or turkey, which is why it is often served with a fruit-based sauce. The meat is also good to use in salads.

Beef is a traditional English favourite which offers many cuts suitable for a number of different cooking methods. Casseroles are particularly suitable for the winter months, and the addition of vegetables and a little alcohol makes them even more welcoming. Minced beef is a great favourite with children and very versatile. As it can be rather fatty, it is worth buying a better quality from your butcher. Minced beef can be extended with lentils, beans, rice and pasta to further reduce fat intake.

Lamb and pork are available frozen all year round and English lamb is available fresh in the autumn. The traditional flavourings for lamb are mint, rosemary and redcurrant, but it is also good with spices and dried fruits. Pork also blends particularly well with spices and fruits, such as apples, pineapple, prunes and apricots.

Some of the dishes included in this section are very simple, while others will be a little more time-consuming, but all of them will be rewarding to make.

Marinating: Soaking or steeping meat, fish and vegetables in an acid-based liquid (water with vinegar or lemon juice, wine) or sometimes yogurt, flavoured with seasonings, herbs and spices. This tenderizes and adds succulence and flavour before cooking, which is often by grilling or roasting. Certain fish and shellfish are marinated instead of being cooked. Game such as venison may be marinated for up to two weeks.

Simmering: Generally long, slow cooking in a liquid 'to cover' at a low temperature, not above 205F (96C), when the liquid barely moves – with perhaps a bubble breaking the surface at one point. This technique is used for less tender meat and you will also see the term used for sauces, where it is important to cook them for as long as possible, without losing volume through evaporation, to develop flavour and thickening.

Chicken

Chicken is one of the most economical meats, and although this may be the main reason for its popularity, it can also be attributed to the fact that it is extremely versatile in both the method of cooking and in the various ingredients with which it can be incorporated.

Chilled poultry, oven-ready and cut into various joints as well as the whole bird are available all the year round. There is also the advantage of frozen poultry too, but care must be taken in thawing completely before removing the giblets and cooking.

There are different sized birds available. Poussin or baby chickens weigh between ¾lb and 1lb (350g-500g) and will serve one or two persons. Spring chickens are somewhat larger than poussins, weighing between 1½lb and 2lb (700g-1kg) and are usually cut in half to serve. Most chickens sold are roasters and their weight starts at around 3lb (1.5kg). Boiling chickens are older and more flavoursome and should not be overcooked. Their weight starts at around 3lb (1.5kg) and their cooking time will be longer than that required for other types.

Curried Spring Chickens.

Curried Spring Chickens

Serves 4

Preparation and cooking: 50 minutes

2oz (50g) butter
2 onions, peeled and chopped
1 clove garlic, chopped
1 tablespoon curry powder
2 × 1½lb (700g) chickens, skinned and jointed
¼ pint (150ml) Chicken Stock
1 tablespoon tomato purée
1 tablespoon brown sugar
1 bay leaf
salt and freshly ground black pepper
lemon slices to garnish

Melt the butter in a frying pan and fry the onions, garlic and curry powder for 2 minutes.
☐ Add the chicken pieces and continue to fry for 5 to 6 minutes. Moisten the chicken pieces with the stock and add the tomato purée, sugar, bay leaf and salt and pepper to taste. Cover and simmer gently for 40 minutes or until the chicken is cooked.
☐ Remove the bay leaf and adjust the seasoning. Garnish with lemon slices and serve with plain boiled rice.

Poulet à l'Estragon

If you use fresh tarragon try to obtain the French variety which has much more flavour than the tasteless Russian kind. Dried tarragon is a good herb to have and is used with egg and fish dishes as well as poultry. It is also one of the four herbs, the others being parsley, chervil and chives, with perfectly balanced flavours which are incorporated into omelette fines herbes.

Poulet Basquaise

The customs and cuisine of the south-western corner of France are linked with the area around its Spanish borders—collectively known as the Basque country. There, onions, garlic, peppers and tomatoes are dominant features of the cooking.

Poulet à l'Estragon
Chicken with tarragon butter sauce

Serves 4   ☆☆☆
Preparation: 10 minutes
Cooking: 1 hour 40 minutes

4oz (100g) butter
1 × 4lb (2kg) oven-ready chicken
4 cloves garlic, peeled
2 tablespoons freshly chopped tarragon or 1 tablespoon dried tarragon
salt and freshly ground black pepper
2 tablespoons plain flour
¾ pint (450ml) dry white wine and water, mixed

Set oven to 375F (190C) gas 4.
☐ Put half the butter inside the cavity of the chicken with 2 whole garlic cloves, half the tarragon and salt and pepper to taste. Truss with thread or fine string, then put in a roasting tin.
☐ Crush the remaining garlic cloves with ½ teaspoon salt. Beat into the remaining butter with the rest of the tarragon until soft, then spread the mixture all over the skin of the chicken. Sprinkle with salt and pepper.
☐ Roast in the oven for about 1½ hours or until the juices run clear when the thickest part of the thigh is pierced with a skewer. Turn the chicken over a quarter turn every 15 minutes during roasting, and baste with the cooking juices.
☐ Transfer the chicken to a warmed serving platter and keep hot in the lowest possible oven. Pour off all but 2 tablespoons of the excess fat and juices from the roasting tin.
☐ Place the roasting tin on top of the stove over moderate heat and sprinkle in the flour. Cook for 1-2 minutes until golden brown, stirring constantly, then gradually stir in the wine and water mixture.
☐ Bring to the boil, then lower the heat and simmer until thickened, stirring all the time.
☐ Taste and adjust the seasoning, then pour into a warmed sauceboat. Serve the chicken immediately, with the sauce handed separately.
Tip: Use as much white wine as you can spare for the sauce, and for a dinner party main course swirl in ¼ pint (150ml) double cream just before serving. For an economical meal, the sauce can be made with chicken stock rather than the mixture of white wine and water.

Poulet Basquaise
Chicken Basque style

Serves 4
Preparation and cooking: 1 hour

---

4 tablespoons olive oil
4 chicken portions, skinned
1 medium onion, peeled and finely chopped
1 clove garlic, peeled and crushed with ½ teaspoon salt
½ red pepper, cored, seeded and finely chopped
½ green pepper, cored, seeded and finely chopped
12oz (350g) tomatoes, skinned, seeded and chopped
¼ pint (150ml) Chicken Stock or water
4 tablespoons brandy or medium sherry
2 teaspoons freshly chopped rosemary or 1 teaspoon dried rosemary
2 teaspoons freshly chopped thyme or 1 teaspoon dried thyme
salt and freshly ground black pepper

Heat the oil in a large flameproof casserole, add the chicken and fry gently until browned on all sides. Remove from the casserole and set aside.
☐ Add the onion to the casserole and fry gently until soft. Add the garlic and peppers and fry for a further few minutes, then stir in the tomatoes, chicken stock or water and brandy or sherry and bring to the boil.
☐ Lower the heat, add the rosemary, thyme, and salt and pepper to taste, then return the chicken to the casserole. Simmer gently, uncovered, for 45 minutes or until the chicken is tender and the liquid and vegetables are reduced.

Poulet à l'Estragon and Poulet Basquaise.

Chicken Marengo

There are countless recipes for this dish which takes its name from the battle at which Napoleon defeated the Austrians in 1800. The dish was created on the battlefield by Napoleon's chef, Dunard, and probably explains the large quantity of Marsala wine incorporated. If you prefer, use sweet sherry in place of the Marsala or use half quantities of chicken stock.

Chicken with Grapefruit

If you use the empty shells of grapefruit, the shell can be shredded, blanched and frozen until required, thus saving time when preparing the dish. Canned, drained grapefruit segments could be used instead of fresh.

Chicken Marengo

Serves 4   ☆☆☆
Preparation: 10 minutes
Cooking: about 1½ hours

4oz (100g) butter
1 × 3½lb (1.75kg) chicken, quartered
6 shallots, peeled
2 cloves garlic, crushed
4oz (100g) plain flour, seasoned
6 tomatoes, skinned and quartered
6oz (175g) button mushrooms
1 bay leaf
1 teaspoon dry oregano
⅓ bottle Marsala
3 fl oz (100ml) brandy

Melt 3oz (75g) of the butter in a flameproof casserole. Add the chicken pieces, shallots and garlic and fry until the chicken is browned.

☐ Sprinkle over 2oz (50g) of the flour. Cook, stirring, for 1 minute.

☐ Add the tomatoes, mushrooms, bay leaf, oregano and Marsala. Bring to the boil, skim and cover. Simmer for 1¼ hours.

☐ Ten minutes before the chicken is ready, add the brandy and stir well.

☐ Mix together the remaining butter and flour to a paste. Stir small pieces into the sauce until thickened.

Chicken with Grapefruit

Serves 4   ☆☆☆
Preparation: 15 minutes
Cooking: about 1½ hours

2oz (50g) butter
1 × 3lb (1.5kg) chicken
2 shallots, peeled and chopped
salt and freshly ground black pepper
1 or 2 grapefruit, according to size

Set oven to 400F (200C) gas 6.

☐ Melt the butter in a roasting tin over a gentle heat and add the chicken and shallots. Fry, turning the chicken until lightly browned, then season with salt and pepper to taste. Cook in oven for 1¼ hours.

☐ Meanwhile, peel the rind from the grapefruit. Cut the rind into thin shreds. Blanch in boiling water for 3 minutes, then drain.

☐ Remove pith from the grapefruit and discard. Separate the fruit into segments, cutting between the membrane.

☐ Transfer the chicken to a serving platter and keep hot. Pour the fat from the roasting tin. Stir in the fruit and shredded rind. Heat through and serve with the chicken.

Chicken with Bacon Dumplings

Serves 4   ☆☆☆
Preparation: 15 minutes
Cooking: about 1¼ hours

---

1 tablespoon olive oil
1 × 3½lb (1.75kg) chicken, cut into joints
2 large onions, peeled and chopped
1 clove garlic, crushed
1oz (25g) plain flour
1 pint (600ml) Chicken Stock
1 bay leaf
salt and freshly ground black pepper

The dumplings:
8oz (225g) self-raising flour
a pinch of salt
1oz (25g) butter
4oz (100g) finely chopped suet
4oz (100g) streaky bacon, rinded and finely chopped
1 small onion, peeled and finely chopped
a pinch of dried thyme
1 egg, size 2, beaten
milk to moisten
1½ pints (900ml) Chicken Stock

Heat the oil in a flameproof casserole. Add the chicken, onions and garlic and fry until browned.

☐ Sprinkle over the flour and cook, stirring, for 1 minute. Stir in stock, add bay leaf and salt and pepper. Simmer for 1 hour.

☐ Meanwhile, make the dumplings: Sift the flour and salt into a mixing bowl and rub in the butter. Mix in the suet, bacon, onion and thyme, beaten egg and milk. Form dumplings.

☐ Bring the stock to the boil in another saucepan. Add the dumplings, cover and poach for 20 minutes.

☐ Serve with the casserole.

Turkey

Turkey need no longer be confined to Christmas and Easter family gatherings. Smaller birds and various joints such as breasts and legs are available, fresh or frozen, all year round and can make economical yet special meals.

Turkey Breasts in Aspic

Serves 6 ☆
Preparation: 20 minutes plus chilling

1-1½lb (500-700g) cooked turkey breast
1½ sachets aspic jelly powder, each 2½oz (70g)
1½ pints (900ml) turkey or Chicken Stock
fresh tarragon sprigs to garnish

Slice the turkey and arrange on a shallow dish.
☐ Make up the aspic with the stock, according to the directions on the packet. Allow to cool until on the point of setting.
☐ Pour most of the aspic over the turkey and the remainder into a separate dish. Chill until set.
☐ Chop the reserved aspic jelly finely. Garnish the turkey with the chopped aspic and sprigs of tarragon.

Turkey Breasts in Aspic
Use boneless chicken breasts and poach them gently in well-flavoured stock for 15 minutes. Cool in the stock then chill before slicing.

Slow roasting
Oven 325F (160C) gas 3
6-8lb (2.75-3.6kg) 3-3½ hours
8-10lb (3.6-4.5kg) 3½-3¾ hours
10-14lb (4.5-6.25kg) 3¾-4½ hours
14-18lb (6.25-8kg) 4¼-4¾ hours

Turkey Breasts in Aspic

Turkey à l'Orange

Serves 2 ☆☆
Preparation: 30 minutes
Cooking: about 20 minutes

---

1 orange
1oz (25g) butter
1 onion, peeled and sliced
8oz (225g) turkey meat, cubed
2oz (50g) mushrooms, sliced
8oz (225g) can tomatoes, drained
4 tablespoons orange juice
salt and freshly ground black pepper

Finely pare the rind from half the orange and cut into julienne strips. Blanch in boiling water for about 10 minutes until tender. Drain well. Grate the remaining orange rind. Squeeze the juice into a separate bowl and reserve.

☐ Melt the butter in a saucepan and fry the onion until lightly coloured. Add the turkey and continue cooking for about 5 minutes or until evenly browned.

☐ Stir in the mushrooms and cook for 2 minutes, stirring frequently.

☐ Add the tomatoes, grated orange rind and juice and seasoning to taste. Bring to the boil. Cover, reduce the heat and simmer for about 20 minutes until the turkey is tender and the juices well reduced and thickened.

☐ Adjust the seasoning and serve on a bed of rice sprinkled with the orange rind strips.

Turkey and Courgette Casserole

Serves 4 ☆
Preparation: 10 minutes plus 1-2 hours draining
Cooking: about 30 minutes

1lb (450g) courgettes, thinly sliced
salt and freshly ground black pepper
1lb (450g) turkey meat, sliced or cubed
a pinch of ground nutmeg
4 tablespoons Chicken Stock
2oz (50g) Parmesan or Cheddar cheese, grated

Sprinkle the courgette slices with salt and leave to drain for 1-2 hours.

☐ Set oven to 400F (200C) gas 6.

☐ Place a layer of courgettes in a casserole dish then cover with a layer of turkey. Repeat the layers until all the turkey and courgettes have been used, ending with courgettes.

☐ Add salt, pepper, nutmeg and stock. Sprinkle with the Parmesan or Cheddar cheese.

☐ Bake for about 30 minutes or until the turkey is tender.

Turkey Mexicana

Chilli powder is very hot and varies in strength according to the brand used, so use it cautiously. Serve this spicy dish with rice and a crisp green salad.

Serves 4 ☆☆
Preparation: 30 minutes
Cooking: 50 minutes

---

4 turkey breast fillets
2oz (50g) seasoned flour
3 tablespoons oil
1 medium onion, peeled and thinly sliced
1 small red pepper, cored, seeded and sliced
½ pint (300ml) Chicken Stock
1oz (25g) seedless raisins
a pinch of ground cloves
a pinch of ground cumin
½ teaspoon ground cinnamon
3 tomatoes, skinned, seeded and sliced
1 teaspoon chilli powder
1 tablespoon sesame seeds
1oz (25g) plain dark chocolate, grated
salt and freshly ground black pepper

To garnish:
lime or lemon wedges
4 sprigs of parsley or coriander leaves

Coat the turkey fillets with the seasoned flour.

☐ Heat the oil in a frying-pan, add the turkey and cook until lightly browned. Transfer to a casserole.

☐ Add the onion and red pepper to the frying-pan and cook gently until they begin to soften. Sprinkle in any remaining seasoned flour and cook for 2-3 minutes.

☐ Set oven to 325F (160C) gas 3.

☐ Stir in the stock, raisins, cloves, cumin, cinnamon, tomatoes, chilli powder, sesame seeds and chocolate. Season lightly, bring to the boil and simmer for 10 minutes.

☐ Pour the sauce over the turkey. Cover the casserole and cook in the oven for 50 minutes. Adjust the seasoning, then garnish with lime or lemon and parsley or coriander.

Turkey Veronique

Serves 4 ☆☆☆
Preparation: 15 minutes
Cooking: 30 minutes

2oz (50g) butter
4 shallots or 1 small onion, peeled and sliced
4 small turkey breasts, skinned
¼ pint (150ml) Chicken Stock
¼ pint (150ml) dry white wine
a few sprigs of parsley
6oz (175g) green grapes, halved and seeded
salt and freshly ground black pepper

To finish:
1oz (25g) butter, softened
1 tablespoon plain flour
4 tablespoons single cream

Melt the butter in a sauté pan. Add the shallots or onion and the turkey and fry until the turkey is lightly browned on both sides.

☐ Add the stock, wine, parsley, half of the grapes and salt and pepper to taste.

☐ Cover the pan, reduce the heat and simmer for 20 minutes.

☐ Remove the turkey and keep hot. Discard the parsley.

☐ Mix the butter with the flour to make a paste. Stir into the cooking liquid in small pieces and cook, stirring constantly, until the sauce thickens.

☐ Add the remaining grapes and cook for 2 minutes. Stir in the cream. Taste and adjust the seasoning.

☐ Pour the sauce over the turkey and serve.

Tip: Turkey steaks, made from raw turkey breasts cut by a machine, are a useful alternative. They are available in many supermarkets.

Duck

Duck is simply delicious and can transform a meal into a special occasion. Both the French and Chinese treat duck with justice – the French invariably include fruit in the ingredients (as in Duck in Orange Sauce, page 195) and the Chinese cook the skin to crisp perfection (as in Peking Duck, page 270). Ducks range in size from 2lb-5lb (1kg-2.25kg). Be sure to buy a duck that is large enough as size is deceptive. A 5lb (2.25kg) bird will serve 4. Ducks are fatty birds, but careful cooking will allow you to really enjoy the incomparable flavour.

Canard au Citron

Serves 3-4   ★★☆
Preparation: 10 minutes
Cooking: about 1½ hours

---

1 × 4lb (2kg) oven-ready duck
salt and freshly ground black pepper
2 lemons
2oz (50g) sugar
2 tablespoons water
4 tablespoons gin
watercress to garnish

Set the oven to 400F (200C) gas 6.

☐ Put the duck on a rack in a roasting tin. Prick with a fork all over skin and rub with salt and pepper. Roast for 1 hour 20 minutes or until cooked.

☐ Meanwhile, remove the rind from one of the lemons, being careful not to take any of the white pith with the rind. Cut the rind into slivers. Peel both lemons, removing all the white pith, and separate into segments.

☐ Put the sugar and water in a saucepan and stir over low heat to dissolve the sugar. Bring to the boil and cook until caramelized to a golden brown. Remove from the heat and add the lemon segments and shredded rind.

☐ When the duck is ready, joint it and place on a warmed serving dish. Surround with the caramelized lemon segments and keep hot.

☐ Pour off most of the fat and juices from the roasting tin and place over low heat on top of the stove. Add the caramel and lemon rind mixture and gin and heat through gently.

☐ Pour over the duck and serve, garnished with watercress.

Variation: This recipe is equally delicious made with grapefruit instead of the lemon.

Tip: Dry the lemon segments before adding them to the caramel so that the caramel sticks together much more easily.

Canard aux Cerises à l'Aigre-Doux
Duck with sweet and sour cherries

Serves 4   ★★☆
Preparation: 15 minutes
Cooking: about 2¼ hours

---

1 × 4½-5lb (2-2.5kg) oven-ready duck
salt and freshly ground black pepper
2 oranges
1 onion, peeled and quartered
1 bouquet garni
1oz (25g) butter, softened
1 × 15oz (425g) can sweetened red or
    black cherries
3 tablespoons red wine vinegar
finely grated rind and juice of 1 orange
2 tablespoons cherry brandy (optional)
1 tablespoon arrowroot

Set the oven to 425F (220C) gas 7.

☐ Sprinkle the inside of the duck with salt and pepper. Cut 1 orange into quarters, then place inside the duck with the onion quarters and the bouquet garni. Truss with fine string.

☐ Place the duck on a rack in a roasting tin and prick the skin all over with a fork. Spread the softened butter all over the bird, then sprinkle with salt and pepper and the juice of the remaining orange.

☐ Cover the duck with foil and roast for 30 minutes. Reduce the oven temperature to 350F (180C) gas 4 and roast for a further 1¾ hours or until the duck is tender and the juices run clear when the thickest part of the thigh is pierced with a skewer. Remove the foil for the last 30 minutes of the cooking time so that the skin becomes crisp and golden brown, sprinkling with more salt if necessary.

☐ During the last 15 minutes of the cooking time, make the sauce. Drain the cherries, reserving half the juice from the can. Put the cherry juice, wine vinegar, orange rind and juice in a measuring jug with the cherry brandy, if using. Make up to ¾ pint (450ml) with water.

☐ In a separate jug, mix the arrowroot to a paste with a little of the measured liquid. Pour the remaining measured liquid into a pan and bring to the boil. Stir in the arrowroot paste and boil vigorously until the sauce thickens. Reduce the heat, add the cherries and seasoning to taste, then simmer gently for 2-3 minutes until the cherries are heated through. (Do not overcook or the cherries will lose their shape.)

☐ Remove the string from the duck and place on a warmed serving platter. Pour a little of the sauce over the breast. Serve with remaining sauce handed separately.

Tips: Unpitted cherries look better in the sauce, but pitted ones are easier to eat. Choose whichever you prefer.

● Arrowroot is used as a thickener when a clear sauce or glaze is required, as cornflour and flour will leave the liquid looking cloudy.

Duck with Orange and Port Wine
If possible include the juice of at least 1 Seville orange in the sauce. The sourness complements the richness of the duck particularly well.

Duck Rouennais
Rouennais is a classic French sauce served with duck or poached eggs.

Duck with Orange and Port Wine

Serves 4 ☆☆☆
Preparation: 10 minutes
Cooking: about 1½ hours

4lb (1.8kg) oven-ready duck
salt and freshly ground black pepper
½ pint (300ml) unsweetened orange juice
4 small oranges
4 tablespoons port wine

Set the oven to 400F (200C) gas 6.
☐ Put the duck on a rack in a roasting tin and prick all over skin with a fork. Rub with salt and pepper. Roast in the oven for 1 hour 20 minutes or until cooked.
☐ After 1 hour, pour off almost all the fat and juices from the tin and baste the bird with the orange juice.
☐ Remove the rind from two of the oranges, being careful not to take any of the white pith with the rind. Cut the rind into slivers and blanch in boiling water for 3 minutes. Drain.
☐ Peel all the oranges, removing the pith, and separate into segments.
☐ When the duck is done, joint it and keep it hot on a warmed serving platter. Place the roasting tin over low heat on top of the stove and add the orange segments and rind. Heat through gently.
☐ Arrange the orange segments around the duck. Stir the port into the tin, scraping up any sediment, then pour the sauce over the duck. Serve immediately.

Duck Rouennais

Serves 6
☆ ☆ ☆
Preparation: 10 minutes
Cooking: about 1½ hours

---

2 × 3lb (1.5kg) oven-ready duck with giblets
1 medium onion, peeled and quartered
2 medium carrots, peeled and halved
2 celery stalks
2 bay leaves
1 tablespoon tomato purée
½ pint (300ml) dry red wine
½ pint (300ml) water
salt and freshly ground black pepper
1½oz (40g) butter
1oz (25g) flour
3 fl oz (100ml) port

Put the duck giblets (reserving the liver), onion, carrots, celery, bay leaves, tomato purée, wine and water into a saucepan and bring to the boil. Simmer for 1 hour, skimming when necessary. Add salt and pepper to taste, then strain the stock.

☐ Meanwhile, set oven to 425F (220C) gas 7.

☐ Put the duck on a rack in a roasting tin and prick skin all over with a fork. Roast in the oven for 45 minutes.

☐ Pre-heat grill to moderate.

☐ Remove duck from the oven and cut off the legs.

☐ Keep the rest of the duck warm. Score the legs and finish cooking them under the grill for about 20 minutes.

☐ Melt the butter in a saucepan and

Duck with Orange and Port Wine (left) and Duck Rouennais.

add the flour. Cook, stirring, for 1 minute, then gradually stir in the strained stock. Simmer, stirring, until smooth and thickened. Put the sauce in a blender with the raw duck liver and the port. Blend until smooth. Adjust the seasoning then return to the pan and simmer gently for 5 minutes.

☐ Slice the duck breasts thinly. Serve a leg and as much breast as possible to each guest and hand the sauce separately.

Variation: If preferred, sauté the duck liver in a little butter, dice it finely and add to the thickened sauce.

Cold roast duck
Often it is worth roasting 2 ducks to be sure that you have enough to serve 4. Use the extra meat to make one of the salads. The meat can be frozen until required.

Somerset Duck Casserole
Carefully skim any fat from the top of the casserole before serving.

Duck, Pasta and Cheese Salad

Serves 4   ★☆☆
Preparation: 15 minutes

12oz (350g) cooked pasta
2 tablespoons oil
12oz (350g) cold roast duck meat, shredded
5oz (150g) Parmesan cheese, grated
salt and freshly ground black pepper
chopped fresh parsley to garnish

Toss the pasta with the oil, then fold in the remaining ingredients with salt and pepper to taste. Add more oil if necessary.
☐ Sprinkle with parsley before serving.

Duck, Green Pepper and Green Pea Salad

Serves 4   ☆☆☆
Preparation: 15 minutes plus 1 hour standing

12oz (350g) cold roast duck meat, shredded
8oz (225g) green peas, cooked
1 large green pepper, cored, seeded and chopped
3 tablespoons Vinaigrette
1 tablespoon chopped fresh mint

Mix together the duck, peas, green pepper and dressing and sprinkle with the mint. Allow to stand for 1 hour before serving.

Duck, Orange and Rice Salad

Serves 4   ☆☆☆
Preparation: 15 minutes

---

2 egg yolks from size 2 eggs
6oz (170g) can mandarin orange segments
salt and freshly ground black pepper
6 fl oz (175ml) oil
10oz (275g) cold, cooked rice
12oz (350g) cold roast duck meat, shredded

Beat the egg yolks with about 3 tablespoons of the syrup from the oranges to flavour.
☐ Season to taste then beat in the oil a drop at a time to make an orange-flavoured mayonnaise. If the mayonnaise is really thick, add more of the syrup to thin it.
☐ Mix the drained oranges with the rice and duck and lightly fold in the mayonnaise. Serve immediately.

Somerset Duck Casserole

Serves 4   ☆☆☆
Preparation: 15 minutes
Cooking: about 1 hour

1oz (25g) butter
2 tablespoons cooking oil
1 large onion, peeled and chopped
4 oven-ready duck portions, skinned
¾ pint (450ml) dry cider
salt and freshly ground black pepper
1 tablespoon demerara sugar
2 dessert apples, peeled, cored and chopped
2 teaspoons cornflour
finely chopped fresh parsley to garnish

Heat the butter and oil in a flameproof casserole and fry the onion until soft and transparent.
☐ Add the duck and brown evenly all over.
☐ Carefully drain off the butter and oil. Add the cider, salt, pepper and sugar and stir well.
☐ Cover the casserole and simmer gently for about 45 minutes.
☐ Transfer the duck to a warmed dish and keep hot. Add the apples and cornflour, blended with a little water, to the sauce. Cook, stirring, until the sauce has thickened, then simmer for 1 minute.
☐ Taste and adjust the seasoning, if necessary, then pour the sauce over the duck. Garnish with chopped parsley to serve.

Beef

Beef is the most popular meat and also the most versatile. The cuts vary considerably, and many lend themselves to a variety of cooking methods including roasting, braising, boiling, frying and grilling. Each nation likes to treat beef differently: the British are keen on roasted joints, the Americans love steaks and burgers, the French prefer their beef braised in wine and the people of the Middle East prepare their beef with spices and shape it into meatballs.

Estouffat de Boeuf

Brisket of beef with red wine

Serves 4 ☆☆☆
Preparation: 15 minutes
Cooking: about 3½ hours

3 tablespoons vegetable oil
2-2½lb (1-1.25kg) joint brisket of beef
1 large onion, peeled and chopped
1 clove garlic, peeled and crushed with
    ¼ teaspoon salt
½ pint (300ml) red wine
½ pint (300ml) Meat Stock
1 bouquet garni
¼ teaspoon ground cinnamon
¼ teaspoon ground allspice
salt and freshly ground black pepper
4 large carrots, peeled and sliced
4 leeks, sliced

To finish:
3 tablespoons brandy
1 tablespoon softened butter
2 tablespoons plain flour

Set the oven to 300F (150C) gas 2.
☐ Put the oil in a large flameproof casserole, add the beef and fry over brisk heat until browned.
☐ Remove from the pan and set aside.
☐ Reduce the heat, add the onion and garlic and fry gently until soft.
☐ Add the wine and stock and bring to the boil.
☐ Add the bouquet garni, cinnamon, allspice and seasoning to taste. Return beef to the pan.
☐ Cover and transfer to the oven.
☐ Cook, basting occasionally, for 3 hours or until the beef is tender.
☐ 30 minutes before the end of cooking add the carrots and leeks.
☐ Remove beef from pan, discard string and place on a warmed serving dish.
☐ Warm the brandy in a small pan, remove from heat and ignite. When the flames subside, pour over beef.
☐ Work the butter and flour to a paste (beurre manié) in a bowl.
☐ Remove bouquet garni from the pan.
☐ Add beurre manié slowly, whisking vigorously over high heat until sauce boils and thickens.
☐ Pour a little sauce over the beef. Serve the rest separately.

Tomatar Gosht

Beef with tomatoes

Serves 4 ☆☆☆
Preparation: 10 minutes
Cooking: 1 hour

2oz (50g) ghee or 4 tablespoons oil
1 onion, peeled and chopped
1oz (25g) fresh ginger root, peeled and crushed
4-5 cloves garlic, crushed
½ teaspoon ground turmeric
1 teaspoon ground coriander
1½ teaspoons ground cumin
1lb (450g) braising steak
salt
1-2 green chillies, seeded and very finely chopped, or 1 teaspoon chilli powder
1 × 14oz (396g) can tomatoes
2-3 sprigs of coriander leaves, chopped

Heat the ghee or oil in a pan and fry the onion until light brown.
☐ Add the ginger, garlic, turmeric, coriander, cumin, the beef and salt.
☐ Mix together well, then cover and cook gently for 10-12 minutes.
☐ Add the chillies, or chilli powder, the tomatoes and coriander leaves.
☐ Cover and cook for 50 minutes.
☐ Serve with naan bread.

Estouffat de Boeuf

Braised Beef with Orange

Serves 4   ★☆
Preparation: 15 minutes
Cooking: 2 hours

---

2 tablespoons oil
1lb (450g) braising steak, trimmed and cut
    into 1in (2.5cm) cubes
1 large onion, peeled and thinly sliced
1 clove garlic, peeled and crushed
3oz (75g) long-grain rice
½ pint (300ml) Meat Stock
finely grated rind and juice of 2 oranges
salt and freshly ground black pepper
2oz (50g) pimiento-stuffed green olives,
    rinsed and drained

To garnish:
1 orange, peeled and thinly sliced
1 tablespoon chopped fresh parsley

Set the oven to 300F (150C) gas 2.
□ Heat the oil in a large pan, add the steak and onion and fry gently until lightly coloured.
□ Stir in the garlic and rice and cook for 2 minutes.
□ Add the stock and grated orange rind, mix well and season with salt and pepper.
□ Bring to the boil, then transfer to a casserole.
□ Cover and cook in the oven for 1½ hours.
□ Stir in the olives and orange juice and return the casserole, uncovered, to the oven for a further 30 minutes.
□ Adjust the seasoning.
□ Serve garnished with twisted orange slices and parsley.

Royal Beef

Serves 6   ★★☆
Preparation: 30 minutes
Cooking: 1¼ hours

2lb (1kg) braising steak, cut into thin strips
2oz (50g) seasoned flour
4 tablespoons oil
3 onions, peeled and thinly sliced
2 bay leaves
2 cloves
½ pint (300ml) red vermouth
¼ pint (150ml) Meat Stock
salt and freshly ground black pepper

½ pint (300ml) soured cream
2 tablespoons chopped fresh parsley

Set the oven to 325F (160C) gas 3.
□ Toss the steak strips in the seasoned flour.
□ Heat the oil in a large frying-pan. Add the steaks and brown gently. Transfer to a casserole.
□ Add the onions to the pan and cook gently until soft and golden. Add any remaining flour, mix well and cook for 2 minutes.
□ Stir in the bay leaves, cloves, vermouth and stock and bring slowly to the boil.
□ Season to taste, then pour the sauce over the steak.
□ Cover the casserole and cook in the oven for 1 hour or until the steak is tender.
□ Stir in the soured cream and parsley and adjust the seasoning.
□ Return the casserole to the oven to heat through.
□ Remove the bay leaves and cloves.
□ Pour into a heated serving dish and surround with the potato nests filled with peas.

Sliced Beef in Oyster Sauce

Serves 2   ★★★
Preparation: 5 minutes plus
20 minutes marinating
Cooking: 5 minutes

---

2 tablespoons oyster sauce
1 tablespoon sherry
1 tablespoon cornflour
8oz (225g) rump steak, thickly sliced
4 tablespoons oil
1in (2.5cm) piece ginger root, grated
2 spring onions
4oz (100g) broccoli, cut into florets
4oz (100g) bamboo shoots, thinly sliced
1 carrot, peeled and thinly sliced
4oz (100g) button mushrooms, wiped
1 teaspoon salt
1 teaspoon sugar
2 tablespoons Chicken Stock

Mix together the oyster sauce, sherry and cornflour. Use to marinate the steak for 20 minutes.

□ Heat half of the oil in a wok and stir-fry the beef for 10-15 seconds, then remove.
□ Heat the remaining oil in the wok, add ginger, onions and vegetables.
□ Add the salt, sugar and beef and stir-fry for about 1½ minutes. Add the stock, stir and serve.

Beef and Pepper Casserole

Serves 4   ★★☆
Preparation: 25 minutes
Cooking: about 1¾ hours

8oz (225g) unsmoked streaky bacon,
    rind removed, diced
2 onions, peeled and sliced
1½lb (700g) braising steak, trimmed and cut
    into 2½in (6cm) cubes
2 carrots, scraped and sliced
2 cloves garlic, peeled and crushed
¾ pint (450ml) Brown Stock
2 teaspoons wine vinegar
2 teaspoons caraway seeds

2 large green peppers, cored, seeded
    and sliced
salt and freshly ground black pepper
2 teaspoons cornflour

To garnish:
1 tablespoon walnut halves, lightly toasted
1 tablespoon chopped fresh parsley

Set the oven to 300F (150C) gas 2.
☐ Fry the bacon in a dry flameproof
casserole over a gentle heat until the
fat runs.
☐ Add the onions, meat and carrots
and stir over a high heat until the
meat is browned.
☐ Stir in the garlic, stock, wine
vinegar, caraway seeds, green
peppers and salt and pepper to taste.
☐ Bring to the boil, then cover and
cook in the oven for 1½ hours.
☐ Dissolve cornflour in 2
tablespoons water and stir into the
stew. Bring to the boil, stirring,
until thickened.
☐ Sprinkle with walnuts and
parsley and serve.

Spiced Moussaka

Serves 4   ☆☆☆
Preparation: 25 minutes
Cooking: 35 minutes

---

1 large aubergine, thinly sliced
3 tablespoons oil
5oz (141g) natural yogurt
1 egg, size 2
3oz (75g) Cheddar cheese, grated
oil for greasing

The meat sauce:
1 medium onion, peeled and finely chopped
1lb (450g) minced beef
1 tablespoon paprika
1 clove garlic, crushed
2 tablespoons tomato purée
4oz (100g) mushrooms, chopped
½ pint (300ml) Chicken or Meat Stock
salt and freshly ground black pepper

Set the oven to 375F (190C) gas 5.
☐ Arrange the aubergine slices on
lightly oiled baking sheets, then
bake for 15 minutes.
☐ Meanwhile, make the meat sauce:

*Braised Beef with Orange (left) and
Beef and Pepper Casserole.*

Fry the onion in most of the oil for
2 minutes.
☐ Add the minced beef and cook,
stirring, until lightly browned. Stir
in the paprika, and cook for
1 minute.
☐ Add the garlic, tomato purée,
mushrooms, stock and seasoning.
Cover and simmer sauce for
15 minutes.
☐ Arrange the aubergine slices and
meat sauce in alternate layers in a
greased ovenproof dish, starting
with sauce and finishing with
aubergine.
☐ Brush the top layer of aubergine
slices with oil and cover the dish
with foil. Bake for 20 minutes.
☐ Beat the yogurt with the egg and
grated cheese and spoon the mixture
over the top of the moussaka. Bake
for 15 minutes.

Paprika Braised Beef

Serve with buttered noodles and a green salad.

Paprika Braised Beef

Serves 4 ☆☆☆
Preparation: 15 minutes
Cooking: about 1½ hours

2oz (50g) lard
1 onion, peeled and thinly sliced
2 red peppers, cored, seeded and sliced
1¾lb (700g) braising steak, cut into 1in (2.5cm) thick slices
1 tablespoon paprika
¾ pint (450ml) Brown Stock
4oz (125g) sweetcorn kernels
salt and freshly ground black pepper

Set the oven to 325F (160C) gas 3.
☐ Heat the lard in a flameproof casserole and fry the onion and peppers until both are beginning to soften. Lift out and drain well.
☐ Brown the meat on both sides. Lift out and drain off the excess fat from the casserole.
☐ Add the paprika, stock and vegetables to the casserole, put the meat on top and season well.
☐ Cook in the oven for about 1½ hours until the meat is tender.

Beef and Bean Casserole

Serves 4 ☆☆☆
Preparation: 15 minutes plus 1 hour soaking
Cooking: about 3 hours

3oz (75g) haricot beans
boiling water
2oz (50g) lard
1 large onion, peeled and sliced
2 carrots, peeled and sliced
1lb (500g) shin of beef, trimmed and cubed
1 pint (600ml) hot Brown Stock
2 tablespoons tomato purée
salt and freshly ground black pepper
1 bay leaf
finely chopped parsley to garnish

Put the haricot beans into a bowl, cover with boiling water and leave to stand for 1 hour.
☐ Set the oven to 300F (150C) gas 2.
☐ Melt the lard in a flameproof casserole. Add the onion and carrots and fry until lightly coloured.
☐ Add the meat and sauté until evenly browned.

Paprika Braised Beef (left) and Beef and Bean Casserole.

☐ Remove from the heat, stir in the stock, tomato purée, salt, pepper, bay leaf and the drained haricot beans.

☐ Return to the heat and bring to the boil.

☐ Cook in the oven for about 3 hours until the meat is very tender.

☐ Taste and adjust the seasoning as necessary. Sprinkle with a little chopped parsley to serve.

Beef and Egg Goulash

Serves 4 ☆☆☆
Preparation and cooking: 2½ hours

---

1 medium onion, peeled and finely chopped
4 celery sticks, finely chopped
4 tablespoons oil
1lb (500g) stewing steak, cubed
1oz (25g) seasoned flour
2 tablespoons paprika
1 tablespoon tomato purée
¾ pint (450ml) Chicken Stock
salt
¼ pint (150ml) soured cream
4 hard-boiled eggs, halved

Set the oven to 325F (180C) gas 4.

☐ Fry the onion and celery gently in the oil until beginning to soften.

☐ Dust the cubed meat with flour and add to the vegetables.

☐ Cook over moderate heat until the meat is lightly browned on all sides.

☐ Stir in the paprika and cook for 1 minute. Add the tomato purée, chicken stock, and salt and bring to the boil.

☐ Cook in the oven for 1½ hours.

☐ Stir in the soured cream and the hard-boiled eggs. Return to the oven for 10 minutes then serve.

Beef Java

Serves 6 ☆☆☆
Preparation: 15 minutes
Cooking: 2¼-2¾ hours

1oz (25g) dripping or lard
2 onions, peeled and sliced
1½-2lb (700-1kg) stewing steak, cut into 1in (2.5cm) cubes
1½ pints (900ml) Brown Stock
1 clove garlic, peeled and crushed
6 parsley stalks
salt and freshly ground black pepper
8oz (225g) long-grain rice
2oz (50g) seedless raisins
2oz (50g) blanched almonds, sliced
1 tablespoon paprika
finely chopped fresh parsley to garnish
mango chutney to serve

Melt the dripping or lard in a large frying-pan, add the onions and cook gently until golden brown. Remove and put into a casserole.

☐ Add the meat to the frying-pan and cook over a brisk heat for 3-4 minutes to brown. Drain and mix with the onions in the casserole.

☐ Add the stock, garlic, parsley stalks, and salt and pepper to taste. Cover and cook in the oven for 1¾-2 hours.

☐ Stir in the rice, raisins, almonds and paprika. Re-cover and continue cooking for 30-45 minutes or until the meat and rice are tender.

☐ Serve sprinkled with chopped parsley and accompanied by mango chutney.

Beef and Bean Casserole
The gravy can be thickened with a little cornflour if liked.

Beef Java
For a more quickly cooked dish, substitute lean minced beef for the stewing steak and cook for about 15 minutes before adding the rice, raisins, almonds and paprika.

Beef and Egg Goulash
Do not overcook once the eggs have been added or they will toughen. Serve with noodles or rice and green beans.

Burgundy Pot Roast
The beef can be marinated in the wine for up to 24 hours before cooking. This adds flavour and helps to tenderize the meat. Dry the meat well before browning.

Burgundy Pot Roast

This is an excellent way to cook the less tender cuts of beef as it retains all the flavour and juices of the meat.

Serves 8
Preparation: 10 minutes
Cooking: 2½-2¾ hours

2¼lb-3lb (1.25kg-1.5kg) topside or aitchbone of beef
salt and freshly ground black pepper
1oz (25g) butter
1 onion, peeled and sliced
2 carrots, peeled and sliced
2 sticks celery, scrubbed and chopped
1 clove garlic, peeled and crushed
¼ pint (150ml) Burgundy
¼ pint (150ml) Brown Stock
bouquet garni
1 bay leaf

To finish:
watercress sprigs

Set the oven to 325F (160C) gas 3.
☐ Season the joint well with salt and pepper.
☐ Heat the butter in a flameproof casserole and quickly fry the meat to brown it lightly on all sides.
☐ Remove and set aside. Add the onion, carrots, celery and garlic to the pan and cook for 2-3 minutes until lightly browned.
☐ Replace the meat on top of the vegetables and pour over wine and stock. Add the bouquet garni and bay leaf and season lightly.
☐ Cover and cook in the oven for about 2¼-2½ hours until the beef is tender and cooked through.
☐ Place joint on a serving plate and spoon the vegetables around it.
☐ Remove bouquet garni and bay leaf. On top of the cooker boil the liquid in the casserole and reduce until slightly thickened, pour over the meat or serve separately.
☐ Garnish with watercress sprigs and serve with braised leeks and baked potatoes.
Tip: Ten minutes before serving increase the oven temperature to 400F (200C) gas 6. Remove the lid of the casserole to allow the joint to brown and crisp slightly.

Steak, Kidney and Mushroom Pie

Serves 4 ☆☆☆
Preparation: 15 minutes
Cooking: about 4 hours

12oz (350g) stewing steak, trimmed and cubed
3 lambs' kidneys, trimmed and cubed
1 medium onion, peeled and thinly sliced
1oz (25g) seasoned flour
¼ pint (150ml) port or red wine
¼ pint (150ml) Brown Stock
salt and freshly ground black pepper
4oz (125g) mushrooms, wiped and sliced
8oz (225g) frozen puff pastry, thawed
flour for rolling out
1 egg, beaten, for glazing

Set the oven to 300F (150C) gas 2.
☐ Toss the stewing steak, kidneys and onion in the flour and place in a 1½ pint (900ml) pie dish.
☐ Add the port or wine and the stock, cover tightly and cook in the oven for about 3½ hours until the meat is very tender. Top up with a little stock or water if necessary. Cool.
☐ Increase oven temperature to 400F (200C) gas 6.
☐ Stir the sliced mushrooms into the pie filling.
☐ Roll out the pastry to 1½in (4cm) larger than the rim of the pie dish. Brush the rim with water and cut a ½in (1cm) strip of pastry to fit. Press into place and brush with water.
☐ Place the pastry lid on the pie and press to seal.
☐ Trim, knock up and flute the edges. Use the trimmings to make leaves to decorate the pie.
☐ Glaze with the beaten egg and cut a steam hole in the centre.
☐ Stand the dish on a baking sheet and bake for 35-40 minutes until well risen and browned.
☐ Serve the pie hot with braised leeks.
Tip: ❄ As the pie filling takes a long time to cook, it is well worth making a large quantity at a time. Pack in small portions and freeze for up to 1 year.

Pork

Pork rivals beef as a favoured meat for a main meal. Although it is considered to be fatty, many of the cuts are quite lean. The most popular cooking methods are roasting and grilling, but in fact pork also lends itself to stir-frying, barbecuing, braising, and for use in casseroles or making kebabs. Because pork is essentially a bland meat, it can take on the taste of its sauces and stuffings – be they mild, creamy, herby or highly spiced. Pork teams well with fruit – apples, prunes, apricots, pineapples and peaches. Pork takes longer to cook than other meats. Unlike beef, it must be thoroughly cooked – test by piercing with a skewer: it is cooked when the juices run clear and no hint of pink remains.

Clockwise from the top: Pork and Tomato Pot Roast; Pork and Tomato with Kasha; Spare Ribs with Beans. For recipes see pages 132-3.

Pork and Tomato with Kasha

The pork rind can be cooked under the grill until crisp if preferred.

Spare Ribs with Beans

The beans absorb flavour from the pork ribs and other ingredients to make particularly tasty 'baked beans'. Remember not to salt the beans during their initial boiling as this will toughen them.

Pork Vindaloo-style

This is a mildly spiced dish, but you can add chilli powder or fresh chillis to taste if preferred. Because of the quantity of vinegar in the recipe use an enamelled or non-stick pan if possible.

Pork and Tomato with Kasha

Kasha (buckwheat groats) is available from wholefood and health food shops and some large supermarkets.

Serves 4   ☆☆☆

Preparation: 25 minutes

Cooking: 1½ hours

1¼lb (700g) pork shoulder
2oz (50g) butter
2 onions, peeled and finely chopped
3oz (75g) kasha
1 teaspoon ground cumin
6 tomatoes, skinned and sliced
1 pint (600ml) Chicken Stock
salt and freshly ground black pepper
sprigs of parsley to garnish

Set the oven to 325F (160C) gas 3.
□ Remove the rind from the pork and cut it into very thin strips. Cut the pork into 2in (5cm) pieces.
□ Melt the butter in a frying-pan, add the pork rind strips and fry carefully, until crisp. Drain on kitchen paper and reserve.
□ Add the pork pieces to the pan and brown lightly on all sides, then transfer to a casserole. Add the onions to the pan and cook gently until soft and golden.
□ Stir in the kasha, cumin, tomatoes, stock and salt and pepper to taste. Bring to the boil and pour over the meat in the casserole.
□ Cover and cook in the oven for 1½ hours or until the pork is tender.
□ After 1 hour check that the casserole is not drying out – add a little more stock if necessary.
□ Arrange the reserved pork rind strips over the dish with parsley sprigs and serve with a green vegetable in season or a salad.

Spare Ribs with Beans

Serves 4   ☆☆☆

Preparation: 1¼ hours plus overnight soaking

Cooking: about 3-3½ hours

6oz (175g) dried haricot beans, soaked overnight in water
2lb (1kg) pork spare ribs, cut into pieces
3 tablespoons soy sauce
1 onion, peeled and finely chopped
1 tablespoon soft brown sugar
2 tablespoons molasses
1 teaspoon dry mustard
1 teaspoon Worcestershire sauce
salt and freshly ground black pepper
about 1 pint (600ml) Chicken Stock
spring onion brushes to garnish

Drain the soaked beans, put them into a saucepan, cover with plenty of cold water, bring to the boil, cover and simmer for 1 hour.
□ Meanwhile, arrange the spare ribs on the rack in the grill pan, lightly brush them with the soy sauce and grill until brown on both sides.
□ Set oven to 300F (150C) gas 2.
□ Mix together the beans, onion, brown sugar, molasses, mustard, Worcestershire sauce and a little salt and pepper.
□ Layer the spare ribs and the bean mixture in a casserole, finishing with spare ribs. Pour in enough of the stock barely to cover. Cover casserole and cook in the oven for 2 hours.
□ Uncover and continue cooking for 1-1½ hours or until the beans are tender and the rib topping is crisp. (Check from time to time to see if more stock is needed. Do not allow to become dry.)
□ Serve garnished with spring onion brushes.

Pork Vindaloo-style

Serves 4   ☆☆☆

Preparation: 15 minutes

Cooking: 45 minutes

---

3 tablespoons oil
1 tablespoon coriander seeds
1 tablespoon cumin seeds
1 tablespoon sesame seeds
4 cloves
1¼lb (700g) pork fillet, cubed
1 tablespoon turmeric
2 tablespoons soft brown sugar
¼ pint (150ml) wine vinegar
¼ pint (150ml) Chicken Stock

salt and freshly ground black pepper

To serve:
chopped onion
chopped green pepper
wedges of tomato
rice
natural yogurt

Heat the oil in a pan and fry the coriander, cumin and sesame seeds and the cloves for 2 minutes.
□ Add the cubed pork fillet and fry over moderate heat until lightly browned on all sides, then add the turmeric and cook for 1 minute.
□ Stir in the brown sugar, vinegar, stock and salt and pepper. Cover and simmer gently for 45 minutes.
□ Transfer to a flat serving dish, and serve with small dishes of chopped onion, chopped green pepper, wedges of tomato, a bowl of chilled yogurt and boiled rice.
Tip: There should not be very much juice with this dish, but if it becomes too dry during cooking add a little extra stock or water.

Pork and Tomato Pot Roast

Serves 4 ☆☆☆
Preparation: 10 minutes
Cooking: 2¾ hours

---

2 tablespoons oil
salt and freshly ground black pepper
3lb (1.5kg) blade bone of pork, well trimmed of fat
1 large onion, peeled and chopped
14oz (396g) can tomatoes, chopped, with their juice
1 teaspoon dried marjoram
½ pint (300ml) Brown Stock
1 teaspoon cornflour

Set the oven to 350F (180C) gas 4.
□ Heat the oil in a flameproof casserole. Season the pork well with salt and pepper. Place the pork in the casserole and brown on all sides. Remove from casserole and set aside.
□ Add the onion to the casserole and fry gently until transparent.

Pork Vindaloo-style

□ Remove from the heat and stir in the tomatoes, marjoram and stock. Return the pork to the casserole.
□ Cover and cook in the oven for about 2½ hours.
□ Lift out the pork. Slice it thickly and arrange on a heated serving dish. Keep hot.
□ Return the casserole to the heat and mash the vegetables into the cooking liquid. Blend the cornflour with a little cold water and add to the vegetable mixture. Bring to the boil and simmer, stirring, for 1-2 minutes or until the sauce has thickened. Taste and adjust the seasoning.
□ Pour the sauce over the meat and serve immediately.
Tip: For a smoother sauce rub the vegetables through a sieve before thickening.

Stuffed Courgettes
with Neapolitan Sauce

Serves 4-6   ☆ ☆ ☆
Preparation: about 20 minutes
Cooking: 40 minutes

8 large courgettes
2 tablespoons oil
1 onion, peeled and chopped
4 streaky bacon rashers, rinds removed, chopped
8oz (225g) minced pork
2oz (50g) fresh white breadcrumbs
1 egg, size 2, beaten
3 tablespoons chopped fresh parsley
salt and freshly ground black pepper
oil for greasing

The sauce:
2 tablespoons oil
1 onion, peeled and sliced
1lb (450g) tomatoes, roughly chopped
¼ pint (150ml) red wine
the grated rind and juice of 1 lemon
1 tablespoon tomato purée
2 teaspoons caster sugar
1 clove garlic, crushed

Set the oven to 375F (190C) gas 5.
☐ Trim the ends off the courgettes, then cut the courgettes in half lengthways and scoop out the flesh to make boat shapes.
☐ Roughly chop flesh and set aside.
☐ Meanwhile, heat oil in a frying-pan and fry onion for 2 minutes. Add the bacon and minced pork and cook, stirring, until lightly browned.
☐ Add the courgette flesh and cook for a further 2 minutes. Stir in the breadcrumbs, beaten egg, chopped parsley, and salt and pepper to taste.
☐ Fill the courgettes with the meat mixture and arrange in a greased ovenproof dish. Sprinkle a little oil over each one and cover. Bake for 30 minutes.
☐ Meanwhile, make the sauce: Heat oil in a pan and fry onion for 2 minutes. Add the tomatoes, wine, lemon rind and juice, tomato purée, sugar, garlic and salt and pepper. Bring to the boil, then simmer for 10 minutes.

Stuffed Courgettes with Neapolitan Sauce (left) and Braised Pork in Orange Sauce.

☐ Remove the courgettes from the oven and pour over the sauce. Return to the oven for a further 10 minutes before serving.

Braised Pork in Orange Sauce

Serves 4　　☆☆☆
Preparation: 15 minutes
Cooking: about 1 hour

3 tablespoons oil
2 medium onions, peeled and chopped
1¼lb (575g) pork fillet, cubed
1oz (25g) seasoned flour
½ pint (300ml) orange juice
¼ pint (150ml) Chicken Stock
8oz (225g) carrots, peeled and grated
a pinch of ground cinnamon
salt and freshly ground black pepper
2 oranges, peel and pith removed, cut into segments
¼ pint (142ml) double cream
2 tablespoons chopped walnuts

Heat oil in a pan and fry onion for 3 minutes over low heat.
☐ Toss the cubed pork in seasoned flour and add to the onion. Cook over moderate heat until the meat is lightly browned on all sides.
☐ Gradually stir in the orange juice and stock. Bring to the boil and add the carrot, cinnamon, and salt and pepper. Cover and simmer gently for 45 minutes.
☐ During the last 10 minutes of cooking, stir in the orange segments, the double cream and the walnuts. Transfer to a serving dish and serve immediately.

Braised Pork in Orange Sauce
✳ When freezing this dish, do not add the cream and walnuts. Pack in shallow freezer boxes and store for up to 3 months. Thaw and reheat, then continue as in recipe.

Cidered Pork Chop Parcels

Wrapping the chops in foil with a little liquid keeps the meat moist and tender. Serve still wrapped in the parcels.

Pork Fillet with Apricots

✳ To freeze: Cool completely and pack in shallow containers. The pork can be stored in the freezer for up to 3 months. Reheat from frozen in the oven set to 350F (180C) gas 4.

Pork Fillet 'en Croûte'

Pork fillet is a very lean cut of meat and cooking it enclosed in pastry ensures that it remains succulent. The bacon adds flavour and bastes the meat as it cooks.

Cidered Pork Chop Parcels

Serves 4 ☆☆☆
Preparation and cooking: 40 minutes

2oz (50g) butter
2 tablespoons oil
4 pork chops, each about 8oz (225g) trimmed
1oz (25g) seasoned flour
4 pineapple rings, fresh or canned
4 tablespoons cider
salt and freshly ground black pepper
4 sage leaves
butter for greasing

Set the oven to 400F (200C) gas 6.
☐ Heat the butter and oil in a frying-pan. Coat the chops with the flour and fry until browned.
☐ Place each chop on a square of buttered foil with a pineapple ring, a tablespoon of cider, seasoning and a sage leaf.
☐ Fold foil around chops to make 4 parcels and place on a baking sheet.
☐ Cook the parcels in the oven for 25 minutes. Serve.

Pork Fillet with Apricots

Serves 4 ☆☆☆
Preparation and cooking: 35 minutes

1lb (450g) pork fillet, diced
2 tablespoons seasoned flour
2oz (50g) butter
14oz (396g) can apricot halves, drained and juice reserved
2 tablespoons Worcestershire sauce
2 tablespoons demerara sugar
2 teaspoons vinegar
2 teaspoons lemon juice
8 tablespoons water

Toss pork pieces in seasoned flour then fry in the butter until browned.
☐ Chop all but 3 apricot halves. Mix the apricot juice with the remaining ingredients. Stir into the pork with the chopped apricots.
☐ Bring to the boil, stirring.
☐ Cover and simmer for 15 minutes.
☐ Serve garnished with the reserved apricots, on a bed of boiled rice.

Pork Fillet 'en Croute'

Serves 2 ☆☆☆
Preparation and cooking: 1 hour

1 pork fillet about 8oz (225g) cut in half
salt and freshly ground black pepper
½ teaspoon dried sage
4-6 streaky bacon rashers, rinds removed
1 tablespoon oil
6oz (175g) frozen puff pastry, thawed
beaten egg to glaze
parsley sprigs to garnish

The mushroom sauce:
1oz (25g) butter
2oz (50g) mushrooms, chopped
1oz (25g) flour
½ pint (300ml) Chicken Stock
a pinch of ground mace

Put one piece of the fillet on top of the other. Season lightly and sprinkle with sage.
☐ Wrap the bacon around the pork and secure with wooden cocktail sticks.
☐ Heat the oil in a frying-pan, add the pork and brown it all over. Remove cocktail sticks and cool.
☐ Set oven to 425F (220C) gas 7.
☐ On a lightly floured surface roll out the pastry thinly.
☐ Wrap the pork in the pastry to enclose completely. Dampen the edges and press together to seal.
☐ Place on a dampened baking sheet, seam side down, and decorate with the pastry trimmings. Glaze with the beaten egg and bake for 15 minutes.
☐ Reduce the heat to 350F (180C) gas 4 and continue cooking for 20 to 25 minutes.
☐ Just before the pork is ready, make the sauce. Melt the butter and fry the mushrooms for 2-3 minutes. Stir in the flour then gradually stir in the stock and bring to the boil. Simmer for 2-3 minutes. Season to taste, add the mace.
☐ Serve the pork sliced, garnished with parsley, with the sauce handed separately.
Variation: Spread the pork with a little pâté before wrapping with the pastry.

Lamb

Lamb is a tender, succulent and tasty meat, and lamb dishes are part of the cuisine of nearly every country in the world. It is tender because it comes from a young animal and all the meat fibres are short and fine-grained. To be considered lamb, the animal must have been slaughtered at under one year of age – the usual practice being at nine months. The most delicious lamb is spring lamb, which is marketed here when it is between five and seven months old; it is in short supply and therefore rather expensive. Lamb slaughtered when older than one year is called hogget, and its meat is mutton; it is virtually unobtainable in this country. When buying lamb look for pink flesh – avoid dark red or greyish meat – and a fine, white fat which gives the meat its characteristic juiciness and flavour. Lamb is delicious roasted, grilled or fried, barbecued and casseroled. The traditional accompaniments are mint sauce or jelly, redcurrant jelly and onion sauce.

Lamb, Leek and Potato Casserole

Serves 4 ☆☆☆
Preparation: 10 minutes
Cooking: 1½ hours

1¼lb (700g) potatoes, peeled and cut into ¼in (5mm) thick slices
2 medium leeks, thinly sliced
salt and freshly ground black pepper
2 tablespoons oil
8 large best end of neck lamb chops
½ teaspoon dried rosemary
½ pint (300ml) hot Brown Stock

Put the potatoes in the bottom of an ovenproof casserole. Add the leeks and season well.

☐ Heat the oil in a frying-pan. Add the chops and brown on both sides then add to the casserole.

☐ Add the rosemary and the stock, cover and cook in the oven for 1½ hours. Serve.

Lamb with Cheese Scalloped Potatoes

Serves 4 ☆☆☆
Preparation: 15 minutes
Cooking: about 2 hours

---

2 tablespoons oil
4 carrots, peeled and sliced
4oz (100g) mushrooms, wiped and sliced
1 clove garlic
8 large best end of neck lamb chops
14oz (396g) can tomatoes
4 tablespoons water
1 bouquet garni
salt and freshly ground black pepper
1¼lb (700g) potatoes, peeled and thinly sliced
4 tablespoons single cream
a little grated nutmeg
3oz (75g) Cheddar cheese, grated
chopped fresh parsley to garnish

Set the oven to 325F (170C) gas 3.
☐ Heat the oil in a flameproof casserole. Add carrots, mushrooms and garlic and fry until carrots are beginning to colour. Remove with a slotted spoon and drain well.

☐ Add the chops to the casserole and brown on both sides. Return the fried vegetables with the tomatoes and their juice to pan. Add

the water, bouquet garni, and salt and pepper to taste.

☐ Arrange the potatoes in a layer on top. Cover and cook in the oven for 1½ hours.

☐ Increase the oven temperature to 400F (200C) gas 6.

☐ Mix together the cream, nutmeg and cheese. Spoon over the potatoes and return the casserole to the oven. Cook, uncovered, for about 20 minutes until the cheese has browned.

☐ Serve garnished with parsley.

Spinach-stuffed Breast of Lamb

Serves 4 ☆☆☆
Preparation: 20 minutes
Cooking: about 1 hour

1¼lb (700g) breast or loin of lamb, boned
1oz (25g) butter
1 teaspoon French mustard
1 tablespoon orange juice
2 tablespoons redcurrant jelly
Espagnole Sauce to serve

The stuffing:
1oz (25g) ham, finely diced
2 lamb's kidneys, peeled, cored and finely chopped
3oz (75g) fresh spinach, finely chopped
1oz (25g) fresh white breadcrumbs
1 small onion, peeled and finely chopped
3 tablespoons double cream
salt and freshly ground black pepper
a little grated nutmeg

Set the oven to 325F (160C) gas 3.
☐ Place the breast or loin of lamb flat on a board and trim off the excess fat.

☐ Combine all the stuffing ingredients and spread over the lamb.

☐ Roll up the lamb and secure with string.

☐ Place the lamb in a roasting tin, and coat lightly with the butter. Season then loosely cover with greaseproof paper or foil.

☐ Cook in the oven for 45 minutes.

☐ Gently heat the mustard, orange juice and redcurrant jelly until the jelly has melted.

☐ Remove greaseproof or foil from

lamb and pour over the redcurrant glaze.

☐ Increase the oven temperature to 400F (200C) gas 6 and cook the lamb for a further 10-15 minutes, basting with the glaze 2 or 3 times.

☐ Serve with Espagnole Sauce.

Spicy Lamb Chops

Serves 4 ☆☆☆
Preparation: 20 minutes
Cooking: about 1¼ hours

---

2 tablespoons oil
4 lamb chump chops
1 Spanish onion, peeled and sliced
1 green pepper, cored, seeded and sliced
1 teaspoon ground cumin
1 teaspoon chilli powder
1 tablespoon apricot jam
1 teaspoon tomato purée
1 teaspoon Worcestershire sauce
1 tablespoon wine vinegar
½ pint (300ml) Chicken Stock
4 tomatoes, peeled, seeded and chopped
2oz (50g) salted peanuts
salt and freshly ground black pepper
1 tablespoon cornflour
2 tablespoons water

Set the oven to 325F (160C) gas 3.
☐ Heat the oil in a large frying-pan, and quickly fry the chops on both sides, then transfer them to a casserole.

☐ Fry the onion and pepper in the pan juices until lightly browned.

☐ Add the cumin and chilli powder and cook over a high heat for 2-3 minutes, stirring constantly.

☐ Reduce the heat, and add the apricot jam, tomato purée, Worcestershire sauce, vinegar, stock, tomatoes and peanuts to the pan, and bring to the boil. Add seasoning then pour over the chops.

☐ Cover and cook in the oven for 1 hour.

☐ Remove the chops from the casserole and arrange them in a deep serving dish.

☐ Mix the cornflour and water together, and stir into the sauce. Cook, stirring, until it is thickened, then pour over the chops.

Spinach-stuffed Breast of Lamb

SNACKS

There are many occasions when a light snack meal is required. During a busy week, members of a family may be eating at different times and these situations often demand something quick and easy. When children arrive home from school, or one of the family returns late from work, it is better to tempt them with a nutritious snack than to give in to demands for biscuits.

Snack meals can be based on dairy products, store-cupboard ingredients and 'leftovers'. Eggs are particularly versatile as they can provide a meal as simple as a boiled or poached egg, or form the basis of soufflés, pancakes, omelettes and sandwich fillings.

Cheese is another food which can be transformed into many savoury snacks. It is highly nutritious and an ideal food for children and vegetarians. Most supermarkets stock a wide range of cheeses, both home-produced and imported. Low-fat cheeses are becoming popular with the weight-conscious and those watching cholesterol levels. They are not ideal for cooking and a better flavour is obtained by using less of a strong mature Cheddar cheese. However, they are useful in salads, for spreading on crispbreads or cheese biscuits, and for blending with fish or vegetables to make savoury moulds or pâtés.

Kebabs make a quick, satisfying snack meal, and can be made with a variety of meats, vegetables and fish. The flavour and texture of the meat is improved with marinating but this requires a little forward planning.

Quiches are an ideal way to use up leftover meat and vegetables. To save time, keep ready-made pastry cases in the freezer. Try replacing some of the plain flour with wholemeal flour for added fibre and a coarser, nuttier texture. It is always a good idea to make several quiches if you have the ingredients available and the time to spare, as they can be stored in the freezer for three to four months.

Stuffed vegetables make a healthy, light meal and are another useful idea for vegetarians. Many vegetables can be used for stuffing, including potatoes, peppers, tomatoes, aubergines.

Rice and pasta are often served as an accompaniment, but they can also make quick, all-in-one meals, such as risotto, kedgeree, lasagne or macaroni. Although it takes longer to cook, the brown variety of both rice and pasta has more texture and flavour.

Grilling and barbecuing: Grilling cooks by fierce direct heat, and a very little fat is brushed on to the outside of the food to prevent it drying before the heat seals the surface. Pieces of fish, some vegetables such as tomatoes and small, tender cuts of meat are suitable. Remember to pre-heat the grill to hot before placing the food beneath it. This rule also applies when you use the grill for browning the tops of dishes that have been cooked in the oven.
On a barbecue, you can cook larger pieces of meat, depending on the type and style of your equipment. The heat is less fierce – often provided by charcoal, which burns more slowly and imparts its own subtle flavours. Basting with a marinade or fat is often essential when barbecuing.

Egg Dishes

Eggs are among the most versatile of snacks and they can be used in numerous imaginative recipes. They can be stuffed, mixed with other ingredients, made into toppings for sandwiches and served as the basis for many quick-to-prepare and economical dishes.

Open Sandwiches

To live up to its Scandinavian reputation, an open sandwich should be colourful, nutritious and attractive enough to be a meal in itself. Use any combination of meat, fish, cheese, fruit and vegetables on any choice of bread or crispbread.

Though the sandwiches can be prepared in advance, they taste far better freshly made.

Serves 2   ☆☆☆
Preparation: 10 minutes

Pâté and Cream Cheese
1 crispbread, buttered
2oz (50g) smooth liver pâté
1 hard-boiled egg, sliced
1oz (25g) cream cheese
parsley sprigs to garnish

Egg and Bacon
1 slice of white bread, buttered
slices of Cheddar cheese
1 egg, lightly scrambled
1 bacon rasher, rinds removed
parsley sprig to garnish

To make the Pâté and Cream Cheese: Cover the crispbread with pâté. Garnish with the sliced hard-boiled egg, pipe the cream cheese over and garnish with parsley sprigs. To make the Egg and Bacon: Cover the bread with the cheese. Cut the bacon rasher in half, roll up and secure with a wooden cocktail stick. Grill until crisp. Top with scrambled egg and rolls of bacon and garnish with parsley.

Variation: As it is usual to eat these sandwiches with a knife and fork the toppings can be piled on. Other delicious mixtures are:
● Sliced, cold roast meat with relish and canned pimiento.
● Prawns, mayonnaise and cucumber.
● Canned salmon or tuna fish with mayonnaise and salad ingredients.
● Blue cheese, grapes and lettuce.
● Rollmop herring with raw onion and tomato.
● Rolled tongue, cottage cheese and orange slices.
● Cream cheese, chopped nuts and sliced apple.
● Salt beef and potato salad.
● Salami, Camembert and tomato slices.

Two open sandwiches—Pâté and Cream Cheese; Egg and Bacon.

Welsh Rarebit

Serves 4 ☆☆☆
Preparation and cooking: 15 minutes

½oz (15g) butter
1 tablespoon plain flour
2 tablespoons milk
4 tablespoons brown ale or dark beer
2 teaspoons Worcestershire sauce
1 teaspoon prepared English mustard
salt and freshly ground black pepper
8oz (225g) Cheddar cheese, grated

To serve:
4 slices hot buttered toast

Melt the butter in a saucepan.
Remove from the heat and stir in
the flour to make a smooth paste.
☐ Gradually stir in the milk, ale or
beer, Worcestershire sauce,
mustard, and salt and pepper.
Return to a low heat and cook,
stirring constantly, for 2 to 3
minutes or until the mixture is thick
and smooth.
☐ Add the cheese and cook, stirring
constantly, for a further 1 minute or
until the cheese has melted.
☐ Pre-heat grill to high.
☐ Place the toast on four flameproof
serving plates. Divide the cheese
mixture between the toast. Grill for
3 to 4 minutes or until the mixture
is golden brown. Serve at once.

Eggs Benedict

Serves 4 ☆☆☆
Preparation and cooking: 15 minutes

8 muffins
8 thick slices of cooked ham
1oz (25g) butter
8 eggs, size 2, poached and kept warm

The Hollandaise sauce:
3 egg yolks from size 2 eggs
1 tablespoon cold water
4oz (100g) butter, softened
a large pinch of salt
a pinch of cayenne pepper
1 teaspoon lemon juice
1 tablespoon single cream

Pre-heat grill to medium.
☐ Prepare sauce: Beat together egg
yolks and water over a pan of hot

water, until mixture is pale.
☐ Beat in butter in small pieces and
beat until mixture thickens.
☐ Add salt, cayenne and juice. Stir
in cream. Remove from heat. Keep
warm.
☐ Place the muffins beside slices of
ham on the grill pan. Grill for 4
minutes, turning after 2 minutes.
☐ Butter muffins and place on
warmed plates. Put a slice of ham
and poached egg on each. Spoon a
little sauce on top.

Yorkshire Rarebit

Serves 2 ☆☆☆
Preparation and cooking: 15 minutes

½oz (15g) butter
1 tablespoon plain flour
2 tablespoons milk
2 tablespoons brown ale
½ teaspoon prepared French mustard
a large pinch of salt
½ teaspoon freshly ground black pepper
4oz (100g) Cheddar cheese, grated

To serve:
2 slices of hot buttered toast
2 thick slices of lean cooked ham
2 poached eggs, size 2, kept hot

Melt butter in a pan. Remove from
heat and stir in flour to make a
paste. Stir in milk, ale, mustard,
seasoning.
☐ Return to a low heat and cook,
stirring, for 2 to 3 minutes until
thick and smooth.
☐ Add cheese and cook, stirring, for
2 minutes.
☐ Pre-heat grill to high. Place toast
on two flameproof serving plates.
Divide mixture, top with ham and
grill for 3-4 minutes. Remove from
heat and top with eggs.

Aubergines and Eggs with Parsley

Serves 4 ☆☆☆
Preparation and cooking: 20 minutes

1 large aubergine, sliced
6 eggs, size 2

salt and freshly ground black pepper
1oz (25g) butter
2 cloves garlic, crushed
4 tablespoons chopped fresh parsley
2 tablespoons sesame seeds
oil for frying

Fry the sliced aubergine in a
generous amount of oil in a large
pan for 3 to 4 minutes on each side.
☐ Drain the aubergine thoroughly
and put into a hot serving dish and
keep warm. Reserve the remaining
fat.
☐ Beat the eggs with salt and
pepper. Heat the butter in a heavy
saucepan and stir in the beaten eggs.
Cook over gentle heat, stirring
constantly, until the eggs scramble.
Spoon evenly over the aubergines.
☐ Fry the garlic, chopped parsley
and sesame seeds quickly in the
reserved fat. Pour the parsley
mixture over the eggs and
aubergines and serve immediately.

Egg Fu-yung

Serves 2 ☆☆☆
Preparation and cooking: 15 minutes
plus 20 minutes standing

2 Chinese dried mushrooms
1oz (25g) prawns, peeled
1oz (25g) cooked ham
1oz (25g) bamboo shoots
2-3 water chestnuts
4 eggs, size 2, beaten
1 tablespoon cornflour
3 tablespoons water
1 teaspoon salt
1 tablespoon sherry
3 tablespoons oil

Soak dried mushrooms in warm
water for about 20 minutes, then
squeeze dry and discard hard stalks.
☐ Finely chop the mushrooms,
prawns, ham, bamboo shoots and
water chestnuts. Mix together with
the beaten eggs. Add the cornflour,
water, salt and sherry to the egg
mixture and stir.
☐ Heat the oil in a wok or frying
pan until smoking, then pour in the
egg mixture. Scramble with a fork
until set. Serve hot.

Kebabs

Charcoal-grilled kebabs are the best known of all Middle Eastern dishes. A huge choice of ingredients can be used – meat, chicken, fish and shellfish, plus a variety of vegetables and even fruit. Kebabs are steeped in a marinade for some hours before grilling and this gives them their distinctive flavour and succulence. Serve kebabs with sauces, dips, breads and rice and salad.

Spiedini di Scampi

Scampi and Mozzarella kebabs

Serves 4   ☆☆☆
Preparation: 20 minutes plus 1 hour chilling
Cooking: 4-5 minutes

16 large fresh or frozen scampi, thawed
12oz (350g) Mozzarella cheese, cut into
   ¾in (1.75cm) cubes
salt and freshly ground black pepper
flour
2 eggs, size 2, beaten
6 tablespoons fine white breadcrumbs
oil for deep-frying
the grated rind and juice of 1 lemon
3 bay leaves, finely crushed
Bagna Cauda to serve

Cut the heads and tails from the scampi and remove the outer shells.
☐ Thread the scampi lengthways with the cubes of cheese on to 4 kebab skewers.
☐ Season with salt and pepper, and dust with flour.
☐ Dip each kebab into the beaten egg and coat thoroughly with breadcrumbs. Chill for 1 hour.
☐ Heat a pan of oil to 355-365F (180-182C) or until a cube of bread browns in 20 seconds.
☐ Lower the prepared kebabs into the pan of oil and deep-fry for 4-5 minutes until crisp and golden. Drain the kebabs on kitchen paper and put on to a heated serving dish.
☐ Sprinkle with lemon rind and juice and the bay leaves. Serve with Bagna Cauda.

Preparing the skewers
Metal skewers are best to use as they help to ensure that the meat cooks in the centre. It is a good idea to oil the skewers lightly before threading on the food.

Barbecuing kebabs
This is one of the best and traditional ways of cooking skewers of food. Make sure the coals are hot (they will be grey in colour), so the food seals quickly and juice does not escape.

Bagna Cauda
This Italian dip is delicious with crispy vegetables but it can also be used as a buttery, anchovy sauce with shellfish. Heat together equal amounts of butter and olive oil, then add chopped anchovies and garlic to taste. Simmer for 10-15 minutes.

Italian-style kebabs – Spiedini di Scampi.

Lamb Kebabs

Serves 4 ☆☆☆
Preparation: 15 minutes plus
6 hours marinating
Cooking: 12 minutes

2¼lb (1.25kg) leg or shoulder of lamb,
    boned and cubed
1 green pepper, cored, seeded and diced
2 small onions, peeled and quartered
3 tomatoes, quartered

The marinade:
2 teaspoons olive oil
3 tablespoons natural yogurt
the juice of 2 lemons
2 cloves garlic, peeled and crushed
1 teaspoon dried mint
½ teaspoon dried rosemary or 1 fresh
    rosemary sprig
¼ teaspoon sea salt
freshly ground black pepper
1 teaspoon paprika
¼ teaspoon dry mustard

Combine all the marinade
ingredients in a shallow bowl. Stir
well, then add the cubed lamb.
Cover and leave to marinate for at
least 6 hours, or preferably
overnight.
☐ When ready to cook, drain the
lamb cubes, reserving any marinade.
Thread meat on to skewers with the
pepper, onions and tomatoes.
☐ Heat grill to high. Cook kebabs
for about 12 minutes, turning and
brushing with the reserved marinade.
☐ Serve with boiled rice.

Shami Kebabs

Serves 4 ☆☆☆
Preparation: 25 minutes
Cooking: about 1 hour

1lb (450g) leg of lamb, boned and cubed
1 small onion, peeled and sliced
1in (2.5cm) stick cinnamon
1 bay leaf
5oz (150g) chick peas
1 egg, size 5 or 6, beaten
2 teaspoons garam masala powder
1 tablespoon ground almonds
salt and freshly ground black pepper
oil for frying

The filling:
½ small onion, peeled and finely chopped
½oz (7g) fresh root ginger, grated
1 sprig of coriander leaves, chopped
1 green chilli, seeded and finely chopped
2 teaspoons lemon juice

Put the meat in a large pan and
cover with water. Add the sliced
onion, cinnamon stick, bay leaf and
chick peas. Cover and simmer for
about 50 minutes or until dry and
the meat is very tender.
☐ Remove the cinnamon stick and
bay leaf. Process or mince the
mixture to a sausagemeat
consistency. Add the egg, garam
masala, almonds, salt and pepper.
Mix well.
☐ Make filling: Mix together the
chopped onion, ginger, chopped
coriander leaves, chilli, lemon juice
and a pinch of salt.
☐ Make kebabs: Take a small
portion of the meat paste and make
a hollow in the middle. Put about ¼
teaspoonful of filling in the hollow
and pat the meat paste into a
rounded shape to enclose it.
Continue with remaining mixture.
☐ Heat oil in a frying-pan and fry
kebabs for 5 minutes, turning until
golden.

Liver Kebabs

Serves 4 ☆☆
Preparation: 15 minutes
Cooking: 15 minutes

1lb (450g) lamb's liver, cubed
4 onions, peeled and quartered
4 tomatoes, quartered
4oz (100g) mushrooms, wiped
8 bay leaves
salt and freshly ground black pepper
2 tablespoons lemon juice

Thread the liver pieces, onions,
tomatoes, mushrooms and bay
leaves alternately on to 4 skewers.
☐ Sprinkle with salt and pepper.
Heat grill to high.
☐ Cook kebabs under grill for 15
minutes, turning occasionally and
spooning over the lemon juice to
prevent burning.
☐ Serve immediately.

Lamb Kebabs
There is plenty of meat on a boned leg or
shoulder of lamb, and if you intend serving
other foods such as sausages and salads
you will find that there is sufficient meat for
up to 12 skewers.

Liver Kebabs
In many Middle Eastern countries, the kebab
stall is quite commonplace. People on their
way to work will stop for a breakfast of small
kebabs, made of tiny pieces of meat, liver
and kidney, which are cooked on a charcoal
brazier while they wait.

Shami Kebabs
More like flat rissoles, these kebabs are
filled with a spicy mixture before patting into
shape and frying. Serve with rice and salad
for a complete meal.

*Opposite: Lamb Kebabs for a summer
barbecue served with brown rice salad
with almonds and apple and celeriac
salad.*

Vegetable Kebabs

Ideal for slimmers, these are a light and tasty way to serve vegetables. You can also try them as a starter with a spicy sauce or as a novel way to serve accompanying vegetables.

Moules en Brochette

Mussel kebabs

Serves 4   ☆ ☆ ☆
Preparation: 30 minutes plus soaking
Cooking: 10-15 minutes

3lb-4lb (1.5kg-1.8kg) fresh mussels, scrubbed with beards removed
¼ pint (150ml) dry white wine
¼ pint (150ml) water
1 medium onion, peeled and chopped
1 bouquet garni
8oz (225g) unsmoked back bacon, rind removed, cut into chunks
1 red pepper, cored, seeded and cubed
1 green pepper, cored, seeded and cubed
4oz (100g) unsalted butter, softened
2 cloves garlic, crushed
2 tablespoons freshly chopped parsley
salt and freshly ground black pepper

Soak the mussels in cold water for about 1 hour.

☐ Drain the mussels and discard any which are open. Place the closed mussels in a large saucepan with the wine, water, onion and bouquet garni. Bring to the boil, cover with a tight-fitting lid and simmer for 10 minutes, shaking the pan frequently during this time.

☐ Drain and discard any mussels which have not opened. Remove the mussels from their shells.

☐ Thread the mussels on to skewers, alternating them with pieces of bacon and red and green pepper.

☐ Heat grill to high.

☐ Put the softened butter in a bowl with the garlic, parsley, and salt and pepper to taste. Beat well to mix, then spread over the kebabs to cover them thickly.

☐ Grill the kebabs on a rack for 10-15 minutes until sizzling hot. Turn them frequently during this time, brushing and basting them with any remaining butter and the juices from the grill pan.

☐ Serve immediately.

Tip: If fresh mussels are not available use frozen, shelled or half shelled instead. Thaw the mussels before cooking them.

Marinated Pork Kebabs

Serves 2   ☆ ☆
Preparation: 10 minutes plus 2 hours marinating
Cooking: about 15 minutes

---

2 tablespoons wine vinegar
1 teaspoon made mustard
salt and freshly ground black pepper
1-2 tablespoons soy sauce
2 tablespoons oil
1 tablespoon finely chopped onion
1 large pork fillet, cubed
1 green pepper, cored, seeded and cubed

Mix together vinegar, mustard, salt and pepper, soy sauce, oil and onion in a bowl. Add pork and marinate for 2 hours, turning often.

☐ Drain the pork, reserving the marinade. Thread on to skewers, alternating with pieces of pepper.

☐ Heat grill to high. Cook kebabs for 5-8 minutes on each side or until cooked and browned, basting with the marinade.

Vegetable Kebabs

Serves 4   ○
Preparation: 15 minutes
Cooking: 10-15 minutes

---

1 medium onion, peeled and quartered
4 courgettes, thickly sliced
4 tomatoes, skinned and quartered
8 button mushrooms, wiped
1 eating apple, cored and cut into eighths
8 bay leaves
salt and freshly ground black pepper
3 tablespoons unsweetened apple juice

Boil the onion for 5 minutes until tender but firm. Add the courgette slices for the last 1 minute.

☐ Heat the grill to high.

☐ Thread the vegetables, fruits and bay leaves on to 4 skewers.

☐ Season apple juice. Brush kebabs with the juice.

☐ Grill kebabs, turning frequently and brushing with apple juice, for 10-15 minutes until cooked. Serve hot.

Quiches

Everyone loves quiches – especially busy cooks! The pastry can be quickly produced and the fillings varied according to taste, time available and ingredients to hand. Indeed quiches are a good way to stretch left-overs or small quantities of food, and the results will always be filling and flavoursome.

Salmon Quiche with Tarragon Dressing

Serves 4   ☆☆☆

Preparation: 30 minutes plus
15 minutes chilling
Cooking: 45 minutes

The pastry:
8oz (225g) flour
2oz (50g) butter, diced
2oz (50g) lard, diced
1 egg, size 2, beaten

The filling:
the head and shoulders of a medium
    salmon, poached and cooled
2 eggs, size 2
¼ pint (150ml) single cream
4 spring onions, finely chopped
1 tablespoon chopped fresh fennel
salt and freshly ground black pepper

The dressing:
1 egg yolk from size 2 egg

½ teaspoon chopped fresh tarragon or pinch
    of dried tarragon
¼ pint (150ml) soured cream
1oz (25g) sugar
1 clove garlic, crushed
2 teaspoons wine vinegar
salt and freshly ground black pepper

Set the oven to 400F (200C) gas 6.

☐ Make the pastry: Sift the flour into a bowl then lightly rub in fats until mixture resembles fine breadcrumbs. Stir in enough beaten egg to make a soft dough.

☐ Wrap the pastry in cling wrap then chill for 15 minutes.

☐ Meanwhile, remove the flesh from the salmon and flake with a fork.

☐ Roll out the pastry on a lightly floured surface, and use to line an 8in (20cm) flan dish.

☐ Prick the base and sides with a fork, and then line with greaseproof paper, add baking beans and bake blind for 15 minutes.

☐ Meanwhile, make the filling: Beat together the eggs and cream, add the onions and fennel. Season to taste.

☐ Remove pastry case from oven. Take out baking beans and greaseproof paper. Return to oven and bake for a further 10 minutes.

☐ Spread flaked salmon over base of quiche and pour over the egg mixture.

☐ Reduce oven temperature to 350F (180C) gas 4 and cook for about 20 minutes or until the filling is golden and just firm to the touch.

☐ Meanwhile, make the dressing: Beat together the egg yolk and tarragon in a bowl. Stir in the soured cream, sugar and garlic.

☐ Place the bowl over hot water and cook gently, stirring, for about 15 minutes, until it thickens.

☐ Remove from the heat, stir in the vinegar and season to taste. Chill.

☐ Remove quiche from the oven and allow to cool. Serve with the dressing.

Salmon Quiche

Chicken Flan

Serves 4 ☆☆☆
Preparation: 10-15 minutes plus
15 minutes chilling
Cooking: 45 minutes

The pastry:
6oz (175g) flour
4oz (100g) butter
2-3 tablespoons cold water

The filling:
6oz (175g) cooked chicken
1oz (25g) butter
1oz (25g) flour
½ pint (300ml) milk
salt and freshly ground black pepper
1 tablespoon finely chopped parsley
the finely grated rind of ½ lemon

Set the oven to 400F (200C) gas 6.
☐ Make the pastry: Sift the flour into a bowl then lightly rub in the butter until mixture resembles fine breadcrumbs.
☐ Gradually add water and mix to form a soft dough. Wrap pastry in cling wrap then chill for 15 minutes.
☐ Roll out the pastry on a lightly floured surface and use to line an 8in (20cm) flan dish.
☐ Prick the base and sides with a fork and then line with greaseproof paper, add baking beans and bake blind for 15 minutes.
☐ Meanwhile, make the filling: Cut chicken into bite-sized pieces.
☐ Melt the butter in a saucepan, add the flour and mix well, stirring constantly for 1-2 minutes.
☐ Gradually add the milk, stirring constantly. Bring to the boil.
☐ Season well and add the parsley and lemon rind.
☐ Stir in the chicken until well mixed.
☐ Remove pastry case from oven. Take out greaseproof paper and baking beans and return the pastry to the oven for a further 10 minutes.
☐ Pour chicken mixture into flan.
☐ Reduce oven to 350F (180C) gas 4 and cook the flan for about 20 minutes.
☐ Serve hot with a tossed green salad.

Sausage and Tomato Quiche

Serves 4 ☆☆☆
Preparation: 30 minutes plus
15 minutes chilling
Cooking: about 1 hour

The pastry:
6oz (175g) flour
4oz (100g) butter
2-3 tablespoons cold water

The filling:
8oz (225g) chipolata sausages
2 eggs, size 2
7 fl oz (200ml) milk
½ teaspoon dried basil
salt and freshly ground black pepper
3oz (75g) mature Cheddar cheese, coarsely grated
2 tomatoes, skinned and sliced

Heat grill to moderate.
☐ Grill sausages until lightly browned. Set aside.
☐ Make the pastry: Sift the flour into a bowl then lightly rub in the butter until mixture resembles fine breadcrumbs.
☐ Gradually add water and mix to form a soft dough. Wrap pastry in cling wrap then chill for 15 minutes.
☐ Set oven to 400F (200C) gas 6.
☐ Roll out the pastry on a lightly floured surface, and use to line an 8in (20cm) flan dish.
☐ Prick the base and sides with a fork and then line with greaseproof paper, add baking beans and bake blind for 15 minutes.
☐ Remove pastry case from oven. Take out baking beans and greaseproof paper and return the pastry to oven for 10 minutes.
☐ Meanwhile, make the filling: In a mixing bowl beat together the eggs, milk, basil and seasoning.
☐ Sprinkle half of the cheese over the base and arrange the cooked sausages on top with the tomatoes.
☐ Pour egg mixture over filling and sprinkle with the remaining cheese.
☐ Reduce oven temperature to 350F (180C) gas 4 and bake quiche for 30-35 minutes, until the top is golden.
☐ Serve hot or cold.

Mushroom and Bacon Quiche

Serves 4 ☆☆☆
Preparation: 25 minutes plus
15 minutes chilling
Cooking: about 45 minutes

The pastry:
6oz (175g) flour
4oz (100g) butter
2-3 tablespoons cold water

The filling:
½oz (15g) butter
1 rasher streaky bacon, rind removed, chopped
4oz (100g) button mushrooms, wiped and sliced
2 eggs, size 2
6 fl oz (175ml) milk
salt and freshly ground black pepper
chopped fresh parsley to garnish

Make the pastry: Sift the flour into a bowl then lightly rub in the butter until mixture resembles fine breadcrumbs.
☐ Gradually add water and mix to form a soft dough. Wrap pastry in cling wrap then chill for 15 minutes.
☐ Set oven to 400F (200C) gas 6.
☐ Roll out the pastry on a lightly floured surface and use to line an 8in (20cm) flan dish.
☐ Prick the base and sides with a fork and then line with greaseproof paper, add baking beans and bake blind for 15 minutes.
☐ Meanwhile, make the filling: Melt the butter in a pan, add the bacon and mushrooms and cook for 2 minutes. Remove and drain.
☐ Beat together the eggs, milk and seasoning.
☐ Remove pastry case from oven. Take out baking beans and greaseproof paper. Return to the oven for a further 10 minutes.
☐ Fill quiche with mushroom and bacon, then pour in the egg mixture.
☐ Reduce oven to 350F (180C) gas 4 and cook for 20 minutes.
☐ Garnish with fresh parsley.

Clockwise: Mushroom and Bacon Quiche; Chicken Flan; Sausage and Tomato Quiche.

Camembert Quiche

Serves 4-6 ☆☆☆
Preparation: about 20 minutes plus
30 minutes chilling
Cooking: 35 minutes

6oz (175g) flour
a pinch of salt
4oz (100g) butter, chilled
1 egg yolk from size 2 egg

The filling:
12oz (350g) ripe Camembert cheese, rinded
  and cubed
2 eggs, size 2, beaten
¼ pint (150ml) double cream
salt and freshly ground black pepper

Make pastry: Sift flour and salt into a bowl. Rub butter into flour.

☐ Add the egg yolk to the flour and mix to form a dough. Wrap in cling wrap. Chill for 30 minutes.

☐ Set oven to 400F (200C) gas 6.

☐ Roll out the dough on a lightly floured surface and use to line a loose-bottomed 9in (23cm) fluted flan tin.

☐ Prick the base and sides with a fork and then line with greaseproof paper, add baking beans and bake blind for 15 minutes.

☐ Meanwhile, make the filling: Place Camembert in a heatproof bowl. Stand the bowl in a pan of gently simmering water and heat, stirring constantly, until cheese has melted.

☐ Remove the bowl and gradually stir in the beaten eggs and cream. Add salt and pepper to taste.

☐ Remove pastry case from oven. Take out greaseproof and baking beans. Pour the filling into the pastry case, return to the oven and bake for 20 minutes until puffed and golden. Serve immediately.

Pissaladière

Serves 4-6 ☆☆☆
Preparation: about 1 hour plus chilling
Cooking: 35 minutes

6oz (175g) flour
½ teaspoon ground cinnamon
a pinch of salt
1½oz (40g) butter or margarine
1½oz (40g) lard
1 egg yolk from size 2 egg

The filling:
4 tablespoons oil
1lb (450g) onions, peeled and thinly sliced
2 cloves garlic, crushed
1lb (450g) tomatoes, peeled and chopped
1 teaspoon caster sugar
1 bouquet garni
2 tablespoons tomato purée
freshly ground black pepper
1 × 1¾oz (50g) can anchovy fillets
8 black olives

First make the filling: Heat the oil in a frying-pan, add the onions and garlic and fry gently for about 10 minutes. Stir in the tomatoes, sugar, bouquet garni, tomato purée, and salt and pepper and bring to the boil. Reduce the heat and simmer, uncovered, for about 40 minutes.

☐ Meanwhile, make the pastry: Sift the flour, cinnamon and salt together in a bowl. Add the fats and rub them in until the mixture resembles breadcrumbs. Mix in the egg yolk with a little cold water if necessary to make a fairly firm dough.

☐ Knead the dough on a lightly floured surface until smooth. Wrap dough in cling wrap and chill for 15 minutes.

☐ Set oven to 400F (200C) gas 6.

☐ Roll out pastry on a lightly floured surface and use to line a 8in (20cm) plain flan ring. Place tin on a baking sheet, prick dough base with a fork, then line with greaseproof paper and fill with baking beans. Bake blind for 15 minutes.

☐ Remove the paper and beans. Remove bouquet garni from the filling. Spoon the tomato mixture into the flan case.

☐ Lattice the surface with anchovy fillets and place an olive in each diamond. Return to the oven for a further 20 minutes, brushing the anchovies and olives with a little extra oil if they become dry. Serve with a fresh green salad.

Variation: If preferred, a shortcrust pastry can be used instead of dough.

Quick Skillet Quiche

Serves 4 ☆☆☆
Preparation and cooking: about
25 minutes

The pastry:
6oz (175g) flour
1½oz (40g) butter
1½oz (40g) lard
2-3 tablespoons cold water

The filling:
3 eggs, size 2
½ pint (300ml) single cream
6oz (175g) Cheddar cheese, grated
salt and freshly ground black pepper
2 large tomatoes, sliced

Make the pastry: Sift the flour into a bowl. Lightly rub in the fats until mixture resembles fine breadcrumbs.

☐ Gradually add water and mix to form a soft dough.

☐ Roll out pastry on a lightly floured surface and cut a circle 10in (25cm) in diameter. Line a non-stick frying-pan with the pastry, pressing it up the sides well. Prick the base all over with a fork.

☐ Put the pan over a gentle heat and cook for 3 to 4 minutes.

☐ Meanwhile, make the filling: Beat the eggs, with the cream, in a bowl. Add 4oz (100g) of the cheese and season well.

☐ Pour cheese mixture into pastry case, cover pan and continue to cook over a gentle heat for a further 3 to 4 minutes.

☐ Heat the grill to high.

☐ Uncover the pan and arrange the tomato slices on top, then sprinkle with the remaining cheese.

☐ Place frying-pan under the grill for 5 minutes until filling is puffed and golden.

☐ Slide the quiche carefully out of the pan on to a serving plate.

☐ Serve immediately.

Variation: Use any other hard cheese in place of the Cheddar.

Stuffed Vegetables

Stuffed vegetables make light meals with a difference. Many vegetables can be used – potatoes, peppers, cauliflowers, mushrooms, aubergines and more and, with the addition of a meat, fish, egg, cheese or rice filling, or even a combination of these, they can be transformed into tasty dishes. Serve either on their own or with a salad for a more filling meal.

Mock Dolmas

Serves 4 ☆
Preparation and cooking: 50 minutes

3oz (75g) long-grain rice
salt and freshly ground black pepper
12 large cabbage leaves
4oz (100g) cooked shoulder ham, chopped
1 hard-boiled egg, chopped
¼ teaspoon grated nutmeg
1 × 14oz (396g) can tomatoes
oil for greasing

Set the oven to 350F (180C) gas 4.
☐ Cook the rice in boiling salted water in a saucepan for about 10 minutes or until tender. Drain and rinse with boiling water.
☐ Meanwhile, blanch the cabbage leaves in boiling water for 1 minute. Drain and pat dry with kitchen paper.
☐ Mix together the cooked rice, ham, egg, nutmeg, and salt and pepper to taste.
☐ Divide mixture equally between the cabbage leaves, placing the

filling in the centre. Fold over the edges of the leaves and the stalk end, then roll up to form parcels, tucking the ends in well to enclose the filling.
☐ Place parcels close together in a lightly greased ovenproof dish.
☐ Chop the tomatoes, then pour them with their juice over the cabbage.
☐ Cover with foil or a lid and cook in the oven for 30 minutes. Serve hot.
Variations: Replace the ham and egg with 4oz (125g) chopped cooked lamb and 1½oz (40g) sultanas.
● For a vegetarian dish, substitute 2oz (50g) chopped hazelnuts for the ham and include 1-2oz (25-50g) grated Cheddar cheese.

Mock Dolmas

Stuffed Tomatoes

Uncooked tomatoes are delicious stuffed with a mixture of smoked mackerel, rice and mayonnaise.

Spinach Ring

To make a more substantial meal serve the ring on a bed of rice and fill the centre with diced cooked chicken. A tomato sauce makes a good substitute for the cream sauce.

Cheese and Bean Stuffed Peppers

For a colourful dish use contrasting peppers such as red and yellow or yellow and green. The kidney beans can be replaced by sweetcorn or salted peanuts.

Stuffed Tomatoes

Serves 4 ☆☆☆
Preparation: 10 minutes
Cooking: about 15 minutes

---

4 large tomatoes
1oz (25g) butter
4oz (100g) mushrooms, finely chopped
1 large onion, finely chopped
1oz (25g) white breadcrumbs
2 teaspoons mixed dried herbs
salt and freshly ground black pepper
1 tablespoon Parmesan or Cheddar cheese, finely grated
oil for greasing
fresh parsley to garnish

Set the oven to 375F (190C) gas 5.
☐ Slice the top off each tomato and scoop out the seeds. Turn upside-down and allow to drain.
☐ Melt the butter in a pan. Add the mushrooms and onion and cook for a few minutes until softened. Stir in the breadcrumbs, herbs, salt and pepper and cheese.
☐ Fill the tomatoes with the mixture and replace tops.
☐ Place in a lightly greased oven dish. Bake for about 15 minutes.
☐ Serve garnished with fresh parsley.

Spinach Ring

Serves 6 ☆☆☆
Preparation: 25 minutes
Cooking: 40 minutes

3lb (1.5kg) fresh spinach, washed, stalks removed
salt and freshly ground black pepper
3oz (75g) butter
2oz (50g) flour
1 pint (600ml) milk
a pinch of ground nutmeg
3 eggs, size 2, beaten
4oz (100g) button mushrooms, wiped and chopped
2oz (50g) cooked ham, diced
butter for greasing
¼ pint (150ml) single cream, warmed and seasoned, to serve

Set the oven to 350F (180C) gas 4.
☐ Butter a 10in (25cm) ring mould.
☐ Cook the spinach with just the water clinging to the leaves and a little salt, until just tender.
☐ Drain spinach very thoroughly, pressing with the back of a spoon to remove excess moisture.
☐ Use a few spinach leaves to line the mould and chop the remainder.
☐ Melt 2oz (50g) of the butter in a pan. Stir in the flour then gradually blend in the milk. Season well with salt, pepper and nutmeg. Simmer for 3 minutes.
☐ Remove from heat and beat in eggs.
☐ Sauté the mushrooms in the remaining butter.
☐ Stir the spinach, ham and mushrooms into the sauce.
☐ Pour the mixture into the mould, cover and bake for 40 minutes.
☐ Turn the ring out on to a serving dish and pour over the warm cream.

Cheese and Bean Stuffed Peppers

Serves 4 ☆☆☆
Preparation: about 15 minutes
Cooking: 15 minutes

---

4 small green peppers, cut in half lengthwise, cored and seeded
salt and freshly ground black pepper
1oz (25g) butter
1oz (25g) flour
8 fl oz (250ml) milk
2 eggs, size 2, separated
8oz (225g) cottage cheese
1 × 6oz (170g) can red kidney beans, drained
3oz (75g) Cheddar cheese, grated
a pinch of ground nutmeg
1½oz (40g) flaked almonds
oil for greasing

Set the oven to 375F (190C) gas 5.
☐ Blanch the pepper halves for 7 minutes in boiling salted water. Drain and dry with kitchen paper.
☐ Meanwhile, make the filling: Melt the butter in a saucepan, stir in the flour and cook for 2-3 minutes. Gradually stir in the milk, bring to the boil and season well. Simmer for 2-3 minutes.
☐ Remove pan from heat and beat in the egg yolks. Stir in the cottage cheese, kidney beans, grated cheese,

nutmeg, and salt and pepper.

☐ Whip the egg whites until stiff then fold into the mixture.

☐ Arrange peppers in a greased ovenproof dish and fill with cheese mixture. Sprinkle with almonds and cook for 15 minutes, until the filling has risen slightly and is golden. Serve at once.

Stuffed Aubergines

Serves 4   ☆ ☆
Preparation: 25 minutes plus
20 minutes standing
Cooking: 25 minutes

2 medium aubergines, stalks removed
salt and freshly ground black pepper
oil for greasing
chopped fresh chives to garnish

The filling:
1½oz (40g) butter
2 onions, peeled and finely chopped
1½oz (40g) flour
8 fl oz (250ml) milk
3oz (75g) Gruyère cheese, grated
1 egg yolk from size 2 egg

Cut the aubergines in half lengthwise. Slash the inner flesh in a criss-cross fashion and sprinkle with salt. Place the halves, flesh-side down, on a wire rack and leave for 20 minutes.

☐ Set oven to 325F (160C) gas 3.

☐ Rinse and dry the aubergines and place in a greased ovenproof dish. Bake for 20 minutes.

☐ Meanwhile, make the filling: Melt the butter in a saucepan and gently fry the onions until transparent. Stir in the flour and cook for 2-3 minutes. Gradually stir in the milk, bring to the boil and season well. Simmer for 2-3 minutes.

☐ Remove from the heat and stir in 2oz (50g) cheese and the egg yolk.

☐ Remove aubergines from oven. Scoop out the flesh and chop roughly.

☐ Add flesh to onion sauce and mix well. Fill the aubergine shells and sprinkle the remaining cheese on top.

☐ Bake in oven for 20 minutes.

☐ Heat grill to high.

☐ Remove aubergines from oven and place under grill for 5 minutes until the topping is golden.

☐ Serve garnished with chives.

Clockwise: Stuffed Aubergines (top); Spinach Ring; Cheese and Bean Stuffed Peppers.

Caernarvon Cauliflower

If the cauliflower breaks up while you are removing the stalk, cook it until tender then reshape it in a well-buttered bowl. Fill with the stuffing, press it into the bowl then turn out on to the serving dish and finish as in the recipe.

Stuffed Mushrooms

The freshest flat mushrooms have clean, dry white tops with pale brown gills underneath. As they age the tops discolour and the gills become darker.

Caernarvon Cauliflower

Serves 4
Preparation: 20 minutes
Cooking: 20 minutes

---

1 medium cauliflower

The sauce:
1oz (25g) butter
1oz (25g) flour
½ pint (300ml) milk
4oz (100g) Cheddar cheese, finely grated
salt and freshly ground black pepper

The stuffing:
½oz (15g) butter
1 leek, washed and finely sliced
6oz (175g) ham, finely chopped
4oz (100g) wholemeal breadcrumbs
2oz (50g) walnuts, finely chopped
butter for greasing

bacon rolls to garnish

Set the oven to 400F (200C) gas 6.
☐ Grease an ovenproof dish.
☐ Make the sauce: Melt the butter in a saucepan, then add the flour, stirring, and cook for a few minutes.
☐ Gradually add the milk, stirring constantly. Bring to the boil. Simmer for 2-3 minutes then remove from heat.
☐ Stir in 3oz (75g) grated cheese and season well.
☐ Wash and trim the cauliflower. Cook for 5 minutes in a pan of boiling, salted water, until tender but still firm. Drain and allow to cool slightly.
☐ Meanwhile, make the stuffing: Melt the butter in a pan. Add the leek and cook, covered, for 5 minutes or until tender.
☐ Add the ham and 3oz (75g) of the breadcrumbs and season well. Stir in the chopped walnuts.
☐ Take 2 tablespoons of cheese sauce, and stir into the stuffing mixture.
☐ Turn over the cauliflower and, using a sharp knife, remove the whole of the stalk, ensuring that the head remains intact.
☐ Fill the cauliflower cavity with the stuffing. Place in the prepared dish with the head up.
☐ Pour over the cheese sauce and sprinkle with the remaining cheese and breadcrumbs. Cook in the oven for 20 minutes.
☐ Serve hot, cut into quarters, garnished with bacon rolls.
Tip: The cooked stalk of the cauliflower is not needed for this recipe and can be puréed and used for soups.
Variation: For a more exotic meal, stuff the cauliflower with minced beef flavoured with curry powder. Omit the walnuts, ham and sauce and serve with tomato or curry sauce.

Stuffed Mushrooms

Serves 4
Preparation: 10 minutes
Cooking: 15-20 minutes

---

4 large open mushrooms, wiped

The stuffing:
½oz (15g) butter
1 rasher streaky bacon, rind removed, chopped
1oz (25g) fresh white breadcrumbs
2 teaspoons freshly chopped parsley
½ teaspoon grated lemon rind
a few drops lemon juice
2oz (50g) Cheddar cheese, finely grated
salt and freshly ground black pepper
oil for greasing

watercress to garnish

Set the oven to 325F (160C) gas 3.
☐ Remove stalks from mushrooms and chop them finely.
☐ Make stuffing: Melt butter in a pan and fry mushroom stalks and bacon for a few minutes.
☐ Remove pan from heat. Stir in breadcrumbs, parsley, lemon rind, juice and cheese. Season well.
☐ Place mushroom caps in a lightly greased ovenproof dish. Divide the stuffing between each one.
☐ Cook in oven for 15-20 minutes.
☐ Serve garnished with watercress.
Tip: For a more substantial meal, serve these delicious mushrooms with lightly scrambled eggs and crisp fried bread.

Rice

Rice can form the basis of many tasty and filling snacks. Combine it with meat, fish, poultry, vegetables and fruits, perhaps some stock, and herbs and spices and, in a very short time, you have produced risottos, pilaffs, curries and a variety of salads. Always use the correct rice for a recipe for the best results.

Kidney Risotto

Serves 4 ☆☆☆
Preparation and cooking: 30 minutes

---

2 tablespoons oil
1 onion, peeled and finely chopped
1 green pepper, cored, seeded and chopped
8 lambs' kidneys, halved, cored and chopped
8oz (225g) long-grain rice
1 pint (600ml) Chicken Stock
salt and freshly ground black pepper
2oz (50g) butter
2 tablespoons chopped fresh parsley
2 tablespoons grated Parmesan cheese

Heat the oil in a frying-pan and fry the onion and green pepper for 2-3 minutes.
☐ Add the kidneys and fry, stirring, for a further 2 minutes.
☐ Stir in the rice and cook for 1 minute.
☐ Gradually stir in the stock, bring to the boil, then add salt and pepper to taste.
☐ Cover the pan and simmer gently for 20 minutes until the rice has absorbed all the liquid.
☐ Stir in the butter, parsley and Parmesan cheese.
☐ Serve with a tossed green salad.
Variations: Add 4oz (100g) sliced mushrooms to the mixture with the stock.
● Add 6oz (175g) lightly fried and chopped chicken livers with the stock.

Kipper Kedgeree

Serves 2 ☆☆☆
Preparation and cooking: 20 minutes

4oz (100g) long-grain rice
salt and freshly ground black pepper
6oz (175g) packet frozen kipper fillets
2oz (50g) butter
2 hard-boiled eggs, chopped
2 teaspoons lemon juice

To garnish:
paprika
1 hard-boiled egg, quartered

Cook the rice in boiling salted water for 15 minutes or until tender. Drain well.
☐ Meanwhile, cook the kipper fillets according to instructions on packet.
☐ Remove from the bag and reserve the liquid. Skin and flake the fish.
☐ Melt the butter in a saucepan.
☐ Add the rice, flaked fish, fish liquid and the chopped hard-boiled eggs.
☐ Heat together gently.
☐ Season to taste with salt and pepper and add the lemon juice.
☐ Transfer to a serving dish. Garnish with the paprika and the quartered hard-boiled egg.
☐ Serve with toast fingers.

Kidney Risotto

Italian risotto

An Italian risotto is usually served on its own with butter and cheese. Its texture should be rich and creamy rather than dry. Risottos are usually served as a starter or as a light supper dish with green salad.

Italian rice

It is important to use the correct rice for the recipe. The short, round-grain rice known as Arborio is ideal for risottos because it is able to absorb large quantities of stock without becoming soft.

Risotto con Gamberetti

Prawn risotto

Serves 4-6 ☆☆☆
Preparation and cooking: about 1¼ hours

1lb (500g) unshelled prawns
1 small head fennel
a few parsley stalks
½ onion, peeled and roughly chopped
1 small carrot, peeled and roughly chopped
1¾ pints (1 litre) water
½ pint (300ml) dry white wine
4oz (100g) butter
2 tablespoons olive oil
1lb (500g) short-grain Italian rice
salt and freshly ground black pepper
1 clove garlic, peeled and crushed
the grated rind of ½ lemon
2oz (50g) grated Parmesan cheese

Shell the prawns. Put the shells, heads and any eggs into a pan. Reserve prawns.
☐ Remove the feathery tops from the fennel and reserve for garnish.
☐ Slice the bulb of fennel and add to the prawn trimmings, together with the parsley stalks, chopped onion and carrot and 1¾ pints (1 litre) water.
☐ Simmer gently for 25-30 minutes.
☐ Strain the prawn stock and make up to 2¾ pints (1.5 litres) with the white wine and some water.
☐ Heat half the butter and the oil in a pan and gently cook the rice for 5 minutes, making sure that the rice does not colour. Add ¼ pint (150ml) stock to the rice and cook until the stock has been absorbed.
☐ Add another ¼ pint (150ml) stock and continue cooking steadily until the rice has absorbed the stock.
☐ Continue adding the stock in this way, until all the stock has been used up and rice is tender.
☐ Add salt and pepper to taste.
☐ Melt the remaining butter in a small pan and add the prawns, garlic and rind. Cook for 5-10 minutes.
☐ Stir into the cooked risotto, together with the Parmesan cheese.
☐ Garnish with the feathery tops from the fennel and serve.

Italian-style Fish Risotto

Serves 2 ☆☆
Preparation and cooking: 45 minutes

1oz (25g) butter
1 onion, peeled and chopped
4oz (100g) long-grain rice
1¼ pints (750ml) Fish or Chicken Stock
½ teaspoon dried dill
salt and freshly ground black pepper
2 plaice fillets, skinned
2oz (50g) peeled prawns
2oz (50g) mushrooms, wiped and sliced
3oz (75g) peas, cooked

To garnish:
a few strips of canned pimiento
a few bottled mussels

Melt the butter in a frying-pan and fry the onion until soft.
☐ Add the rice and cook for 1-2 minutes, stirring well, then add the stock, dill and salt and pepper to taste.
☐ Bring to the boil.
☐ Cover and simmer for 20 minutes.
☐ Cut the fish into narrow strips and add to the pan with the prawns and mushrooms.
☐ Stir well, re-cover and continue simmering gently for a further 10-15 minutes, stirring occasionally and adding a little more boiling stock if necessary.
☐ Adjust the seasoning, stir in peas and cook for a further 2-3 minutes.
☐ Serve hot, garnished with strips of pimiento and mussels.

Risotto Verde

Risotto with spinach and herbs

Serves 4-6 ☆☆☆
Preparation and cooking: 40 minutes

1lb (500g) spinach, fresh or frozen
2 tablespoons olive oil
4oz (100g) butter
1 small onion, peeled and finely chopped
1lb (500g) short-grain Italian rice
2¾ pints (1.5 litres) Chicken Stock
1 tablespoon chopped fresh oregano
1 clove garlic, peeled and crushed
salt and freshly ground black pepper
3oz (75g) grated Parmesan cheese

Cook the spinach in a large pan, with only the water that clings to leaves, for 5-10 minutes until tender.
□ Drain the spinach and chop.
□ Heat the oil and half the butter in a pan and gently fry the onion for 3 minutes.
□ Add the rice and stir over a gentle heat for 5 minutes, making sure that the rice does not colour.
□ Add ¼ pint (150ml) of the stock to the rice and cook until the stock has been absorbed.
□ Add another cup of stock, the chopped spinach, oregano and garlic.
□ Cook again until the stock has been absorbed. Continue adding the stock in this way until it has all been absorbed.
□ Add the salt and pepper to taste and stir in the remaining butter and the Parmesan cheese.
□ Serve immediately.
Variation: If liked garnish with lemon wedges.

Saffron Rice

This superb rice is one of the most useful of all recipes. Saffron is expensive but makes the subtle difference. Use a heavy saucepan or an iron casserole for absolutely carefree cooking.

Serves 8
Preparation and cooking time:
35-40 minutes

½ teaspoon crumbled saffron
10oz (310g) long-grain rice
½oz (15g) butter
1 tablespoon oil
1 small onion, finely chopped
1¼ pints (750ml) boiling chicken
    stock or water
salt

Soak the saffron in sufficient water to cover.
□ Rinse the rice in a sieve under cold running water until the water runs clear. Drain thoroughly.

□ Heat the butter and oil in a deep saucepan and cook the onion until soft but not coloured. Add the rice and cook for a further few minutes, stirring all the time, until the rice is well coated in butter and oil.
□ Pour on the stock or water, and add the saffron and water in which it was soaked. Add a large pinch of salt (or less if the stock is salty). Stir once, then cover tightly and cook gently for 15-20 minutes or until the rice is tender and the liquid has been absorbed.
□ Remove the lid and stand for a few minutes to allow steam to escape. Fluff up with fork and serve.

From the top (clockwise): Risotto Verde; Risotto con Gamberetti; Saffron Rice.

Creole Banana Salad

This salad can also be served as a main course in a vegetarian buffet. It is more colourful than the North African Salad and has a higher fruit content, but the two make a good combination.

Rice salads

Leftover rice need never be wasted as it can always be added to a selection of finely chopped fruit or vegetables to make a tasty and attractive rice salad. As an accompaniment, allow 2oz (50g) cooked rice per person.

Rice Balls in Tomato Sauce

For this recipe only use raw rice, and not pre-processed rice such as easy-to-cook, parboiled, pre-cooked or instant. In pre-processed rice the grains remain separate, which makes it unsuitable for this dish.

Serves 4 ☆☆☆
Preparation and cooking: 45 minutes

8oz (225g) long-grain rice
1 egg, size 2, lightly beaten
1 tablespoon flour
4oz (100g) Mozzarella cheese, cubed
1 tablespoon finely chopped fresh parsley

The sauce:
1oz (25g) butter
1 large onion, peeled and finely chopped
1lb (500g) tomatoes, skinned, seeded and
    chopped, or 14oz (396g) can tomatoes,
    drained and chopped
1 teaspoon dried basil
½ teaspoon dried thyme
1 teaspoon salt and ½ teaspoon freshly
    ground black pepper
5 tablespoons dry white wine
½ pint (300ml) Chicken Stock

First make the sauce: Melt the butter in a saucepan, add the onion and fry for 5 minutes or until soft.
☐ Add the tomatoes, basil, thyme, and salt and pepper and cook for a further 3 minutes.
☐ Stir in the wine and the chicken stock.
☐ Bring to the boil, then simmer, covered, for 15 minutes.
☐ Meanwhile, cook the rice in boiling salted water for 15 minutes or until tender.
☐ Drain well and allow to cool.
☐ Mix rice with egg and flour.
☐ Take a large spoonful of the mixture, roll into a ball and insert a cube of cheese. Continue making the rice balls until all the mixture and cheese have been used.
☐ Add the rice balls to the sauce and simmer gently for a further 10 minutes.
☐ To serve: Turn the rice balls and the sauce into a warmed serving dish and sprinkle with the parsley.

Creole Banana Salad

Serves 4 ☆☆☆
Preparation and cooking: 30 minutes

8oz (225g) long-grain rice
salt
4 large bananas, peeled and sliced
1 tablespoon lemon juice
1 medium red eating apple, cored and chopped
4oz (100g) seedless green grapes
3oz (75g) canned or fresh pineapple, chopped
2 tablespoons finely chopped walnuts
1 tablespoon sultanas
2 tablespoons desiccated coconut to serve
4 large lettuce leaves

The dressing:
4 fl oz (125ml) mayonnaise
2 tablespoons lemon juice
a large pinch of hot chilli powder
½ teaspoon dry English mustard

Cook the rice in boiling salted water for 15 minutes. Drain and cool.
☐ Stir the bananas, lemon juice, apples, grapes, pineapple, walnuts and sultanas into the rice.
☐ Mix dressing and stir into rice.
☐ Serve, sprinkled with coconut on a bed of lettuce.

North African Salad

Serves 2 ☆☆☆
Preparation and cooking: 30 minutes plus 30 minutes chilling

6oz (175g) long-grain rice
salt
1 small cucumber, sliced
2 medium bananas, peeled and sliced
2 tablespoons seedless raisins
1 tablespoon chopped almonds
4 tablespoons olive oil
the juice and grated rind of 1 lemon
a large pinch of ground coriander
a large pinch of ground cumin
a large pinch of cayenne pepper
1 teaspoon clear honey

Cook the rice in boiling salted water for 15 minutes. Drain and cool.
☐ Stir the rice, cucumber, bananas, raisins and almonds together in a bowl.
☐ Mix together oil, lemon juice and rind, salt, coriander, cumin, cayenne and honey. Pour over the rice and mix well. Chill for 30 minutes.

Pasta

Pasta is immensely popular and, whether you use dried or fresh, you can produce some delicious, filling and speedy snacks. The range of pasta is quite vast and really worth experimenting with—as are the various sauces you can prepare.

Lasagne

Serves 4   ☆☆☆
Preparation: 45 minutes
Cooking: 30-35 minutes

8oz (225g) lasagne
1 tablespoon oil
butter for greasing

The filling:
1 tablespoon oil
2oz (50g) carrots, diced
2oz (50g) onion, peeled and diced
4oz (100g) bacon, rinds removed, diced
1lb (500g) minced beef
8oz (226g) can tomatoes
1 tablespoon tomato purée
1 teaspoon French mustard
2 teaspoons Worcestershire sauce
1 teaspoon caster sugar
salt and freshly ground black pepper
1 tablespoon cornflour
3 tablespoons water
3oz (75g) ricotta or cottage cheese
6oz (175g) fresh spinach, cooked and well
    drained

The topping:
½ pint (300ml) Mornay Sauce
1oz (25g) Cheddar cheese, grated
1oz (25g) grated Parmesan cheese

First make the filling: Heat the oil in a pan, add the carrots, onion and bacon and fry gently for 5 minutes.
☐ Add the minced beef and continue cooking, stirring occasionally, until the meat is browned.
☐ Stir in the tomatoes, tomato purée, mustard, Worcestershire sauce, sugar, and salt and pepper.
☐ Simmer for 30 minutes.
☐ Mix the cornflour with the water and stir into the sauce. Cook, stirring, for 3-4 minutes, then remove from the heat and allow to cool.

☐ Cook the lasagne in a large pan of boiling salted water, adding 1 tablespoon of oil. Cook for 12 minutes, making sure that the lasagne does not stick together while cooking.
☐ Drain the lasagne and pat dry with kitchen paper.
☐ Set oven to 325F (160C) gas 3.
☐ Grease a 3 pint (1.75 litre)

ovenproof dish and place a layer of lasagne in the bottom.
☐ Cover the lasagne with a layer of sauce, then a thin layer of ricotta or cottage cheese, followed by a layer of spinach.
☐ Continue layering, finishing with a layer of lasagne.
☐ Pour sauce over the top and sprinkle over the grated Cheddar and the Parmesan cheeses.
☐ Bake for 30-35 minutes.

Lasagne and Noodles with Italian Meat Sauce.

Noodles with Italian Meat Sauce

Serves 4 ☆☆☆
Preparation and cooking: 1 hour

8oz (225g) pasta noodles
1 tablespoon oil

The sauce:
3 tablespoons oil
1 Spanish onion, peeled and diced
1 small green pepper, cored, seeded and diced
1lb (450g) minced beef
2 cloves garlic, crushed

14oz (396g) can tomatoes or 1lb (450g) fresh tomatoes, skinned and chopped
3 tablespoons tomato purée
¼ pint (150ml) red wine
¼ pint (150ml) Meat Stock
1 teaspoon oregano
1-2 teaspoons caster sugar
2 bay leaves
salt and freshly ground black pepper
4oz (100g) button mushrooms, wiped and thinly sliced

First make the sauce: Heat 3 tablespoons oil in a saucepan, add the onion and green pepper and fry gently until the onion is soft.

☐ Stir in the minced beef and continue cooking until the meat is browned.

☐ Add the garlic, tomatoes, tomato purée, wine, stock, oregano, sugar, bay leaves, and salt and pepper.

☐ Simmer gently, uncovered, for 30 minutes, stirring occasionally.

☐ Stir in the mushrooms, cover and simmer for a further 15 minutes.

☐ Put the pasta noodles in a large pan of boiling salted water and add 1 tablespoon of oil. Cook the pasta for 12-15 minutes until just tender. Drain well.

☐ Serve immediately with the sauce.

Seafood Spaghetti; Pasta Carbonara; Spaghetti con Funghi.

Seafood Spaghetti

Serves 4 ☆☆☆
Preparation and cooking: 25 minutes

4 tablespoons oil
1 onion, peeled and finely chopped
½ pint (300ml) dry white wine
1 clove garlic, crushed
10oz (275g) spaghetti
salt and freshly ground black pepper
7 fl oz (200ml) double cream
2 tablespoons chopped chives
6oz (175g) peeled prawns
6oz (175g) mussels, cockles or crabmeat

Heat 2 tablespoons oil in a frying-pan and fry onions until soft.
☐ Add the wine and garlic and simmer gently until reduced by ⅓.
☐ Lower spaghetti into a large pan of boiling salted water and add 1 tablespoon of oil. Cook for 8 minutes.
☐ Meanwhile, add the cream, chives, prawns and other shellfish to the wine mixture. Heat through gently and add seasoning to taste.
☐ Drain the spaghetti well and stir in the remaining oil and the sauce.

Pasta Carbonara

Serves 4 ☆☆☆
Preparation and cooking: 15 minutes

12oz (350g) pasta noodles
salt and freshly ground black pepper
1 onion, peeled and finely chopped
3 tablespoons oil
6oz (175g) bacon, rinds removed, chopped
4 eggs, size 2
4 tablespoons cream
chopped fresh parsley to garnish

Cook noodles in boiling salted water for 6-8 minutes.
☐ Fry onion in 1 tablespoon of oil, add bacon and fry for 2 minutes.
☐ Beat eggs with seasoning and add to onion and bacon. Cook gently, stirring, until eggs scramble. Remove from heat. Drain noodles well and stir in the remaining oil.
☐ Turn on to a warm serving dish.
☐ Add the cream to the scrambled egg and heat for a few seconds.
☐ Spoon over pasta. Sprinkle with parsley and serve immediately.

Spaghetti con Funghi

Serves 4 ☆☆☆
Preparation and cooking: 15 minutes

4 tablespoons oil
1 onion, peeled and finely chopped
6oz (175g) mushrooms, wiped and chopped
8oz (225g) ham, chopped
1 clove garlic, crushed
4 tablespoons Marsala
3 tablespoons chopped fresh parsley
salt and freshly ground black pepper
12oz (350g) spaghetti

Heat 2 tablespoons of oil in a pan and fry the onion for 2 minutes.
☐ Add the chopped mushrooms, ham, garlic, Marsala, parsley, and salt and pepper to taste.
☐ Cover and simmer for 10 minutes.
☐ Meanwhile, cook the spaghetti for about 8 minutes in a large pan of boiling salted water.
☐ Drain the spaghetti well and stir in the remaining oil.
☐ Stir the mushroom and ham sauce into the spaghetti and serve.

Macaroni Topkapi

Serves 2   ☆☆☆
Preparation and cooking: 45-50 minutes

3-4oz (75-100g) macaroni
1 tablespoon oil
salt and freshly ground black pepper
butter for greasing

The sauce:
1½oz (40g) butter
1 onion, peeled and sliced
2oz (50g) mushrooms, wiped and sliced
1oz (25g) flour
½ pint (300ml) milk
½ teaspoon dried mixed herbs
3oz (75g) Cheddar cheese, grated
2 hard-boiled eggs, sliced
1 tomato, sliced, to garnish

Cook the macaroni in a large pan of boiling salted water and add oil. Cook for 15 minutes until tender, stirring occasionally. Drain.
☐ Set oven to 400F (200C) gas 6.
☐ Melt the butter in a saucepan and fry the onion until soft.
☐ Add the mushrooms and continue cooking for 2 minutes, then stir in the flour and cook for 1 minute.
☐ Gradually stir in the milk, bring to the boil and simmer for 2 minutes. Season well.
☐ Stir in the herbs and 2oz (50g) of the cheese then mix in the macaroni.
☐ Pour half the mixture into a greased ovenproof dish.
☐ Cover with most of the sliced eggs, then the remaining macaroni.
☐ Sprinkle with remaining cheese and bake for 25-30 minutes until brown.
☐ Garnish with egg and tomato.

Tagliatelli Bake

Serves 4   ☆☆
Preparation and cooking: 40 minutes

8oz (225g) green tagliatelli
salt and freshly ground black pepper
1 tablespoon oil
butter for greasing

The sauce:
1 tablespoon oil
1 large onion, diced
1 clove garlic, crushed
1 green pepper, cored, seeded and diced
2 tomatoes, skinned and chopped
1 large potato, peeled, cooked and chopped
4oz (100g) ham, chopped
1 teaspoon fresh or dried chives

To finish:
2oz (50g) Cheddar cheese, grated

Set the oven to 400F (200C) gas 6.
☐ Cook tagliatelli in a pan of boiling salted water and add 1 tablespoon of oil. Cook for 8-10 minutes. Drain.
☐ Meanwhile, make the sauce: Heat the oil in a frying-pan and fry the onion and garlic until soft and lightly browned. Add the pepper and continue to cook until soft.
☐ Add the tomatoes, potato, ham and chives and cook for 10 minutes, stirring occasionally. Season.
☐ Grease an ovenproof dish. Mix the tagliatelli with the sauce and pour into the dish.
☐ Sprinkle with the grated cheese and bake for 20 minutes. Serve.

Pasta Soufflé

Serves 4   ☆☆☆
Preparation and cooking: 55 minutes

6oz (175g) pasta shells
salt and freshly ground black pepper
1 tablespoon oil
2oz (50g) butter
1 onion, sliced
8oz (226g) can tomatoes, drained
7oz (198g) can sweetcorn kernels, drained
4oz (113g) can tuna, drained and flaked
1oz (25g) flour
¼ pint (150ml) milk
½ teaspoon made mustard
½ teaspoon dried basil
2oz (50g) Cheddar cheese, grated
3 eggs, size 2, separated
butter for greasing

Set the oven to 350F (180C) gas 4.
☐ Put the pasta shells in a large pan of boiling salted water and add 1 tablespoon of oil. Cook the pasta shells for 10-15 minutes until just tender. Drain well.
☐ Melt 1oz (25g) of the butter in a frying-pan and fry the onion until soft and lightly browned. Add the tomatoes and cook for 1-2 minutes.
☐ Season well with salt and pepper.
☐ Put the pasta, sweetcorn and tuna into the bottom of a greased 6in (15cm) soufflé dish and spoon the onion mixture on top.
☐ Tie a piece of greased foil around the dish to come 2in (5cm) above rim.
☐ Melt remaining butter in a pan. Stir in flour and cook for 1 minute.
☐ Gradually stir in the milk and bring to the boil. Simmer for 1 minute. Season well, then beat in the mustard, basil and cheese, followed by the egg yolks. Cook until smooth, stirring constantly.
☐ Whisk the egg whites in a bowl to stiff peaks. Fold evenly through the sauce.
☐ Spoon into the dish and bake for 35-40 minutes.

Pasta with Ricotta Cheese

Serves 4   ☆☆
Preparation and cooking: 20 minutes

12oz (350g) wholemeal pasta rings
salt and freshly ground black pepper
1 tablespoon oil
1oz (25g) butter
8oz (225g) ricotta or curd cheese, chopped
a pinch of grated nutmeg
1 clove garlic, peeled and crushed
2 tablespoons chopped fresh parsley
2oz (50g) grated Parmesan cheese

Put pasta rings in a large pan of boiling salted water, add a tablespoon of oil and cook for 10-15 minutes.
☐ Drain well and transfer to a warmed serving dish.
☐ Add the butter, ricotta or curd cheese, nutmeg, garlic and salt and pepper to taste.
☐ Mix and sprinkle with parsley.
☐ Serve with grated Parmesan cheese.

Macaroni Topkapi; Tagliatelli Bake; Pasta Soufflé.

DESSERTS

The British are well known for their love of puddings and desserts. For many this is the climax to a meal, the finale and the favourite. For others it is a pleasant way to complete a meal. The traditional English pudding, based on sponge, pastry and grains, is no longer served daily in the average household. More efficient heating and a less active lifestyle mean that we now require lighter meals.

However, a special occasion is always a good excuse to take more trouble with a dessert or pudding. Basic ingredients used in desserts include eggs, milk, fruit, liqueurs, nuts, dried fruit, chocolate, honey, sugar and gelatine. The first three are usually purchased on a regular basis and stored in the refrigerator. It is worth keeping a few liqueurs, as they can give a real lift to many desserts. The remaining ingredients should be bought from a supermarket or store with a high turnover to ensure that they have a maximum shelf life. They are best kept in airtight containers in a cool, dark, dry cupboard.

Mousses and moulds provide a light and refreshing end to a meal. They can be based on chocolate, coffee or fruits. For quick and easy preparation, store fruit purées in the freezer to use whenever required.

Custards and cream desserts date back many centuries in English households. They were particularly popular in the farming areas where milk and cream were always available fresh from the dairy. As these desserts can be rather rich, try replacing whole milk with semi-skimmed, and double cream with some whipping or a cream replacement product based on vegetable fats. The latter whip well and have a good flavour in desserts.

Crêpes and pancakes are nutritious desserts as they are made from milk, eggs and flour, and can be served with many different fillings. The batter can be lightened with an extra egg white, or some of the plain flour can be replaced with wholemeal or buckwheat flour. Pancakes keep in the refrigerator for several days or in the freezer for up to three months. They are quickly reheated in a conventional or microwave oven.

Hot puddings may require a little extra planning, but often a complete meal can be cooked in the oven at the same time. Puddings can be rather filling, but some of the old favourites make meal times at home especially enjoyable for everyone.

Baking: Cooking in the oven, without added liquid or fat, by dry direct heat which circulates around the food. This term is usually applied to cakes, pastries and breads, and not to meat or poultry. Food is usually baked on metal trays or containers to conduct heat efficiently, though ovenproof glass and ceramic dishes are popular for puddings and desserts.

Au bain-marie (in a water bath). This is for cooking or keeping dishes hot at a constant temperature by gentle, indirect heat. The food, in its pan or dish, is placed in a larger pan half-filled with hot water and usually put into the oven or else on top of the stove. This is the method for delicate egg-based custards and temperamental hollandaise sauces which curdle or scorch if subjected to fiercer, direct heat.
You can use the same technique on top of the stove for custards or sauces by placing a heatproof basin over a saucepan of boiling water, or using a double-boiler.

Mousses & Moulds

Creamy mousses and light airy soufflés are delightful desserts to make *and* eat. Transform a simple milk jelly into something special by setting it in a mould. You'll turn out a treat!

Orange and Yogurt Jelly

Serves 4 ○
Preparation and cooking: about 25 minutes plus 4 hours chilling

4 large oranges
¼ pint (150ml) water
4oz (100g) caster sugar
1 sachet (1 tablespoon) powdered gelatine
the juice of 1 lemon
¼ pint (150ml) natural yogurt
2 small oranges, sliced, to serve

Remove rind from oranges with a vegetable peeler, then put rind in a pan. Squeeze juice from oranges and measure ½ pint (300ml), making up the volume with extra water.

☐ Pour orange juice into pan, add measured water and sugar and heat gently until sugar has dissolved.

☐ Bring slowly to the boil, then remove from the heat and leave to infuse for at least 10 minutes.

☐ Meanwhile, sprinkle gelatine over lemon juice in a small heatproof bowl, then leave until spongy.

☐ Stand bowl in a pan of hot water and heat gently until gelatine has dissolved, stirring occasionally.

☐ Strain juice mixture to remove rind. Reserve rind. Stir gelatine liquid into juice. Leave until cold, then stir in the yogurt.

☐ Pour into a wetted 1 pint (600ml) mould. Chill in refrigerator for at least 4 hours or until set.

☐ To serve: Turn jelly out on to a serving platter and decorate with orange slices and rind.

Orange and Yogurt Jelly and Fresh Lemon Blancmange.

Strawberry Mousse

This is ideal to make using over-ripe strawberries. It is best eaten on the day it is made.

Serves 4 ☆☆☆
Preparation: 20 minutes plus cooling and chilling

8oz (225g) fresh or frozen strawberries, thawed
2 eggs, separated, plus 1 egg yolk, from size 2 eggs
1oz (25g) caster sugar
¼ pint (150ml) whipping or double cream
a little red colouring (optional)

To finish:
toasted flaked almonds

Process or liquidize the strawberries and then pass through a nylon sieve to remove the pips.
☐ Put the purée, 3 egg yolks and caster sugar in a heatproof bowl and stand over a pan of hot water. Heat gently, whisking constantly, until thick enough to leave a trail.
☐ Remove from the heat and whisk until cold.
☐ Lightly whip the cream and fold into the strawberry mixture.
☐ In a separate bowl whisk the egg whites to soft peaks and fold into the strawberry mixture.
☐ Spoon into a serving bowl or individual dishes and chill.
☐ Serve decorated with toasted flaked almonds.

Country Cream

Serves 4 ☆☆☆
Preparation: 15 minutes plus chilling
Cooking: 1¼-1½ hours

---

1 pint (600ml) milk
2oz (50g) sugar
4 eggs, size 2, beaten

To finish:
3 tablespoons raspberry or apricot jam
7 fl oz (200ml) whipping cream
1oz (25g) dark cooking chocolate, grated

Set the oven to 325F (160C) gas 3.
☐ Put the milk and sugar in a saucepan and heat gently to just below boiling point.
☐ Pour on to the beaten eggs and then strain into a 2 pint (1.2 litre) ovenproof dish. Cover with foil and stand in a bain marie or baking tin with sufficient water to come half-way up the dish.
☐ Bake for 1¼-1½ hours until the custard is set. Allow to cool.
☐ Beat the jam until soft and spread over the surface of the custard.
☐ Whip the cream and spread a little over the surface. Put the remainder in a forcing bag fitted with a star pipe and decorate the edge of the dish.
☐ Top with the grated chocolate and chill until required.

Lemon Mousse Tart

Serves 6 ☆☆☆
Preparation and cooking: about 15 minutes plus chilling

The biscuit crumb case:
4oz (100g) butter
8oz (225g) gingernut biscuits, finely crushed

The filling:
1 sachet (1 tablespoon) gelatine
3 tablespoons cold water
the grated rind and juice of one lemon
2 eggs, size 2, separated
2oz (50g) caster sugar

To finish:
¼ pint (150ml) whipping cream
3 slices of lemon, cut into butterflies

First make the biscuit crumb case: Melt the butter in a pan over a low heat and stir in the crumbs. Mix well and use to line a 9in (22cm) loose-bottomed flan tin. Chill.
☐ Meanwhile, make the filling: Mix the gelatine and the water together in a heatproof bowl with the lemon rind and juice, caster sugar and egg yolks. Heat over a pan of hot water, stirring, until almost at boiling point. Remove from the heat and allow to cool and thicken.
☐ Whisk the egg whites to stiff peaks and gradually add the sugar. Whisk again until glossy.
☐ Fold in the lemon mixture and spoon into the biscuit case.
☐ Chill until required. Serve decorated with whipped cream and lemon butterflies.

Fresh Lemon Blancmange

Most children like blancmange, and it's a quick and easy dessert to prepare for them at teatime. The tangy taste of blancmange made with fresh lemons is particularly good.

Serves 4 ☆
Preparation and cooking: 10 minutes plus chilling

---

4 tablespoons cornflour
2oz (50g) caster sugar
1 pint (600ml) milk
a knob of butter
the finely grated rind of 1 lemon
the juice of 2 lemons
a few drops of yellow food colouring (optional)

Mix the cornflour and sugar to a paste with a little of the milk in a large heatproof bowl.
☐ Heat the remaining milk to just below boiling point, then stir gradually into the cornflour paste. Return the mixture to the rinsed-out pan, bring to the boil, then lower the heat.
☐ Add the butter and simmer for 3 minutes until thick, stirring constantly.
☐ Remove from the heat and leave to cool for a few minutes, then add the lemon rind and gradually stir in the lemon juice and food colouring, if using, until they are evenly blended.
☐ Pour the blancmange into a wetted 1 pint (600ml) mould. Cool, then chill in the refrigerator until set. Serve chilled.

Country Cream, Strawberry Mousse and Lemon Mousse Tart.

Coeurs à la Crème

Small heart-shaped moulds are traditionally used for making this dessert but clean yogurt cartons, pierced with a few holes in the base, serve the purpose just as well.

Gooseberry Soufflé

To dissolve the gelatine: sprinkle over the water in a small heatproof bowl and allow to become spongy. Stand the bowl in a pan of hot water and heat gently until the gelatine has dissolved.

Coeurs à la Crème

Serves 4-6 ☆☆☆
Preparation: 25-30 minutes plus
6-8 hours chilling

8oz (225g) cottage cheese
a pinch of salt
$\frac{1}{2}$ pint (300ml) double or whipping cream

To serve:
$\frac{1}{2}$ pint (300ml) double or whipping cream
strawberries or raspberries
granulated sugar

Rinse 4-6 heart-shaped moulds or yogurt cartons in cold water; do not dry them.
☐ Put the cottage cheese into a clean piece of muslin or thin cloth and squeeze to remove as much excess moisture from the cheese as you can.
☐ Put the cheese into a bowl with the salt and mix together.
☐ Press the cheese through a sieve. Lightly whip the double cream and stir in the sieved cheese.
☐ Spoon the cheese and cream

mixture into the moulds or yogurt cartons and stand them on a tray to catch any liquid that drains off. Chill for 6-8 hours.
☐ To serve: Unmold and serve with cream, fruit and sugar.

Gooseberry Soufflé

Serves 6 ☆☆☆
Preparation and cooking: about
45 minutes plus 4 hours chilling

8oz (225g) fresh gooseberries, prepared
3 eggs, size 2, separated
4oz (100g) caster sugar
1 sachet (1 tablespoon) powdered gelatine,
   dissolved in 4 tablespoons water
¼ teaspoon almond essence
¼ pint (150ml) double cream, softly whipped
whipped cream and ratafias to decorate

Prepare a 5in (13cm) soufflé dish: Cut a strip of double greaseproof paper 3in (8cm) higher than the dish. Tie securely around the dish, then lightly brush the inside of the paper above the dish with oil.
☐ Put the gooseberries into a heavy-based pan and cook for 10-15 minutes over a gentle heat until soft. Rub fruit through a fine sieve and measure ¼ pint (150ml) of purée.
☐ Put the egg yolks and caster sugar in a heatproof bowl standing over a pan of gently simmering water. Whisk until thick and creamy and mixture leaves a trail. Remove bowl from the heat and whisk occasionally until cool.
☐ Cool the gelatine slightly (see sidelines) and beat into the gooseberry purée with the almond essence.
☐ Combine the gooseberry mixture with the whisked egg mixture.
☐ Fold the cream into the soufflé mixture.
☐ Whisk the egg whites until stiff and fold into the soufflé mixture.
☐ Pour mixture into prepared soufflé dish and chill for 4 hours.
☐ To serve: decorate with whipped cream and ratafias.

Coeurs à la Crème with raspberries.

Custards & Creams

Many mouthwatering desserts are either cream or custard based and so have wide appeal. Try any of the following cool concoctions – they'll go down a treat after a substantial meal.

Gooseberry Yogurt Fool

Serves 4 ☆

Preparation and cooking: 15 minutes plus cooling and chilling

---

1lb (500g) gooseberries, topped and tailed
¼ pint (150ml) milk
1 tablespoon custard powder
½ tablespoon sugar
5oz (141g) carton natural yogurt
a few drops green colouring (optional)

To finish:
1oz (25g) plain chocolate, grated

Put the prepared gooseberries into a pan with enough water to cover the base of the pan. Simmer over a low heat until fruit is soft.

☐ Pass through a sieve or process until smooth. Allow to cool.

☐ Meanwhile, make the custard by mixing a little of the milk with custard powder in a bowl. Heat the remaining milk to just below boiling point. Stir slowly into the custard powder with the sugar.

☐ Return to the pan and cook until thick, stirring constantly. Allow to cool.

☐ Combine the gooseberry purée, cold custard, yogurt and a few drops of colouring to make the fool a pale green colour if liked.

☐ Test for sweetness and, if liked, add a little extra sugar.

☐ Pour the fool into a bowl or individual serving dishes and chill in the refrigerator.

☐ Serve chilled, decorated with grated chocolate.

Tip: This is an ideal recipe for using frozen fruit purée. Make the purée and freeze when fresh fruit is in abundance for use later in the year.

Winter Prune Fool

Fruit fools are usually associated with soft summer fruits, but there is no reason why they cannot be made in the winter with dried fruit. Dried apricots or figs could be substituted for the prunes used here.

Serves 4

Preparation and cooking: 20 minutes plus soaking and chilling

---

4oz (100g) pitted prunes
2oz (50g) caster sugar
the juice of 1 orange
2 tablespoons redcurrant jelly
1 tablespoon custard powder
¼ pint (150ml) milk
¼ pint (150ml) whipping or double cream
1-2oz (25-50g) chopped nuts, walnuts and almonds to finish

Place the prunes in a bowl and cover with cold water. Allow to stand overnight.

☐ Drain the prunes, then chop the flesh roughly. Put in a pan with the sugar, orange juice and redcurrant jelly, then heat gently for 10 minutes until soft, stirring occasionally.

☐ Meanwhile, make the custard by mixing a little of the milk with the custard powder in a bowl. Heat the remaining milk to just below boiling point, then stir slowly into the custard powder.

☐ Return mixture to the pan and cook until thick, stirring constantly. Allow to cool.

☐ Reduce the prune mixture to a smooth purée in a food processor or liquidizer, then fold into the cooled custard.

☐ Whip the cream until thick, then fold into the prune custard until evenly blended.

☐ Spoon into the individual glasses or bowls, then chill in the refrigerator until firm.

☐ Sprinkle with the nuts. Serve chilled.

Tipsy Freezer Trifle

Serves 6

Preparation: 25 minutes plus 5-6 hours freezing

---

1 × 4oz (100g) packet trifle sponges or stale sponge cake
4 tablespoons raspberry jam
¼ pint (150ml) sherry
3oz (75g) ground almonds
2oz (50g) ratafia or macaroon biscuits, crumbled
3 tablespoons double cream
1 pint (600ml) hot custard

To serve:
¼ pint (150ml) double cream, whipped
glacé cherries
angelica leaves
toasted almonds to decorate

Line a straight-sided china or freezer-proof glass serving dish with foil, leaving a border just above the rim of the bowl.

☐ Halve the trifle sponges and spread them with the raspberry jam. Cut each sponge into 4 and arrange in the bottom of the dish.

☐ Pour over sherry and sprinkle almonds and biscuits on top.

☐ Stir the cream into the hot custard and pour the mixture over the trifle. Cover the dish with cling film to prevent a skin from forming while the custard is cooling.

☐ To freeze: Allow to go cold, then open freeze for 5-6 hours. When frozen, lift out of the dish by the foil border and place in a polythene bag. Seal and return to freezer for up to 4 months.

☐ To serve: Peel the foil away from the frozen trifle and return to the original dish. Allow to thaw at room temperature for at least 6 hours. Decorate the top with whipped cream, glacé cherries, angelica leaves and toasted almonds.

Variation: Make the trifle but omit lining the bowl with foil. Serve immediately without freezing.

Mango and Lemon Cream

Fresh peaches may be used in place of mangoes but the flavour will not be quite so distinctive. You will need 4-6 peaches to make up the required weight.

Peach Brûlee

This recipe is equally delicious with other fresh fruits. Try plums, strawberries or a fruit salad mixture.

Old-fashioned Junket

Rennet can be bought in liquid form from chemist shops. It is colourless and comes both unflavoured and flavoured. Junket is formed when warm milk heats with an enzyme in the rennet. If the milk is too hot, the enzyme will become inactive and the junket will not set.

Mango and Lemon Cream

Serves 4-6 ☆☆
Preparation and cooking: 30 minutes plus overnight chilling

---

1 sachet (1 tablespoon) powdered gelatine
the juice of 1 lemon
2 ripe fresh mangoes (about 8oz (225g) each), peeled and stoned
2oz (50g) caster sugar
¼ pint (150ml) double or whipping cream
2 egg whites from size 2 eggs

Sprinkle the gelatine over the lemon juice in a small heatproof bowl then leave until spongy. Stand the bowl in a pan of hot water and heat gently until the gelatine has dissolved, stirring occasionally. Leave to cool completely.

☐ Meanwhile, put the mango flesh and caster sugar in a liquidizer and blend to a smooth purée.

☐ Stir the cooled gelatine liquid into the mango purée, then leave the mixture until just beginning to set.

☐ Whip the cream until it just holds its shape, then fold into the purée. Beat the egg whites until stiff, then fold in until evenly blended.

☐ Pour the mixture into a wetted 1½ pint (900ml) mould, then chill in the refrigerator overnight until set.

☐ To serve: Loosen the edge of the cream with a sharp knife, then turn the cream out on to a serving plate. Serve chilled.

Peach Brûlée

Serves 4-6 ☆☆☆
Preparation and cooking: 15 minutes plus 2 hours chilling

---

6 fresh peaches, peeled, halved and stoned
½ teaspoon ground cinnamon
½ pint (300ml) double or whipping cream, chilled
1oz (25g) icing sugar, sifted
6oz (175g) demerara sugar

Pre-heat grill to moderate.

☐ Put the peach halves, cut side down, in a single layer in a shallow heatproof dish. Sprinkle with the cinnamon.

☐ Whip the cream and icing sugar together until thick, then spread over the peaches.

☐ Sprinkle the demerara sugar over the cream to cover it completely, then grill for 10 minutes until the topping is dark and bubbling.

☐ Remove from the heat, leave until cold, then chill in the refrigerator for at least 2 hours before serving.
Variation: If you like the flavour of molasses, this simple dessert can be made with dark soft brown sugar instead of the demerara sugar that is used here.

Old-fashioned Junket

Serves 4 ☆
Preparation: 5 minutes plus 1 hour setting

---

1 pint (600ml) fresh milk
1 tablespoon caster sugar
1 teaspoon essence of rennet
1 egg, size 2, beaten
¼ teaspoon grated nutmeg

Heat the milk to 100F (38C) on a sugar thermometer, then pour into a dish.

☐ Stir in the sugar, rennet and beaten egg, then sprinkle the top with the grated nutmeg.

☐ Cover with a clean cloth and leave in a cool place for about 1 hour until cool and set. The setting time will vary according to the room temperature and time of year.

☐ Serve at room temperature.
Variation: To make this dessert a little more special, leave the junket plain until set, cover the surface with ¼ pint (150ml) lightly whipped cream then sprinkle with the nutmeg just before serving. Junket should *not* be chilled in the refrigerator.

Mango and Lemon Cream, Peach Brûlée and Old-fashioned Junket.

Caramel Cream with Fruits

Vanilla sugar is available in sachets from most large supermarkets and some delicatessens. Alternatively, you can make your own by burying a vanilla pod in a jar of caster sugar. Leave it for at least one week before using.

Scots Flummery

This is another quick and easy dessert to make but it is also very rich.

Caramel Cream with Fruits

Serves 8   ★★☆

Preparation and cooking: 1½ hours plus chilling

8oz (225g) granulated sugar
½ pint (300ml) water
1 pint (600ml) milk
½ pint (300ml) whipping or double cream
4 eggs, size 2
2 egg yolks from size 2 eggs
2oz (50g) vanilla sugar

To serve:
2 oranges, peeled, divided into segments and halved
4oz (100g) black grapes, halved and seeded
1 large banana, peeled and thinly sliced

Set the oven to 350F (180C) gas 4.

☐ Put the granulated sugar and water in a pan and heat gently until the sugar has dissolved. Bring to the boil, then boil rapidly, without stirring, until thick and golden brown in colour.

☐ Pour the caramel immediately into a 2 pint (1.2 litre) ring or kugelhopf mould, tipping the mould so that the caramel covers the bottom and sides. Set aside.

☐ Put the milk and cream in a heavy pan and bring slowly to just below boiling point. Put the eggs, egg yolks and vanilla sugar in a bowl and stir well.

☐ Stir in the scalded milk and cream, then strain the mixture into the mould.

☐ Stand mould in a bain marie or a roasting tin half-filled with hot water, cover loosely with foil, then bake in the oven for 1 hour 10 minutes or until set.

☐ Remove the mould from the bain marie and leave until cold, then chill in the refrigerator for several hours, preferably overnight.

☐ To serve: Loosen the edges of the caramel cream with a sharp knife, then turn out on to a large deep serving dish. Mix the fruits together, then pile them into the centre of the caramel cream. Serve chilled.

Little Cream Pots

Serves 6-8   ★★☆

Preparation and cooking: 30 minutes

1 pint (600ml) milk
2oz (50g) caster sugar
4 egg yolks
1 whole egg
½ teaspoon vanilla essence
1 teaspoon instant coffee powder
1 tablespoon warm water

Set the oven to 350F (180C) gas 4.

☐ Scald the milk with the sugar.

☐ Lightly beat the egg yolks with the whole egg.

☐ Add the milk and vanilla, then strain and divide into two equal parts.

☐ Flavour one part with the coffee dissolved in the warm water; and leave the other half plain.

☐ Pour carefully into 8 little pots. Stand in a shallow baking tin and fill the tin with hot water to come half-way up the pots. Cover and bake for 12-20 minutes or until set.

Scots Flummery

Serves 4   ★★☆

Preparation and cooking: 15 minutes plus soaking and cooling

2oz (50g) fine oatmeal
4 tablespoons whisky
2 tablespoons thick honey
½ pint (300ml) double cream
4-8 shortbread fingers to serve

Put the oatmeal, whisky and honey in a heavy pan and stir well. Leave to soak for about 15 minutes.

☐ Heat gently for about 1 minute until thick, stirring constantly with a wooden spoon. Transfer to a bowl and leave to cool.

☐ Pour the cream on to the oatmeal, then beat gently until thick and evenly blended. Spoon into 4 individual glasses, then press 1 or 2 shortbread fingers into the top of each or hand the shortbread separately. Serve chilled with fresh raspberries.

Crêpes

Crêpes or pancakes are delightful to eat and, contrary to opinion, they are simple to make. All you need is flour, eggs and a water or milk batter plus a delectable variety of flavourings and fillings. Once you perfect the pancake-making skill you can transform them into lacy French crêpes, flavoured with liqueur and soaked in syrup; into gâteaux filled with fruit; or, for an extra taste of luxury, and some drama, into flaming desserts to be served at the table. Also, by adding yeast and chocolate you can turn pancakes into the Russian delicacy blinis.

Gâteau de Crêpes aux Abricots

Apricot pancake gâteau

Serves 6   ☆ ☆ ☆
Preparation: about 35 minutes plus 30 minutes standing
Cooking: 35-45 minutes

4oz (100g) plain flour
a pinch of salt
1 egg, size 2
½ pint (300ml) milk
oil for greasing

The filling:
2-3oz (50-75g) sugar, or to taste
¼ pint (150ml) water
4 tablespoons brandy
2lb (1kg) fresh apricots, halved and stoned
2oz (50g) ratafias

pouring cream to serve

Sift the flour and salt into a bowl. Make a well in the centre, add the egg, then gradually whisk in the milk until the batter is smooth.

☐ Make the apricot filling: Put 2oz (50g) sugar in a heavy-based pan with the water. Heat gently until the sugar has dissolved, then stir in half the brandy. Add the apricots and simmer gently for 10-15 minutes or until they are just tender.

☐ Remove apricots with a slotted spoon, reserving the syrup. Leave the apricots to cool slightly, then process or liquidize to a purée, reserving 6 for decoration.

☐ Crush the ratafias finely, reserving a few whole ones.

☐ Make the crêpes: Heat a little oil in a 6in (15cm) crêpe or frying-pan until very hot. Ladle in enough batter to cover the bottom of the pan and rotate to coat the bottom as thinly as possible. Cook for 1-2 minutes until set, then turn the crêpe over and cook for 1 minute on the other side.

☐ Slide the crêpe out of the pan on to a warm plate and cover with a sheet of greaseproof paper. Keep warm while making the remaining 7 crêpes, greasing the pan when necessary.

☐ To assemble the gâteau: Heat the apricot purée and the reserved

apricot syrup gently in separate pans. Taste the purée for sweetness and add more sugar if necessary. Place 1 crêpe on a serving platter and spread with about 1 tablespoon hot apricot purée. Sprinkle a little of the crushed ratafias over the top. Repeat these layers until all the pancakes, purée and crushed ratafias are used, finishing with a pancake.

☐ Decorate the top of the gâteau with the reserved whole apricots and ratafias. Stir the remaining brandy into the hot apricot syrup. Serve the gâteau immediately, cut into wedges, with the syrup and cream handed in separate jugs.

Gâteau de Crêpes aux Abricots

Pancake Parcels

Pancake Parcels

Once filled, these pancakes can be frozen for up to 6 months. Pack in rigid containers, cover and freeze. To serve: Place frozen parcels in a large frying-pan with the sauce and cook, turning, for 10-15 minutes until crisp and heated through.

Pancake Parcels

Serves 4 ☆☆
Preparation: 20 minutes
Cooking: 25 minutes

4oz (100g) plain flour
¼ teaspoon salt
1 egg, size 2
½ pint (300ml) milk
oil for frying

The filling:
3 bananas
juice of 1 lemon
2 tablespoons apricot jam

The sauce:
4 tablespoons orange juice
2 tablespoons soft brown sugar
1oz (25g) butter or margarine
½ teaspoon ground cinnamon

pouring cream to serve

Sift the flour and salt into a bowl. Make a well in the centre and add the egg, then gradually whisk in the milk until the batter is smooth.

☐ Make the pancakes: Heat a little oil in a frying-pan until very hot. Pour in a few spoonfuls of batter, tilting the pan so that it spreads evenly, and cook over high heat until golden brown. Turn over the pancake and cook the underneath until golden brown. Remove from the pan and keep warm while cooking the remaining batter to make 8 pancakes in all.

☐ Make the filling: Peel the bananas, then mash the flesh with the lemon juice and jam. Divide the filling equally between the pancakes, then fold each pancake around the filling to make a parcel.

☐ Make the sauce: Make the orange juice up to ¼ pint (150ml) with water, then pour into a large frying-pan. Add the remaining ingredients and bring to the boil, stirring

Pancake Parcels

constantly. Boil for 5 minutes until reduced, then lower the heat.

☐ Arrange the pancake parcels in a single layer in the pan, then heat through for about 10 minutes, spooning the sauce over the pancakes from time to time.

☐ Serve hot, with cream.

Crêpes à la Crème

Serves 6-8   ☆☆☆
Preparation: 25 minutes plus cooling
Cooking: 30 minutes

3oz (75g) plain flour
¼ teaspoon salt
2oz (50g) caster sugar
4 eggs, size 2
about 1 pint (600ml) milk
2oz (50g) unsalted butter, melted
2 tablespoons brandy
oil and butter for greasing

The filling:
4 egg yolks from size 2 eggs
2½oz (65g) sugar
1½oz (40g) vanilla sugar
½ pint (300ml) double cream
2 tablespoons fresh breadcrumbs
7oz (200g) walnuts, finely chopped
8oz (225g) grated chocolate

whipped cream to serve

Sift the flour, salt and sugar into a bowl. Make a well in the centre, gradually add the eggs, then whisk in the milk until the batter is smooth. Stir in the melted butter and brandy. The batter should have the consistency of single cream; add more milk if necessary.

☐ Make the crêpes: Heat a 6in (15cm) pancake or omelette pan over a medium heat with a small amount of oil. Ladle in enough batter just to cover the bottom of the pan and rotate to coat the bottom as thinly as possible. Pour out any excess batter and trim away the trail.

☐ After about 10 seconds, when the surface of the crêpe appears dry and the edges free themselves from the sides, turn the crêpe over. Cook for a few seconds and slide the crêpe on to a plate. Repeat until all the batter is used. If the surface of the pan looks dry, wipe with an oiled piece of kitchen paper.

☐ Make the filling: Beat the egg yolks and sugars until pale and creamy. Beat in the cream and mix well.

☐ Set oven to 325F (160C) gas 3.

☐ Butter a 7in (18cm) cake tin and sprinkle it with the breadcrumbs. Place the crêpes in the tin in layers, spooning some of the filling and sprinkling some of the walnuts and chocolate over each layer. Finish with a crêpe and cover with a round of buttered greaseproof paper.

☐ Bake for 30 minutes or until the filling has set. Remove and leave to cool for 15-20 minutes. Turn out and serve with whipped cream.

Crêpes Soufflés

This is an elegant and exciting show-piece for everyone to enjoy at the table. It is simple and quick to prepare if the crêpes are made in advance and then reheated when they are required.

Serves 6   ☆☆☆
Preparation: 30 minutes
Cooking: 8 minutes

4oz (100g) plain flour
a pinch of salt
1oz (25g) caster sugar
2 eggs, size 2
about ½ pint (300ml) milk
1oz (25g) unsalted butter, melted
oil and butter for greasing

The filling:
4 fl oz (120ml) milk
1oz (25g) vanilla sugar
2oz (50g) lightly roasted almonds, finely chopped
2oz (50g) plain chocolate, broken into pieces
1 tablespoon plain flour, mixed with 2-4 tablespoons cold milk
a knob of unsalted butter
3 egg yolks from size 2 eggs
4 egg whites from size 2 eggs, stiffly beaten

whipped cream to serve

Sift the flour, salt and sugar into a bowl. Make a well in the centre, add the eggs, then gradually whisk in the milk until the batter is smooth. Stir in the melted butter. The batter should have the consistency of single cream; add more milk if necessary.

☐ Make the crêpes: Heat a 6in (15cm) pancake or omelette pan over a medium heat with a small amount of oil. Ladle in enough batter just to cover the bottom of the pan and rotate to coat the bottom as thinly as possible. Pour out any excess batter and trim away the trail.

☐ After about 10 seconds, when the surface of the crêpe appears dry and the edges free themselves from the sides, turn the crêpe over. Cook for a few seconds and slide the crêpe on to a plate. Repeat until all the batter is used. If the surface of the pan looks dry, wipe with an oiled piece of kitchen paper.

☐ Make the filling: Bring the milk, vanilla sugar and almonds just to the boil in a small saucepan. Add the chocolate pieces and the flour to the milk mixture; stir until the chocolate melts and the mixture is smooth.

☐ Remove from the heat and leave to cool for a few minutes, then whisk in the butter and the egg yolks.

☐ Gently fold a quarter of the egg whites into the chocolate mixture and pour this over the remaining egg whites. Gently fold the mixtures together.

☐ Set oven to 400F (200C) gas 6.

☐ Butter a large ovenproof dish. Place a generous spoonful of the soufflé mixture on to one half of each crêpe. Fold over the other half and place on the dish. Rest a piece of kitchen foil lightly over the top of each crêpe to prevent it from burning.

☐ Bake the crêpes in the oven for 8 minutes.

☐ Serve the crêpes with whipped cream.

Tip: As you make each crêpe, layer it between sheets of kitchen paper. Allow to cool before wrapping in cling film. Make early in the day and fill just before baking or, if preferred, cool the crêpes, layer between greaseproof paper, and wrap in foil to freeze. Defrost before filling and continue as for fresh.

Crêpes à la Crème; Chocolate Blinis; Crêpe Soufflé.

Blinis

Blinis are traditionally served in Russia with soured cream and caviar. They are small pancakes made from yeast batter, similar to drop scones and have been adapted for a dessert by adding cocoa powder.

Chocolate Blinis

Serves 6-8   ☆ ☆

Preparation: 25-30 minutes plus 3½ hours rising

Cooking: 10-15 minutes

1½ tablespoons warm water
1½ teaspoons dried yeast
1½oz (40g) buckwheat or wholewheat flour
2oz (50g) plain flour
1oz (25g) cocoa powder
¼ pint (150ml) warm milk
2 eggs, size 2, separated
¼ teaspoon salt
2oz (50g) caster sugar
1oz (25g) unsalted butter, melted
5 fl oz (142ml) soured cream

Mix the warm water and yeast and leave for 15 minutes.

☐ Sift ½oz (15g) of the buckwheat or wholewheat flour, all of the plain flour and cocoa powder together into a mixing bowl.

☐ Make a well in the centre and add the yeast and 3½ fl oz (100ml) of the warm milk. Stir to combine the ingredients and beat until smooth and creamy.

☐ Cover with cling film and leave to rise for about 1 hour or until doubled in bulk.

☐ Knock back and stir in the remaining buckwheat or wholewheat flour. Cover with cling film and leave in a warm place for about 2 hours.

☐ Stir the batter, add the remaining milk, egg yolks, salt, sugar, melted butter and 2½ tablespoons of the soured cream. Stir until thoroughly blended.

☐ Whisk the egg whites to stiff peaks. Gently fold ⅓ into the batter, then fold in the rest. Cover with cling film and leave for 30 minutes.

☐ Make blinis: Heat the butter in a heavy frying-pan over a medium heat. Place spoonfuls of batter in the frying-pan, leaving enough room between each pancake to turn them. Cook the pancakes about 2 minutes on each side or until lightly coloured.

☐ Serve hot with the remaining soured cream.

Puff & Choux Pastry Desserts

Desserts made with puff and choux pastry are really rather special. They are light, crisp, richly flavoured, with an attractive appearance and a melt-in-the-mouth texture. Puff pastry can be used to create dramatic gâteaux, pretty plaits, fruit-filled tranches and pies; choux pastry can be made into creamy puffs and éclairs. Making these two types of pastry requires just a little more skill (and patience) than other pastry, but once this is perfected the most delightful desserts can be produced. If short of time, ready-made frozen puff pastry is a useful standby, and it is well worth keeping a supply in the freezer. (For more delicious puff and choux pastry recipes see Pastry chapter, pages 78-82.)

Torta di Noci e Canditi

Walnut and candied peel pie

Mascherpone is a soft, creamy, bland Italian cheese whose flavour closely resembles that of clotted cream. If you find it difficult to buy, use a good quality full-fat soft cheese – most supermarkets and some food stores sell it either loose or pre-packed.

Serves 6-8 ☆☆☆
Preparation: 20 minutes
Cooking: 35-40 minutes

1lb (450g) frozen puff pastry, thawed
6oz (175g) Mascherpone cheese or any full-fat soft cheese
2oz (50g) caster sugar
2 tablespoons apricot jam
3 egg yolks from size 2 eggs
2oz (50g) walnuts, chopped
4oz (100g) chopped candied mixed peel
the finely grated rind of 1 lemon

To decorate:
2 tablespoons coarsely chopped walnuts
icing sugar

Set the oven to 400F (200C) gas 6.
☐ Roll out the puff pastry fairly thinly. Line a 9in (23cm) fluted flan tin with half the pastry.
☐ Beat the soft cheese with the sugar, apricot jam, 2 of the egg yolks, chopped walnuts, peel and lemon rind.
☐ Spoon into the pastry case.

☐ Cover the filling with the remaining pastry, trimming off the edges. Pinch the edges together to seal.
☐ Beat the remaining egg yolk with a little water and brush over the top of the pie to glaze.
☐ Bake for 35-40 minutes until risen and deep golden brown.
☐ Sprinkle with the walnuts and dust with icing sugar and serve hot or cold.

Torta di Noci e Canditi
The Italians love desserts but rarely make them at home. They reserve the pleasure for when they are in restaurants and cafés, where they consume delicious concoctions such as this, combining creamy cheese, nuts and candied peel in a puff pastry case.

Torta di Noci e Canditi

Paris-Brest

This gâteau, named after the famous cycle race, is filled with a rich Crème au Beurre Meringuée flavoured with praline. It can be served for tea-time, buffet parties or dinner parties and is best eaten the day it is prepared. If left overnight, the crunchy texture of the praline in the filling is lost as the sugar coating dissolves.

❄ Freeze ahead

Make your choux rings in advance and freeze them. They will keep for up to 6 months wrapped in polythene bags. To crisp after thawing, put on a baking sheet and warm through in an oven preheated to 425F (220C) gas 7 for 2 minutes. Cool and fill as before.

Gâteau Pithiviers

The town of Pithiviers in the Orleanais area of France is renowned for several gastronomic specialities. Traditionally the surface is scored like the spokes of a wheel.

Paris-Brest

Serves 6-8 ☆☆☆
Preparation: 40 minutes
Cooking: 30-35 minutes

18oz (500g) Basic Choux Pastry
1 egg, size 2, beaten
1oz (25g) flaked almonds
icing sugar for dusting
oil for greasing

The filling:
2 egg whites from size 2 eggs
4½oz (140g) icing sugar, sifted
8½oz (240g) unsalted butter, at room temperature
4 tablespoons coarsely crushed Praline

Set the oven to 425F (220C) gas 7. Lightly grease a baking sheet.
☐ Place the choux pastry in a forcing bag fitted with a large star pipe and pipe the pastry in a continuous line to form a thick 8in (20cm) ring.
☐ Brush with the beaten egg and sprinkle the almonds over the top. Bake for 10 minutes. Reduce the oven temperature to 375F (190C) gas 5 and continue cooking for a further 20-25 minutes until the ring is golden brown and crisp.
☐ Remove from the oven, cut the ring in half, making 2 circles, and cool on a wire tray.
☐ Meanwhile, make the filling: Put the egg whites and icing sugar into a large bowl and mix together.
☐ Place over a pan of hot water on a gentle heat and whisk until the mixture is stiff and stands in peaks. Remove from the heat and continue whisking until it is completely cold.
☐ Cut the softened butter into small pieces. Whisk into the meringue a piece at a time. Continue whisking until the mixture is smooth and then fold in the crushed praline. Place in a forcing bag fitted with a ½in (1cm) plain pipe and pipe into the bottom half of the pastry ring.
☐ Cover with the other pastry ring and sift icing sugar liberally over the the top.
☐ Serve on the day of making.

Gâteau Pithiviers

Serves 6 ☆☆☆
Preparation: 25 minutes plus
10 minutes chilling
Cooking: 30 minutes

2oz (50g) butter
2oz (50g) caster sugar
1 egg yolk from size 2 egg
2oz (50g) ground almonds
13oz (375g) frozen puff pastry, thawed
beaten egg to glaze
icing sugar for dusting

cream to serve

Set the oven to 425F (220C) gas 7.
☐ Cream the butter with the sugar. Add the egg yolk and mix well, then stir in the ground almonds.
☐ Roll out the pastry to a thin rectangle and cut out 2 circles, each 7in (18cm) in size.
☐ Place one of the pastry circles on a wetted baking sheet and pile the almond mixture into the centre, leaving a 1in (2.5cm) edge.
☐ Roll out the pastry trimmings and cut a thin strip ¼in (5mm) wide: Brush the border of the almond filled pastry circle with beaten egg and place the pastry strip around the edge. Brush with the beaten egg and place the second pastry circle over the top of the almond filling.
☐ Crimp the edges of the gâteau to seal and, with the back of a knife, scallop the edges. Using the point of a knife, make a small hole in the centre to allow the steam to escape. Prick the surface with a fork and brush lightly with beaten egg, taking care not to brush over the sealed edges as this will prevent the pastry from rising.
☐ Chill for 10 minutes.
☐ Meanwhile, set oven to 425F (220C) gas 7.
☐ Bake pastry for 25 minutes until well risen and golden brown.
☐ Sift icing sugar over top of pastry and return to oven for a further 5 minutes. Dust lightly again before serving warm with cream.

Apple and Blackberry Plait

Serves 6-8   ☆☆☆
Preparation: 25 minutes
Cooking: 35-40 minutes

13oz (375g) frozen puff pastry, thawed
8oz (225g) blackberries
1 large cooking apple, peeled, cored and
   diced
1 tablespoon caster sugar
2oz (50g) flaked almonds
beaten egg to glaze
1 tablespoon demerara sugar

cream to serve

Set the oven to 400F (200C) gas 6.
☐ Roll out the pastry to form a
9in × 12in (23cm × 30cm) rectangle.
☐ With the rectangle upright, make
diagonal slashes at ¾in (2cm)
intervals down both sides, leaving
a 4in (10cm) panel down the centre.
☐ Mix together the blackberries,
apple, caster sugar and almonds, and
spread evenly down the centre panel.
☐ Turn in the 2 ends of the pastry,
then plait the pastry strips over the
filling, securing the last two strips
under the plait with a little beaten
egg.
☐ Place on a baking sheet, brush
with beaten egg and sprinkle with
demerara sugar.
☐ Bake for 15-20 minutes, until
well risen, then reduce the heat to
350F (180C) gas 4, and continue
cooking for 20 minutes.
☐ Serve with cream.
Variations: For Apple and
Mincemeat Plait omit the sugar and
replace the blackberries with
mincemeat.
● For Apple and Raspberry Plait
replace the blackberries with fresh
raspberries.
● For Apple and Apricot Plait
replace the blackberries with 10oz
(275g) fresh apricots, halved and
stoned.

*Apple and Blackberry Plait; Gâteau
Pithiviers.*

Apple and Blackberry Plait

Brambles (wild blackberries) are to be seen
from September to October. If they appear
any later they are not really worth picking.
Cultivated blackberries will keep their flavour
longer. They are particularly good cooked
with apples as this fruit adds to the texture
and accentuates the delicious acid flavour of
the blackberries.

Tranche aux Fruits

The centre piece of pastry which is removed to make the border can be marked in a lattice pattern and cooked on a second baking tray. Use as a lid for the tranche, dusted with icing sugar. Alternatively cut out small shapes, bake and use for decorations. If you do not have a large enough plate for this dessert, place it on a wooden board or tray to serve.

Ring the changes

Strawberries are excellent to use for the tranche but other fruits such as grapes, orange segments, raspberries, or fresh or canned pineapple can also be used. An attractive way to arrange the fruit is in lines of contrasting colours. Use redcurrant glaze for red fruits and apricot jam for other fruits.

Choux aux Fraises

For a special dessert macerate the sliced strawberries in a little orange liqueur before filling the buns. Drain the fruit and add the liqueur to the whipped cream.

Choux aux Fraises

Makes 8   ☆☆☆
Preparation: 1 hour plus chilling
Cooking: 40 minutes

18oz (500g) Basic Choux Pastry
lard for greasing

The sauce:
¼ pint (150ml) milk
2 egg yolks from size 2 eggs
1½oz (40g) caster sugar
½ teaspoon vanilla essence
8oz (225g) strawberries, hulled and puréed
¼ pint (142ml) double cream, whipped

To finish:
4 tablespoons double or whipping cream
8oz (225g) strawberries

Set the oven to 425F (220C) gas 7. Grease a baking sheet.
☐ Place the choux pastry in a forcing bag fitted with a ½in (1cm) plain pipe. Pipe 8 large oval shapes on to the baking sheet.
☐ Bake for 15 minutes. Reduce oven temperature to 375F (190C) gas 5 and continue cooking for a further 25 minutes until well risen, crisp and golden brown.
☐ Cut the choux ovals across in half before placing on a wire tray to cool.
☐ Make the sauce: Warm the milk in a saucepan.
☐ Cream the egg yolks, sugar and vanilla essence together. Pour the warm milk on to the mixture and stir together.
☐ Return mixture to the pan and stir constantly until thickened sufficiently to coat the back of a wooden spoon.
☐ Remove from the heat and strain into a bowl. Cool.
☐ Stir in the puréed strawberries and cream and chill.
☐ To finish: Whip the cream and hull and slice the strawberries. Divide the cream between the choux ovals and top with the strawberries. Replace the lids and chill in the refrigerator.
☐ To serve: Pour over the chilled sauce and serve immediately.

Tranche aux Fruits

Serves 6   ☆☆☆
Preparation: 25 minutes plus chilling
Cooking: 20 minutes

6oz (175g) frozen puff pastry, thawed
3 tablespoons apricot jam
½ pint (284ml) double cream, whipped
8oz (225g) strawberries, hulled
2 tablespoons redcurrant jelly
beaten egg to glaze
flour for dusting

Roll out the pastry to a 12in × 14in (30cm × 36cm) rectangle.
☐ Trim the edges of the pastry and cut across the shortest width.
☐ Place one piece of pastry on a dampened baking sheet and brush the edge with a little beaten egg.
☐ Sift a little flour over the surface of the other piece of pastry and fold in half lengthwise. With a small knife cut out the centre, leaving a 1in (2.5cm) border.
☐ Open out the pastry, brush off the surplus flour and carefully lift on to the larger piece of pastry. Press the edges together all the way round. Knock up edge of the pastry. Brush border with beaten egg.
☐ With a sharp knife, mark the top of the border in a lattice pattern and prick the base of the tart well.
☐ Leave to chill for 20 minutes in the refrigerator.
☐ Set oven to 450F (230C) gas 8.
☐ Bake pastry for 20 minutes or until golden brown and cooked through. Cool on a wire rack.
☐ Meanwhile, heat the apricot jam gently in a small pan. Sieve and brush over the pastry base. Cool.
☐ Pipe or spoon the cream in an even layer over the bottom of the tart. Cut the strawberries into halves or quarters, according to size, and arrange in diagonal lines on top.
☐ Heat the jelly in a small pan. Reheat the jam. Brush the top and sides of the pastry with apricot jam and glaze the fruit with redcurrant jelly.
☐ Allow to cool before serving.

Hot Puddings

Hot puddings are very much a part of traditional British cooking. Their popularity rests on their peculiarly warm and comforting nature – perfect for damp climates – and the fact that they cater for people's taste for rich, sweet desserts.

Steamed Apricot and Apple Mould

Serves 4-6 ☆☆☆
Preparation: 20 minutes
Cooking: 2 hours

6oz (175g) self-raising flour
a pinch of salt
2oz (50g) caster sugar
3oz (75g) shredded suet
about 6 tablespoons milk
butter for greasing

The filling:
1 cooking apple
6oz (175g) dried apricots, soaked overnight
   in cold water
2oz (50g) seedless raisins
½ teaspoon ground mixed spice
4 tablespoons golden syrup

demerara sugar, to finish

Make the pastry: Sift the flour and salt into a bowl.

☐ Stir in the sugar and suet, then gradually add the milk. Knead lightly to form a firm dough.

☐ Wrap in greaseproof paper, then chill in the refrigerator.

☐ Meanwhile, make filling: Peel and core the apple, then grate it into a bowl.

☐ Drain the apricots and chop them finely, then stir in with the other filling ingredients using only 3 tablespoons of the syrup.

☐ Grease a 1½ pint (900ml) pudding basin thoroughly with butter. Spoon in the remaining syrup.

☐ Roll out the dough on a lightly floured surface, then cut out a circle large enough to fit the bottom of the basin.

☐ Place the circle of dough in the basin, then cover with a layer of filling.

☐ Continue cutting out circles of dough and layering them with the filling until all the ingredients are used up, making 3 layers of filling and finishing with a circle of dough.

☐ Cover the top of the pudding with a circle of buttered greaseproof paper, then cover the top of the basin with foil, making a pleat in the centre to allow for the expansion during steaming. Tie securely with string.

☐ Place the basin in the top of a steamer or double boiler, or in a pan half-filled with gently boiling water.

☐ Cover and steam for 2 hours.

☐ Remove the foil and greaseproof paper, then leave the pudding to stand in the basin for 5 minutes.

☐ Turn out carefully on to a warmed serving dish and sprinkle liberally with demerara sugar.

☐ Serve hot, with thin pouring cream or custard.

Steamed Apricot and Apple Mould

Mincemeat and Apricot Plait

Serves 4 ☆☆
Preparation: 15 minutes
Cooking: about 20 minutes

8oz (225g) frozen puff pastry, thawed
6oz (175g) mincemeat
15oz (425g) can apricots, drained
beaten egg to glaze

Set the oven to 425F (220C) gas 7.
☐ Roll out the pastry to an oblong
9in × 13in (23cm × 33cm).
☐ Place on a baking sheet. Roughly
mark into three sections, lengthwise,
and spread the mincemeat down the
centre section.
☐ Arrange the apricots over the
mincemeat, make diagonal cuts ½in
(1cm) apart along the uncovered
pastry at each side, to within ¼in
(5mm) of the filling.
☐ Brush pastry strips with egg and
plait over apricots.
☐ Brush outside of pastry with egg
glaze and cook for about 20 minutes
until golden.
☐ Serve hot, in slices, with cream.

Syrup Tart

Serves 4 ☆☆
Preparation: 15 minutes
Cooking: 20 minutes

8oz (225g) frozen shortcrust pastry, thawed
9 tablespoons golden syrup
3oz (75g) fresh white breadcrumbs
finely grated rind of 1 lemon

Set the oven to 425F (220C) gas 7.
☐ Line an 8in (20cm) flan ring or
pie plate with the pastry.
☐ Warm the syrup in a pan and
pour on to the breadcrumbs and the
lemon rind.
☐ Spoon breadcrumb mixture onto
the pastry and cook in a hot oven for
about 20 minutes.
☐ Serve the tart hot, with a custard
sauce.

Lemon Sponge Pudding

A creamy base with a sponge top.

Serves 4
Preparation: 20 minutes
Cooking: 1 hour

2oz (50g) margarine
4oz (100g) caster sugar
finely grated rind and juice of 2 lemons
2 eggs, size 2, separated
½ pint (300ml) milk
2oz (50g) self-raising flour
butter for greasing

Set the oven to 350F (180C) gas 4.
☐ Cream the margarine and sugar
together with the lemon rind until
pale and fluffy.
☐ Add egg yolks and beat in well.
☐ Stir in half the milk and flour.
☐ Pour in the rest of the milk and
the lemon juice.
☐ Whisk egg whites until just stiff
and fold into mixture. Pour into a
greased 2 pint (1.2 litre) ovenproof
dish and put in a roasting tin half-
filled with water.
☐ Cook in centre of oven for
1 hour, until golden brown and
firm.
☐ Serve hot, with custard or ice
cream.

Hot Spicy Fruit Salad

Serves 4 ○
Preparation: 5 minutes
Cooking: 45 minutes

1oz (25g) soft brown sugar
1 pint (600ml) water
1 tablespoon clear honey
1 teaspoon powdered cinnamon
1 teaspoon powdered nutmeg
2 cloves
2 tablespoons lemon juice
1 tablespoon brandy (optional)
4oz (100g) dried apricots, washed
1lb 12oz (822g) can peach halves, drained
2oz (50g) sultanas

Dissolve sugar in water in a pan.
☐ Add the honey, cinnamon,

nutmeg, cloves, lemon juice and
brandy.
☐ Bring to boil, then reduce heat.
☐ Add the apricots, cover, and
allow to simmer for 15 minutes.
☐ Stir in the peaches and simmer
for a further 30 minutes.
☐ Remove the cloves. Just before
serving add the sultanas.
☐ Serve hot, with whipped cream.

Pear and Ginger Upside-down Pudding

This is a spicy and slightly unusual
variation of pineapple upside-down
pudding and is a family favourite.

Serves 4 ☆☆☆
Preparation: 15 minutes
Cooking: 45-55 minutes

4 tablespoons golden syrup
14½oz (411g) can pears, drained with
      juice reserved
4 glacé cherries
4oz (100g) soft margarine
4oz (100g) caster sugar
2 eggs, size 2
6oz (175g) self-raising flour
2 teaspoons powdered ginger
a little milk
2 teaspoons cornflour

Set the oven to 350F (180C) gas 4.
☐ Grease an 8in (20cm) round cake
tin.
☐ Heat the syrup and pour into the
tin to cover the base.
☐ Arrange the pears and glacé
cherries in the syrup.
☐ Cream the fat and sugar together
until light and fluffy.
☐ Beat in the eggs then stir in the
sifted flour and ginger.
☐ Add a little milk to the mixture
to give a dropping consistency.
☐ Spread the mixture over the fruit
and cook in oven for 45-55 minutes.
☐ To make the pear sauce: Blend
the cornflour with a little pear juice
and heat with the rest of the juice to
boiling point, stirring all the time.
☐ Pour over the hot pudding.

*From top to bottom: Lemon Sponge
Pudding; Hot Spicy Fruit Salad;
Pear and Ginger Upside-down
Pudding.*

Beignets with Cherry Sauce
If fresh cherries are not available use canned red or black cherries. Drain them well and use the syrup in place of the water to make the sauce.

Banana Fritters
Apricots, pears, apples and pineapples are examples of some of the firm fruit which also make successful fritters.

Almond-stuffed Peaches
Cointreau or Grand Marnier would make good alternatives to brandy or sherry in this recipe.
Crushed macaroons can be substituted for the ground almonds in the filling.

Beignets with Cherry Sauce

Serves 2   ☆ ☆ ☆
Preparation and cooking: 45 minutes

1oz (25g) butter
4 tablespoons water
1½oz (35g) flour, sifted
a pinch of salt
1 egg, size 2, beaten
oil for deep-frying
a little caster sugar mixed with
    ground cinnamon

The cherry sauce:
1oz (25g) sugar
4 fl oz (125ml) water
the finely pared rind of ½ lemon
1½ teaspoons lemon juice
a pinch of ground cinnamon
4oz (100g) fresh cherries, halved and stoned
1½ teaspoons arrowroot dissolved in
    1 tablespoon water

Melt butter with water in a pan.
☐ Boil, then remove from heat. Beat in flour and salt until the mixture leaves the sides of pan clean.
☐ Cool, beat in egg until smooth.
☐ Make sauce: Dissolve sugar in water. Add rind, juice and cinnamon. Boil for 2 to 3 minutes.
☐ Add cherries. Simmer for 5 minutes.
☐ Remove rind and stir in arrowroot. Simmer until thickened.
☐ Heat the oil in a deep frying-pan to 355F (180C).
☐ Pipe the dough, in 1in (2.5cm) lengths, into the fat.
☐ Cook, turning, until golden.
☐ Drain well, toss in sugar and cinnamon and serve with sauce.

Banana Fritters

Serves 2   ☆ ☆ ☆
Preparation and cooking: 20 minutes

1½oz (40g) flour
a pinch of salt
1 teaspoon oil
3 tablespoons water
1 egg white from size 2 egg
3 bananas
3-4 tablespoons oil for deep-frying
1-1½oz (25-40g) caster sugar mixed with
    a large pinch of ground cinnamon

Sift the flour and salt into a bowl and make a well in the centre.
☐ Add the oil and water and gradually work in the flour to make a smooth batter.
☐ Beat the egg white until stiff and fold into the batter.
☐ Cut the bananas in half or into 1in (2.5cm) pieces and coat evenly in the batter.
☐ Heat the oil in a deep frying-pan to 355F (180C).
☐ Deep-fry the fritters until golden brown.
☐ Remove fritters with a slotted spoon and drain on kitchen paper. Serve hot, sprinkled with spiced sugar.

Almond-stuffed Peaches

Serves 2   ☆ ☆ ☆
Preparation and cooking: 40 minutes

1oz (25g) butter
½oz (15g) icing sugar, sifted
1½oz (40g) ground almonds
a few drops of almond essence
½ teaspoon finely grated orange rind
2 large fresh peaches, peeled, halved and
    stoned
1 tablespoon brandy or sherry
2 tablespoons orange juice
1-2oz (25-50g) caster sugar

Set the oven to 375F (190C) gas 5.
☐ Cream half the butter with the icing sugar until soft, then beat in ground almonds, almond essence and grated orange rind.
☐ Form into 4 equal balls.
☐ Press the filling into the cavities in the peach halves, then press the peach halves back together again.
☐ Place in a small ovenproof dish.
☐ Melt the remaining butter in a pan and add the remaining orange rind, brandy or sherry and juice.
☐ Spoon over the peaches and sprinkle thickly with the caster sugar.
☐ Bake for 25-30 minutes or until the sugar forms a syrupy glaze and the peaches are tender.
☐ Serve with cream or ice cream.

Fruited Bread and Butter Pudding

Serves 2 ☆☆☆

Preparation: 25 minutes plus
15 minutes standing
Cooking: 35-40 minutes

2-3 slices of bread, brown or white
1½oz (40g) butter
2oz (50g) raisins
1oz (25g) chopped mixed candied peel
½ teaspoon grated orange rind
2-3 tablespoons demerara sugar
1 egg, size 2
8 fl oz (250ml) milk
a little mixed spice or ground cinnamon
3-4 glacé cherries, halved (optional)

Set the oven to 350F (180C) gas 4.
☐ Spread the bread with most of
the butter. Use the remainder to
grease a 1 pint (600ml) ovenproof
dish.
☐ Cut the bread into strips and
arrange in layers, buttered side
upwards, in the dish, sprinkling
each layer with the raisins, peel,
orange rind and most of the sugar.
☐ Beat the egg and milk together
and strain into the dish. Leave to
stand for 15 minutes.
☐ Sprinkle with spice and the
remaining sugar and dot with glacé
cherries, if using.
☐ Bake for 35-40 minutes or until
set and lightly browned. Serve hot.

Fruited Bread and Butter Pudding;
Beignets with Cherry Sauce; Banana
Fritters; Almond-stuffed Peaches.

Fruited Bread and Butter Pudding
Try using currants or sultanas in place of the
raisins and 1oz (25g) chopped nuts in place
of the candied peel.

Hot Fruit Soufflé

In the summer a variety of soft fruits can be used to make delicious hot soufflés. Try blackberries, raspberries, redcurrants or a combination of soft fruits.

Brown Betty

Traditionally this recipe includes lemon rind and juice instead of orange rind and cider. The addition of mincemeat is also a variation which makes the pudding more interesting.

Sussex Puddle Pudding

Although lemon puddings are popular, try using a lime or an orange for delicious alternative flavours.

Hot Fruit Soufflé

Serves 2 ☆☆
Preparation: 15 minutes
Cooking: 35-40 minutes

---

1 small banana, sliced
1 × 7oz (198g) can apricot halves, drained
1oz (25g) caster sugar
2 eggs, size 2, separated
2 tablespoons flour
¼ pint (150ml) milk
½ teaspoon vanilla essence
a little icing sugar
butter for greasing

Set the oven to 350F (180C) gas 4.
☐ Lightly grease a 1½ pint (900ml) soufflé dish.
☐ Cover the bottom with banana slices, then with the apricots.
☐ In a saucepan, beat together the sugar and one egg yolk until creamy.
☐ Beat in the flour.
☐ Gradually beat in the milk and bring slowly to the boil, stirring.
☐ Simmer for 2 minutes.
☐ Remove from the heat and cool slightly, then beat in the other egg yolk and the vanilla essence.
☐ Beat the egg whites until stiff and fold through the sauce.
☐ Spoon over the fruit. Bake for 35-40 minutes.
☐ Serve immediately, sprinkled with icing sugar.

Brown Betty

Serves 4 ☆☆
Preparation: 20 minutes
Cooking: 1 hour

---

4 cooking apples, peeled, cored and
   thinly sliced
4oz (100g) mincemeat
4oz (100g) fresh brown breadcrumbs
4oz (100g) soft brown sugar
1 teaspoon ground cinnamon
2 teaspoons grated orange rind
2oz (50g) butter, cut into pieces
2 tablespoons cider

To decorate:
icing sugar
4 small macaroons

Set the oven to 375F (190C) gas 5.
☐ Place a layer of half the apple slices on the bottom of a casserole and spread over half the mincemeat.
☐ Mix together breadcrumbs, sugar, cinnamon and rind and sprinkle half over mincemeat.
☐ Scatter over half the butter.
☐ Repeat layers. End with butter.
☐ Pour in the cider.
☐ Cover the casserole and cook in the oven for 45 minutes.
☐ Remove the lid and continue cooking for 15 minutes to brown.
☐ Dust with icing sugar and serve decorated with macaroons.

Sussex Puddle Pudding

Serves 4 ☆☆☆
Preparation: 10 minutes
Cooking: 1¾ hours

8oz (225g) self-raising flour
4oz (100g) shredded suet
pinch of salt
1oz (25g) granulated sugar
1 lemon, washed, cut into 8 pieces
4oz (100g) soft brown sugar
4oz (100g) butter, cut into pieces
1 tablespoon sifted icing sugar
butter for greasing

Set the oven to 325F (160C) gas 3.
☐ Mix together the flour, suet, salt and granulated sugar, add water and mix to a soft dough.
☐ Turn on to a floured surface.
☐ Cut off two-thirds of the dough, roll out and use to line a 2 pint (1.2 litre) casserole dish.
☐ Layer lemon pieces in the dish with the brown sugar and butter.
☐ Roll out the remaining dough and cover the filling.
☐ Cover with buttered greaseproof paper, then cover the top of the basin with foil, making a pleat in centre. Tie securely with string.
☐ Place the casserole in a roasting tin half-filled with hot water and cook for 1¾ hours.
☐ Remove foil and greaseproof and dust pudding with icing sugar. Serve.

INTERNATIONAL CUISINE

International cuisine is one of the most exciting areas for a cook to explore. Each of the following chapters takes a country or region and includes at least one complete menu of traditional dishes, plus several extra specialities.

France is renowned for its cuisine and regional specialities, and because it has such an enormous variety of dishes to offer, it has been divided into two chapters: in the North, soups, pâtés and dairy foods predominate, while in the sunnier South there is a more Mediterranean influence with use made of garlic, herbs and vegetables. Similar ingredients are used in Italy and Spain, although each country has its specialities. Pasta, pizza and rice dishes abound in Italy, while Spain is known for its paella, tortilla (vegetable omelette) and tapas (small appetizers).

The Greeks use oregano, lemon and olive oil to flavour their stews. Lamb is the most popular meat and they serve it in the form of meatballs, moussaka and kebabs. No one visits Greece without trying feta cheese and salad or the honey-based sweet delights, such as halva and baklava.

Switzerland, Austria and the Scandinavian countries all enjoy a very high standard of living and consume a high proportion of meat and dairy products. The Swiss make excellent cheese dishes such as fondue and raclette, while the Austrians specialize in sweet strudel pastries and sachertorte (rich chocolate cake). In Scandinavia, fish is used as widely as meat and cheese. Their speciality is the smörgåsbord, which is a wonderful selection of food set out as a cold table.

Dishes from the Middle East are particularly tasty and healthy as they make good use of vegetables, pulses, spices and yogurt. These are made into delicious soups, stews, pancakes, pickles and salad vegetable dishes.

The increasing number of Indian, Chinese and Japanese restaurants reflect the growing interest in foods from the Far East. Indian cookery, with its subtle blend of spices, is a fascinating cuisine; Chinese food is less spicy, but varied, tasty and healthy. We also enjoy the delicacy of Japanese dishes which rely on fresh ingredients exquisitely presented and garnished.

This section on International Cuisine will give you an insight into the traditions and eating habits of many nations and is sure to inspire the imagination and stimulate the appetite.

The cuisine of Japan is one of the newest to be tried in Western homes, although it has already influenced the way restaurant chefs present food in the *Nouvelle Cuisine* style – arranged simply but very prettily on the plate. The Japanese chapter tells you exactly how to prepare a meal – starting with *Suimono* (clear soup with prawn and chicken dumplings), followed by *Tori no Teriyake* (chicken) and *Awajukikan* (snow jelly with strawberries).

Nearer to home, the chapter on Italian cooking shows how to create *Spaghetti con Cozze* with that useful store-cupboard standby, a jar of mussels. That's followed by *Braciolette Ripiene* (slices of stuffed veal) and finally, a light cake layered with low-fat cheese, maraschino cherries, angelica and kirsch, then coated with toasted nuts!

Chicken round the World

As well as using local ingredients, each different land cooks its chickens in a different way. Long, slow simmering is typical of France; Greeks love to roast their meats and poultry; in Northern India they either bake or—as here—grill their kebabs, and the Chinese use their classic and delicate stir-frying technique.

Since chicken is such a versatile basic ingredient, it is used the world over in a variety of ways, each country flavouring it with locally available ingredients and cooking it according to the traditions of the region. Here are four delicious recipes—two from the East and two from the West—to give you some idea of the contrast in cooking styles . . .

Lemon, olive oil and herbs for an authentic Greek flavour

Simple vegetables and belly pork from France

A variety of spicy sauces with hot chillies from China

Typically Indian— the aromatic spices with ginger and yogurt

188 INTERNATIONAL CUISINE/Introduction

First, there's Chicken Oregano, a fine example of simple Greek cooking. It makes lavish use of olive oil – and here it is important to use a good-quality *green* olive oil for a truly authentic flavour – with lashings of lemon and oregano, all of which grow in profusion under the hot sun.

Then move to China, where the southern province of Szechuan is renowned for its hot, spicy food. Its traditional dishes, such as Chilli Chicken, combine liberal amounts of different spices in such perfect balance that no single flavour should predominate in the finished dish.

Indian cooking, too, gains characteristic qualities from the imaginative and subtle use of spices, but this is not to say that the food is always hot. Like many dishes from the north of India, Chicken Tikka is mild and aromatic and in its homeland would be cooked in a *tandoor* (clay oven).

Lastly, to France, where the thrifty French cook their traditional Chicken in the Pot: the bird need not be young; the long, slow cooking allows the flavours to mingle; the meal is cooked all in one large pot – and it makes a delicious broth as well.

Koutopoulo Rigani

Chicken oregano

This simple Greek recipe produces a crisp-skinned, succulent roast chicken and tender potatoes with a delightful lemony flavour. Serve it with a mixed Greek salad.

Serves 4 ★★☆
Preparation: 35 minutes
Cooking time: 1½ hours

3½lb (1.6kg) oven-ready chicken
salt and freshly ground black pepper
2 teaspoons dried oregano
1 teaspoon dried thyme
1 small onion, peeled
2lb (1kg) small old potatoes, peeled and
    quartered lengthways
juice of 2 small lemons
3 tablespoons olive oil
¼ pint (150ml) cold water
2oz (50g) butter

Heat the oven to 425F (220C) gas 7.
☐ Wipe the chicken inside and out with kitchen paper, then season it inside and out with salt and pepper. Combine the dried herbs, then sprinkle 1 teaspoon of the mixture inside the chicken. Put in the whole onion. Truss the chicken.
☐ Place it, breast down, in a large roasting tin and surround it with the potatoes. Pour the lemon juice and olive oil over the chicken and sprinkle with 1 teaspoon dried herbs. Pour the water into a corner of the tin, then roast it in the oven for 30 minutes.
☐ Remove the tin from the oven. Turn the chicken over, breast upwards, dot with the butter and sprinkle with the remaining dried herbs. Baste the potatoes.
☐ Turn the oven down to 400F (200C) gas 6 and continue roasting for a further hour, until the chicken is golden brown. The potatoes will be slightly less brown.
☐ Transfer the chicken to a heated serving platter and surround it with the potatoes. Skim the fat from the tin juices and pour the juices into a heated small jug to serve.

Koutopoulo Rigani
Choose small potatoes – they should weigh about 4oz (100-125g) each. New potatoes can also be used for this recipe; they hold their shape well during cooking but absorb a little less of the flavoured cooking juices than old potatoes.

In Greek households a small piece of Feta, or similar, cheese is sometimes placed inside the chicken.

If fresh herbs are available, use 4 teaspoons oregano and 2 teaspoons thyme.

For an authentic Greek salad, serve sliced tomatoes and olives, dressed with olive oil and plenty of salt and pepper; top each portion with a generous sprinkling of Feta, Halloumi or other sheep's cheese. Add some lettuce if you like.

Koutopoulo Rigani from Greece

Chicken Tikka

This dish serves 6 as a main course with chapatis and a vegetable dish, or 8 as a first course.

Serves 6-8 (see above) ☆☆
Preparation: 40 minutes plus
  marinating
Cooking time: 15 minutes

2¾lb (1.25kg) chicken breast meat, skinned
  and boned
1 teaspoon salt
juice of 1 lemon
6 tablespoons natural yogurt
1in (2.5cm) piece fresh root ginger,
  peeled and finely grated
2-3 cloves garlic, crushed
1 teaspoon ground cumin
¼ teaspoon cayenne pepper
¼ teaspoon garam masala or curry powder
4oz (100g) ghee or unsalted butter,
  melted, or oil

To garnish:
raw onion rings
sprigs of fresh coriander, or flat-
  leaved parsley
lemon wedges
tomato roses (optional)

Remove any fat from the chicken and cut the meat into 2in (5cm) cubes. Lay the cubes in a single layer on a large platter and sprinkle with half the salt and half the lemon juice. Turn the cubes over and sprinkle with the rest of the salt and lemon juice. Leave to stand for 20 minutes.

☐ Meanwhile, put the yogurt in a small bowl and beat it with a fork until it is smooth. Mix in the ginger, garlic, cumin, cayenne pepper and garam masala.

☐ When the chicken has been standing for 20 minutes, tip it and its juices into a bowl. Strain the yogurt mixture over the chicken, pressing it through the sieve with a rubber spatula. Turn the chicken in this marinade until evenly coated, then cover tightly and leave it in the refrigerator for 8-24 hours.

☐ Remove the chicken from the refrigerator 2 hours before you intend to grill it, and leave it to stand at room temperature.

☐ Preheat the grill to its highest temperature. Thread the cubes of chicken on to long, oiled skewers, leaving a little space between each piece. Balance the skewers on the rim of the grill pan. Brush the chicken with melted ghee, unsalted butter or oil, then grill for about 15 minutes, turning the skewers and brushing the chicken with the rest of the ghee, butter or oil.

☐ Using a fork, slide the chicken off the skewers onto heated plates. Garnish each serving with raw onion rings, sprigs of coriander, a wedge of lemon and a tomato rose. Serve immediately.

Chicken Tikka from Northern India

Szechuan Hot Chilli Chicken

This dish serves 4-5 if it is one of several dishes in a Chinese menu, or 3 if served alone, with boiled rice. The unusual ingredients in this recipe are available from oriental food stores.

Serves 3-5 ☆☆
Preparation: 20 minutes
Cooking time: 15 minutes

1lb (500g) chicken breast meat, skinned and boned
½ teaspoon salt
1 tablespoon cornflour
2 teaspoons vegetable oil
4 spring onions
½ red pepper
2 small dried red chillies
1lb 3½oz (553g) can bamboo shoot pieces
2 tablespoons dry sherry
1 tablespoon sesame oil
sprigs of coriander, or flat-leaved parsley, to garnish

The sauce:
2 cloves garlic, crushed
1 tablespoon soy bean paste
2 tablespoons soy sauce
1 tablespoon hoisin sauce
2 tablespoons tomato purée
2 teaspoons sugar
4 tablespoons chicken stock
½ teaspoon Tabasco sauce
vegetable oil for shallow frying

Remove any fat from the chicken and cut the meat into 1in (2.5cm) cubes. Sprinkle them with the salt, cornflour and oil and rub it into the chicken with the fingertips.

Chilli chicken from China

☐ Trim the spring onions then cut each one into 3 pieces. Cut the red pepper into ⅓in (1cm) dice. Cut off the stalk ends of the chillies and carefully tip out and discard *all* the seeds. Drain the canned bamboo shoots, halve them lengthwise and slice thickly.

☐ Put all the sauce ingredients together in a small bowl. Mix well.

☐ Pour enough oil into a large frying-pan to give a depth of ¼in (5mm). Heat the oil until it is very hot, then add the chicken cubes, spreading them out flat in the pan. Fry over a high heat for 3-4 minutes, turning them, until lightly golden. Remove them from the pan with a slotted spoon.

☐ Allow the oil to cool a little, then pour away all but 2 tablespoons of it. Add the spring onion, red pepper and whole dried chillies to the pan and stir-fry over a medium heat for 1 minute. Add the sauce and stir over the heat until smooth. Add the bamboo shoots and stir-fry for 1 minute, until heated through and coated with the sauce. Add the chicken and cook for a few seconds until just heated through. Finally, stir in the sherry and sesame oil.

☐ Transfer to a heated serving dish, garnish with sprigs of coriander and serve immediately.

Chicken tikka

The word *tikka* means 'noisette' a 'nut-sized' piece of meat, and in this recipe noisettes of spiced chicken are threaded on skewers and cooked quickly under a very hot grill. It is aromatic rather than 'hot'.

Garam masala is a mixture of ground spices (cardamoms, cloves, ginger, coriander etc.), the exact constituents and proportions of which often depend on the supplier. Curry powder can be used instead.

The coriander shown as a garnish in these recipes is fresh and sold in bunches, like watercress, in Indian grocers' shops. It can also be obtained in some supermarkets.

Szechuan Hot Chilli Chicken

Szechuan (pronounced *Sechwan*), in the west of China, is well known for its spicy and flavoursome food. This is cooked by the *yu-xiang* method; the chicken is first stir fried, then cooked with plenty of garlic, soy paste, ginger and chillies, giving the meat a hot flavour and a deep, characteristic, reddish brown colour.

Part of the aesthetic pleasure of Chinese food is its preparation—and the appearance of the finished dish; that is why the instructions for chopping and slicing are given so exactly.

Beware of chilli seeds; they contain a pungent, burning substance which can cause an irritation of the skin. Wear rubber gloves for safety; don't touch your face or eyes after preparing chillies, and wash your utensils, hands—and the gloves—immediately before going on to the next stage.

In Indian and Chinese dishes, chicken is usually skinned. This allows the spices to penetrate the meat during marinating or cooking.

To make a tomato rose for the garnish, pare the peel from a tomato very thinly (chilling the tomato first makes it easier to peel), then wind it around a finger to form a rose. Secure it with a small piece of cocktail stick, if necessary.

Poule au Pot

Chicken in the pot

Serves 6-8 ★★☆
Preparation: 1 hour
Cooking time: 3 hours

3½-4lb (2kg) chicken, giblets removed
salt and pepper
1 large green cabbage
oil or fat for shallow frying
1½lb (750g) potatoes, peeled

The stuffing:
3 slices white bread, crusts removed
4 tablespoons milk
9-10oz (250g) bacon in the piece
9-10oz (250g) lean pork
6oz (150g) belly pork
liver from the chicken
2oz (50g) butter
2 large onions, finely chopped
2 cloves garlic, finely chopped
a sprinkling of nutmeg

The stock:
1 large carrot, sliced
1 onion stuck with 5 cloves
2 sticks of celery, sliced
1 clove of garlic, chopped
1 pint (500ml) chicken stock
3½-4 pints (2 litres) water

Make the stuffing: Crumble the bread into a large bowl and stir in the milk. Mince or process the bacon, pork and belly pork with the chicken liver and add them to the bowl. Melt the butter and cook the onion and garlic over a low heat until transparent. Stir the cooked onion into the bowl with the seasoning. Knead with wet hands to mix thoroughly. Cover and chill.

☐ Make the stock: Place the prepared vegetables in a large saucepan or flameproof casserole. Add the stock and water and bring to the boil. Remove the scum which rises to the surface.

☐ Blot the chicken dry, then sprinkle generously inside and out with salt and pepper. Fill with half of the stuffing, then close the opening (use cocktail sticks or safety pins). Place the chicken in the pan with the stock, cover, reduce the heat and cook very gently for 2½ hours.

☐ Meanwhile, prepare the cabbage rolls. Trim the cabbage and remove 12 large leaves. Slice the remainder of the cabbage and set aside in a bowl of cold water. Blanch the whole leaves for 3-5 minutes until just supple. Rinse immediately in cold water.

☐ Form the rest of the stuffing into 12 little sausages. Fry lightly in a little hot fat in a frying pan. Drain well, then set one on each of the blanched cabbage leaves. Roll up and secure with cocktail sticks.

☐ Cut the potatoes into thick slices. After 2½ hours cooking time, add the potatoes to the chicken and cook for another 10 minutes.

☐ Add the cabbage rolls, then drain and add the shredded cabbage. Cook just long enough to soften the potatoes and cabbage, but do not let them overcook.

☐ Transfer the chicken to a heated serving platter then carefully lift out the vegetables with a slotted spoon and arrange them around the chicken. You can strain off the stock and serve it as a soup.

Tip : Use a stockpot or deep covered roasting tin.

A traditional French Poule au Pot

Northern & Central France

If you are ever fortunate enough to visit a French food market, you will be dazzled by the beauty and perfection of the display. All over the country, the attention to food is the same. Impeccable cuts of meat, dozens of cheeses, bright vegetables lovely enough to inspire an artist and all being carefully inspected by local housewives intent on buying nothing but the best.

To recapture the elegance of the haute cuisine dishes of France, or the comforting qualities of the more homely regional cookery, it's worth emulating this care and attention to detail. Most of the ingredients for the dishes of northern and central France in this chapter are readily available, and a major part of the art of French country cooking is to make the best of whatever is in season, economical, and to hand.

France is a gourmet's paradise, overflowing with a wonderful variety of ingredients which give rise to many simple or spectacular dishes.

FRENCH MENUS

French meals often start with a bowl of soup, ranging from clear consommés through thick creamy and puréed soups known as potages, to thick broths packed with vegetables, known as garbures.

Alternatively, the meal may start with an hors d'oeuvre. This may be a homemade pâté, a salad of blanched, cold vegetables with a vinaigrette, or raw sliced vegetables (crudités) with vinaigrette or a mayonnaise. On the coast, the meal may start with a plate of freshly cooked shellfish.

For a simple family supper, a hearty soup with crusty bread, followed by cheese and fruit may be all that is served, or an omelette may be included after the soup. For a more substantial meal, there will be fish, poultry, game or meat as a main course. Some of these dishes come with a classic vegetable accompaniment, for the French pay particular attention to vegetables, cooking them in many different ways and serving them separately from the main course.

An everyday meal will probably end with one or two cheeses, carefully chosen to be at exactly the right stage of ripeness, and served with more red wine. The cheese may be eaten on its own, or with a few grapes, or some crusty French bread, followed perhaps by a piece of fresh fruit.

On special occasions there will be a beautiful gâteau or fruit-filled tart, either homemade or bought from the pâtissier.

Haute cuisine

We think of France as being the home of haute cuisine, but in fact France owes a great deal of its reputation to Italy. When Catherine de Medici came to Paris from Florence in 1533 to marry the future King Henry II, she brought with her a retinue of Italian pastrycooks, sauce-makers and chefs who proceeded to transform the cuisine of the French court.

The French chefs were quick to learn and since then they have been experimenting, refining, and dictating what a truly classic dish should be. Today, a fine sauce, truffles or foie gras can be the hallmark of a haute cuisine dish.

Regional dishes

In the brasseries, cafés and homes of France, you will find a simpler, less expensive style of cooking.

Often this will include local specialities, working on the wily French principle that cheap, fresh, local ingredients are the best and that nothing, but nothing, is ever wasted. Broth is made from a poaching liquid, potatoes may be cooked in fat from a goose or duck, and nutritious bone marrow is scraped out and spread on bread or toast. Petite Marmite (page 197) is one example.

France is a country which benefits from having several different climates. Olives, citrus fruits, grapes and peaches are abundant in the sunny south, while the cooler northern regions and the areas close to the mountains are famed for their cattle. In this chapter, there are recipes and menus from the north and central parts of France, including Bordeaux. (The Mediterranean region, the Dauphiné Alps and the area around Lyons are covered in a later chapter.)

Cattle give both excellent dairy produce and high quality meat. Add to this the numerous rivers and streams with their trout, salmon and crayfish and the miles of coastline where fine seafish can be caught and where shellfish lie among the rocks for the taking, and you can already see why France is renowned as one of the gastronomic leaders of the world. In woods are treasure troves of chestnuts, nuts, edible fungi and game, while a marvellous variety of vegetables, fruit and herbs are grown all over the country. It is sheer delight to make a gastronomic tour through France, enjoying the specialities which the different regions have to offer.

In **Normandy,** dairy produce is of prime importance and local products such as cream, butter and cheese are all incorporated into the regional specialities. Fish and shellfish play an important role and the coast is full of fishing villages. Vineyards are almost non-existent but there are plenty of apple orchards, and you will find dishes including apples, cider or Calvados (apple brandy) on almost every restaurant menu in the district.

In **Brittany,** the dairy products and meat are slightly less renowned than their counterparts in Normandy. However, Brittany is washed on three sides by the Atlantic Ocean and fish and shellfish are abundant. The Bretons prefer uncomplicated meals—the natural flavour of the main ingredient is of prime importance, and most food is prepared as simply as possible.

Around **Poitiers** with its lush green meadows, cows, lambs and goats, roast kid is one of the local specialities. This area also produces excellent little goats' cheeses in different shapes. In the rainy **Limousin** region, around Limoges, there are heart-warming, filling puddings such as Clafoutis.

In the region of **Bordeaux** you enter one of the most famous wine districts of France. This area is famed for eels poached in red wine and goose liver recipes. Mushrooms abound in the woods of the region and the prized 'cèpes' are included in many dishes.

In Saint Emilion, entrecôte steaks are barbecued over fires made with vine branches and the quality of lamb in the area around Pauillac cannot be bettered.

Traditional stews and casseroles abound all over France and they are very much alike, probably because *the* classic French recipe for a casserole is Boeuf Bourguignonne. The flavour is so good that it has been copied all over France, with regional variations of course. Every chef or housewife has his or her own version: one uses more onion, while another will include a favourite herb or spice. This also applies to the pâté à la maison (house pâté), found on the menus of every small restaurant.

You don't have to visit a star-rated restaurant in France to be able to experience the culinary delights of a particular region. In fact 'starred' restaurants usually prepare the kind of dishes which are already well-known abroad. Instead, choose a small restaurant in a provincial town or village where the landlord's wife does the cooking, where grandfather still tends the vegetable garden and the children help to peel the vegetables. It is in restaurants such as these that you will discover the true flavour of French regional cuisine which has long been the source of inspiration for the world's most famous chefs.

Canard à la Bigarade is a fine example of a French 'haute cuisine' dish.

Canard à la Bigarade

Duck in orange sauce

Often the whole duck is roasted and served with the orange sauce. Here, the succulent breast fillets alone are used.

Serves 4   ★ ★ ☆
Preparation: 25 minutes
Cooking time: 2½ hours

2 large ducks
salt and pepper
2oz (50g) butter
orange slices to garnish (optional)

The stock:
2 tablespoons oil
1 small onion, finely chopped
2 small carrots, diced
9fl oz (250ml) dry white wine
9fl oz (250ml) cold water
juice of 3 Seville oranges or 2 sweet oranges
    and 1 lemon

The sauce:
stock from above
1 tablespoon cornflour
salt and pepper
2 teaspoons sugar
1 tablespoon orange liqueur

Remove the breast fillets from the ducks. Pat them dry. Rub with salt and pepper. Set aside. Cut the carcasses into portions.

☐ To make the stock, heat the oil in the saucepan and lightly sauté the onion and carrot. Do not allow them to brown. Add the carcass pieces and continue stirring over a low heat for 5 minutes. Add the wine and water and bring to the boil. Remove scum, cover the pan, reduce the heat and simmer gently for 2 hours.

☐ Strain the stock and return it to the saucepan. Boil vigorously until reduced to about half the original volume. Squeeze the oranges (and lemon if used) then strain the juice into the stock. Allow to simmer for a further 10 minutes.

☐ Heat the butter in a large frying pan and brown the duck fillets on both sides—about 5 minutes if you like the duck pink and rare, or longer until the duck is cooked to taste. Transfer to a serving dish and keep hot.

☐ To finish the sauce, drain any excess fat from the pan, pour in the stock and boil to loosen the residue from the base of the pan. Mix the cornflour smoothly with 2 teaspoons cold water. Stir into the pan and cook until thickened. Adjust the seasoning to taste with salt and pepper, sugar and orange liqueur.

☐ Spoon a little sauce over the duck and serve the rest in a sauceboat. Garnish the duck, if liked, with slices of orange poached for a minute in the sauce just before serving (and before adjusting its seasoning).

☐ Serve with sautéed new potatoes and a green vegetable or salad.

Tip: For a less extravagant dish, use duck portions on the bone. A well-flavoured duck or chicken stock may be used instead of the cold water in the recipe, then you do not need a duck carcass.

Petite Marmite

Beef soup with vegetables

The name 'marmite' is taken from the traditional metal or earthenware pot in which the soup is cooked, then served. The 'petite marmite' is said to be a speciality of Paris. The marmite is made with whatever everyday vegetables are available added to a rich stock of beef bones. The usual, and delicious, accompaniment for this hearty soup is fried bread spread with the marrow from the bones.

Serves 4

Preparation: 30 minutes

Cooking time: 3 hours

The soup:
1lb (450g) shin of beef with the bone, chopped
3 pints (1½ litres) cold water
1 large onion
8oz (225g) carrots, chopped
1 clove of garlic, chopped
2 leeks, green parts only, sliced
2 celery stalks, sliced
8 parsley stems
1 bay leaf, crumbled
1 blade of mace
2 cloves
8 black peppercorns
1-2 chicken portions, together weighing about 8oz (225g)

The garnish:
8oz (225g) carrots, diced
2 leeks, white parts only, sliced
1 small turnip, diced
salt
chopped parsley

Put the beef into a large pan with the water. Bring to the boil, then carefully skim off any scum.

☐ Add the rest of the soup ingredients except the chicken. Cover and simmer gently for 2½-3 hours, or until the meat comes away from the bones easily.

☐ Add the chicken and continue to cook for a further 20-30 minutes, or until it is tender. Remove the chicken and the meat from the pan and strip all the flesh from the bones. Set the bones aside. Cut the meat into small pieces.

☐ Skim off any surface fat from the liquid, then boil it vigorously until

reduced by about half. Meanwhile, prepare the garnish vegetables. Add them to the reduced stock and simmer for 10 minutes, or until the vegetables are just tender but still crisp.

☐ Finally, add the chopped chicken and beef and reheat. Season to taste. Just before serving, sprinkle with chopped parsley.

Marmite Croûtes

Marrow toasts

This classic accompaniment to the Petite Marmite ensures that not a scrap is wasted.

Preparation and cooking time: 10 minutes

3oz (75g) butter
4 slices white bread, crusts removed
marrow from the cooked beef bones
a little chopped parsley

Lightly butter the bread. Put a large knob of butter into a frying-pan and heat until just turning brown. Add the bread, buttered side up, and fry until brown. Turn and brown the buttered side.

☐ Scoop the marrow from the bones with the tip of a small spoon. Mix well with the remaining butter and a little chopped parsley. Season to taste then spread over the fried bread. Serve hot.

Sole à la Normande

Sole, Normandy style

The essential element of this dish is sole poached in the oven, with a sauce made from fish stock. Plaice or flounder can be used instead of sole, though in the classic dish sole is always used. You can vary the garnish to taste: mushrooms, mussels and prawns are added here. Canned mussels may be used if fresh are not available. Drain them well.

Serves 4

Preparation and cooking time: 1¼ hours

Petite Marmite
Instead of Marmite Croûtes, serve the petite marmite with slices of crusty French bread which has been baked in the oven for about 10 minutes alongside the fish. For a lighter soup, you can strain off some of the broth and serve this on its own.

Marmite Croûtes
The marrow bones are sometimes wrapped in muslin before cooking so that the marrow cannot escape, or a simple flour and water paste is used as a 'stopper'.

Left: Petite Marmite served with Marmite Croûtes, followed by Sole Normande and Gâteau au Chocolat.

8 sole fillets
salt and pepper
5 tablespoons white wine

The sauce:
2oz (50g) butter
3 tablespoons flour
½ pint (300ml) Fish Stock
cooking liquor from the sole
1 egg yolk
3 tablespoons cream
salt and pepper
squeeze of lemon juice

The garnish:
4oz (100g) button mushrooms
squeeze of lemon juice
12 mussels
3oz (75g) peeled prawns

Prepare the garnish. Wash the mushrooms and trim the bases of the stems. Slice the mushrooms and place in a saucepan with a little salted water and a squeeze of lemon juice. Simmer for 3-4 minutes until just tender. Drain.

☐ To prepare the mussels, scrub them well and remove the hairy beards. Steam them open in a little water in a wide, shallow pan over high heat. Remove them from their shells. Discard any that do not open.

☐ Wrap mushrooms, mussels and prawns in separate foil parcels and set on a baking tray.

☐ Pre-heat the oven to 350F (180C) gas 4. Butter a shallow ovenproof dish large enough to hold all the fillets when folded. Season them, fold them in half crossways and arrange them in the dish. Pour the wine over, and cover the dish with foil. Place the garnishes in the oven to warm through while the fish is cooking. Check the fish after 10 minutes to ensure it doesn't overcook. When the fish looks white and opaque, it is ready.

☐ Meanwhile, prepare the sauce. Melt the butter slowly in a heavy-based saucepan. Add the flour and cook gently for a minute or two, stirring. Off the heat, stir in a little fish stock. Return to the heat and cook, stirring constantly, until the mixture thickens. Add the rest of the stock in batches, off the heat, and cook, stirring, until the sauce is

smooth. Simmer the sauce gently for about 5 minutes.

☐ Take the fish from the oven and pour the cooking liquor into the sauce. Mix in well. Turn the oven to low and keep fish and garnishes warm until ready to serve. Keep this time as short as possible or the fish will dry out.

☐ Finish the sauce by blending the egg yolk with the cream in a small basin. Stir 3 tablespoons of the hot sauce into the egg mixture (liaison) then, off the heat, add this to the pan of sauce. Season with salt, pepper and lemon juice.

☐ Spoon some of the sauce over the fish, and garnish with the mushrooms, mussels and prawns. Pour the rest of the sauce into a sauceboat and serve.

Tip: If you like, you can make the sauce a day in advance, omitting the cooking liquor from the fish. When it is cool, store it in a covered container in the fridge. Ten to fifteen minutes before serving time, pour it into a small covered dish to heat in the oven while the fish is cooking. Add the cooking liquor from the sole just before serving. Take care not to over-thin the sauce.

Gâteau au Chocolat

Chocolate cake
A typically French dessert cake with the added texture of ground almonds and a subtle flavour of brandy. As it is rather rich, the helpings should be small, and it can be cut into 10-12 portions.

Serves 10-12   ☆☆☆
Preparation: 20 minutes
Cooking time: 55 minutes
Decoration: 15 minutes

The cake:
4oz (125g) butter
4oz (125g) caster sugar
2 eggs, size 2
3oz (75g) ground almonds
2oz (50g) plain flour
1oz (25g) cocoa
1½ teaspoons baking powder
3 tablespoons brandy

The icing:
4oz (125g) plain dessert chocolate
1 tablespoon caster sugar
1oz (25g) butter
1 tablespoon water

To finish:
5floz (150ml) double cream
2 tablespoons brandy

To make the cake, beat the butter and sugar together until very light and creamy. Add the eggs one at a time and beat in well. If the mixture curdles at this point, don't worry—it won't hurt the cake. Add the rest of the ingredients and stir sufficiently to mix well together.

☐ Turn the cake mixture into a greased 8in (20cm) cake tin and bake at 350F (180C) gas 4 for about 55 minutes or until baked in the centre. Leave to cool in the tin then turn out and spread with the icing.

☐ While the cake is cooling, make the icing. Break the chocolate into small pieces and put them into a basin with the sugar, butter and water. Place over a pan of hot but not boiling water and stir until the chocolate melts.

☐ Put the cooled cake upside-down on a serving plate and spread the chocolate over evenly with a palette knife. Leave to set in a cool place for about 30 minutes.

☐ Whip the cream and the brandy together and pipe rosettes on top of the cake, using a ½in (1cm) star pipe.

Variation: The French prefer a single layer, but you can split the cake and fill it with whipped cream or a thick fruit purée before coating it with chocolate.

❋ *To freeze:* either before or after icing but before piping cream, set on a tray in the freezer until hard. Remove, and wrap in foil or freezer wrap. Store in the freezer for not more than one month.

☐ To thaw, remove the wrapping, set the gâteau on a serving plate and leave to thaw at room temperature for about 2 hours. The icing will be covered with beads of moisture at first but these will dry out when the cake has come to room temperature.

Speciality

Tarte de Cambrai

Cambrai apple flan

Serves 4-5 ☆ ☆ ☆
Preparation: 20 minutes
Cooking time: 45 minutes

The batter:
1oz (25g) butter
4oz (100g) self-raising flour
4 tablespoons icing sugar
2 eggs, size 2
5 tablespoons milk

The topping:
2-3 dessert apples
2oz (50g) butter
3 tablespoons caster sugar

Pre-heat the oven to 400F (200C) gas 6. Place 1oz (25g) butter in a 9in (23cm) diameter cake tin and put this in the oven to melt.

☐ Mix the flour and icing sugar together in a basin and make a well in the centre. Break the eggs into the well, then add the milk. Remove the cake tin from the oven and pour the melted butter into the batter mixture. A film of butter will remain in the tin to grease it. Stir to mix well together and beat finally for a minute or so.

☐ Pare and core the apples and cut into thin rings. Cut the butter into small pieces.

☐ Pour the batter into the buttered tin and arrange the apple rings on top. Sprinkle with the sugar, and dot with the butter. Bake for about 45 minutes. The batter will bake beneath and around the apples to form a springy base for them. When cooked, the pudding will be a lovely rich brown with an appetizing sugary top. Serve immediately with cream or custard.

TARTE DE CAMBRAI

This traditional dessert goes back many centuries and has long been a favourite, particularly in northern France. A small glass of cognac or Calvados used to be poured over each serving. Nowadays, however, people usually content themselves with lightly whipped cream.

This flan or tart is really a batter pudding with fruit and a delicious sugary-buttery top. It is very easy to make and is equally good as a winter pudding or a summer dessert. Serve it lukewarm straight from the tin.

Variations

Pears, cherries, apricots, peaches, strawberries, raspberries or blueberries can be prepared, stoned or sliced and used instead of apples.

Tarte de Cambrai.

Terrine Tante Marie

Boeuf Bourguignonne
with
Mixed Salad

Clafoutis aux Cerises

Red wine: Côte de Nuits (Bergundy)

────────

*Quantities given serve 6
(except for the terrine)*

Terrine Tante Marie

If you want to make the authentic terrine illustrated, line the dish with thinly sliced speck. This fat from the back of the pig is to be found on delicatessen counters.

To stretch bacon rashers Lay each rasher flat and grasp one end with your left hand. Press the blade of a cook's knife firmly across the rasher, with the back of the blade towards your left hand. Slowly pull the rasher up against the back of the blade to stretch it. This helps prevent the bacon from shrinking during cooking.

Leftover terrine can be stored, wrapped, in the fridge for up to two days. It also freezes well for up to three months.

Carefully line the terrine mould with stretched bacon rashers before filling.

Add the minced meat mixture to the dish, fold the ends of the bacon strips over and finish with reserved bacon.

Terrine Tante Marie
Pork and chicken liver pâté

────────

Serves 10-12 ☆☆☆
Preparation: 1¼ hours
Cooking time: 2 hours

────────

1lb (450g) chicken livers
a little milk
8oz (225g) thinly sliced streaky bacon,
    rinds removed
1lb (450g) boned shoulder of pork
5oz (150g) lean chicken flesh
3oz (75g) white bread, crusts removed
1 onion
2 cloves of garlic
4 tablespoons brandy
3 tablespoons red wine
2 eggs, lightly beaten
salt and pepper
pinch of dried thyme
3 tablespoons finely chopped parsley
1 tablespoon finely chopped chives
sprig of thyme to garnish

────────

Rinse the chicken livers in cold water then soak them in just enough milk to cover for an hour. This removes the slightly bitter taste.

☐ Reserve a few bacon rashers for the top of the pâté. Stretch the rest and use to line the sides and base of a 3 pint (1.5 litre) terrine.

☐ Drain the livers, discarding the milk, and mince finely with the pork, chicken, bread, onion and garlic. This can be done in a mincer or food processor. With your hand, mix thoroughly with all the other ingredients, except the thyme sprig, to be sure you have an even mixture.

☐ Pack the pâté mixture into the lined dish, pressing it well into the corners. Cover with the remaining bacon rashers. Add the sprig of thyme. Cover the dish with a lid or a piece of foil and stand it in a roasting tin. Place in the oven, then carefully pour hot water into the tin until it reaches halfway up the sides of the pâté dish.

☐ Heat the oven to 350F (180C) gas 4. Cook the pâté for about 2 hours, checking after 1½ hours: insert the tip of a sharp knife into the pâté. If it is cooked, the knife will come out clean and feel hot to the touch. Make sure the level of the water

doesn't drop during cooking, and if the water shows any hint of bubbling, lower the temperature.

☐ Remove the pâté from the water bath (bain marie) when it is cooked, and pour off the juices which have collected. Set the pâté on a rack to cool. Store, covered, in the refrigerator for several hours before serving with crusty bread and butter.

Boeuf Bourguignonne
Burgundian beef stew
Serve with a mixed salad dressed with vinaigrette.

────────

Serves 6-8 ☆☆☆
Preparation: marinate overnight,
    plus about 30 minutes
Cooking time: 2½-3 hours

────────

2lb (900g) lean braising or stewing steak

The marinade:
¾ pint (450ml) red wine
6 tablespoons brandy
1 large onion, roughly chopped
1 clove of garlic, crushed
6 parsley stems, chopped
1 stick of celery, chopped
1 bay leaf, crumbled
2 small carrots, chopped
8 black peppercorns
pinch of dried thyme or a large sprig of
    fresh thyme
1 teaspoon salt

The sauce:
2oz (50g) butter
2 tablespoons oil
8oz (225g) streaky bacon, chopped
2 large onions, finely chopped
2 cloves of garlic, crushed
1 tablespoon flour
1 pint (600ml) beef stock
salt and pepper

The garnish:
2-3 tomatoes
8oz (225g) butter
12oz (350g) button mushrooms
3 tablespoons oil
8 slices of white bread, crusts removed
9oz (250g) button onions, peeled
2 tablespoons sugar
2 tablespoons water
salt and pepper
3 tablespoons finely chopped parsley
    to garnish

────────

Trim the meat and cut it into bite-
continued on page 202

Boeuf Bourguignonne

This is an excellent recipe to make with one of the less expensive cuts of beef, such as stewing steak. You can make it in advance and it will mellow if kept overnight. It can be frozen for up to 6 months. Though the list of ingredients may look daunting, it is a very simple casserole to make, and a very good one even if you don't add the final garnish of tiny onions, tomatoes and fried bread croûtes. It is easy to make double the quantity and freeze half for another dinner party.

Clafoutis aux Cerises

When baking the pudding, use a shallow dish. If the dish is too deep, the pudding will not cook through to the centre. And a metal dish may mean that the Clafoutis cooks too quickly at the sides, leaving the middle uncooked.

When baking Remember that metal dishes conduct heat more quickly than earthenware, porcelain or ovenproof glass.

sized pieces. Mix all the ingredients for the marinade together in a large bowl, add the meat, and stir. Cover and leave for 8-12 hours in a cool place. Turn the meat from time to time, if possible.

☐ Remove the meat from the bowl and pat dry with kitchen paper. Strain the marinade and reserve.

☐ For the sauce, heat the butter and oil in a large frying-pan and sauté the bacon to render the fat. Remove the bacon to a saucepan.

☐ Quickly fry the beef in the hot fat then add it to the saucepan. Sauté the onion and garlic until they just begin to brown. Stir in the flour and gradually add half the stock, stirring all the time. Simmer for 5 minutes.

☐ Stir the reserved marinade into the pan and mix well, bringing it to the boil. Pour over the meat and add just enough of the remaining stock to cover the meat. Season, cover, and simmer for 2-2½ hours or until tender.

☐ Prepare the garnish just before serving. Cut the tomatoes in wedges (peel them first if you like), and add to the pan. Heat 2oz (50g) of the butter in a large frying-pan and lightly sauté the mushrooms. Add them to the stew.

☐ Heat the oil in the frying-pan and use to fry the bread on both sides, adding a little butter or more oil if necessary. Remove, cut the bread into triangles and keep hot.

☐ Put the button onions into the frying-pan, making sure they are not more than one layer deep. Cut the rest of the butter into small pieces and dot over the onions. Sprinkle with the sugar and the water, and a little salt and pepper. Shake the pan gently over a low heat until all the liquid has evaporated. Continue to cook gently until a caramel-coloured sauce forms. Remove from the heat immediately to prevent scorching.

☐ Arrange the stew in a heated serving dish, place the onions on top, and garnish with the bread. Sprinkle with parsley.

Variation: If you prefer, you can serve this with French bread in place of the fried bread croûtes.

Clafoutis aux Cerises

Cherry batter pudding

Firm canned fruits are suitable for this dessert and the batter is similar to that made for Yorkshire pudding. It's easy to make and rather good to eat: crusty on the outside with a light but firm texture inside, and the juicy cherries spread throughout.

Serves 4-5 ☆☆☆
Preparation: 20 minutes
Cooking time: 35 minutes

15oz (425g) can cherries
2oz (50g) butter
4oz (125g) plain flour
4oz (125g) caster sugar
4 eggs, size 2
½ pint (300ml) milk
icing sugar to dust

Pre-heat the oven to 375F (190C) gas 5.

☐ Drain the cherries and reserve the syrup for another use. Put half the butter into an ovenproof dish about 8in (20cm) in diameter and 2in (5cm) deep, and place in the oven. Remove the dish as soon as the butter is melted.

☐ Mix the flour and sugar together in a large basin and make a well in the centre. Break the eggs into the well, then add the milk and the melted butter. Stir slowly until the flour is all mixed in, then beat well until smooth.

☐ Pour a thin layer of batter into the hot dish; cook for about 5 minutes until set. Meanwhile, cut the remaining butter into small cubes.

☐ Remove the dish from the oven and scatter the cherries over the surface of the set batter. Pour in the rest of the batter and dot with the cubes of butter. Bake for a further 25-30 minutes. The pudding is ready when it is well puffed up with a firm, golden brown crust. Remove from the oven and dust with icing sugar. Serve immediately.

The South of France

No survey of the food of France, however brief, would be complete without a mention of the sunny south. The region of Languedoc is famed for its grapes and the variety of soft fruits that are now grown on the well-irrigated plains that sweep down to the Camargue. This is the only part of France where rice is grown. The famous Cassoulet stew is just one example of the use that is made of dried beans and any available local meat or sausage. The Languedoc is the true home of Roquefort cheese. To the east is the popular region of Provence, rocky and fragrant with herbs, its name synonymous with olives, garlic and tomatoes.

Both provinces enjoy a plentiful supply of fish and shellfish from the Mediterranean – and the Languedoc fish soup, or Bourride, is cousin to the more familiar Provençal Bouillabaisse. Whereas the latter is traditionally served with the red-hot Rouille sauce, a Bourride will have a spoonful of thick garlic mayonnaise, or aïoli, stirred into each bowl.

Olive oil and peppers are found in both styles of cooking. Instead of the traditional Provençal dish of Ratatouille, make a 'stew' of red, green and yellow peppers, sliced and cooked in olive oil with a hint of onion, to serve with the roast meats of the region.

In Provence, much use is made of thyme and rosemary, and the tuna fish and anchovy-flavoured Salade Niçoise is a universal favourite. While the cooking of Languedoc leans towards Spain, Provence is under a more Italian influence – not surprising, as it once was annexed by Italy, whose borders are not far away.

The food is simple, the 'rôti' or roast being a favourite way of cooking meat – particularly lamb, pork and poultry. Dessert is either fresh fruit or a fruit flan, or perhaps a cooling sorbet in the brilliant summer sun, served in the orange or lemon skin in which it was frozen. Local wine is rough but plentiful, and with after-dinner coffee you may be served with chewy sweet nougat.

Speciality
Salade Niçoise

Serves 4 ☆☆☆
Preparation: 10-20 minutes

2 lettuce hearts, separated into leaves
8oz (225g) canned tuna, drained and flaked
4 tomatoes, cut into wedges
4 hard-boiled eggs, quartered
4oz (100g) cooked or canned French beans
2oz (50g) canned anchovy fillets, soaked in a little milk
2oz (50g) black olives, stoned

The garlic vinaigrette:
¼ pint (150ml) olive oil
2 tablespoons wine vinegar
a pinch of sugar
½ garlic clove, crushed
salt and freshly ground black pepper

Line a salad bowl with lettuce leaves. Arrange the flaked tuna on the lettuce with the tomatoes and egg slices, and the beans.
☐ Drain and add the anchovy fillets and scatter with olives.
☐ Put the olive oil, vinegar, sugar and garlic in a screw-topped jar. Season well and shake to emulsify the dressing.
☐ Just before serving, pour over the salad and toss gently.
Tips: Season the vinaigrette carefully. Remember that anchovies and black olives can be very salty.
● Small cubes of dry bread fried until crisp in garlic-flavoured oil make a delicious addition to the salad.

Salade Niçoise

Ratatouille

For a main course, add some cooked chicken or pork and serve hot. Ratatouille can also be made into a delicious vegetarian supper: Add 2oz (50g) shelled nuts about 20 minutes before the end of cooking.
❇ Ratatouille freezes very well for up to 12 months and can be gently reheated from frozen. Be sure to heat until bubbling hot, though, before serving.

Tapenade

A savoury spread which is a speciality of Southern France, this is a particularly useful addition to the store cupboard. Made from olives, anchovies and capers, it can be spread on toast or biscuits and served with crudités, or spread on bread instead of butter when making salad sandwiches. To serve 6, put 8oz (225g) stoned olives, a small can of anchovies – about 2oz (50g) – a large garlic clove, 1 teaspoon well drained capers and 2 tablespoons olive oil in a blender. Process to a smooth paste, then pack into small jars, covering surface with olive oil to seal. Store in the fridge for up to 3 months.

Lyonnaise potatoes

Sautéed potatoes and onions are combined to make this regional speciality. Serve as an additional accompaniment to the lamb, or with any roast, grilled or fried meat. For 4 people, boil 1¼lb (700g) even-sized potatoes in their skins until just tender. Peel and cut into ½in (1cm) slices, then sauté gently in 1½oz (40g) dripping or butter until evenly browned. In a second pan, sauté 1 finely sliced large onion in 1½oz (40g) fat until lightly browned. Just before serving, mix the onions and potatoes and season well.

Artichaut au Crabe Vinaigrette

Artichaut au Crabe Vinaigrette

Artichoke and crab salad

—————

Serves 4　　　　　
Preparation: about 1 hour

—————

4 medium globe artichokes, trimmed
salt
crab legs to garnish (optional)

The filling:
2 tablespoons lemon juice
¼ pint (150ml) olive oil
freshly ground black pepper
8oz (225g) white crabmeat
2oz (50g) rice, cooked
1 tablespoon cream
1 tablespoon finely chopped parsley
1 tablespoon finely chopped tarragon

—————

Cook the artichokes in boiling, salted water to cover, until just tender. The exact cooking time will depend on the size, age and freshness of the artichokes – 20-40 minutes. They are cooked when a leaf can be pulled off easily. Plunge into cold water to cool.
☐ Drain the artichokes and trim off any stalk from the base so that they sit steady. Remove the cone of leaves from the centre of each, then the hairy 'choke' from below to leave a cup to hold the filling.
☐ Mix together the lemon juice and oil and season well.
☐ Toss the crabmeat and rice in half of the dressing and divide the mixture between the artichokes, putting some between the outer leaves as shown.
☐ Stir the cream and herbs into the remaining dressing and spoon a little over each. Garnish with the crab legs, if available, and serve with thinly sliced brown bread and chilled butter.

Gigot d'Agneau Rôti avec Tomates de Provence

Roast lamb with Provençal tomatoes

—————

Serves 4　　　　　
Preparation: about 5 minutes
Cooking: 1½-2 hours

—————

½ leg of lamb, weighing about 2½-3lb
(1.25-1.5kg)
2 garlic cloves
¼ pint (150ml) red wine

The tomatoes:
1 medium onion, finely chopped
6 medium tomatoes
10 tablespoons fresh white breadcrumbs
1 tablespoon finely chopped basil
1 tablespoon finely chopped parsley
1 teaspoon finely chopped thyme
3oz (75g) butter, melted
salt and freshly ground black pepper

—————

Gigot d'Agneau Rôti avec Tomates de Provence

Set the oven to 350F (180C) gas 4.

☐ Pat the meat dry with kitchen paper. Cut each garlic clove into four, lengthways. With a small sharp knife, make eight deep incisions at intervals in the surface of the lamb and push a piece of garlic into each.

☐ Roast for 20-25 minutes per lb (450g) plus 30 minutes for pink meat, or allow 30 minutes per lb (450g) plus 30 minutes for well-done meat.

☐ Meanwhile simmer the onion in a little salted water until tender. Drain.

☐ Cut each tomato in half and scoop out the seeds. Strain and discard them, reserving the juice to add to the gravy.

☐ Mix together the breadcrumbs, herbs and butter and season well. Stir in the onion, then pack the mixture into the tomatoes. About 15 minutes before the meat is cooked, arrange the tomatoes in the roasting tin.

☐ At the end of cooking time, remove the meat and tomatoes and keep hot.

☐ Pour off any excess fat from the pan, add the wine and the reserved juice from the tomatoes. Bring to the boil, scraping up any sediment from the pan. Reduce the gravy slightly.

☐ Carve the meat into thick slices to serve, adding any extra juices to the gravy before serving.

Note: The traditional way of making gravy, as demonstrated in this recipe, reflects the French preference for unthickened pan juices, skimmed and reduced with a little wine or stock. The gravy can be thickened if you prefer with a little flour or cornflour in the usual way. The lamb can be served with crusty French bread and a green salad instead of potatoes.

Ratatouille

Serves 4-6 ☆☆
Preparation: 20 minutes
Cooking: about 1 hour

---

2 large aubergines
salt and freshly ground black pepper
6 tablespoons olive oil
2 large onions, sliced
2 medium red peppers, cored, deseeded
  and chopped
1 medium green pepper, cored, deseeded
  and chopped
3 courgettes, sliced or diced
2 garlic cloves, crushed
8oz (225g) ripe tomatoes, chopped
2 tablespoons finely chopped basil and
  parsley

Thickly slice the aubergines and sprinkle with salt. Leave to drain while preparing other vegetables.

☐ Heat the oil in a large, shallow pan (a sauté pan is ideal). Add the onion, peppers, courgettes and garlic and stir well.

☐ Drain, rinse and pat the aubergines dry, then add to the pan.

☐ Cover and cook gently for about 1 hour, until vegetables are tender but still hold their shape. Add the tomatoes 15 minutes before the end of the cooking time.

☐ Season well and stir in the herbs. Serve hot.

Tip: Chilled Ratatouille makes an excellent first course.

Tarte aux Fruits

It is important not to over-brown the pastry during baking. The high proportion of sugar means that it scorches easily which would spoil the flavour.

Citron pressé

Seen on the tables of every pavement café in southern France during hot weather, this refreshing and thirst-quenching drink is very simple to make. For 1 large glass, squeeze a juicy lemon, and add ice, water and sugar (1-2 teaspoons) to taste.

Tarte aux Fruits

Tarte aux Fruits
Mixed fruit tart

For a large 'tarte' choose four contrasting fruits or use just one favourite – strawberries, raspberries or stoned cherries, for instance. If you prefer, use the pastry to make 4-6 'tartelettes', using 3-4in (7.5-10cm) fluted tins and fill each one with a different fruit.

Serves 4-6   ☆☆☆
Preparation: 1¼ hours, including chilling
Cooking: 20 minutes

The French flan pastry:
6oz (170g) flour
3oz (85g) butter, at room temperature
3oz (85g) caster sugar
3 egg yolks

The filling:
4oz (100g) raspberries
3 ripe apricots, halved and poached until tender
4oz (100g) redcurrants
4oz (100g) white grapes, skinned and deseeded

The glaze:
6 tablespoons apricot jam
2 teaspoons lemon juice

Put the flour on the work surface and make a well in the centre.

☐ Place the butter, sugar and egg yolks in the well and work them together with the finger tips of one hand, gradually drawing in the flour.

☐ Continue to work until a smooth, even paste is formed, but be careful not to overwork the dough. Wrap and chill for about 1 hour.

☐ Set the oven to 375F (190C) gas 5. Roll out the pastry and use to line an 8in (20cm) flan ring set on a baking sheet, or a sandwich tin, or 3-4 small tartlet tins. Prick the base all over with a fork and line with foil and baking beans.

☐ Bake blind for about 20 minutes, removing the foil and beans after 10 minutes, until the pastry is a light golden brown and moves easily in the tin. Cool.

☐ Gently heat the jam with the lemon juice and rub through a sieve. Brush the base of the pastry with a little of the glaze and arrange the fruit on top. Brush the remaining glaze over the fruit and leave to set before serving.

Italy

The cuisine of Italy is varied, fragrant and very often beautiful to look at. Every town and region has its own culinary traditions, some of which travel the world to reach trattorias in New York, London and Sydney–others you can only discover by visiting Italy yourself. This chapter brings home just a few of the specialities for you to recreate in your own kitchen.

Among Europeans, Italians spend the highest percentage of their income on food and drink and in their own homes they have high standards. These standards start in the market place where critical housewives choose only the best from the bright array of tomatoes, melons, aubergines and courgettes (known as zucchini). You will find that good Italian food is seldom oily, while garlic is used with discretion except in some of the most rustic dishes. The quality of the olive oil is one of the golden secrets of Italian cookery so try to find some of the greenish oil labelled 'first pressing' (vergine) and use it to give an authentic flavour to Italian dishes.

ITALIAN MENUS

Italian meals follow a relaxed pattern, where courses can be added or dropped as appetites dictate.

The first course is antipasto–usually a delectable collection of cold morsels on a platter.

The second course may be a light soup garnished with egg, thin noodles (vermicelli) or herbs. Or it can be a more substantial vegetable soup served with finely grated Parmesan cheese–the hard, strong cheese that is an essential ingredient in Italian cooking. For everyday occasions, such hearty soups may be the only main course.

A pasta dish may be served instead of soup–a smaller helping than if it were the main course. There are literally hundreds of different pasta shapes in Italy, varying from the thin ribbon noodles like tagliatelle to the wide tubes of pasta such as cannelloni stuffed with meat or vegetables, or plump mouthfuls of filled pasta such as ravioli and tortellini.

The main course usually consists of roast, fried or grilled meat, poultry or fish and is accompanied by rice, polenta or different vegetables such as broccoli, or a green salad.

Many Italians finish the meal with fresh fruit or a sorbet, although some prefer cheese–with an extra glass of wine. Italy boasts a wide range of cheeses, including the blue-veined Gorgonzola, creamy Bel Paese, Fontina and Taleggio. Alternatively, there may be an extravagant dessert, accompanied by sweet white wine.

Left: Map of Italy showing the main centres for regional specialities.

Italy–region by region

Each region still has its own culinary traditions–fish and shellfish in the coastal regions, rice dishes in the area around Milan, roast meat in Tuscany, artichokes, aubergines and tomatoes in Rome and the more southern regions, and sweet specialities in Sicily.

Bologna is the centre for cooked meats and is considered to be the gastronomic heart of Italy. The famous Bolognese meat sauce which is served with pasta varies from kitchen to kitchen. Its basic ingredients–tomato purée, white wine and minced beef–may be supplemented with chicken livers or slices of local bacon and sausage. One of the best known Bolognese sausages is the plump, pink, pistachioed Mortadella. Green pasta–egg pasta coloured green with spinach–also originated in Bologna.

Modena has an aroma of fresh fruit and vinegar–there are over 300 vinegar factories! Here a little vinegar is often added to meat, game and poultry sauces to give extra piquancy to local dishes.

Parma is famous not only for its ham and its Parmesan cheese, but also for its sausages.

Venice and Genoa (Venezia and Genova), two great seaports, have dozens of fish dishes including their own versions of Fritto Misto (deep-fried seafood). A delicious sauce for fish or pasta is Pesto from Genoa, which is made with fresh basil, pine nuts, olive oil and grated cheese. The Venetians also make a feature of liver, serving it lightly sautéed with sage, or with onions when it is known as Fegato alla Veneziana.

Milan (Milano) is the centre for risotto and polenta dishes. Polenta, made by boiling a coarse corn meal, is served plain, or shaped into squares, fried in oil and garnished with Parmesan. Round-grain rice is also popular–the uncooked rice is usually sautéed in butter or oil, then simmered in stock and served rather moist.

Tuscany (Toscana) is the home of Chianti wines. Some of the best olive oil is also produced in Tuscany, while oregano, tarragon, rosemary, thyme and fennel are used as flavourings.

Florence (Firenze) is renowned for its specialities and the name of the city is often used to indicate the origins of the dish. Arista Fiorentina is roast pork seasoned with rosemary, garlic and cloves. Bistecca alla Fiorentina is a thick, succulent steak, charcoal-grilled to crispness on the outside but rare within, and sprinkled with a drop of green Tuscan olive oil just before serving. Around **Siena,** hunting is popular and favourite dishes include barbecued pigeon, served with a fragrant fennel salad, and noodles with hare sauce. Almonds feature in both savoury and sweet dishes because some of the best almond orchards in the world are to be found in the region.

In **Norcia** truffles are added to sausages and hams.

And so to **Rome** (Roma), a centre of good food for the past 2000 years. Many restaurants serve regional specialities from the rest of Italy, but there are some uniquely Roman recipes, such as artichokes stuffed with garlic and herbs or grilled lamb prepared with rosemary, peppers, garlic and red wine. The veal that plays such a prominent role in Italian cookery here figures in Salt-imbocca alla Romana, piquant pieces of meat with a wine sauce.

Naples (Napoli) is the home of tomato sauce, pizzas and Mozzarella cheese. In many delicious recipes, tomatoes or aubergines take the place of meat.

Sardinia (Sardegna) boasts its own wines and cheeses and also produces fine olive oil and lemons.

In Sicily (Sicilia) many dishes are prepared with nuts and candied fruits (a legacy of Arab influence long ago) and complemented by the fine dessert wines of the region, including Marsala.

Ossobuco alla Milanese
Braised shin of veal Milan-style

Serves 4 ☆☆☆
Preparation and cooking time: about 3 hours

2lb (1kg) shin of veal, cut into 2in (5cm) pieces complete with bone and marrow
salt and pepper
3 tablespoons flour
2oz (50g) butter
1 tablespoon olive oil
1 onion, chopped
2 sticks of celery, chopped
4 tomatoes, quartered
2 cloves garlic, peeled and crushed
7 floz (200ml) dry white wine
7 floz (200ml) meat stock
1 bay leaf
sprig of parsley

The gremolata (traditional garnish):
2 anchovy fillets
1 teaspoon lemon juice
1 clove garlic, finely chopped
1oz (25g) butter
1 tablespoon finely chopped parsley
a little grated lemon peel

Pat meat dry with kitchen paper. Put it into a plastic bag with the salt, pepper, and flour. Shake to coat the meat.

☐ Heat the butter and oil in a large heavy pan. Add the meat and brown all over. Remove from the pan and set aside. Add vegetables to the pan and stir over a low heat for 5 minutes to soften but not brown. Place the meat upright on top of the vegetables, and add the remaining ingredients.

☐ Bring to the boil, then reduce the heat, cover the pan and cook gently for 1½-2 hours. Turn the bones once during cooking. The meat should be tender enough to be eaten without a knife when the dish is cooked.

☐ Remove the meat with the bones to a serving dish and keep hot. Rub the sauce through a sieve. If necessary, re-boil to reduce a little. Serve separately. And provide spoons for eating the marrow.

☐ *For the gremolata*, pound together all the ingredients to form a paste. Spread over the cooked meat before serving.

Risotto alla Milanese

Risotto Milan-style

Serves 4 ☆☆
Preparation and cooking time:
35-40 minutes

a pinch of saffron strands
about 1¼ pints (750ml) hot chicken stock
2oz (50g) butter
1 small onion, finely chopped
8oz (225g) rice
¼ pint (150ml) dry white wine
1oz (25g) grated fresh Parmesan cheese
salt and freshly ground black pepper
extra Parmesan cheese, to serve

Put the saffron in a cup with 2 tablespoons of the hot stock and leave to stand, pressing the strands with a teaspoon from time to time.
☐ Melt half the butter in a heavy saucepan or frying-pan and soften the onion for 2-3 minutes. Add the rice and stir to coat it with butter.
☐ Pour in the wine and cook over a medium heat for about 1 minute, until the wine has almost evaporated. Reduce the heat, add about 4fl oz (100ml) of the hot stock and cook, stirring occasionally with a fork, until the stock is absorbed. Continue adding stock a little at a time, and stirring frequently, until the rice is cooked–about 25

minutes. Strain the saffron liquid into the pan for the last minute of cooking.
☐ Add the remaining butter and the Parmesan cheese, season and serve.

Zabaglione

Marsala 'custard'

Serves 4 ☆
Preparation and cooking time:
about 15 minutes

4 large egg yolks
3oz (75g) caster sugar
6 tablespoons Marsala

Cream together the egg yolks and caster sugar in a bowl. Set the bowl over a pan of barely simmering water–the water should not touch the base of the bowl–and whisk in the Marsala, or other strong-tasting sweet dessert wine. Continue

whisking–by hand or with an electric beater–until the mixture is pale, creamy and thick. Do not allow to boil. Pour into glasses and serve while still warm, with thin crisp biscuits.
Note: This classic dessert can be served as a sauce for fruit dishes or a fruit salad.

Below left: Ossobuco alla Milanese made with slices of shin of veal cooked slowly in their own juices and served with gremolata — made with anchovies, garlic, parsley and lemon. Right: Risotto alla Milanese, served with tomato sauce, as an alternative to pasta.

Menu

Antipasti

Spaghetti con Cozze

Braciolette Ripiene

Cassata alla Siciliana

White wine: Frascati

————————

*Quantities given serve 4
(except for the cake)*

IDEAS FOR ANTIPASTI

Italians excel at producing the most deliciously light and appetizing first courses, always arranged very decoratively. You can combine two or three–or more–of the ingredients below.

Thin slices of two or three sorts of salami

Olives–black, or stuffed green ones

Anchovy fillets, rolled up with a caper in the middle

Slices of cured ham, such as Parma, can be served on their own or with figs, melon or pears

Artichoke hearts or pimientos in oil

Stuffed tomatoes

Blanched or parboiled vegetables served cold with a little chopped parsley

Tuna, prawns or scampi

Fried or grilled sardines or little pieces of squid

Mussels and clams (fresh or from jars)

Anchovies are sometimes combined with a salad of raw mushrooms, or pimientos

Tuna is traditionally served with cooked French beans or haricot beans and onion rings

Pieces of Mozzarella cheese are alternated with sliced tomato and sprinkled with chopped basil and a few black olives

A vinaigrette or mayonnaise is served with most of these lovely fresh antipasti. You may prefer to substitute lemon juice for vinegar. Antipasti sold ready-made in delicatessen shops often contain too much vinegar–a good reason for making your own antipasti.

Spaghetti con Cozze

In Italy this dish is usually made with vongole, small clams, but in this recipe mussels are used.

Spaghetti con Cozze
Spaghetti with mussels

Serves 4

Preparation and cooking time:
    about 45 minutes

---

3 pints (1.75 litres) mussels in their shells
5 tablespoons olive oil
8oz (225g) spaghetti
1 chilli pepper
2 cloves garlic, finely chopped
2 tablespoons finely chopped shallot or onion
5 anchovy fillets, drained and very finely chopped
4 tablespoons dry white wine
salt and freshly ground black pepper
½ tablespoon finely chopped fresh basil or parsley

Tap any open mussel shells and discard those that do not close, as the mussels inside are no longer alive. Also discard any with cracked shells. Scrub the shells with a stiff brush and scrape them with a knife to remove the encrustations. Tug sharply at the seaweed-like beard to pull it away, and discard it.

☐ Heat 3 tablespoons of oil in a big saucepan. Add the mussels, cover and shake over a medium heat until the mussels have opened. Discard any that do not.

☐ Remove the mussels from their shells, holding them over the pan in order to catch the juices. Keep the mussels warm. Strain the pan juices through a muslin-lined sieve.

☐ Cook the spaghetti in boiling salted water until it is 'al dente', tender but still firm to the bite.

☐ Meanwhile, heat the rest of the oil in a frying-pan and fry the chilli pepper until it just begins to brown. Remove it from the pan. Add the garlic, shallot or onion and the anchovy and turn in the hot oil until the shallot is translucent. Add the strained pan juices and wine and boil until the liquid is reduced by half. Season.

☐ Drain the cooked spaghetti and divide it between 4 heated plates. Put the mussels in the centre, pour over the sauce in the pan and sprinkle with basil. Serve at once.

Braciolette Ripiene
Stuffed veal rolls

Serves 4

Preparation time: 30 minutes
Cooking time: 20 minutes

---

4 veal escalopes, each weighing 3oz (75g)
freshly ground black pepper
8 small thin slices of Parma ham, or 4 large thin slices of cooked ham, halved
2 tablespoons olive oil
1oz (25g) butter
6 tablespoons dry white wine
extra olive oil for frying
4 slices of French bread

The filling:
bunch of parsley, weighing about 2oz (50g), stalks removed, finely chopped
2oz (50g) pine nuts or nibbled almonds
1oz (25g) sultanas
2 tablespoons freshly grated Parmesan cheese
salt and freshly ground black pepper

Mix together the filling ingredients and set aside. Beat the veal escalopes out thinly between 2 sheets of cling film using a cutlet bat or rolling pin. Cut each escalope into 2 equal pieces and season with pepper.

☐ Put a slice of ham on each piece of veal, trimming the ham so that it does not overlap the veal. Spoon some filling onto each piece and press it down keeping it in from the edges. Roll each piece up and tie it in 2 places with fine string.

☐ Heat the oil and butter in a large frying-pan. Fry the veal rolls gently until golden brown–about 10 minutes. Add the wine, let it bubble for 1 minute, then lower the heat, cover the pan and cook for 4-5 minutes, until the veal is tender.

☐ Transfer the rolls to a heated dish and remove the strings. Keep the veal warm in a low oven. Boil the pan juices to reduce them to a glaze. Meanwhile, heat some oil in a separate frying-pan and fry the slices of bread until golden brown on both sides. Drain on absorbent kitchen paper. Spoon the glaze over the rolls and serve with the croûtes.

☐ If you wish, before spooning over the glaze you can place the rolls briefly under a hot grill.

Cassata alla Siciliana

Sicilian layer cake

A simple Madeira cake, layered with a ricotta cheese and fruit filling and coated with toasted almonds, makes a most delicious dessert. It is rich but not overwhelming, and not at all difficult to make.

Certainly you may use a commercially made Madeira cake, but you will have to adapt the quantities of filling and coating for the size of cake you buy. Of course, your homemade cake will have its own special flavour.

Serves 9-10   ☆ ☆ ☆
Preparation time: 1 hour
Cooking time: 1 hour

The cake:
7oz (200g) butter, softened
7oz (200g) caster sugar
4 eggs, size 2
11oz (300g) plain flour
1 tablespoon baking powder
4 tablespoons sherry or milk

The filling and coating:
14oz (400g) ricotta cheese
4oz (100g) caster sugar
2 tablespoons maraschino liqueur
3oz (75g) glacé cherries, chopped
¼oz (7g) angelica, finely chopped
2oz (50g) dried apricots, chopped
2oz (50g) raisins
finely grated zest of ½ lemon
4oz (100g) chopped almonds, toasted
4 tablespoons apricot jam, melted and sieved

First make the cake: heat the oven to 325F (160C) gas 3. Grease and line a loaf tin measuring about 9 × 5 × 3in (23 × 13 × 7.5cm). Beat the butter and sugar together until light and creamy. Beat in the eggs, one at a time. Sift together the flour and baking powder and stir into the cake mixture. Add the sherry or milk and mix in well. Turn the mixture into the prepared loaf tin and level the top. Bake for about 1 hour, or until the cake is well risen, a good golden colour, and beginning to shrink away from the sides of the tin. A skewer inserted in the centre of the cake should come out clean.

☐ Allow the cooked cake to cool in the tin for a short while, then turn it carefully on to a wire rack and leave it to get cold.

☐ Make the filling: beat the ricotta cheese with the sugar until fluffy and stiff. Mix in the liqueur, fruits and lemon zest.

☐ Slice the cold cake horizontally into four layers, then sandwich the layers with the ricotta filling. Press down lightly. Put the toasted almonds on a sheet of greaseproof paper. Brush the sides of the cake with the warm jam, then, holding the cake by the top and bottom, dip the sides of the cake in the toasted almonds. Brush the top of the cake with more jam and sprinkle with the remaining almonds.

☐ Transfer the cake to a plate or board and cut into thick slices to serve.

Cassata alla Siciliana
This delicious cake is best served on the day it is made.

Variations
● Vary the filling by using a different liqueur, or sweet sherry, or by altering the proportions of fruit. Instead of apricot jam you can use marmalade for the coating.

● Another popular version of cassata is made with a coating of melted chocolate, rather than jam and toasted nuts. Heat 2 tablespoons of orange juice in a small saucepan, add 4oz (100g) dark dessert chocolate, grated, and stir until melted. Remove the pan from the heat and with a small palette knife coat the cake completely with chocolate. Set the cake on the serving plate or board and chill to set the chocolate.

Top to bottom: Spaghetti con Cozze, Cassata alla Siciliana, Braciolette Ripiene.

Minestrone

Minestrone

This is as varied as the kitchens where it is born. It is one of the great rustic soups into which goes whatever bits of vegetables and meat are available, along with either pasta or dried beans. The thing which distinguishes the Italian country soup from others is the lavish use of freshly ground pepper and grated cheese on top of the soup.

Ragù Bolognese

This sauce, served with spaghetti, is one of the most universally popular of all Italian dishes. It can be most economical, but for this recipe the delicious—but expensive—Parma ham has been used for its unique flavour. For every day, use streaky bacon.

Minestrone, Ragù Bolognese.

Minestrone

Serves 8   ☆☆☆
Preparation time: 30 minutes
Cooking time: 30 minutes

1oz (25g) butter or bacon fat
1 onion, chopped
2 carrots, sliced
8oz (225g) green beans, sliced
a few cauliflower or broccoli florets
9oz (250g) Parma ham or streaky bacon, diced
2¼ pints (1.25 litres) beef stock
2 courgettes, thinly sliced
11oz (300g) fresh spinach, shredded
2 tablespoons finely chopped parsley
8oz (225g) short pasta
salt and pepper

Heat the fat in a large saucepan and sauté the onion until transparent. Add the carrots, beans, cauliflower or broccoli and ham, and cook for a further 5 minutes, stirring occasionally.

☐ Pour in the stock and bring the contents of the pan to the boil, then add the remaining vegetables, the parsley, and the pasta.

☐ Cook gently until the pasta is 'al dente'– cooked but firm to bite. Season to taste and serve immediately.

Ragù Bolognese

Bolognese meat sauce

Serves 6   ☆☆☆
Preparation time: 15 minutes
Cooking time: about 50 minutes

2oz (50g) bacon fat or butter
1 tablespoon olive oil
1 onion, finely chopped
1 carrot, finely chopped
2 sticks celery, sliced
4oz (100g) minced raw pork
4oz (100g) minced raw beef
4oz (100g) Parma ham or streaky bacon, diced
5 tablespoons tomato purée
¼ pint (150ml) beef stock
6 tablespoons red wine
4oz (100g) button mushrooms, sliced
pinch of dried oregano
salt and pepper

Heat the bacon fat and oil in a large saucepan and use to sauté the vegetables until the onion turns translucent.

☐ Crumble the pork and beef into the pan, add the ham or bacon, quickly turning the mixture with a fork.

☐ Blend the tomato purée with a little of the stock, then add with the rest of the stock and the wine to the pan. Stir in the mushrooms and oregano, reduce the heat, cover, and simmer for 30 minutes.

☐ For a thicker ragù, remove the lid after 20 minutes.

☐ Adjust the seasoning and serve with spaghetti allowing about 3oz (75g) pasta per person.

Spain

Many a visitor has returned from Spain with memories of a cuisine which caters primarily for visiting foreigners' tastes. But, as any well-informed Spanish traveller knows, not far behind the high-rise tourist hotels lie the bars, cafés and inland villages where the true Spanish culinary tradition still thrives, where the real Spanish food is served, and where the Spaniards themselves choose to eat.

Perhaps the best way of exploring what Spain has to offer is to visit the bars serving 'tapas'–small tasty morsels of food to be eaten with the fingers, accompanied by a glass of local wine or dry sherry. These attractive dishes are eaten as snacks, though a gastronomic 'crawl' of a city's tapas bars would provide a substantial and delicious midday meal.

Tapas serve to introduce the abundance of fresh foods used in Spanish dishes–the fish and shellfish, found also in rich stew-like soups and in the famous Paella; the vegetables, most delicious in the iced Gazpacho soup so welcome on a hot Spanish day, or folded into the Spanish omelette or Tortilla; and the eggs, fresh meats, herbs, spices, dried sausages and stews which are all part of a strong, creative and thriving national cuisine.

Meals in Spain

There are two main daily meals in Spain. The first, a late lunch at about 2pm, consists normally of a soup, a meat or fish dish, then a salad and perhaps cheese. This is accompanied by lots of freshly baked crusty bread, a suitable local wine or two, and is usually followed by a siesta!

Tapas are served freshly made at all times of the day, but it is perhaps in the early evening before dinner (served not earlier than 9pm) that they are most indulged in, when work finishes, and friends meet to relax, talk, drink–and nibble.

Dinner is a meal similar to lunch, but is often slightly more elaborate, with interesting 'entremeses', good-looking salads, and many wonderful homemade sauces. It ends occasionally with a dessert (especially on feast days) when the Spanish can indulge their sweet tooth–inherited from the Moorish strain in their ancestry. Apart from almond cakes, pastes and sweetmeats, there are delicious flans, caramel egg custards, shortbreads and deep-fried pastries.

Types of Spanish sausage

Butifarra Made with pork, white wine, cloves, nutmeg, salt and pepper.

Chorizo Made with beef, pork, peppers and garlic, and used in stews.

Salchichon Lightly smoked, made with pork, fat bacon and pepper and eaten raw.

Longaniza Made with pork, garlic and marjoram.

The map of Spain (and Portugal) shows the principal regions of the country and their gastronomic specialities.

Spain–region by region

The history of culinary influences in Spain is an interesting one. Cut off by the Pyrenees from the strong nearby influence of France, the Spaniards–already separated into geographical regions by chains of mountains, plateaux and river gorges–developed individual regional dishes and specialities, dependent on climate, agriculture, and access to river or ocean. The seven-hundred-year rule of the Moors was undoubtedly the strongest culinary influence and indeed changed the nature of the country itself in no small way.

The Moorish invaders, Muslim peoples from countries along the coast of North Africa, brought wealth, culture, their architecture, and helped a peasant Spain to a new sophistication. Agriculturally, they introduced exotic spices and herbs, and cultivated acres of almond plantations, orange groves, rice fields and vegetable gardens.

The Spanish themselves, great travellers and explorers, in turn passed on their knowledge, and language, to the countries they discovered or visited, and many dishes of Mexico, the Philippines and parts of South America show traces of regional Spanish influence. Many products were introduced into Spain, too, from the Americas–tomatoes, peppers and chocolate, for instance.

In the wealthy, green northern provinces of Galicia, and the Basque country (on the border between France and Spain), cattle and sheep thrive on rich pastures, and an abundant supply of seafood comes from the cold northern waters of the Bay of Biscay. Some of the coastal towns in **Galicia** offer what are considered to be the best shellfish tapas in Spain. **Asturias** has delicious black smoked sausages, and the beef, lamb, pork and dairy foods are unequalled elsewhere in the country. Inland from the Basque country is **Navarre** with its trout rivers and famous Rioja vine-

yards–Spain's best-known wine, increasingly available in Britain–which stretch down into Old Castile.

In **Catalonia** to the east, particularly in the large port of Barcelona, the cuisine is varied and interesting, offering the first tastes of the Mediterranean. The cooking is nearer to the French traditions here than elsewhere in the country, using fragrant herbs, garlic, hot red peppers, local olive oil, and specializing in pungent sauces which are uniquely Spanish.

Further south in **Valencia**, the influence of the Moors reveals itself most clearly. Here it was that they planted huge rice fields, and because there was also a plentiful supply of vegetables, poultry and seafood, Valencia, so tradition has it, became the birthplace of one of Spain's great national dishes, the Paella.

Andalucia, in south Spain, is olive oil, citrus, fish and sherry country, and is also renowned for its Gazpacho. The quality of meat available here has led to the development of slow-cooking stews or 'cocidos', often containing chickpeas and sausage,

The Spanish love cooking outside, and purists claim that a Paella must be cooked this way, preferably over a wood fire when the flames licking round the pan will cook the rice properly.

usually the chorizo, the best-known of Spain's many delicious dried sausages. Cocidos are occasionally served in three courses: the cooking liquid is served first as a soup, the vegetables are eaten next, followed by the meats. Sherry or 'jerez' is produced in a small area of chalky soil around the town of Jerez de la Frontera, from which the wine takes its name.

In **Extremadura**, bordering on Portugal, the climate is hard, and pies and pasties, often made with locally caught game, are filling specialities.

Old and New **Castile**, in the central plains of Spain, produce one of the best Spanish cheeses, Manchego, and is famous for its roast baby lambs and piglets. And **Madrid**, the gastronomic hub as well as the geographical centre of Spain, has many regional restaurants for the gourmet to explore.

Tapas

Tapas are a way of life in Spain. Many different types are available—meat, fish and vegetable—and they are appetizingly displayed in rows on bar counters. The hungry customer chooses a selection from those on offer. These include hot and cold tapas. This representative selection, when served together, serves 8 as a starter or 6 as a snack.

Mejillones en Salsa Verde
Mussels in green sauce

Serves 4 ☆☆
Preparation and cooking time:
  10 minutes

8oz (225g) canned mussels, drained

The sauce:
3 tablespoons mayonnaise
1 teaspoon lemon juice
1 tablespoon finely chopped parsley
1 small green pepper, seeded and very finely chopped
salt and pepper
1-2 teaspoons dry sherry

Mix all the sauce ingredients together, seasoning to taste with salt, pepper and sherry.

☐ Pat the mussels dry on kitchen paper, then stir them into the sauce. Transfer to a small serving dish, cover and chill well.

Alcachofas en Salsa Verde
Artichoke bottoms in green vinaigrette

Serves 3-4 ☆☆
Preparation and cooking time:
  10 minutes

1 can artichoke bottoms, about 6oz (175g) drained weight
2 tablespoons chopped chives

The sauce:
3 tablespoons olive oil
1 tablespoon lemon juice
1 tablespoon finely chopped parsley
pinch of rosemary
salt and pepper

Mix all the sauce ingredients together by shaking them in a small clean glass jar with a lid.

☐ Arrange the drained artichoke bottoms on a small serving dish and pour a little of the sauce over each. Sprinkle with chopped chives, cover and chill until required.

Mussels in Pink Sauce
Make a pink mayonnaise sauce instead of green for seafood such as mussels, prawns and shrimps. Make the mayonnaise with lime juice instead of lemon, then stir in enough tomato purée to colour it a delicate pink.

Vegetables in Green Vinaigrette
As an alternative to artichoke bottoms, serve lightly cooked broccoli spears or cauliflower florets.

A delicious display of tapas, clockwise from top right: Artichoke Bottoms in Green Vinaigrette, Meatballs with Ham, Chicken Croquettes, Mussels in Green Sauce, and Prawns (Scampi) with Garlic.

Chicken Croquettes

These can be made with cold poached fish, shrimps, or leftover roast meat instead of chicken.

Prawns with Garlic

You can cook the prawns or scampi with or without their shells. Peel away the shell with your fingers before eating.

The Spanish are great lovers of seafood. Mussels, squid and octopus often appear on restaurant menus. These too are good to serve with the garlic sauce. If you like the taste of garlic and olive oil you can do as the Spanish would, and mix some—or all—of the garlicky hot oil into the sauce.

Meatballs with Ham

These meatballs may be served either hot or cold and are particularly delicious when accompanied by a spicy sauce. Add a few drops of Tabasco to tomato-flavoured mayonnaise or homemade tomato sauce and serve in a small bowl. Spear the meatballs on wooden cocktail sticks and dip into the sauce.

❋ Freezing tapas

Chicken Croquettes and Meatballs can be prepared in large quantities and frozen before the cooking stage. Cooked from frozen they provide quick, hot snacks at short notice. Fry them more slowly and for a longer time than usual to be sure that they are thoroughly cooked in the centre.
The other tapas recipes are not suitable for freezing.

Pastéis de Pollo
Chicken croquettes

Makes 10 croquettes ☆☆☆
Preparation and chilling:
  20 minutes
Cooking time: 10 minutes

---

2 slices of white bread, crusts removed
2 egg yolks
2 tablespoons milk
about 10oz (275g) cooked chicken, finely
    minced
salt and pepper
1 tablespoon finely chopped onion
1 tablespoon cream cheese
1 tablespoon chopped parsley
4-5 tablespoons dry breadcrumbs
oil for frying

Crumble the bread into a basin and mix in the egg yolks and milk. Place the chicken, salt and pepper, onion, cream cheese and parsley into the basin and mix everything together with your hands.

☐ Form into 10 little log shapes, then roll in the breadcrumbs until completely coated. Chill for at least 30 minutes until firm.

☐ Heat the oil in a frying pan and quickly fry the croquettes, turning them to brown on all sides. Drain on kitchen paper and serve piping hot, or cool, chill, and serve cold.

Gambas al Ajillo
Prawns (scampi) with garlic

Serves 4 ☆☆
Preparation: 10 minutes
Cooking time: 10 minutes

---

8 scampi or large prawns, thawed if
necessary
7 fl oz (200ml) olive oil
2 large cloves garlic, crushed with
    a little salt

The sauce:
3 egg yolks, beaten
2 cloves garlic, crushed
4 tablespoons fine fresh white breadcrumbs
4 tablespoons olive oil
1 tablespoon finely chopped parsley
pinch dried thyme or small sprig of fresh
    thyme, chopped
a few drops of lemon juice
salt and pepper

To make the sauce, blend together the egg yolks, garlic and breadcrumbs, then gradually whisk in 3 tablespoons oil, a little at a time, until smooth. Stir in the herbs, then add lemon juice, salt and pepper.

☐ Heat the remaining oil in a frying pan and gently sauté the garlic until golden. Remove garlic shreds from the pan with a slotted spoon, allowing the garlicky oil to run back into the pan.

☐ Pat the scampi or prawns dry on kitchen paper, and fry them quickly in the hot oil (about 30 seconds each side). Remove from the pan and drain.

☐ Serve them hot, with the cold sauce in a separate bowl, or serve them cold with the sauce.

Albondiguillas con Jamón
Meatballs with ham

Makes 15-20 ☆☆☆
Preparation and chilling:
  about 40-45 minutes
Cooking time: 15-20 minutes

12oz (350g) lean raw pork
5oz (150g) Parma ham, thickly sliced
1 egg, beaten
6 tablespoons fine white breadcrumbs
2 tablespoons finely chopped spring onions
1 tablespoon finely chopped parsley
salt and pepper
olive oil for frying
flour for coating

Mince the pork and ham together, then stir in the beaten egg. Add the breadcrumbs, spring onions, parsley, salt and pepper, and mix thoroughly with your hands.

☐ Shape the mixture into small walnut-sized balls, place on a baking sheet and then leave to chill until they are firm.

☐ Heat a little olive oil in a large frying pan. Toss the meatballs in flour until coated, and gently fry them in the hot oil until golden, turning them from time to time. Remove from the pan, drain and serve hot or cold.

Speciality
Paella à la Valenciana

Serves 4-6 ☆☆☆
Preparation: 30 minutes
Cooking time: 30 minutes

6oz (175g) peeled prawns
a few saffron strands
18 fl oz (500ml) warm chicken stock
6 tablespoons olive oil
4 cloves of garlic, crushed
1 large onion, peeled and chopped
1lb (450g) raw chicken, diced
1 red pepper, cut into thin strips
7oz (200g) long-grain rice
3oz (75g) frozen peas
1 pint (600ml) mussels in the shell, cleaned
    and drained
4 tomatoes, peeled, seeded and cut into
    wedges
1 tablespoon finely chopped parsley
salt and pepper
lemon wedges to garnish

Thaw the prawns if necessary. Soak the saffron in the warm stock, and heat the olive oil in a large heavy-based frying pan. Toss the garlic and onion in the hot oil, then add the diced chicken. Sauté gently until the onion is transparent.

☐ Add the pepper strips and rice and stir until coated with oil. Cook for a minute then add the chicken stock and saffron to the pan. Mix well, and cook gently for 15 minutes.

☐ Add the peas, cook for 5 minutes, then add the mussels and tomatoes. Continue to cook gently until all the mussels have opened (discard any that remain closed). Stir in the parsley and prawns and heat through, mixing well together. Season to taste and serve immediately with wedges of lemon as a garnish.

Tip: Leftover cooked chicken can be used. Add with the mussels towards the end of cooking time.

Paellas are normally cooked in a traditional two-handled paëllera (from which Paella gets its name), but a large, heavy-based frying pan is a good substitute, or use two saucepans.

Paella

As in most countries, there are regional variations in the ingredients for traditional dishes. Paella, one of the best known of Spanish national dishes, is no exception. In the coastal areas, the accent is on fish and shellfish as the main ingredients, whereas inland, lamb, pork and rabbit are more often found, perhaps with a few prawns if and when available. Eels, snails, crayfish, squid and clams are other Paella ingredients. This Paella from Valencia is considered to be the most authentic, with its high proportions of chicken and mussels.

Menu

Sopa de Vigilia

*Albóndigas de Bacalao
à la Catalana*

Perdices de Capellán

Torta de Almendras

Wine: White and red Rioja

---

*Quantities given serve 4
(except for soup and cake)*

Cauliflower Fish Soup

Traditionally, the Catholics in Spain eat no meat on Fridays. Instead, fish is served in a variety of ways. This unusual soup, like so many other Mediterranean fish soups, is almost stew-like in consistency.

Clockwise from top: Spanish Almond Cake, Mock Partridges with their sauce (left), Cauliflower Fish Soup and Catalonian Fish Rissoles.

Sopa de Vigilia
Cauliflower fish soup

Serves 6-8 ☆
Preparation: 15-20 minutes
Cooking time: 15-20 minutes

10oz (275g) filleted white fish, cut in strips
2 tablespoons olive oil
1 small onion, finely chopped
1½ pints (900ml) fish or chicken stock
3 tomatoes, peeled and diced
1lb (450g) cauliflower florets
1 cup of boiled rice (about 2oz/50g uncooked)
salt and pepper

Dry the fish on kitchen paper. Heat the oil, then gently sauté the fish and onion until the onion is transparent. Add the stock, tomatoes and cauliflower florets and bring to the boil. Then simmer for 10 minutes. ☐ Add the rice, stirring it through the soup, and season to taste. Serve immediately, with crusty bread, or croûtons fried in olive oil and sprinkled with a little salt.

Albóndigas de Bacalao à la Catalana
Catalonian fish rissoles

Serves 4 ☆☆
Preparation and chilling:
    45 minutes
Cooking time: 15 minutes

12oz (350g) cod fillet, finely minced
1 egg, beaten
3 tablespoons fresh white breadcrumbs
salt and pepper
pinch of ground cloves
1 tablespoon flour
2-3 tablespoons milk
3-4 tablespoons oil for frying

The sauce:
2 slices toasted white bread, crusts removed
few strands of saffron soaked in ¼ pint (150ml) dry white wine
2 tablespoons olive oil
¼ pint (150ml) fish stock
1 tablespoon finely chopped parsley

In a large bowl, mix together all the fish rissole ingredients, apart from the milk and oil, kneading well with

the hands. Add enough milk to bind the mixture, but don't make it too soft.

☐ Flour your hands with extra flour and shape the mixture into walnut-sized balls. Place them on a greased plate and chill for 15-20 minutes until firm.

☐ Now make the sauce. Break up the toasted bread and place in a liquidizer or processor with all the other sauce ingredients except the parsley. Blend until smooth. Transfer to a shallow saucepan and bring gently to the boil. Reduce the heat and simmer for a few minutes.

☐ Heat the oil in a frying pan and lightly fry the fish rissoles, turning, until golden brown. Drain and set aside.

☐ Place the fish rissoles in the sauce and heat through for about 5-8 minutes. Transfer to a hot serving dish, sprinkle with parsley and serve immediately.

Perdices de Capellán
Mock partridges

Serves 4   ☆☆☆
Preparation: 20 minutes
Cooking time: 30-35 minutes

---

8 small veal escalopes, each weighing about 2oz (50g)
8 wafer-thin slices of Parma ham
8 thin slices of salami
2 tablespoons flour sifted with salt and pepper to taste
4 tablespoons olive oil
1 small onion, finely chopped
2 cloves garlic, finely chopped
9 fl oz (275ml) dry white wine
1 tablespoon finely chopped parsley
¼ teaspoon dried thyme or 2 sprigs fresh thyme, finely chopped
¼ teaspoon dried oregano
¼ teaspoon dried basil

Cover each escalope with a slice of ham and a slice of salami, then roll up and secure with wooden cocktail sticks. Coat the meat rolls in the seasoned flour, reserving any excess.

☐ Heat the oil in a frying pan and gently fry the meat until golden brown all over. Add the onion and garlic and sauté for a few minutes,

then add 2 teaspoons of the remaining seasoned flour, the wine and herbs. Bring to the boil, reduce the heat, cover and simmer gently for 20 minutes.

☐ Take the meat rolls out of the pan, drain and transfer to a hot serving plate. Remove the cocktail sticks. Serve immediately, accompanied by boiled new potatoes, a crisp mixed salad, and the sauce.

Torta de Almendras
Spanish almond cake

Serves 8-10   ☆☆☆
Preparation: 20 minutes
Cooking time: 1¼-1½ hours

7oz (200g) butter, at room temperature
7oz (200g) caster sugar
4 eggs, size 2
7oz (200g) plain flour, sifted
3½oz (100g) ground almonds
3 teaspoons baking powder
1 tablespoon milk
1 teaspoon almond essence
4oz (125g) glacé cherries, quartered

Grease and line a loaf tin about 9 × 7 × 3in (23 × 18 × 7.5cm). Pre-heat the oven to 325F (160C) gas 3.

☐ Cream the butter and sugar together until very light and fluffy. Beat in the eggs, one at a time, then fold in the flour, ground almonds and baking powder. Stir the milk, almond essence and cherries into the mixture and turn it into the prepared cake tin.

☐ Bake for 1¼-1½ hours. When cooked, the cake is golden in colour and will have shrunk away from the sides of the tin. To test if it is cooked through, insert a thin skewer into the centre. If the skewer comes out clean, the cake is ready.

☐ Stand the cake in the tin for 5 minutes, then turn out on to a cooling tray and leave until cold. Store in an airtight container.

Almond Cake
Almond trees grow in abundance in mainland Spain and in the Balearic islands, and the nuts are used often in cooking. Cold soups are thickened with ground almonds, meat and fish are occasionally accompanied by toasted almonds, and the Spanish sweet tooth is indulged in many jams, pastes, cakes, biscuits and nougat-like sweetmeats made from almonds.

Saffron in Spanish cooking
Saffron, the dried stigmas of the saffron crocus–a legacy of the Moors–is grown in Spain and is therefore used a great deal in the country's cooking. It comes in threads (the stigmas) or powdered form; either way it is expensive. Turmeric, the ground root of a plant of the ginger family, costs less and colours food with a similar, though brighter, yellow.

'a la Catalana'
Poultry or meat is sautéed in oil, then braised in a prepared sauce made with chopped shallots, mushrooms, tomatoes, garlic and white wine. It is then served with small slices of fried Spanish sausage and braised button onions.

Gazpacho

Gazpacho is often accompanied by separate small bowls of extra chopped salad vegetables and hard-boiled eggs as a garnish. Sometimes cubes of bread are added instead of breadcrumbs, and a few ice cubes added at the last minute ensure its refreshing qualities on a hot Spanish day. Make ice cubes of tomato juice to add to Gazpacho without diluting the flavour.

Spanish Omelette

The Spanish eat their Tortillas hot or cold and often do not fold them, but cut and eat them in wedges—or in strips, as tapas. Many things can be put into this basic recipe—cooked vegetables such as peas, pepper strips and beans, and a little chopped cooked chicken or ham adds taste and texture. Traditionally the Spanish Omelette is flatter and not as fluffy as the French equivalent.

Left: Gazpacho; and right: Spanish Omelettes for two.

Speciality
Gazpacho
Iced vegetable soup

Serves 4   ☆☆
Preparation: 10 minutes
Chilling time: 1 hour

---

2 tablespoons white breadcrumbs
1 clove garlic, crushed
1 tablespoon red wine vinegar
4 tablespoons olive oil
1 green pepper, seeded and chopped
1 small onion, finely chopped
10oz (275g) tomatoes, peeled and seeded
½ cucumber
1 tablespoon ground almonds
½ pint (300ml) chicken consommé or stock, chilled
1-2 tablespoons coarsely chopped parsley
salt and pepper

Put the breadcrumbs, garlic, vinegar, olive oil, green pepper, onion and tomatoes into a blender and process until smooth. Grate the cucumber and stir this into the mixture.

☐ Stir in the ground almonds and consommé or stock, then transfer to a tureen. Cover and chill for at least 1 hour. Sprinkle the chopped parsley over the soup and season just before serving.

Speciality
Tortilla à la Española
Spanish omelette

Makes 2 omelettes   ☆☆☆
Preparation: 5-10 minutes
Cooking time: 20 minutes, including potatoes

---

6 tablespoons olive oil
4 small potatoes, peeled and thinly sliced, or diced
1 onion, finely chopped
1 clove garlic, crushed
6 eggs
2 tablespoons milk
salt and pepper

Heat half the oil in a frying pan and sauté the potatoes over a medium heat. Do not allow to brown.

☐ Add the onion and garlic and cover the pan. Cook gently until potatoes are soft—about 10 minutes.

☐ Beat the eggs with the milk, and season lightly. Heat half the remaining oil in an omelette pan and pour in half the egg mixture. Arrange half the potato and onion mixture over the egg as it sets, and cook gently until the underside is golden brown and the top is set.

☐ Fold the omelette in half and slide on to a heated plate. Make a second omelette, using the rest of the oil. Serve hot, with a salad.

Switzerland

Financial wizardry, clockwork ingenuity, mountains, cheese and chocolate are – to many – the principal characteristics of Switzerland. An Alpine country landlocked by Germany, Austria, Italy and France, its cuisine is split roughly into three divisions which represent the neighbouring nations and the language spoken in those areas – French, German or Italian. These major influences apart, the Swiss have still managed to produce some specialities of their own, which are loved the world over: fondue, raclette, and the most nutritious breakfast of all, muesli.

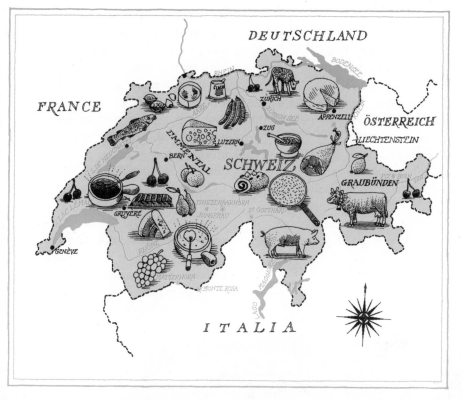

The map of Switzerland shows the diverse regional specialities.

With its Alpine heights, lakes and great rivers, Switzerland is a rich agricultural country. The river Rhine flowing north into Lake Constance (Bodensee), forms the borders with Austria and Germany, and here, predictably, the cuisine is most German: fish are eaten from river and lake; a major growing area, there are cabbage tarts, onion tarts, a unique onion soup, Sauerkraut, and carrot cakes; potatoes, cheese, apples and pears (sometimes cooked together) all feature in local specialities. Basle is famed for gourmet pastries, salmon dishes, and Rhine wines, and from Zürich, the largest Swiss city, comes the veal in wine sauce, Geschnitzeltes, traditionally served with Rösti, a shredded potato cake. Zürich is also the birthplace of muesli, the mixture of cereal, nuts and dried fruit which brought health to the breakfast tables of Europe.

Appenzell, towards Austria, produces a famous cheese, and from further south comes a particular Swiss treat: viande séchée or Bindenfleisch. This is beef or pork, brined and air-dried rather like Parma ham, and served in thin slices with bread and pickles. The area is also known for its game, fruit, nuts and (many claim) the best pâtissiers in Europe – of whose art the Engadiner Nusstorte (nut tart) is a prime example.

On the other side of the St Gotthard Pass lies Ticino, or Italian Switzerland, where pasta, osso bucco, zabaglione, pizza and a delicious risotto flavoured with wild mushrooms, are specialities.

Back over the Alps, from the French-speaking west, comes raclette. A large local cheese is set in front of heat and, as it melts, the cheese is scraped off and eaten with boiled potatoes and pickles. Fondue also stems from here as do Gruyère and Emmental, from the premier Swiss cheese areas which are very close. Each village, if not household, has a different recipe, but basically the cheese should be half Gruyère, half Emmental. Kirsch, Swiss cherry brandy, is an authentic essential. A beef fondue, with chunks of beef dipped in hot oil, is also popular.

Geneva, the French-speaking city on Lac Léman, is the base of many international organizations, and its cuisine is thus more sophisticated. Perch are caught in the lake, and a classic sauce of fish stock and wine is Genévoise. Gratin Dauphinoise, a casserole of potatoes and cheese, Veal Cordon Bleu, and pigs' trotters in Madeira sauce, are all typical.

Further north, from near the capital city Berne, come tripe dishes, cheese tarts, apple and potato mixtures, apple puddings and bilberries. Sbrinz, the Swiss Parmesan, has been made for over 400 years in the Lucerne valley, and this area also makes a stew with bacon and pears, and gingerbreads. Nearby Zug is known for cheese toasts, Käseschnittchen.

Menu

Zuger Käseschnittchen

Geschnitzeltes
or
Zürcher Leberspiessli
with
Rösti
Cucumber Salad

Apfelwähe
or
Cherries in Kirsch

White wine: Swiss Fendant
———————
Quantities given serve 4

From left to right: Zuger Käseschnittchen, Geschnitzeltes, served with Rösti and Cucumber Salad, and Apfelwähe, a creamy apple and grape flan.

Züger Käseschnittchen

Serves 4   ★★☆
Preparation: 10 minutes
Cooking: 10 minutes

4oz (100g) Emmental cheese, grated
4oz (100g) Sbrinz or Parmesan, grated
3 tablespoons milk
2 eggs, separated
1 tablespoon brandy
4 slices white bread, crusts removed
4 slices ham

To garnish:
a few parsley sprigs
2 tomatoes, van-dyked as shown

Mix cheeses together. Add milk, egg yolks and brandy, and mix well.
□ Set the grill to high and toast one side of the slices of bread.
□ Meanwhile, whisk the egg whites until stiff and carefully fold into the cheese mixture.
□ Turn toast over, top with the ham and pile the cheese mixture to within ½ inch (1cm) of the edge.
□ Grill until the mixture has set and is golden brown. Serve hot, garnished with parsley sprigs and tomatoes.

Geschnitzeltes

Serves 4   ★★☆
Preparation: 5 minutes
Cooking: 30 minutes

1lb (500g) veal fillet
3oz (75g) butter
1 small onion, finely chopped
9 fl oz (250ml) dry white wine
9 fl oz (250ml) double cream
salt and freshly ground black pepper
1 tablespoon chopped parsley or chives

Cut the veal lengthways into long slices then cut into strips.
□ Melt the butter in a large frying-pan. When foaming add the meat and cook for 2-3 minutes, stirring, until meat is still pink and not browned. Remove and keep warm.
□ Add the onion to the pan and cook in the juices until softened but not coloured. Add the wine, scrape up any sediment in the pan and boil until liquid has reduced by half.
□ Stir in the cream and simmer for a few minutes until sauce has thickened slightly. Season with salt and freshly ground black pepper.
□ Return the meat to pan and heat through. Serve sprinkled with chopped parsley or chives.

Zürcher Leberspiessli

Serves 4 ☆☆☆
Preparation and cooking: 40 minutes

1lb (500g) calves' or lambs' liver
about 20 fresh sage leaves or 2 tablespoons
    dried sage
freshly ground black pepper
8oz (225g) streaky bacon, rinds removed
4 tablespoons well-flavoured Meat or
    Chicken Stock
4 tablespoons dry white wine
salt

Trim the liver and cut it into $1\frac{1}{2} \times \frac{3}{4}$ in (4×1.75cm) strips.

☐ Cut the sage leaves in half. Place a piece on each strip of liver or sprinkle with a little dried sage. Grind on plenty of pepper.

☐ Stretch the bacon rashers with the back of a knife, cut into four.

☐ Wrap the liver pieces in bacon with the sage and thread on to 4 skewers.

☐ Set the grill to high, then grill until the bacon is brown and beginning to crisp. Remove and keep warm.

☐ Add the stock and wine to the pan juices, scrape up any sediment and boil the sauce for 1-2 minutes. Season to taste.

☐ Spoon the sauce over the liver and serve at once with Rösti.

Rösti

Serves 4 ☆☆☆
Preparation: 15 minutes
Cooking: 25 minutes

2lb (1kg) potatoes
salt and freshly ground black pepper
6 tablespoons oil or clarified butter

Choose potatoes which are of equal size. Bring to the boil in a large pan with water to cover and cook for 10 minutes, until potatoes are almost tender but still just undercooked. Drain and leave to cool.

☐ Peel the potatoes and grate coarsely into a bowl. Season and mix carefully to prevent breaking up the potato shreds.

☐ Heat the oil or butter in a 9 inch (23cm) frying-pan. Add the potato and spread evenly over base of pan, pressing down firmly with a spatula.

☐ Cook over high heat for 4-5 minutes, then reduce the heat to very low and cook for a further 20 minutes.

☐ To serve, place a plate over the pan and invert it, allowing the Rösti to turn out whole. Serve cut into wedges.

Cucumber Salad

Thinly slice a large cucumber and toss it with a punnet of mustard and cress and some Vinaigrette dressing (6 tablespoons olive oil and 3 tablespoons white wine vinegar).

Sbrinz

This is a very hard cheese which is cured for 2-3 years, stored vertically rather than horizontally and rubbed with linseed oil to prevent loss of weight by evaporation. It is therefore very hard and good for grating.

Rösti

Sometimes a little chopped onion or ham is added to the potato before frying.

Geschnitzeltes

Pork fillet or a firm-textured fish such as salmon, turbot or sole could be used instead of veal.

Hot cherries in kirsch

To serve hot, pour the thickened syrup, without the kirsch, over the cherries. Immediately before serving, warm the kirsch slightly, ignite it and pour over the cherries. Serve, still flaming, as a sauce for vanilla ice cream.

Bindenfleisch

A very popular first course or accompaniment to cheese fondue in Switzerland is air-dried beef, known as Bindenfleisch or 'viande séchée'. It is cut in extremely thin slices and eaten with various pickles.

Chocolate Cherries

For a very Swiss after-dinner treat, try chocolate-coated liqueur cherries. Plan ahead, and select fresh cherries that are not over-ripe. Wipe them, trim off all but a short length of stalk and marinate in kirsch to cover in a lidded jar for at least 3 months. Drain, then pat dry. Dip in gently melted chocolate until well and evenly coated. Leave to set in a cool place (not the fridge). Serve in small paper cases.

Glühwein

Hot spiced wine, fortified with a dash of brandy, is a favourite drink of skiers in Switzerland; it is also an ideal drink to serve at the beginning of a winter party. Red or white wine may be used. For 3 bottles: heat about a third of the wine with 8 cloves, 2 sticks of cinnamon, 2 sliced oranges and sugar to taste. Leave to infuse for 45-60 minutes. To serve, add the remaining wine and heat it so that it is pleasantly hot to drink, but not hot enough to evaporate the alcohol or crack the glasses. Just before serving, add brandy to taste and decorate with sliced oranges.

Swiss wines

The Swiss are great wine drinkers, and although they import a great deal of French wine, they also produce their own, to which they are very loyal—so much so that there is very little left to export. Perhaps the best-known Swiss wines are the white, slightly fizzy white wines of Vaud and Valais—Dorin and Fendant. A smaller amount of red wine is also produced, notably the Dôle from Valais and the Merlot from Ticino.

Apfelwähe

Serves 4-6   ☆☆☆
Preparation: 1½ hours
Cooking: 40-50 minutes

The pastry:
6oz (175g) flour
pinch of salt
3oz (75g) chilled butter
2oz (50g) caster sugar
¼ teaspoon white wine vinegar or lemon juice
3 tablespoons iced water

The filling:
¾lb (350g) black or green grapes
2 large cooking apples
2 tablespoons kirsch
2½oz (65g) caster sugar
2 Dutch 'toast' crispbreads or rusks
3oz (75g) hazelnuts, roughly chopped
3 eggs, size 3
4 fl oz (100ml) double cream
a few drops of vanilla essence
½ teaspoon cinnamon (optional)

Sift the flour and salt into a bowl. Add the butter, cut into small dice and rub it into the flour with the fingertips until the mixture resembles fine breadcrumbs. Stir in the caster sugar.

☐ Mix together the vinegar or lemon juice and water and sprinkle over mixture. Using a round-bladed knife press mixture together to form a dough. Turn out on to a floured work surface and knead lightly until smooth and free from cracks. Roll out into a rectangle approximately 10 × 5 inches (25 × 13cm), keeping the edges straight as you roll by patting into shape.

☐ Mark pastry into 3 equal parts with the back of a knife. Fold bottom third up and over centre third, then fold top third down to cover both these layers. Seal edges and give pastry a half turn clockwise. Repeat this process 3 times, chilling pastry for 5 minutes between rollings.

☐ Roll pastry into a circle about 12 inches (30cm) in diameter and line a 8-9 inch (20-23cm) spring-form cake tin. Chill whilst preparing filling.

☐ Set the oven at 375F (190C) gas 5. Peel and de-pip grapes and place in a bowl. Peel and core the apples, cut into ½ inch (1cm) dice and add to grapes. Stir in the kirsch and 1 tablespoon of the caster sugar and mix well.

☐ Crush the rusks and mix together with the hazelnuts. Spread mixture evenly over base of pastry-lined tin and cover with the apple and grape mixture.

☐ Whisk together the eggs, cream, vanilla essence and 1 tablespoon of the remaining caster sugar. Pour over the apple and grapes.

☐ Bake on the centre shelf of the oven for 40-50 minutes until golden brown and the custard is set. Remove from tin and serve warm or cold sprinkled with the remaining caster sugar mixed with the cinnamon.

Cherries in Kirsch

Serves 4   ○
Preparation: 10 minutes
Cooking: 15 minutes, plus about 3 hours chilling

¼ pint (150ml) water
4oz (100g) sugar
1½lb (700g) sweet cherries, rinsed and stalks removed
½ teaspoon arrowroot
6 tablespoons kirsch

Place the water and sugar in a pan over moderate heat. Stir until the sugar has dissolved, then boil for 2 minutes.

☐ Add the cherries and simmer very gently for about 10 minutes until tender.

☐ Remove the cherries with a slotted spoon, draining thoroughly, and place them in a serving bowl.

☐ Blend the arrowroot with a little water and add it to the syrup. Boil for 2-3 minutes, until the mixture thickens and clears. Remove from the heat, stir in the kirsch and pour over the cherries.

☐ Cool, cover and chill the cherries. Serve cold with whipped cream or ice cream.

Speciality
Fondue Neuchâtel

The Swiss cheese fondue is a perfect way of entertaining friends. Cooked in a communal pot which each person dips into, it is prepared with the minimum of fuss and is also great fun. The fondue can be prepared at the table but it is probably easier to cook it in the kitchen and use the fondue burner to keep it hot. The Swiss insist that no extras except wine are needed, but it would be wise to have plenty of salad on hand to help avoid the indigestion known as 'cheese ball'.

Serves 4   ☆☆☆
Preparation: 10 minutes
Cooking: 10 minutes

1 garlic clove, halved
1 tablespoon cornflour
¾ pint (450ml) dry white wine
2 teaspoons lemon juice
¾lb (350g) Emmental cheese, coarsely grated
¾lb (350g) Gruyère cheese, coarsely grated

a pinch of nutmeg
a pinch of ground white pepper
3 tablespoons kirsch
1 French loaf, 1 day old, cut in 1 inch (2.5cm)
   cubes

Rub the inside of the fondue pot with the garlic.

☐ Blend the cornflour with a little of the wine in a small bowl. Bring the rest of the wine to the boil with the lemon juice in the fondue pot, then gradually add the cheese, stirring continuously until it is dissolved. When it is blended and bubbling, add the cornflour mixture and cook for 2-3 minutes until the fondue has thickened.

☐ Season with the nutmeg and pepper, stir in the kirsch and serve with the cubes of bread, a green salad and plenty of dry white wine.
Variation: Try using rosé wine instead of the white – it gives a different flavour and an attractive colour to the fondue.

The fondue pot
Traditionally an earthenware pot, known as a caquelon, is used for cheese fondue, although cast iron is also very good. Thinner metal pots such as copper or enamelled steel can be used, but the mixture must be carefully tended if it is not to burn on to the pan.

Traditions
If you are in a party mood or need to encourage one, the traditional forfeits are fun. If a man drops a piece of bread into the fondue he must either provide another bottle of wine for the company or undertake to hold the next party. Any lady who drops her bread into the fondue is supposed to kiss all the men present.

The traditional Fondue Neuchâtel.

Engadiner Nusstorte

The quantities and types of nuts can be varied. All walnuts are often used, giving a stronger flavour, or alternatively all hazelnuts; all almonds or a mixture of the two could be used.

❋ The Nusstorte freezes very well for up to 6 months, wrapped in foil and sealed in a plastic bag. Thaw for 3-6 hours and warm in the oven before serving.

Engadiner Nusstorte.

Speciality
Engadiner Nusstorte

Serves 6-8   ☆☆☆
Preparation: 1 hour
Cooking: 35 minutes

The pastry:
6oz (175g) flour
a pinch of salt
8oz (225g) butter, chilled
6oz (175g) caster sugar
2 teaspoons finely grated lemon rind
1 egg, lightly beaten

The filling:
6oz (175g) caster sugar
2 tablespoons clear honey
5 tablespoons single cream
4oz (100g) shelled walnuts, roughly chopped
4oz (100g) shelled hazelnuts, roughly chopped
1 egg, lightly beaten
a little beaten egg to glaze

Sift the flour and salt into a bowl and rub in the butter. Stir in the sugar, lemon rind and egg. Press mixture together to form a soft dough. Turn out on to a floured work-surface and knead gently until free from cracks.

☐ Roll out two-thirds of the dough and use to line base and sides of a 9 inch (23cm) diameter loose-based flan tin. Wrap remaining pastry and chill with prepared tin whilst making filling.

☐ Heat a heavy-based frying-pan over moderate heat. Add the caster sugar and stir until melted.

☐ When the sugar is liquid, boil until it is a pale golden brown. Remove from the heat and cool slightly. Add the honey and cream – if the mixture turns into a soft toffee return the pan to a low heat to melt. Mix together the nuts and egg and stir into the mixture in the pan. Spread filling evenly into prepared pastry case. Set the oven at 400F (200C), gas 6.

☐ Roll out two-thirds of the reserved pastry into a circle to cover the flan. Seal the edges.

☐ Roll out the remaining pastry and cut out several crescents and oval shapes using a fluted pastry cutter.

☐ Brush Nusstorte with a little beaten egg and arrange shapes on it. Brush with beaten egg. Bake just above the centre of the oven for about 30-35 minutes, or until golden brown.

☐ Cool slightly, then remove from the tin and serve warm or cold with whipped cream.

Austria

For many hundreds of years the political as well as geographical centre of Europe, Austria shows clearly the influences of its grand European Imperial past in its cuisine. Yet it has developed a style of eating uniquely its own. Thought of as a 'heavy' cuisine, and there *is* a bias towards potatoes, dumplings, noodles and cream, the world would be infinitely poorer without the delights of Apfelstrudel and Sachertorte!

This map of Austria shows the regional specialities and the countries bordering Austria which so influence its food.

A landlocked country dominated by the Alps, Austria is bordered to the north by Czechoslovakia, and then clockwise by Hungary, Yugoslavia, Italy, Switzerland, Liechtenstein, and Germany. Strauss's famous Danube (in reality more murky than blue) flows through the capital Vienna, the source of many Austrian specialities. The origins of Wiener Schnitzel are debated, but the Viennese still claim it as their own. Boiled beef and mutton are popular too, served at midday with herb sauces and crisp vegetables.

From Vienna comes the renowned chocolate cake, Sachertorte, so highly prized that local restaurants have legally contested the 'original' recipe. Vienna is also famed for its coffee houses, where the art of coffee making is taken seriously, each serving at least six different varieties, in many different ways – most, if not all, with lashings of whipped cream. The afternoon Kaffee mit Schlag (with cream) is accompanied by the famous creamy Austrian cakes.

From Czechoslovakia come the widespread Austrian dumplings, both sweet and savoury. Further south, Hungary's paprika spices up the local cooking, which features stuffed peppers and a roast goose eaten at Martinmas. Also notable are thick bean soups with bacon, and robust red wines. Near Yugoslavia, poultry, heavier ragoûts of pork or mutton, and game are popular. On the Italian borders, noodles replace potatoes, while many gastronomes claim that this area produces the best Apfelstrudel in Austria.

Pork and ham are eaten throughout the country, but in the Tyrol, the many sausages, fat-bacon dumplings and smoked loin dishes with sauerkraut are heavier – to keep out the cold!

From around Salzburg, the birthplace of Mozart, come many of the best national puddings: Salzburger Nockerln, a soufflé-omelette; Kaiserschmarrn (a 'torn' pancake, good with local fruit); and further north from Linz, the Linzertorte, a wonderful latticed jam tart. From the banks of the Danube come the light crisp wines, and the famous 'blue' trout which turns blue when cooked.

Menu

Stuffed Cucumber

*Boiled Leg of Lamb
with Marjoram Sauce*

*Kaiserschmarrn
with Fruit*

White wine: Austrian Riesling

Quantities given serve 4

Stuffed Cucumber

Try varying the filling with fish such as sardines, salmon or smoked mackerel instead of the ham, or try this easy version of Liptauer cheese: rub 4oz (125g) curd or cottage cheese through sieve, then beat in 2oz (50g) softened butter, a tablespoon of cream, a few chopped chives, a pinch of paprika, and pepper and salt to taste. Fill the cucumber as in the recipe.

The cucumbers are salted and left to drain to draw out some of their moisture. If this is not done it is possible that the filling may absorb the juice and become too soft.

From left to right: Stuffed Cucumber served with toast and herb butter, Boiled Leg of Lamb with Marjoram Sauce and Kaiserschmarrn, a traditional 'torn pancake' dessert, with fruit.

Stuffed Cucumber

Serves 4 ☆☆☆
Preparation: 2 hours, including chilling

1 large cucumber
salt
3 hard-boiled eggs
4oz (100g) Parma ham or similar smoked ham
4oz (100g) cooked ham
2 tablespoons mayonnaise
½oz (15g) butter, softened
1 tablespoon finely chopped gherkins
1 tablespoon finely chopped onion
1 teaspoon French mustard
2 teaspoons horseradish sauce or ¼ teaspoon freshly grated horseradish (optional)
freshly ground black pepper

The sauce:
4 tablespoons mayonnaise
4 tablespoons soured cream
1 tablespoon finely chopped chives
½ teaspoon freshly grated horseradish

Trim and discard both ends of the cucumber then cut into four equal lengths. Remove strips of the skin with a small knife or a potato peeler.

☐ Carefully hollow out the centre core, then place cucumber pieces on a plate and sprinkle it with a little salt. Leave to drain in a cool place for about 30 minutes.

☐ Meanwhile, shell the eggs, cut them in half and remove the yolks. Chop the whites and rub the yolks through a sieve. Finely chop ham.

☐ Mix together the mayonnaise, butter, egg whites, yolks, ham, gherkins, onion, mustard and horseradish. Season to taste.

☐ Rinse the cucumber pieces and dry well with kitchen paper. Carefully fill the hollowed centres with the stuffing, wrap each piece in foil and chill for at least 1 hour.

☐ Mix together the sauce ingredients.

☐ To serve, cut each portion of cucumber into ½in (1cm) slices and arrange in rings on 4 individual plates. Spoon the sauce into the centres of the rings and serve with thin toast and chive butter.

Boiled Leg of Lamb with Marjoram Sauce

Serves 4 ☆☆☆
Preparation: 25 minutes
Cooking: 2¼ hours

1 small leg of lamb, boned and secured with skewers
2 large onions, roughly chopped
2 garlic cloves, crushed
2 bay leaves
6 parsley stalks
a small sprig of thyme
salt and freshly ground black pepper
1¼lb (700g) small potatoes, peeled and quartered
1lb (500g) carrots, peeled and cut into fingers
6 celery sticks, cut into 3in (8cm) matchsticks
8oz (225g) French beans, topped and tailed
4oz (100g) butter
1½oz (40g) flour
1 teaspoon lemon juice or white wine vinegar

½ teaspoon dried marjoram or 1 tablespoon
finely chopped fresh marjoram
1 tablespoon finely chopped parsley

Bring 3½ pints (2 litres) water to the boil in a large pan. Carefully lower the meat into the pan and bring the water to the boil. Remove any scum.

☐ Add the onion, garlic, bay leaves, parsley stalks and thyme, with salt and pepper to taste.

☐ Reduce the heat, cover and simmer for about 1½ hours, or until the meat is tender and the juices run clear when the joint is pierced.

☐ Remove the meat and keep warm. Strain the cooking liquid, rinse the pan and return the liquid. Bring to the boil, then add the potatoes. Cook for 10 minutes then add the carrots, celery and beans. Continue to cook until all the vegetables are tender, then remove them, drain and keep warm.

☐ Melt 2oz (50g) of the butter in a pan. Add the flour and cook for 2 minutes over a low heat. Remove from the heat and gradually add ¾ pint (450ml) of the cooking liquid. Return to the heat and bring to the boil, stirring constantly, until the sauce is smooth and thickened. Simmer gently for 5 minutes. Whisk in the remaining butter, the lemon juice and marjoram.

☐ Carve the lamb in neat slices and arrange them with the vegetables on a heated serving plate. Spoon a little of the sauce over the meat, sprinkle with the parsley and serve.

Kaiserschmarrn

Serves 4   ☆☆☆
Preparation and cooking: 20 minutes

2oz (50g) raisins or sultanas
4 tablespoons white rum
5oz (150g) flour
a pinch of salt
3 tablespoons caster sugar
4 eggs, separated
a few drops of vanilla essence
½ pint (300ml) milk
3oz (75g) butter
sifted icing sugar to finish

Put the raisins to soak in the rum.

☐ Sift the flour and salt into a large bowl and stir in the caster sugar. Make a well in the centre and add the egg yolks and vanilla.

☐ Stir in half the milk, gradually incorporating the flour to make a stiff batter. Stir in the remaining milk, the soaked raisins and any rum.

☐ Whisk the egg whites until stiff, then fold them carefully into the batter until evenly combined.

☐ Melt half the butter in a frying-pan. Pour in enough mixture to fill the pan to a depth of ½in (1cm). Cook over moderate heat until golden underneath and set on top.

☐ Using two forks, tear the mixture into 5-6 even-sized pieces. Turn the pieces over and cook them until brown. Remove and keep warm.

☐ Repeat with the remaining mixture. Serve hot, sprinkled with icing sugar.

Chive Butter
Cream 4oz (125g) softened butter with a little lemon juice, two teaspoons of chopped chives and seasoning to taste. Shape it in to a roll, wrap, and chill. Serve sliced.

Boiled Leg of Lamb
The same recipe can be used for a boned and rolled shoulder of lamb for a more economical meal.

For a more piquant sauce, add a tablespoon of anchovy paste (but do not add salt to the sauce) or 1½ tablespoons of chopped capers.

Kaiserschmarrn
This crisp, light, omelette-like dessert is traditionally served with stewed fruit such as cherries, apricots, plums or apples. Canned fruit may be used instead. The dessert can also be baked in the oven, pre-heated to 400F (200C) gas 6.

The steps in making a perfect Apfelstrudel.

Apfelstrudel

This is a simplified version of the traditional strudel. Usually it is rolled up like a Swiss roll with the filling inside. To simplify it even more it is possible to buy frozen strudel pastry which is ready-rolled.
Strudels freeze very well uncooked for up to 12 months. Bake from frozen but add about 15 minutes to the cooking time.

Speciality

Apfel strudel

Makes 2, each serving 6 ☆☆
Preparation: 1 hour
Cooking: 40 minutes

The strudel dough:
14oz (400g) plain flour
pinch of salt
1 egg, lightly beaten
4 tablespoons warm water
2oz (50g) butter, melted

The filling:
3lb (1.5kg) cooking apples
4oz (100g) sultanas
2oz (50g) sugar
2 teaspoons ground cinnamon
2 teaspoons finely grated lemon rind
3 tablespoons fine, dry white breadcrumbs
4oz (100g) flaked almonds

To finish:
3oz (75g) flour
2oz (50g) butter, melted
2 tablespoons fine, dry white breadcrumbs
a little icing sugar

Sift the flour and salt into a large bowl and make a well in the centre. Add the egg, water and butter and mix with a wooden spoon or electric mixer until a smooth ball is formed.
☐ Turn out on to a lightly floured work surface and knead for 10 minutes, or until the dough is smooth and elastic. Cover with an inverted bowl and leave to rest for 30 minutes.
☐ Peel, core and thinly slice the apples. Mix them with all the remaining filling ingredients except the almonds.

☐ Pre-heat the oven to 425F (220C), gas 7. Lightly grease 2 large baking sheets.

☐ Spread a large tea towel or a piece of muslin (about 39 × 48in / 1 × 1·2m) on a table and sprinkle it evenly with flour.

☐ Place the dough in the centre and roll it out as thinly as possible. Then holding dough and cloth at one short end with one hand, use the other to carefully stretch dough evenly outwards until very thin. Use small pieces of dough from the edge to patch any holes.

☐ Brush the dough with three quarters of the melted butter and scatter almonds and half the breadcrumbs over half of it lengthways. Spread over apple mixture to within 1in (2·5cm) of the edges. Carefully fold the uncovered dough over the filling, brush the edges with water and press to seal. Cut the strudel in half, push the filling back inside the cut ends and seal.

☐ Transfer the strudels to the baking sheets, brush them with the remaining butter and sprinkle over the remaining breadcrumbs.

☐ Bake for 10 minutes, then reduce the heat to 400F (200C), gas 6 and continue to bake for about 30 minutes or until golden brown and the apples are tender when tested with a skewer.

☐ Dredge with icing sugar and serve, either warm or cold, with cream.

Speciality

Sachertorte

Serves 10-12 ☆☆☆
Preparation: 15 minutes
Cooking: 1 hour

6oz (175g) good quality plain chocolate
6oz (175g) unsalted butter, softened
6oz (175g) caster sugar
6 eggs, size 2, separated
1 tablespoon rum
a few drops of vanilla essence
5oz (150g) self-raising flour, sifted

1oz (25g) ground almonds or hazelnuts
2 tablespoons sieved apricot jam

The chocolate icing:
3oz (75g) sugar
3 tablespoons water
4oz (100g) good quality plain chocolate

Pre-heat the oven to 325F (160C), gas 3. Butter and flour a 10in (25cm) loose-bottomed cake tin.

☐ Break the 6oz (175g) chocolate into pieces and melt it in a bowl over a pan of hot water.

☐ Cream the butter with the sugar until pale and fluffy, then beat in the egg yolks one at a time.

☐ Cool the chocolate slightly, add the rum and vanilla and stir it into the mixture.

☐ Sift together the flour and the ground almonds. Whisk the egg whites until stiff, then fold tablespoons of egg white into the mixture alternately with the flour and ground almonds.

☐ Pour into the prepared tin and bake in the centre of the oven for about 1 hour, or until the cake is firm to touch and has slightly shrunk away from the sides of the tin. Leave to cool in the tin for a few minutes then turn out on to a wire rack to cool.

☐ Brush the cake thinly with the apricot jam and leave to set.

☐ Bring the sugar and water to the boil in a small pan, stirring until the sugar has dissolved. Boil rapidly for 1 minute, then remove from the heat.

☐ Melt the 4oz (100g) chocolate in a bowl over hot water. Stir it into the warm sugar syrup.

☐ Pour the icing over the cake and spread it evenly with a palette knife. If necessary, dip the knife in warm water. Allow to set before serving: do not chill.

Tip: If possible, pour the icing carefully over the top of the cake so that it is not necessary to spread it with the palette knife. This will mean that the icing keeps the shine which is so characteristic of this cake.

Cherry Strudel
Mix together 2lb (1kg) stoned cherries, 1 teaspoon ground cinnamon, 4oz (100g) roughly chopped almonds, 4oz (100g) fine, dry white breadcrumbs and sugar to taste.

Cheese Strudel
Mix together until blended 1lb (500g) curd cheese, a lightly beaten egg, ½ teaspoon vanilla essence, 4oz (100g) sultanas or raisins, 1½oz (40g) melted butter, 2oz (50g) caster sugar and the finely grated rind of half a lemon.

Apricot and Almond Strudel
Split and stone 1½lb (700g) apricots and spread them on the pastry. Mix together 6oz (175g) ground almonds, 4oz (100g) caster sugar, 1 egg and 4 tablespoons double cream. Spread this mixture over the apricots.

Sachertorte
Sometimes the cake is split in two and spread with apricot jam before icing. It could also be filled with cream, chocolate or some extra buttercream icing, although this is not authentic.

Linzertorte

Choose the best jam available, preferably homemade. Alternatively, substitute fresh raspberries for up to half of the jam for a fresher, less sweet filling.

Lining a tin with pastry

Roll out the pastry until it is 1in (2.5cm) bigger than the tin all round, wrap it round the rolling pin and unroll it into the tin. Fit it into the edge by pressing very gently with the knuckles. Trim the top edge by running the rolling pin over the top of the tin.

To help the base of the pastry cook through, heat a baking sheet in the oven and stand the tin on this to bake.

Linzertorte

Speciality
Linzertorte

Serves 6-8   ★★☆
Preparation: 20 minutes plus 1 hour chilling
Cooking: 40 minutes

10oz (275g) flour
a pinch of ground cloves
1½ teaspoons ground cinnamon
4oz (125g) soft light brown sugar
4oz (125g) ground almonds
1 teaspoon finely grated lemon rind
8oz (225g) butter, softened
2 egg yolks
a few drops of vanilla essence
1lb (500g) good quality raspberry jam
egg white to glaze
sifted icing sugar to finish

Sift the flour, cloves and cinnamon into a bowl, then stir in the brown sugar, almonds and lemon rind.

☐ Make a well in the centre and add the butter, yolks and vanilla. Using the fingertips of one hand, gradually work the mixture together to form a dough. Turn out on to a lightly floured work surface and knead lightly until smooth. Wrap and chill for at least 1 hour.

☐ Grease a 10in (25cm) loose-bottomed cake tin or sandwich tin. Pre-heat the oven to 350F (180C), gas 4.

☐ Roll out three-quarters of the pastry and use it to line the tin. Spread the jam evenly over the base.

☐ Roll out the remaining pastry to a rectangle 8 × 10in (20 × 25cm) long. Cut strips about ½in (1cm) wide and arrange them over the jam in a neat lattice. Trim the edges.

☐ Brush the pastry with lightly beaten egg white and bake for 30-40 minutes or until the pastry is golden brown.

☐ Leave to cool slightly in the tin, then cool on a wire rack. Serve warm lightly dusted with icing sugar.

Speciality
Malakofftorte

Serves 6-8   ★★☆
Preparation: 30 minutes, plus about 6 hours chilling

4oz (125g) unsalted butter, softened
4oz (125g) sugar
3 egg yolks
4oz (125g) ground almonds
2 pints (1.2 litres) double cream
30-40 sponge finger biscuits
6 tablespoons brandy or rum, or to taste

Beat the butter with the sugar until light and fluffy. Add the egg yolks one by one, beating well after each addition.

☐ Mix in the almonds and stir in ½ pint (300ml) of the cream until thoroughly blended.

☐ Slice the sponge fingers lengthways and arrange a layer in the bottom of an 8in (20cm) spring-form cake tin. Sprinkle with brandy or rum, then add a layer of butter cream.

☐ Whip the rest of the cream until stiff and spread a layer over the butter cream. Continue layering with sponge fingers sprinkled with brandy or rum, butter cream and whipped cream. Finish with a layer of sponge fingers.

☐ Press lightly, cover with foil and chill for 6 hours before serving.

Scandinavia

There's a well-known saying that 'the Swedes eat to drink, the Norwegians eat to live and the Danes live to eat'. The Finns, too, are known to enjoy their food, and throughout Scandinavia they all make the most of their plentiful supply of fish. Pork, both cured and fresh, is a popular meat and butter, cream and cheese are generously used–especially in the rich dairy country of Denmark. Desserts throughout the region are often based on the berried fruits that grow so well in Northern climes and every Scandinavian loves a snack–biscuit, pastry or open sandwich. Perhaps the widest-known example of their cuisine is the traditional buffet spread, featuring imaginative combinations of meat, fish and salads which are designed to complement their delicious variety of breads and crispbreads. It is known as Smörgåsbord in Sweden, Smørbrød in Norway, Smørrebrød in Denmark and Voileipäpyötä in Finland.

Sweden

The Swedes enjoy a very high standard of living and have a great deal of open country on which to draw for wild foods such as game. They eat a simple breakfast, a light lunch and have their main meal in the evening. This almost always includes a fish course. Crayfish are especially popular, but because stocks are now depleted, catching them is prohibited in Sweden. However, every year on August 7th there is a national feast when crayfish are imported from Poland, Czechoslovakia and Turkey. Specialities from Sweden include Janssons Temptation–a baked dish of potato, anchovy and cream, and Glasmästarsill–spiced, marinated herrings.

Norway

The Norwegians like straightforward, sustaining food and the main characteristic of their cooking is superb natural flavour, undisguised by rich sauces or spices. Fish is always fresh and is usually poached, so that the flavour can be fully appreciated. The long winter means that the Norwegians have perfected the art of preserving. Curing, smoking, pickling and drying are all used to provide stores of meat and fish.

Because of their climate they start the day early, with a hearty breakfast of porridge, eggs, cheese, fish or meat, bread, butter and milk. They then have an early lunch–often just an open sandwich and a hot drink. The main meal of the day is served in the early evening, and has two or three courses. A lot of traditional dishes such as Jansson's Temptation and pickled herring overlap with those of the other Scandinavian countries. Game and dairy produce feature largely in meals, and smoked meats such as reindeer and mutton are also very popular.

A map of Scandinavia, showing the different countries and their specialities.

Finland

Finland is geographically part of Scandinavia but the people are of a different ethnic origin. From the 11th to the 19th centuries, Finland was ruled by Sweden, then annexed by Russia: it also includes part of Lapland. Sweden, Russia and the Lapps have each brought their cultural and culinary influences.

Like the Swedes, the Finns have their open sandwiches, often accompanied by soup and Russsian Blinis (buckwheat pancakes) with soured cream. Finland has vast hunting grounds and autumn game is an important feature of the menu. The meat of elk, reindeer and wild boar is often combined with sauces made from berried fruits.

Specialities from Finland include Lamb with Dill Sauce, dill being a herb which is greatly prized in all the Scandinavian countries. Rikkaat Ritarit (Rich Knights), the Finnish version of the English 'Poor Knights' and the French 'Pain Perdu', is a popular dessert.

Denmark

Denmark is renowned for its pork, dairy produce, open sandwiches and pastries. Like the Norwegians, the Danes love their food, beginning their day with an early breakfast of bread, cheese and coffee or milk.

Lunch invariably takes the form of an open sandwich–highly elaborate, almost a meal in itself and often served with extra salad, cheese or fruit. The afternoon coffee break gives an excuse for eating the delicious Danish pastries and buttery cakes and biscuits for which the Danes are famous. The main meal of the day is in the early evening and it usually consists of two courses. Pork, fish, poultry and veal are all popular and the meal is often rounded off by a fluffy, fruity dessert.

The Danish Smørrebrød, like other Scandinavian cold tables, originates from when it was customary for guests to contribute a dish to the meal.

Planning a Smörgåsbord

This traditional Scandinavian buffet is easy to prepare as most of the ingredients are readily available on delicatessen counters. First serve a hot soup, a dish such as Jansson's Temptation (page 238) and a herring pickle such as Sursild (page 238). Base your selection of open sandwiches on different breads such as light and dark rye, wholemeal crispbreads and toast.

Choose from the following to combine and make open sandwiches, or to serve by themselves:

rollmop herrings	smoked buckling
pickled herrings	smoked eel
spiced herrings	smoked mackerel
lumpfish roe	sild
anchovies	shrimps
Danish salami	liver pâté
Danish ham	smoked pork loin
chicken	eggs

Typically Scandinavian garnishes include mayonnaise, especially when flavoured with curry or horseradish, gherkins, pickled beetroot, sliced onion, radishes, cucumber, tomatoes, lemon, orange. Favourite herbs are dill, chives and parsley.

For each person allow 1 portion of 2 hot dishes, 2-3 open sandwiches and 2-3 small snacks, plus a generous quantity of chilled lager or wine. For a party of 8, try to have about 8 different dishes.

Preparing open sandwiches
Use a variety of breads, cut them into slices and trim away the crusts. Butter thickly (use unsalted butter for pickled fish and smoked meats) and remember presentation is all-important. Give height by rolling meat slices, or by piling ingredients high in the centre. Try these:
Kipper fillets on lettuce, garnished with radish and a raw egg yolk.
Slices of ham topped with scrambled egg and chives.
Prawns topped with lettuce heart and served with a wedge of lemon.

Sherrysill
Marinated herring

Serves 8   ☆
Preparation: 3-4 hours

---

4 pickled herrings, filleted
1 medium onion, sliced
2oz (50g) sugar
freshly ground pepper
2 teaspoons chopped dill
4 tablespoons dry sherry
4 tablespoons white wine vinegar
2 sprigs of dill to garnish

Rinse the herring fillets well in cold water. Place in a small dish with the onion, sugar, pepper, dill, sherry and vinegar. Cover and leave in a cool place for 3-4 hours.
☐ Drain well and serve garnished with sprigs of dill and some of the onion from the marinade.
Variation: Trim the marinated herring into large diamond shapes and roll the pieces in chopped chives.

Pariser Smorgas
Steak tartare toasts

Serves 8   ☆☆
Preparation and cooking: 25 minutes

1lb (500g) minced lean steak
2 raw egg yolks
1 tablespoon finely chopped onion
1 tablespoon finely chopped parsley
2 tablespoons finely chopped gherkins
2 tablespoons capers
2 tablespoons finely diced pickled beetroot
salt and pepper
8 slices bread, crusts removed
3oz (75g) butter
8 slices skinned tomato
8 slices hard-boiled egg

Mix together thoroughly the steak, egg yolks, onion, parsley, gherkins, and capers. Lightly stir in the beetroot and salt and pepper.
☐ Fry 2 slices of bread at a time in the butter until brown both sides.
☐ Spread the meat mixture on the fried bread. Garnish with tomato and egg slices. Serve immediately.

Gravad Lax

Marinated salmon with dill

Buy the piece of salmon to fit the available tin. Usually, the centre cut is used, but the tail end is cheaper and will taste just as good. Make sure that the salmon is well pressed—use as many kitchen weights or cans from the store cupboard as possible, as long as they will fit on to the tin. Fresh dill must be used for this recipe.

Makes 12 slices ☆
Preparation: 15 minutes
Marinating: 4-5 days

---

about 2lb (1kg) fresh salmon in the piece
5 tablespoons salt
4 tablespoons sugar
1 tablespoon green peppercorns
3oz (75g) finely chopped dill

Line a 1lb (450g) loaf tin with foil.
☐ Cut the salmon in half lengthways to produce 2 fillets, scrape out the backbone and free the bones. Remove the skin.
☐ Mix together the salt, sugar, and peppercorns. Rub well into both sides of the fillets then sandwich the two pieces with a generous layer of dill.
☐ Sprinkle half the remaining salt mixture and dill into the lined tin. Press the salmon on top and sprinkle with the rest of the salt and dill.
☐ Place a second tin on to the salmon and weight down. Store in a cool place for 4 days, turning the salmon each day and basting with the liquid which forms.
☐ To serve, scrape the outside of the salmon free of dill and seasoning. Slice diagonally and use to make open sandwiches.
Tip: Gravad Lax also makes a most delicious dinner-party starter. Slice very thinly and serve with brown bread, unsalted butter and lemon wedges.

A typical Smörgåsbord including the potato dish Jansson's Temptation, pickled Sursild, Sherrysill, Gravad Lax and a selection of open sandwiches.

A cheeseboard makes a popular addition to a Smörgåsbord: include Danablu, Esrom, Havarti and a Samsoe cheese. Try Jarlsberg from Norway and a Gjetost. Accompany the cheeses with apples and grapes.

Sherrysill
Make these into spiced herrings by substituting ground cinnamon and cloves for the dill in the recipe.

Menu

Fisksoppa med Bullar

*Kalops
with
Creamed Potatoes
Green Salad*

Plattar med Frukt

Lager or light beer

Quantities given serve 6

Fisksoppa
In Sweden the fishballs are made of salmon but you can make them from any available fresh white fish. Cook the vegetables briefly to retain their colour and texture.

Kalops
In Sweden the stew is served with hot beetroot.

Sweden

Fisksoppa med Bullar

*Clear fish soup
with fish dumplings*

Serves 6   ☆
Preparation: 25 minutes
Cooking: 15 minutes

1¾ pints (1 litre) fish stock
8oz (225g) celeriac, diced
white part of 1 large leek, sliced
celery salt
pepper

The fish dumplings:
8oz (225g) filleted raw white fish
1 egg white
3 tablespoons single cream
3 tablespoons white breadcrumbs
salt and pepper
1 tablespoon finely chopped dill

Bring the stock to the boil in a large pan. Add the vegetables and simmer for about 10 minutes until tender. Season to taste.
□ Cut the fish into small pieces. Work to a smooth paste in a blender or food processor with the egg white, cream, crumbs, salt, pepper and dill.
□ Form the mixture into walnut-sized balls. Add to the fish soup and poach for about 5 minutes or until set.
□ Serve immediately with brown bread.

Kalops

Rich beef stew

Serves 6   ☆☆☆
Preparation: 10 minutes
Cooking: 2¼-2½ hours

1¾lb (800g) chuck steak,
    cut into 1in (2.5cm) cubes
3 tablespoons flour
salt and pepper
about 2oz (50g) oil or cooking fat
1½lb (700g) carrots, cubed
1lb (500g) onions, coarsely chopped
about 15 fl oz (450ml) beef stock
1 bay leaf
small onion stuck with 3 cloves
5 fl oz (142ml) carton soured cream

Put the meat into a plastic bag with

the flour, salt and pepper. Shake until it is coated with flour.

☐ Brown the meat in three separate batches in the hot oil, then remove.

☐ Brown the vegetables, add the meat and the rest of the ingredients except the cream.

☐ Cover and cook very slowly for about 2 hours or until the meat is tender.

☐ Remove the onion and stir in the cream just before serving with creamed potatoes and a green salad.

Plattar med Frukt
Egg pancakes with fruit

Serves 6 ☆☆☆
Preparation: 5 minutes
Cooking: 10-12 minutes

8oz (250g) self-raising flour
6 eggs, size 3
2-4 tablespoons milk
6oz (150g) butter, melted
6 tablespoons oil for frying
icing sugar
12oz (350g) fresh strawberries

Put the flour into a mixing bowl. Whisk together the eggs and 1 tablespoon of milk. Gradually stir into the flour to make a stiff batter. Beat the butter in well, adding a little more milk, if necessary, to make a batter which just drops from a spoon.

☐ Put enough oil into an 8in (20cm) frying-pan to cover the base. Heat until the fat smells hot and trembles. Test with a little batter–it should cook on one side in about 1 minute.

☐ With a serving spoon, drop two spoons of batter well apart into the hot oil. Cook for about 1½ minutes until browned underneath and set on top. Turn, and brown the second side. Add more oil and continue making pancakes with the rest of the batter.

☐ Dust with icing sugar and serve immediately with strawberries or other fresh fruit.

Plattar med Frukt
Swedish pancakes are quite different from other kinds. They are crispy on the outside, and tender and melting inside. For success, the batter must not be too thin so add milk carefully. If the batter is too thin it prevents the top setting before the underside over-browns.
The Swedes cook their pancakes in a special pan with indentations, called a 'plattar'. An ordinary frying-pan may be used, but it must be heated correctly, as in the recipe.

From left to right: Fisksoppa–a clear soup with fresh vegetables and fish balls; Kalops–a typical beef and vegetable stew, served with creamed potatoes and a green salad; and Plattar med Frukt–small, light-textured pancakes with strawberries.

Jansson's Frestelse

This tasty potato dish is served as a hot appetizer in Norway and Sweden. At the Smörgåsbord table it is spooned straight from the oven dish on to large slices of bread.

If anchovies preserved in salt are available, you can use them in place of the canned variety. Be sure to wash off the salt first.

Sursild

In Sweden the marinated herring is called 'Glasmastersill' which means literally 'the glassblower's herring'.

If salted herrings are not available they are easy to prepare at home. Gut fresh herrings, and remove the heads and as many bones as possible. Cut each fish into two fillets and rub well with salt. Put them into a dish (not a metal one), cover tightly and refrigerate for 24 hours, turning the fillets occasionally. Rinse well and pat dry before using.

Sursild–Norwegian spiced and marinated herring.

Norway

Speciality
Jansson's Frestelse

Jansson's Temptation

Serves 6 ☆☆

Preparation: 40 minutes
Cooking: 1 hour

2oz (50g) butter
2lb (1kg) potatoes, peeled and thinly
    sliced
3½oz (99g) can anchovies, chopped
8oz (225g) onions, peeled and sliced
salt and pepper
10 fl oz (284ml) single cream

Grease a 2½ pint (1.4 litre) ovenproof dish with some of the butter. Fill it with alternate layers of potatoes, anchovies, and onions. Sprinkle each layer with salt and pepper, ending with potatoes.

☐ Pour half the cream over the potatoes and dot the remaining butter over top.

☐ Place the dish in the oven, slightly below the centre. Bake for about 50 minutes at 350F (180C) gas 4 until the potatoes are tender. Pour the rest of the cream over and return to the oven for about 10 minutes to finish browning.

☐ Serve as a main course with boiled red cabbage.

Speciality
Sursild

Spiced marinated herring
Serve with toast for a first course or with potato salad as a main course.

Serves 6 ☆☆

Preparation: 45 minutes
Marinating: 5 days

2 large salted herrings
2 large carrots
¾lb (350g) onions
7 fl oz (200ml) water
7 fl oz (200ml) herb vinegar
4 tablespoons sugar
2 teaspoons grated horseradish
1 teaspoon chopped ginger root
12 black peppercorns
3 small bay leaves
1 teaspoon mustard seed, crushed

Soak the herrings overnight in cold water. Rinse well and pat dry with kitchen paper. Slash along the underside and scrape out the backbone. Cut each herring in half lengthways and pick out as many bones as possible. Cut into strips about 1in (2.5cm) wide.

☐ Peel and coarsely chop the carrots and onions.

☐ Put all the ingredients except the vegetables into a saucepan. Bring to the boil, then cool.

☐ Pack alternate layers of herring, carrot, and onion into a tall jar. Pour the marinade over.

☐ Cover the jar closely and store in a cool place for 5 days. Drain off the marinade before serving.

Finland

Speciality

Dillilammas

Lamb with dill sauce

Serves 6   ☆ ☆ ☆
Preparation: 15 minutes
Cooking: 1½-2 hours

3lb (1.5kg) leg of lamb
1 teaspoon salt

The sauce:
2oz (50g) butter
2oz (50g) flour
2 tablespoons brown sugar
2 tablespoons wine vinegar
1 tablespoon finely chopped dill
salt and pepper

Cut the lamb into 1in (2.5cm) cubes, and put into a saucepan with just enough water to cover; add the salt. Bring to the boil and remove any scum which rises to the surface.
☐ Lower the heat, cover and simmer the meat very gently for 1-1½ hours until it is tender.
☐ Remove the meat, strain the cooking liquid and measure it. Reserve 1 pint (600ml), adding a little water if necessary.
☐ Make a roux with the butter and flour, then stir in the warm stock. Bring to the boil, stirring constantly, until the sauce thickens.
☐ Add the lamb and the remaining ingredients, and cook gently for 15 minutes.
☐ Serve with boiled potatoes and carrots.

Speciality

Rikkaat Ritarit

Finnish bread fritters

Serves 4   ☆ ☆ ☆
Preparation: 15 minutes
Cooking: 15 minutes

4 tablespoons ground almonds
6 tablespoons caster sugar

juice of ½ lemon
5oz (150g) butter, softened
1 egg, size 2
7 fl oz (200ml) milk
2 teaspoons ground cinnamon
8 slices day-old bread, crusts removed
½ pint (300ml) hot apple sauce, to serve

Mix together the ground almonds, sugar, lemon juice, and 2oz (50g) of the butter to make a smooth paste.
☐ Whisk together the egg, milk, and cinnamon. Pour into a shallow dish.
☐ Heat a little of the remaining butter in an 8in (20cm) frying-pan over a moderate heat until it begins to turn brown. Turn on the grill.
☐ Quickly dip 2 slices of the bread on either side into the milk mixture. Fry in the hot butter for about 3 minutes altogether, to brown both sides. Set aside, and continue with the rest of the butter, bread, and milk mixture.
☐ Spread each slice of the fried bread with almond paste. Toast for about 1 minute until browned and bubbling. Serve immediately with hot apple sauce.

Denmark

Speciality

Bondepige med Sløla

Veiled country lass

Serves 4   ☆ ☆ ☆
Preparation: 10 minutes

8oz (225g) dark rye breadcrumbs
4oz (125g) plain dessert chocolate, grated
¼ pint (142ml) double cream, whipped
8oz (250g) raspberries or other red fruit
sugar to taste

Mix the breadcrumbs and chocolate.
☐ Put into individual glasses, with alternate layers of cream and sweetened fruit. Reserve some fruit to decorate.
☐ Finish with a layer of cream, and decorate with the reserved fruit.

Lamb with Dill Sauce
This lamb dish is slightly sweet and sour. Served with potatoes it is another dish which would be suitable to serve as part of a Scandinavian-style buffet.

Rikkaat Ritarit
Every country has its own recipes for using leftover dry bread. In North-west Europe, there are many varieties of bread soaked in milk and egg. The Finns serve them with hot apple sauce. It is also common to sprinkle cinnamon over as a final touch.

Speciality
Honningkranse
Honey rings

Makes about 30   ☆
Preparation: 10 minutes
Cooking: 10 minutes

8oz (225g) plain flour
½ teaspoon baking powder
6oz (175g) butter
2oz (50g) caster sugar
2 tablespoons clear honey
1 egg, size 4

Preheat oven to 375F 190C gas 5.
☐ Sieve together the flour and
baking powder. Rub in the butter
until the mixture resembles fine
breadcrumbs.
☐ Stir in the sugar, then blend the
honey and the egg and stir in to
make a soft dough.
☐ Place the mixture in a piping bag
fitted with a medium-star tube. Pipe
rings, about 2in (5cm) in diameter,
on a greased baking sheet and bake
for about 10 minutes, or until firm
and golden. Cool on a wire rack.

Frugtkage–a Danish speciality.

Speciality
Frugtkage
Danish no-bake apple cake

Serves 6-8   ☆☆☆
Preparation: 1½ hours
Chilling: 3-3½ hours

2lb (1kg) cooking apples, cut into pieces
4 tablespoons water
7oz (200g) caster sugar
4 teaspoons powdered gelatine
5oz (125g) butter
7oz (200g) white breadcrumbs
6oz (175g) redcurrant jelly
7 fl oz (200ml) double cream
4oz (100g) redcurrants, washed and
   stemmed

Cook the apples with the water and
3oz (75g) of the sugar until pulpy.
Rub through a sieve into a large
basin.
☐ Sprinkle the gelatine over the
purée. Set the basin over a pan of
hot water and stir for 2-3 minutes to
dissolve the gelatine. Cool for about
1½ hours until beginning to thicken.
☐ Heat the butter in a large heavy
frying-pan until it begins to brown.
Reduce the heat and add the crumbs
and 3oz (75g) of the remaining
sugar. Stir for 10-15 minutes until
browned.
☐ Press half the crumbs into a

greased 8in (20cm) cake tin. As soon
as cool, spoon the apple mixture
over. Chill until set–about 1 hour.
☐ Spread the jelly over the apple
and sprinkle with the rest of the
crumbs. Press lightly. Chill again
for ½-1 hour until quite firm.
☐ Carefully remove the cake to a
flat plate.
☐ Whip the cream with the last of
the sugar to a spreading consistency.
Spread over the cake and decorate
with redcurrants.

Variations: The redcurrant
decoration can be replaced by
different fresh fruits if you choose a
jam to match. Strawberries,
raspberries, or blackcurrant are all
suitable. The apple filling can also
be varied by replacing some of the
apple with an equal quantity of red
fruit–the strong flavours of
raspberries, redcurrants or
blackcurrants are best, and they also
give a good colour. Choose a jam to
match the fruit and sieve it to
remove the pips if your prefer.

Tip: The easiest way to stem
redcurrants is to gently pull the
stems through the prongs of a table
fork. The berries will come off their
stems undamaged.

Greece

The Greeks are famous for their hospitality, and the best Greek cooking is often found in private homes rather than restaurants. Simple methods (charcoal grilling is a favourite) and fresh local ingredients are the basis of Greek cuisine. Some excellent robust wines are produced from the vines which thrive on the Greek hillsides, making the perfect accompaniment to all Greek food.

The Greeks love to socialize in cafés and tavernas, over glasses of ouzo, the anise-flavoured national apéritif, and retsina, a wine with a distinctive tang of pine resin, but they tend to eat at home, with family or friends. They have their main meal at midday, followed by a long siesta; dinner is eaten late and is usually much lighter – a salad, or a platter of stuffed vegetables.

The Greeks like to eat snacks throughout the day, and one of the most popular combinations of these is 'mezze', or a selection of appetizers, which may be served with drinks or, like hors d'oeuvre, to start a main meal. Other favourite starters are Taramasalata, a creamy pâté made with the smoked roe of grey mullet or cod, Hummus, a dip of puréed chick peas, and soups–in particular Fassoulatha (bean soup) and Avgolemono (chicken broth with egg yolk and lemon juice).

The main course might consist of succulent pieces of lamb charcoal-grilled on skewers (Souvlakia); a ragoût (Stifatho); meatballs (Keftethes); fish baked with vegetables (Psari Plaki); Moussaka, minced lamb layered with aubergines and cheese; or Pastitsio, a similar dish using macaroni. These would be accompanied–or followed by–a Greek salad (Elleniki Salata) of shredded crisp lettuce, sliced onion, cucumber and tomato, sprinkled with herbs and olive oil and garnished with olives and diced feta, the most famous of the Greek cheeses.

The meal might end with a pastry – crisp Baklava, with a nut and cinnamon filling, drenched in honey syrup, or Galatoboureko, the Greek version of custard tart, or Ravani (honey cake). Desserts might include Rizogalo, a creamy spiced rice pudding, or a bowl of yogurt with a spoonful of rose petal preserve or the famous Mount Hymettus honey. Every Greek meal is rounded off by a tiny cup of strong, piping hot coffee, perhaps with a metaxa, the finest of the Greek brandies.

Lamb is far more widespread than beef in Greece, sheep being better suited than cattle to the rugged terrain. Not surprisingly in a country with an extensive coastline and innumerable islands, there is a spectacular variety of fish–mullet, tuna fish, sardines, squid and prawns are just a few.

Vegetables are equally abundant. Olive oil, combined with the fragrant herbs which grow profusely in the hills, is used to flavour many Greek savoury dishes. Nuts and honey, both natural products of Greece, are used in a mouthwatering range of desserts and pastries, to satisfy the sweetest tooth.

With the Aegean Sea to the east and the Ionian Sea to the west, Greece offers a wonderful choice of fresh fish and shellfish.

Menu

Fassoulatha

*Moussaka
with
Elleniki Salata*

Ravani

Kafes Ellenikos

*White wine: Retsina or Robola
Cephalonia*

———

*Quantities given serve 4
(except for the cake)*

Start your Greek meal with steaming bowls of soup, or try making you own 'mezze' selection served with freshly baked pitta bread. This might include olives, salted roasted nuts, cubes of feta cheese sprinkled with herbs and olive oil, fried squid, vine leaves stuffed with rice and herbs (dolmathes), a dip of puréed aubergines (melizanosalata), small dishes of taramasalata or hummus.

White Bean Soup

When making soups with pulses, always add the seasoning at the end, as salt toughens the beans during cooking.

Fassoulatha
White bean soup

———

Serves 4 ☆
Preparation: 5 minutes, plus soaking
Cooking: about 1¾ hours

———

2 tablespoons olive oil
2 large onions, finely chopped
1 garlic clove, finely chopped
9oz (250g) white haricot beans, soaked
    overnight and drained
4 large tomatoes, skinned and chopped
1 teaspoon dried oregano
2 pints (1.2 litres) Chicken Stock
salt and freshly ground black pepper

Heat the oil in a large saucepan and fry the onions and garlic for about 5 minutes, until softened and lightly coloured.

☐ Add the beans, tomatoes and oregano and fry gently, stirring, for 5 minutes.

☐ Pour in the stock, cover and simmer for about 1½ hours or until the beans are very soft. Season to taste.

From left to right: Fassoulatha, Moussaka, Elleniki Salata and Ravani.

Moussaka

Serves 4 ☆☆☆
Preparation: 30 minutes
Cooking: about 1 hour

1½lb (700g) aubergines, sliced
salt
2 tablespoons olive oil
1 large onion, finely chopped
1¼lb (575g) minced lamb or beef
2 sprigs of thyme
1 tablespoon finely chopped parsley
2 large tomatoes, skinned and chopped
2 tablespoons tomato purée
4 tablespoons dry white wine
freshly ground black pepper
4oz (125g) feta cheese, crumbled

The sauce:
3 fl oz (100ml) milk
3 fl oz (100ml) double cream
1 egg
3 egg yolks

Put the sliced aubergines into a colander, sprinkle with salt and leave to drain over a plate for 30 minutes.

☐ Set the oven to 350F (180C) gas 4.
☐ Rinse the aubergines and pat dry with kitchen paper.
☐ Heat the oil in a large frying-pan and fry the onion for about 5 minutes until softened and lightly coloured. Add the minced meat and fry, stirring often, until the meat has lost all its pinkness.
☐ Add the herbs, tomatoes, tomato purée and white wine and cook gently, stirring from time to time, for 15 minutes. Season well with salt and pepper.
☐ Make layers of the meat mixture and the sliced aubergines in a large ovenproof dish ending with a layer of aubergines.
☐ In a small bowl, beat together the sauce ingredients and pour over the moussaka. Bake in the oven for about 45 minutes, until the top is crusty.
☐ Heat the grill to high. Sprinkle the moussaka with the feta cheese and grill for 5 minutes, or until the cheese is melting and golden-brown. Serve at once.

Moussaka
A rich and substantial dish, moussaka lends itself to many variations. The feta cheese topping may be omitted, and slices of cheese layered with the meat and aubergines instead. Kasséri, a very popular mild, firm cheese might be used in Greece. Gruyère would also be a good choice. Courgettes may be substituted for the aubergines, and freshly grated nutmeg used to flavour the sauce, if liked. In Greece, some versions of moussaka have a sliced potato topping.

Elleniki Salata

Greek salad

The addition of hard-boiled egg to the Greek salad is not traditional, but makes a tasty and filling combination, which could be served by itself as a light lunch for 2 people.

Serves 4   ☆☆
Preparation: 15-20 minutes

4 tomatoes, skinned and sliced
½ cucumber, sliced
1 small green pepper, de-seeded and cut into strips
1 small red pepper, de-seeded and cut into strips
2 onions, sliced or coarsely chopped
12 black olives to garnish
2 hard-boiled eggs, cut into wedges (optional)

The dressing:
4 tablespoons olive oil
1½ tablespoons lemon juice
salt and freshly ground black pepper
3 anchovy fillets, soaked in milk and cut into strips

Arrange all the salad vegetables in a deep dish or salad bowl.
□ Thoroughly combine all the ingredients for the dressing and pour over the salad.
□ Garnish the salad with olives and wedges of hard-boiled egg.

Ravani

Honey cake

Makes 10 slices   ☆☆
Preparation: 20 minutes
Cooking: about 1 hour

2oz (50g) butter
5 tablespoons caster sugar
2 teaspoons grated lemon rind
4 eggs, separated
3oz (75g) self-raising flour
2oz (50g) fine semolina
5 tablespoons nibbed almonds
butter, for greasing

The glaze:
5 tablespoons clear honey
2 tablespoons lemon juice

Set the oven to 350F (180C) gas 4.
□ Grease and line a 7in (17.5cm)

cake tin with greaseproof paper.
□ Cream the butter and sugar together in a mixing bowl until light and fluffy. Add the lemon rind and gradually beat in the egg yolks. Gradually sift in the flour with the semolina, beating well between each addition. Stir in 4 tablespoons of the almonds.
□ Whisk the egg whites until stiff, then fold them into the cake mixture. Pour into the prepared cake tin, smooth the surface and sprinkle over the remaining almonds.
□ Bake in the centre of the oven for about 1 hour, until the cake is golden and cooked through, and a fine skewer inserted into the centre comes out clean.
□ Leave the cake to cool slightly in the tin, then turn out on to a wire rack set over a plate. Make several holes in the top with a skewer.
□ Put the honey and lemon juice for the glaze into a small saucepan and warm through gently. Pour the glaze over the cake and leave for 8 hours or overnight to cool.

Kafes Ellenikos

Greek coffee

Making Greek coffee is an art in itself. The coffee should be freshly ground to a powder – instant coffee should not be used. It is always served black, never with milk, in demi-tasse cups.

Serves 2   ○
Preparation: 5 minutes

6 fl oz (175ml) cold water
2 teaspoons caster sugar
2 heaped teaspoons very finely ground coffee

Bring the water and sugar to the boil in a breke or small enamelled saucepan. Remove from heat and vigorously stir in coffee. Return to heat and when coffee boils up almost to the top, remove from heat.
□ Repeat twice, add more sugar if necessary and serve at once in small cups, being careful not to disturb the foam on top of each cup.

Speciality
Spanakopita

Greek spinach pie

Serves 6-8   ☆☆☆
Preparation: 20 minutes
Cooking: 1½ hours

8 tablespoons olive oil
6 spring onions, sliced
2lb (900g) fresh spinach, thoroughly rinsed and drained
2 eggs, lightly beaten
8oz (225g) feta cheese, crumbled
2 tablespoons chopped dill
2 tablespoons chopped parsley
salt and freshly ground black pepper
1lb (500g) packet ready-made filo pastry

Heat half the oil in a large saucepan, add the spring onion and fry until soft but not browned.
□ Remove the stems from the spinach and chop it finely. Stir in to the mixture in the pan, cover tightly and cook very gently for 2-3 minutes, or until wilted.
□ Remove the lid and continue to cook, stirring constantly, until the moisture has evaporated.
□ Remove from the heat, leave to cool, then stir in the eggs, cheese, dill, parsley and seasoning to taste.
□ Heat the oven to 350F (180C) gas 4. Oil a 13 × 9in (33 × 23cm) rectangular cake tin.
□ Unroll the pastry. Line the prepared tin with half the sheets, brushing each with oil and pressing them well into the corners and up the sides.
□ Spread the spinach mixture evenly over the pastry. Top the pie with the remaining pastry, again brushing each thin sheet with oil.
□ Press the edges together firmly to seal, trim the edges and bake for 30 minutes. Reduce the oven to 300F (150C) gas 2 and bake for a further 30 minutes, or until the top is brown.
□ Cut the pie in squares and serve hot or at room temperature.
Variation: for a cheese filling, mix 1½lb (700g) crumbled feta cheese with 4 eggs, 7fl oz (200ml) milk, white pepper and nutmeg.

Israel

Israeli food is a fascinating amalgamation of many different cultures. You have dishes from Eastern Europe and countries such as Poland and Russia alongside the foods of North Africa and the Middle East. Though as yet there is no truly national Israeli cuisine, the bounty of the land, due to advanced agricultural techniques which make the most of a favourable climate, gives a plentiful supply of fruit and vegetables and an impressive range of dairy produce. Chicken and fish are often preferred to red meat.

Breakfast is often considered the best meal in Israel, whether served in hotel or kibbutzim. Here you will see an amazing array of dairy foods – cultured milks, soured creams and yogurts, soft cheeses (some flavoured with herbs and peppers), pickled fish, hard-boiled eggs, and wonderful breads including plaited loaves.

The main meal of the day is usually taken at lunchtime and may consist of soup (cold fruit soup, brought by the Central Europeans, makes a delicious summer soup) followed by simply cooked chicken or fish, with a typical Israeli salad of tomatoes and cucumber. Dessert is most likely to be fruit.

In the evening there's a light meal similar to breakfast, with cheeses and salads, hummus (ground chick peas) and tahina (sesame paste).

One of the features of Israeli eating is the street food, found especially in the Arab markets but also all along the main streets. You can buy falafel (chick pea croquettes, deep-fried and stuffed into pitta breads, together with an array of salads and pickles), freshly squeezed fruit juices and sabra, fruit from cacti cooled on ice.

Speciality
Cholent

Cholent (sometimes called Shalet) is a traditional dish which orthodox Jews prepare on the eve of the Sabbath in order for it to cook in the fire without requiring any attention. This is because, according to strict Sabbath observance, no fire may be kindled or work done on that day.

Use a casserole with a tight-fitting lid and cover with foil before putting on the lid. Choose a casserole which is just large enough – if it is too big you will find you have too much liquid.

Serves 4
Preparation: 25 minutes plus soaking beans overnight
Cooking: 12 hours minimum

2 onions, sliced
2 carrots, sliced
1 large garlic clove, crushed
2oz (50g) margarine or 4 tablespoons oil
1lb (500g) brisket of beef, in the piece
3oz (75g) haricot beans, soaked overnight
3oz (75g) chick peas, soaked overnight
2oz (50g) rice or pearl barley
2 bay leaves
salt and freshly ground black pepper

Soften the onion, carrot and garlic in hot fat. Add the meat and brown well on all sides.
☐ Set oven to 225F (110C) gas ¼.
☐ Drain the beans and chick peas and add to the pan together with the rice or pearl barley and bay leaves. Season very generously. Pour on boiling water to cover.
☐ Cover tightly and cook in the oven for a minimum of 12 hours – overnight if possible.
Tip: Season very well. Use one large piece of meat rather than small pieces which are likely to disintegrate with such a lot of cooking. A marrow bone is optional. Pearl barley is more traditional than rice, though rice can be used, as shown.

The traditional Jewish Cholent (Shalet) is perfect for long, slow cooking.

Menu

Melon Appetizer

*Fish Baked in Tahina
with
Sautéed Aubergines*

*Creamy Cheesecake
with fruits*

White Israeli wine

Quantities given serve 4

Melon Appetizer

Mineolas are a variety of easy-peel citrus fruit, a cross between a tangerine and a grapefruit and one of many varieties now being grown in Israel. The flesh of the fruit is very soft, so don't remove the membranes, just any loose white pith.

Baked Fish in Tahina

You can use any fish for this recipe. In Israel they eat a lot of grey mullet and trout is popular too, but white fish such as haddock or cod would be good.

Melon Appetizer served with warm pitta bread, and Fish Baked in Tahina.

Melon Appetizer

Serves 4   ☆☆
Preparation: 15 minutes plus 30 minutes chilling

---

1 medium Galia or honeydew melon
1 large avocado
juice of 1 lemon
3 tablespoons natural yogurt
1 teaspoon curry powder
salt and freshly ground black pepper
1 mineola or small orange, peeled and
    segmented
pitta bread for serving

Halve the melon, scoop out and discard the seeds and remove the flesh. Chop it into even chunks and put it into a bowl.

☐ Halve the avocado, remove the stone and cut the flesh into cubes. Sprinkle with lemon juice.

☐ Mix together the yogurt, curry powder, salt and a little pepper. Add the avocado, mineola and yogurt dressing to the melon in the bowl and mix gently.

☐ Chill for 30 minutes. Serve with hot pitta bread.

Fish Baked in Tahina

Serves 4   ☆☆☆
Preparation: 15 minutes
Cooking: 15-20 minutes

---

4 trout, each about 6-8oz (175-225g), cleaned
    and skinned, heads intact
a little butter for greasing
6 fl oz (175ml) lemon juice
8oz (225g) tahina paste
1 large garlic clove, crushed
salt and freshly ground black pepper
thin lemon slices for garnish
small sprigs of parsley to garnish

Set the oven to 350F (180C) gas 4.

☐ Place the fish in a lightly greased shallow ovenproof dish.

☐ Combine the lemon juice, tahina and garlic. As it thickens, beat in just enough cold water to make a thick, creamy sauce. Season well and pour over the fish, leaving the heads clear. Cover the dish with foil and bake for 15-20 minutes.

☐ Remove the foil from the dish and garnish the fish with lemon slices and sprigs of parsley. Serve with Sautéed Aubergines or a simple salad.

Creamy Cheesecake

Serves 6 ☆☆☆

Preparation: 25 minutes
Cooking: 35 minutes plus chilling overnight

8oz (225g) plain digestive biscuits
3oz (75g) butter, melted
1lb (500g) medium-fat curd cheese
8oz (225g) full-fat soft cheese

4 eggs, size 3
8oz (225g) caster sugar
1 teaspoon vanilla essence
½ pint (300ml) soured cream
fruit, to serve

Set the oven to 350F (180C) gas 4.

☐ Crush the biscuits and mix thoroughly with the melted butter. Press into a 7in (18cm) diameter spring-form cake tin to form a base crust.

☐ Mix all the remaining ingredients except the soured cream, beating until smooth and well blended. Spoon it in to the prepared tin and bake for 25 minutes.

☐ Turn off the heat and leave the cheesecake to cool in the oven with the door ajar.

☐ When cooled, spoon the soured cream over the top. Set the oven at 400F (200C) gas 6, and return the cake for 10 minutes to bake and set the top.

☐ Cool and chill overnight.

☐ Decorate with fruit to serve.

Sautéed Aubergines

Aubergines seem to appear at almost every Israeli meal in some form. They make the perfect accompaniment to Fish Baked in Tahina. For 4 people, allow 1½lb (700g) aubergines, slice them thinly, sprinkle with salt and leave to drain in a colander for 15 minutes. Rinse, pat dry and sauté in hot oil, stirring constantly and adding extra oil as required. Drain well and sprinkle with salt to serve.

Slicing and salting them first helps to draw out the bitter juices.

Creamy Cheesecake

Israelis are great bakers and cheesecake is popular as a traditional dish for both Middle and Eastern European Jews.
This is delicious served on its own, but make it even more special with a topping of fresh fruit, such as mangoes, which are now grown in Israel, or peaches.

As with most cooked cheesecakes, this tastes better the day after it is made. It also freezes well.

Sautéed Aubergines to serve with the fish dish, and a Creamy Cheesecake topped with peaches and served with slices of fresh mango.

White Beans with Apples

An unusual spiced bean dish that is especially good in winter. Serve either as a pudding, or as an accompaniment to plain roast chicken.

Use two 15oz (425g) cans of haricot beans to save time. Add 1-2 tablespoons soaked raisins to the mixture with the apples and sugar.

Crimsels

This recipe is a particular Passover favourite. During this period no flour or bread is eaten in a Jewish home to commemorate the exodus from Egypt when there was no time for the leavening of the bread.

Below: White Beans with Apples.
Right: Crimsels made with matzos.

Speciality

White Beans with Apples

Serves 4-6 ☆
Preparation: 15 minutes plus overnight soaking
Cooking: 1 hour 5 minutes

8oz (225g) haricot beans, soaked overnight
1½lb (750g) cooking apples, peeled, cored and sliced
4oz (100g) demerara sugar
1 teaspoon ground cinnamon
grated rind of 1 lemon, or to taste
2oz (50g) margarine

Drain the beans and cook in plenty of water for about 45 minutes.

☐ Drain the cooked beans and add all the remaining ingredients. Stir together, then cook gently for 20 minutes, stirring from time to time, until the apples are cooked.

☐ Serve warm.

Speciality

Crimsels

Serves 4
Preparation: 15 minutes
Cooking: 15 minutes

---

4 matzos
2 eggs
3 tablespoons caster sugar
grated rind of 2 lemons
1 teaspoon ground ginger
1 cooking apple, peeled and grated
3 tablespoons raisins
2oz (50g) chopped mixed nuts
oil for shallow-frying
a little caster sugar or cinnamon sugar for serving

Crumble the matzos and put them into a large bowl. Pour on water to cover, soak briefly, then squeeze out the water.

☐ Beat the eggs and add to the soaked matzos together with the caster sugar, lemon rind, ginger, apple, raisins and nuts. Mix together thoroughly.

☐ Heat the oil in a large frying-pan. Drop the mixture into the hot oil a tablespoonful at a time, and fry until golden brown on each side.

☐ Drain well on kitchen paper and serve hot, sprinkled with caster sugar or cinnamon sugar.

Eastern Europe

Poland and Czechoslovakia lie behind the Iron Curtain, but patriotic pride and a sense of national identity are very strong in these countries, and the same is true of the 15 republics of the USSR. One of the ways old traditions are best preserved is in cooking: the people of Eastern Europe have always been renowned for their hospitality, and Polish, Czechoslovakian and Russian housewives are justly proud of their recipes for national dishes passed down from generation to generation. There are some striking similarities in the cuisines of the Eastern European countries, including a love of hearty soups, fish and game dishes and sweet and savoury pancakes and dumplings.

Soups feature prominently on every Polish menu, and barszcz (Russian Borsch) is probably the favourite, though krupnik, a meat and barley broth, is also very popular. The characteristic ingredient of barszcz is beetroot, but there are endless different versions. A meatless barszcz is made with the mushrooms which grow profusely in the forests of Poland and are included, fresh or dried, in many dishes, such as bigos, a robust hunter's stew of mixed meats, sausage and cabbage. Since much of Poland is heavily wooded, game dishes are common, and berries from the forests are used to make delicious fruit soups. The Poles are famous for their cakes, particularly doughnuts, gingerbread and honey cakes. As in

Russia, vodka is the national drink, sometimes excitingly flavoured with rowanberries, lemon peel, blackcurrant leaves, anise, peppercorns or buffalo grass (zubrovka).

Unlike Poland, which opens on to the Baltic in the north, Czechoslovakia has no sea coast, but its rivers and lakes teem with fish such as carp, pike and trout, which are as popular as meat. A favourite Eastern European way of cooking fish is with dried fruit, especially raisins and prunes, to make a sweet-sour sauce. Two of the best known drinks in Czechoslovakia are slivovitz, a plum liqueur, and pils, a strong lager.

Russian food is as varied as the country is vast, but can be divided into home cooking and classic dishes that have achieved international renown. Of these, Beef Stroganoff, meat strips in soured cream sauce, Chicken Kiev, fried chicken breasts stuffed with garlic butter, kulebjaka, a raised flaky pastry salmon pie, and Charlotte Russe, a sponge fingerlined moulded creamy dessert are among the most famous. Caviar, the roe of sturgeon, is always associated with Russian cuisine, and is perhaps best eaten as in Russia with Blinis – buckwheat yeast pancakes – and soured cream. Blinis are often included in zakushki, a mouthwatering spread of appetizers to accompany tiny glasses of chilled vodka, along with chopped herring, pickled cucumbers and mushrooms, pâtés and galantines, bitki (meatballs) and pirozhki, little savoury pasties.

Among the more homely Russian dishes are cabbage soup (shchi) and potato soup (pokhlobka), as well as Borsch, accompanied by dark rye bread. Kasha, a kind of buckwheat porridge, is very popular, as are dishes made with soured cream and curd cheese: Russia is famous for its dairy products, and Russian ice cream is delicious. Tea served from the urn or samovar in glasses and kvass, a thin beer made from fermented bread, are the most popular everyday drinks.

Bigos 'Jan'
For a richer stew, stir ¼ pint (150ml) soured cream into the casserole before serving. Chanterelle mushrooms are delicious in bigos, but any mushrooms will do.

Makowiec
Almonds may be used instead of the walnuts and hazelnuts. Try adding 2 tablespoons of seedless raisins, soaked in a little sherry, to the poppy seed mixture.

Poland

Speciality
Bigos 'Jan'
Hunter's stew
Accompany with mashed potatoes and crisp boiled French beans.

Serves 4   ★★☆
Preparation: 15 minutes
Cooking: about 1¼ hours

1 lb (500g) boneless venison, cubed
8oz (225g) belly pork, rinded and cubed
salt and freshly ground black pepper
4oz (100g) goose fat or beef dripping
2 onions, peeled and chopped
¾lb (350g) mushrooms, wiped and trimmed
1lb (500g) sauerkraut
¼ pint (150ml) boiling water
8oz (225g) garlic sausage, sliced

Heat the oven to 400F (200C) gas 6.
☐ Season the meats with salt and pepper. Melt the fat or dripping in a flameproof casserole and fry the meat quickly to seal and brown.
☐ Remove the meat with a slotted spoon and set aside. Add the onion to the casserole and fry gently for 5 minutes, then add the mushrooms and fry for 2-3 minutes, stirring.
☐ Return the meats to the casserole and cover with the sauerkraut. Pour in the boiling water, cover and cook in the oven for about 40 minutes.
☐ Reduce the oven temperature to 350F (180C) gas 4. Stir the contents of the casserole, add a little extra boiling water, if necessary, and top with the garlic sausage. Cook for a further 20 minutes, or until all the ingredients are tender.

Speciality
Makowiec
Poppy seed cake

Makes 12 slices   ★☆
Preparation and cooking: 25 minutes
Chilling: 2-3 hours

1lb (500g) poppy seeds
7oz (200g) clear honey
4oz (100g) butter
2oz (50g) sugar
¼ pint (150ml) water
4oz (100g) shelled walnuts
4oz (100g) shelled hazelnuts

Heat a dry frying-pan over a moderate heat for 2-3 minutes, add the poppy seeds and roast, shaking constantly.
☐ In a saucepan, bring the honey, butter, sugar and water to the boil. Add the poppy seeds and simmer for 10 minutes, stirring constantly.
☐ Finely chop half the nuts and grind the remainder. Stir the chopped nuts into the poppy seed mixture and leave to cool, then shape into a 2½in (6cm) cylinder.
☐ Roll this in the ground nuts to coat thoroughly, then wrap in foil and chill in the refrigerator for 2-3 hours. Serve cut into thick slices.

Speciality
Karp Po Polsku
Polish-style carp
Serve with boiled potatoes, rice or noodles and spinach creamed with a little nutmeg.

Serves 4   ★★☆
Preparation: 10 minutes
Cooking: 35 minutes

½ pint (300ml) lager
4 onions, peeled and chopped
2 bay leaves
2 cloves
6 black peppercorns, lightly crushed
4 carp fillets or steaks about 1¾lb
   (800g) in total
salt and freshly ground black pepper
2 teaspoons lemon juice
2oz (50g) wholemeal breadcrumbs
a pinch of mixed spice
a pinch of sugar
2 teaspoons herb vinegar
3oz (75g) blanched almonds, chopped
2oz (50g) raisins
3oz (75g) chilled butter, diced
parsley sprigs, to garnish

Put the lager, onions, bay leaves, cloves and peppercorns in a pan and boil. Lower the heat, cover the pan and simmer for 15 minutes, then

Karp po Połsku

Carp is considered quite a delicacy by most Eastern Europeans. Its soft, almost glutinous, texture and very fine full flavour are quite distinctive. If carp is not available, the nearest equivalent is small pike.
Other freshwater fish may be cooked in the same way. Small brown trout, cleaned and with the heads removed would be a good choice.

strain through a fine sieve into a clean bowl.

☐ Meanwhile, rinse the carp and pat dry with kitchen paper. Season lightly with salt and sprinkle with the lemon juice. Arrange the carp on a trivet in a large saucepan or fish kettle, and pour in the strained lager mixture.

☐ Bring to the boil, then lower the heat and poach the carp for 15 minutes, or until cooked through (the flesh flakes easily when pierced with a small sharp knife).

☐ Remove the trivet from the pan. Using one or two fish slices, carefully transfer the carp to a warmed serving dish and keep hot while making sauce.

☐ Stir the breadcrumbs into the cooking liquid in the saucepan and season to taste with mixed spice, sugar and salt and pepper, if necessary. Bring the mixture to the boil, stirring constantly.

☐ Strain the mixture through a fine sieve into a clean pan, pressing with the back of a wooden spoon. Add the vinegar, almonds and raisins and simmer for 2-3 minutes. Gradually whisk in the butter, piece by piece, and allow the sauce just to heat through.

☐ Pour the sauce over the carp and garnish with parsley sprigs.

Tip: Try adding a little sugar or honey to the sauce for a more 'sweet-and-sour' effect. Some recipes also put leek or parsnips into the lager mixture for added flavour.

From left to right: Ceške Polevka z Drubeziho Hasé – a creamy chicken and mushroom soup; Koulicky Zjeleniho Masa na Smetané – venison and pork in a soured cream sauce, served with mashed potatoes, lager and a sharp cranberry and apple sauce; and Moravské Kolace – buttery pastries stuffed with a spicy filling.

Czechoslovakia

Ceške Polevka z Drubeziho Hasé

Bohemian chicken soup

Serves 4   ☆ ☆ ☆
Preparation: 15 minutes
Cooking: 25 minutes

2½oz (65g) butter
1 small onion, chopped
1 tablespoon finely chopped parsley
¼lb (100g) mushrooms, finely chopped
1½ pints (900ml) Chicken Stock
1½oz (40g) plain flour
8oz (225g) cooked chicken, very finely
     chopped
salt and freshly ground pepper
1 egg yolk
3fl oz (100ml) single cream

Heat half the butter in a saucepan, add the onion and fry gently for 5 minutes until softened. Stir in the parsley and the mushrooms and add about ¼ pint (150ml) of the stock. Simmer gently for 10 minutes, stirring from time to time.

☐ In a separate saucepan melt the remaining butter and sprinkle in the flour. Cook for 1-2 minutes, stirring, then gradually stir in the remaining stock. Simmer for a further 2-3 minutes, then add the mushroom mixture with the chopped chicken. Stir well and season to taste with salt and pepper.

☐ Beat the egg yolk with the cream in a bowl. Stir in 2-3 tablespoons of the hot soup, then pour the mixture back into the soup and reheat very gently without boiling.

☐ Serve the soup immediately in a warmed soup tureen or individual soup bowls.

Koulicky Zjeleniho Masa na Smetané

Venison meatballs in cream sauce

Serves 4 ☆ ☆ ☆
Preparation: 25 minutes
Cooking: 20 minutes

3oz (75g) streaky bacon rashers, rinds removed and diced
¾lb (350g) venison, finely minced
8oz (225g) lean pork, finely minced
4 juniper berries, crushed
1 small onion, peeled and finely chopped
1 tablespoon finely chopped parsley
6oz (175g) fresh white breadcrumbs
1 egg
3fl oz (100ml) milk
salt and freshly ground black pepper
2oz (50g) butter
1oz (25g) flour
¼ pint (150ml) Game or Meat Stock
¼ pint (150ml) soured cream

Fry the bacon in its own fat in a covered frying-pan set over a moderate heat until it is lightly browned.

☐ Remove the bacon with a slotted spoon and place in a mixing bowl with the venison and pork, juniper berries, onion, parsley and breadcrumbs.

☐ Beat the egg with the milk and stir into the meat mixture. Season to taste with salt and pepper, then mix well. Divide the mixture into pieces the size of a walnut and shape into balls.

☐ Melt the butter with the fat in the frying-pan. Fry the meatballs quickly, turning to brown all over. Lower the heat, partially cover the pan and cook gently for 10 minutes, stirring from time to time, until the meatballs are cooked through. Remove them with a slotted spoon and keep warm while making the sauce.

☐ Pour off all but 1½ tablespoons of the fat from the pan. Sprinkle in the flour and cook for 1-2 minutes, stirring. Remove from the heat and gradually stir in the stock. Return to the heat and cook for a further 2-3 minutes, stirring until thickened.

☐ Remove from the heat, gradually stir in the soured cream and season to taste with salt and pepper. Return the meatballs to the pan and stir to coat in the sauce. Heat through gently before serving, but do not allow to boil.

Tip: Hand a bowl of cranberry or apple sauce separately and serve chilled beer to drink.

Borsch

As well as chunks of rye bread, traditional accompaniments to borsch include finely sliced pickled cucumber, spring onions and chopped hard-boiled egg. Sometimes the soup is garnished with tiny bitkis (meatballs).

Blinis

These are almost as good if made using wholemeal flour. Serve them with chopped hard-boiled eggs, sliced spring onions and soured cream as an interesting starter.

Moravské Kolace
Moravian apple pastries

Makes 16 ☆
Preparation: 1¼ hours, including proving
Cooking: 20 minutes

¼ pint (150ml) tepid milk
1oz (25g) fresh yeast, crumbled
2½oz (65g) caster sugar, plus
    extra for glazing
9oz (250g) flour
a pinch of salt
1 egg, beaten
2oz (50g) butter, softened
½ teaspoon grated lemon rind
1 egg yolk, beaten

The filling:
2 large dessert apples, peeled, cored
    and coarsely grated
1oz (25g) currants
1 teaspoon grated lemon rind
a pinch of ground cinnamon
a pinch of allspice

Pour the milk into a bowl, add the yeast and stir until completely dissolved. Stir in 1 teaspoon of the sugar and leave to stand for 10 minutes until frothy.
☐ Sift the flour with the salt into another mixing bowl and make a well in the centre. Pour in the yeast liquid and egg and add the remaining sugar, butter and lemon rind. Using a wooden spoon, work the dry ingredients into the liquid until blended.
☐ Knead for about 10 minutes to obtain a pliable, elastic dough. Cover the bowl with a clean damp cloth and leave to rise for 30 minutes in a warm place.
☐ Divide the dough into 16 equal pieces and shape each into a 2½in (6cm) round. With a wetted finger, make a hollow in the top of each. Combine all the filling ingredients and spoon into the hollows. Leave to rise for a further 15 minutes in a warm place. Heat the oven to 350F (180C) gas 4.
☐ Brush the pastries with egg yolk and bake for 20 minutes or until golden brown and cooked through. Sprinkle with sugar and serve.

Russia

Speciality
Borsch
Beetroot soup

Serves 4 ☆☆☆
Preparation and cooking: 1 hour

¾lb (350g) raw beetroot, peeled and sliced
    into matchstick lengths
3oz (75g) bacon, rinds removed and diced
2 tablespoons tomato purée
1 tablespoon red wine vinegar
1¼ pints (750ml) Meat Stock
3oz (75g) butter
1 large carrot, thinly sliced
1 onion, chopped
1½ tablespoons flour
4 large potatoes, coarsely cubed
¾lb (350g) cabbage, shredded
1 bay leaf
salt and freshly ground black pepper
¼ pint (150ml) soured cream
1 teaspoon caraway seeds (optional)

Put the beetroot into a large saucepan with the bacon, tomato purée, red wine vinegar and meat stock.
☐ Bring to the boil, then lower the heat, cover the pan and simmer gently for 20-30 minutes.
☐ Meanwhile, melt the butter in a separate large saucepan over a moderate heat and fry the carrot and onion gently for 5 minutes, stirring from time to time, until the onion is soft.
☐ Sprinkle in the flour and stir well to mix. Cook for 1-2 minutes, stirring, then gradually add the beetroot with its cooking liquid. Stir well to incorporate.
☐ Add the potatoes, cabbage and bay leaf and season to taste with salt and pepper. Bring to the boil, then lower the heat, cover and simmer for about 20 minutes or until all vegetables are tender.
☐ Remove and discard the bay leaf. Ladle the borsch into warmed soup plates. Beat the soured cream with a fork until smooth, then swirl over the soup and sprinkle with the caraway seeds, if using.

Blinis

Buckwheat pancakes

A traditional accompaniment—with soured cream—to caviar, these are just as good on their own dressed only with some melted butter.

Serves 4   ☆☆☆

Preparation: about 1½ hours, including rising

Cooking: about 10 minutes

9fl oz (250ml) milk
1oz (25g) fresh yeast, crumbled
1 teaspoon sugar
¼ pint (150ml) water
7oz (200g) buckwheat flour
7oz (200g) plain flour
a pinch of salt
2oz (50g) butter, softened
2 eggs, separated
4oz (100g) butter, for frying

Warm half the milk and pour it into a bowl. Add the yeast and stir until dissolved. Add sugar and leave for 10 minutes, until frothy.

☐ Bring the remaining milk with the water to the boil in a large saucepan. Remove from the heat and add the buckwheat flour. Stir until absorbed. Leave to cool.

☐ Sift the plain flour with the salt into a mixing bowl. Make a well and pour in the yeast liquid. Work all the dry ingredients into the liquid, then knead until the dough is pliable.

☐ Cover the bowl with a clean damp cloth and leave to rise for 30 minutes in a warm place.

☐ Add the butter and egg yolks to the buckwheat mixture and mix well. Stir in the dough to make a thick batter. Cover the bowl and leave to rise for 30 minutes.

☐ Stiffly whisk the egg whites and fold them into the batter lightly and thoroughly.

☐ Heat a small knob of butter in a large frying-pan and drop in tablespoons of batter. Fry the blinis quickly, turning once, until golden brown on both sides. Keep warm while frying remaining batter.

Marinovannye Riba, Russian marinated fish, also makes a delightful summer lunch dish, accompanied by wholemeal bread and butter and a cucumber salad.

Try serving the marinated fish as part of your own selection of Russian-style hors d'oeuvre. You might also like to include some pirozhki, tasty little savoury pasties beloved by the Russians. To make these, cut 2½ inch (6cm) rounds of rich shortcrust pastry, and spoon on to one half of each a mixture of finely flaked cooked fish, chopped hard-boiled egg, finely chopped onion and mushroom, and parsley or dill. Fold over the pastry, press the edges firmly to seal, brush with egg yolk and bake on a lightly greased baking sheet in a hot oven for about 20 minutes, until golden brown.

Speciality
Marinovannye Riba

Marinated fish
Serve as a starter accompanied by toast and butter, or as part of mixed hors d'oeuvre.

Serves 6
Preparation: 10 minutes, plus cooling and chilling
Cooking: 20 minutes

1lb (500g) fillets of pike, carp,
    salmon or sturgeon, skinned
salt and freshly ground black pepper
2 tablespoons flour
¼ pint (150ml) sunflower oil
lettuce leaves, to garnish
1 tablespoon finely chopped chives

The marinade:
3 tablespoons sunflower oil
2 onions, chopped
2 small carrots, scraped and diced
3 tablespoons white wine vinegar
2 tablespoons tomato purée
3 tablespoons dry white wine

Cut the fish fillets into 12 equal pieces, then season with salt and pepper and coat with the flour. Heat the oil in a large frying-pan over a moderate heat and fry the fish, turning once, for 5-10 minutes, or until the fish is cooked through and lightly browned on both sides. Drain on kitchen paper and leave to cool completely.

☐ Make the marinade: heat the oil in a saucepan, add the onion and carrots and fry gently for 5 minutes until softened. Add the vinegar, tomato purée and wine, stir well and season to taste with salt and pepper. Bring to the boil then lower the heat and simmer for 5-6 minutes. Remove from the heat and leave to cool completely.

☐ Line a serving dish with lettuce leaves. Arrange the fried fish pieces on top and spoon over the marinade.

☐ Chill the marinated fish in the refrigerator for 30 minutes, then sprinkle with chives and serve.

India

Because India is so huge, and its faiths, ways of life and languages are so varied, it is not surprising that its cuisine, too, is perhaps the most diverse in the world. Geography itself forms regional differences in cooking styles – the more temperate north is where wheat dominates, while in the wetter south, rice is the staple. Religion, too, is influential: the predominant Hindus will not eat beef, the Muslims will not eat pork and, of course, the poverty of the majority of Indians as well as reverence for life dictate that vegetarianism is the norm. But the common denominator of all of the wide spectrum of Indian food is the use of spices: sometimes mild, usually subtle, often searingly hot – with the addition of hot chilli peppers.

The thousands of miles of Indian coastline – stretching south from the border with Pakistan round to the complex delta of the Ganges at Bangladesh – teems with exotic seafood, caught and eaten principally in the south and north-east. Fish is often cooked 'dry' or, as in Bengal, with tomatoes, their sharpness offsetting any oiliness in the fish.

In southern India, the majority of the population is Hindu, vegetarian and poor. Here meat is a luxury, and vegetable dishes are the staple diet – satisfying dhals (lentil purées) and plain boiled rice. Southern meat dishes are the spiciest and hottest in India – chillies are grown, and used in

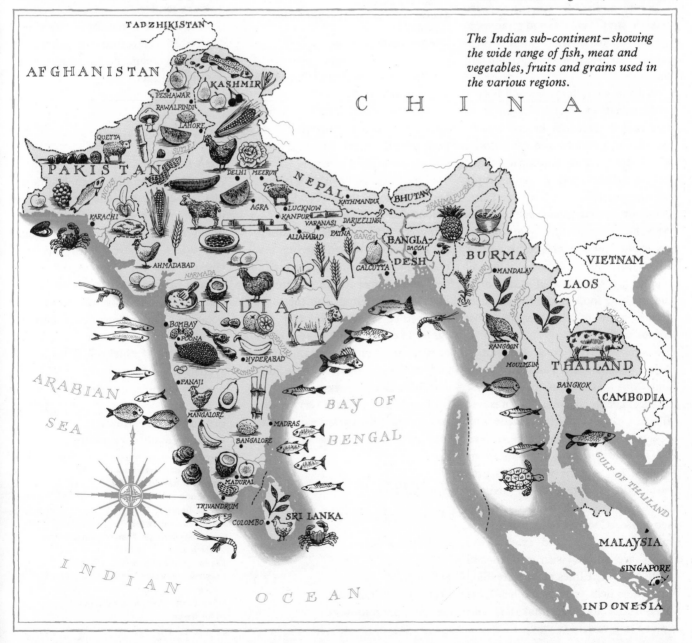

The Indian sub-continent – showing the wide range of fish, meat and vegetables, fruits and grains used in the various regions.

profusion. From here come the searing Madras curry and the vinegar based Vindaloos. But spicing can be less hot, with rich lamb Kormas, the occasional beef and pork dish – the latter often using the wild boar that graze the sugar cane plantations. The most predominant flavourings, though, are coconut (milk and flesh), which grows widely throughout the region, tamarind and curry leaves.

In the centre and north, where the Muslim Moghul emperors once ruled, the emphasis lies on good ingredients, here more readily available, and there are echoes of the Islamic cooking of the Middle East and North Africa. Chicken dishes are supreme, and subtly spiced; eggs are eaten in simple curries and scrambles; lamb is cooked with opulent ingredients such as pistachios, cream and saffron.

With its more temperate climate, a wider variety of vegetables is grown in this region – spinach, broccoli, peas, sweetcorn, potatoes and cauliflower. These are eaten as accompaniments, not main dishes, and rice is not simply boiled, but baked and steamed into elaborate spiced pilaus and biryanis (the latter sometimes – for special occasions – topped with edible gold or silver leaf). Fresh ginger, garlic and onions are the basis of many meat dishes, and food colouring powders create some of the world's most colourful dishes.

From here too come the Indian wheat breads – the Parathas, Naans and Rotis – as well as many popular snacks such as Samosas, Pakoras and Bhajias, pasties and fritters made from vegetables, minced meat and seafood.

The continent which produces the spiciest food in the world also produces the sweetest foods – usually made with rice, semolina and condensed milk. Coconut and carrots are made into fudge, and exotic fresh fruits are spiced with pepper and chilli powder. Limes make refreshing drinks, as does yogurt, and tea (from both India and Sri Lanka) is also spiced in a variety of ways.

Speciality
Rogan Josht
Curried lamb

Serves 4-6
Preparation: 1 hour 10 minutes
including marinating
Cooking: 1 hour

2lb (1kg) boned leg of lamb
½ pint (300ml) natural yogurt
1-1½ teaspoons cayenne
1 teaspoon salt
1in (2.5cm) piece fresh root ginger,
    peeled and grated
½ teaspoon turmeric
4 tablespoons ghee or oil
2 onions, finely chopped
4 garlic cloves, crushed
4 tomatoes, chopped
2 tablespoons chopped fresh coriander
    leaves
½ teaspoon garam masala

Cut the meat into 1in (2.5cm) cubes and put in a bowl.

☐ Mix the yogurt, cayenne, salt, ginger and turmeric together and pour over the meat. Mix well, cover and set aside for 1 hour.

☐ Heat the ghee or oil in a large pan over moderate heat and fry the onions and garlic until lightly coloured. Add the meat and all of the marinade and fry, stirring, until bubbling. Cover the pan, reduce the heat and simmer for 45 minutes.

☐ Add the tomatoes and the chopped coriander leaves and continue cooking uncovered, stirring occasionally, until the sauce thickens and the meat is tender. Taste and add more salt if necessary.

☐ Transfer to a warm serving dish and sprinkle the garam masala on top. Serve with Parathas or pitta bread.

Speciality
Matar Korma
Fresh pea curry

Serves 4 ☆☆
Preparation: 5 minutes
Cooking: 25 minutes

2 tablespoons oil
1 onion, finely chopped
2 garlic cloves, crushed
2 teaspoons grated fresh root ginger
1-2 green chillies, finely chopped
1½lb (700g) ripe tomatoes, skinned and
    puréed
1lb (500g) shelled peas
½ teaspoon salt
½ teaspoon sugar
¼ pint (150ml) soured cream

Heat the oil in a large frying-pan over moderate heat and fry the onion, garlic, ginger and green chillies until soft but not browned.

☐ Add the puréed tomatoes and cook, stirring, for 2 minutes. Add the peas, salt and sugar. Cover and simmer for 20 minutes or until the peas are tender.

☐ If the sauce is too thin, cook uncovered for a few minutes. Stir in the soured cream, heat through for 1 minute and serve.

Speciality
Jhinga Bhajia
Fish fritters

A snack commonly eaten in India, bhajias can be made from many ingredients, cooked or raw. The batter is made from chickpea flour and water flavoured with salt and chillies, and the main ingredient is usually a vegetable such as sliced onions, whole spinach leaves or sliced potatoes. The recipe given here is slightly more elaborate. Use self-raising flour if chickpea flour is not available.

Serves 4 ☆☆
Preparation: 10 minutes
Cooking: about 10 minutes

1½oz (40g) chickpea flour
a pinch of baking powder
½ teaspoon salt
2 eggs, beaten
3-4 tablespoons water
8oz (225g) shrimps, thawed and drained
    if frozen
1 onion, finely chopped
1 tablespoon finely chopped coriander
    leaves
1-2 green chillies, finely chopped
oil for frying

Sift the flour, baking powder and salt into a bowl. Stir in the eggs and enough of the water to make a smooth, thick batter.

☐ Chop the shrimps and mix into the batter with the onion, coriander leaves and green chillies.

☐ Heat enough oil to cover the bottom of the frying-pan until very hot. Drop in tablespoons of the batter mixture and fry for 1-2 minutes on each side or until golden brown.

☐ Drain well and serve hot.

Speciality
Machli Tamatar

Spicy fish with tomatoes

This dish is from the west coast of India which is rich in fine seafood. The fish in this area are firmer-fleshed than haddock or cod, so flour is not used for coating – as it is in this recipe, to prevent disintegration of the fish strips when fried.

Serves 4   ☆☆
Preparation: 10 minutes
Cooking: 12 minutes

1¼lb (700g) thick haddock fillets, skinned
1 tablespoon flour
1 teaspoon salt
1 teaspoon cayenne
4 tablespoons oil
1 onion, finely chopped
2 garlic cloves, crushed
½ teaspoon ground turmeric
2 teaspoons ground coriander
2 large tomatoes, chopped
2 tablespoons chopped fresh coriander
    leaves
juice of ½ a lemon
1 teaspoon garam masala

Cut the fish into strips. Mix the flour, salt and cayenne on a plate and roll the fish strips in the mixture.

☐ Heat 3 tablespoons of the oil in a large, deep frying-pan and fry the fish for 1 minute turning the strips over constantly. Fry in batches if necessary. Using a slotted spoon transfer the fish strips to a plate.

☐ Add the rest of the oil to the pan and fry the onion and garlic, stirring constantly, until they begin to colour. Stir in the turmeric and ground coriander and fry for 2 minutes. Add the tomatoes and half the chopped coriander leaves and cook until slightly softened.

☐ Return the fish to the pan, squeeze the lemon juice over and stir gently to mix. Taste and add more salt and cayenne, if necessary. Cover the pan and cook for 5 minutes.

☐ Turn out into a serving dish. Sprinkle the garam masala on top and then the remaining chopped coriander leaves.

☐ Serve with plain boiled rice.

Ghee
A kind of clarified butter which is a favourite cooking medium in northern India and is now readily available in many large supermarkets. To make your own ghee melt 8oz (225g) unsalted butter in a heavy pan. Cook very gently for about 20 minutes or until the butter is beginning to change colour and has stopped spitting. Strain through muslin and store in a screw-top jar.

Garam Masala
A blend of spices which is added to a dish during the last minutes of cooking, this is often made at home. In a dry frying-pan, stir-fry separately 4 tablespoons whole coriander seeds, 2 teaspoons whole cumin seeds, 1 tablespoon whole black peppercorns, 2 teaspoons cardamom seeds, 4 pieces cinnamon stick each about 2½in (6cm) long and 1 teaspoon whole cloves. When the spices release their aroma set aside to cool. Grind them together in a blender or coffee grinder, then stir in half a grated nutmeg. Store in a screw-top jar.

Machli Tamatar – spicy fish fried with tomatoes.

Basmati rice

One of the best kinds of long-grain rice, with a good flavour and firm texture. To cook it successfully: First pick over to remove any small stones or debris, then rinse thoroughly in several changes of water until the water remains fairly clear. Leave rice to soak for about 30 minutes then drain. Bring to the boil in 1⅓ cups of salted water to every cup of rice, cover and simmer for 20 minutes.

Kitchri

A mixture of rice and lentils, cooked together. There are many recipes for kitchri, the simplest being to boil equal quantities in salted water and serve with butter. For a more elaborate version soak 6oz (175g) each of rinsed long-grain rice and orange lentils in water for 30 minutes. Meanwhile, fry 1 chopped onion, 2 crushed garlic cloves and 2 teaspoons grated root ginger in 4 tablespoons ghee until soft. Stir in ½ teaspoon turmeric, ½ teaspoon cayenne pepper and a little salt. Add the rice and lentils, fry for 2 minutes, cover then simmer in ¾ pint (450ml) water for 20 minutes. Serve garnished with fried onion.

Cardamom

Whole cardamom pods are used in several of the recipes given here. Remove them from the cooked dish before serving or leave on the side of the plate as although they impart flavour, they are not very nice to eat. Or just use the seeds from the pods.

Murgh Biryani

Speciality
Murgh Biryani

Spiced chicken with rice
Biryanis can be served on their own with yogurt or a yogurt salad, or as part of an Indian meal with various other dishes.

Serves 6 ☆☆☆
Preparation: 30 minutes plus 30 minutes soaking
Cooking: about 1 hour

1lb (500g) basmati rice
salt
5 tablespoons oil
2 cinnamon sticks
10 whole cloves
10 whole cardamoms
8 peppercorns
2 onions, finely chopped
2 garlic cloves, crushed
1-in (2.5cm) piece of fresh root ginger, peeled and grated
2 small chickens, each cut into 6 pieces
½ pint (300ml) natural yogurt
1 teaspoon cayenne pepper
¼ pint (150ml) cold water
½ teaspoon saffron powder
3 tablespoons hot water

The garnish (optional):
2 tablespoons oil
onion rings
slivered almonds
raisins

Wash the rice in several changes of cold water. When the water runs clear leave the rice to soak for 30 minutes, then drain.

☐ Bring a large pan of salted water to the boil. Tip in the rice and boil for 1½ minutes. Drain and set aside.

☐ Meanwhile, in another large pan heat 4 tablespoons of the oil over a moderate heat. Add the cinnamon, cloves, cardamom and peppercorns and fry, stirring, for 30 seconds. Add the onions, garlic and ginger and fry, stirring, for 3-4 minutes or until coloured. Put in the chicken pieces and cook, turning them to brown on all sides.

☐ Stir in the yogurt a spoonful at a time, allowing each addition to be absorbed before adding the next. Mix in the cayenne, 1 teaspoon salt and the cold water. Bring to the simmer, cover the pan and cook gently for 25-30 minutes or until the chicken is cooked.

☐ Set oven to 350F (180C) gas 4. Brush a large ovenproof casserole dish with the remaining oil. Dissolve the saffron powder in the hot water and mix it into the rice.

☐ Put one-third of the rice in the casserole. Cover with half the chicken pieces. Repeat the layers finishing with a layer of rice. Pour any juices and gravy left in the pan over the top. Cover tightly and bake for 25-30 minutes.

☐ Meanwhile, if you are going to garnish the dish, heat the oil in a frying-pan and fry the onion rings until brown. Remove from the pan with a slotted spoon and drain on kitchen paper. Put the almonds and raisins in the pan and fry until the almonds colour and the raisins puff.

☐ Serve the biryani in the casserole or serving dish, with the garnish.

Speciality
Spicy Basmati Rice

Serves 4   ☆ ☆
Preparation: 5 minutes plus
30 minutes soaking
Cooking: 20-25 minutes

12oz (350g) basmati rice
3 tablespoons ghee or oil
5 whole cardamoms
5 cloves
2-in (5-cm) piece of cinnamon stick
1 medium onion, finely chopped
1 teaspoon salt
½ teaspoon saffron powder
¾ pint (450ml) boiling Chicken Stock,
    skimmed of all fat

The garnish:
ghee or oil
flaked almonds
raisins

Wash the rice in several changes of cold water. When the water runs clear leave the rice to soak for 30 minutes, then drain.

☐ Heat the ghee or oil in a large pan. Add the cardamoms, cloves and cinnamon and fry, stirring, for 30 seconds. Add the onion and fry until it begins to colour.

☐ Add the rice and salt and fry, stirring until all the rice grains are coated with the oil. Add the saffron powder and mix in with a fork. Pour in the stock, cover the pan tightly, and simmer very gently for 20-25 minutes, or until the rice is cooked and all the stock absorbed.

☐ While the rice is cooking prepare the garnish. Heat a little ghee or oil in a frying-pan and gently fry the almonds and raisins until the nuts are lightly coloured and the raisins puffed up.

☐ To serve, turn the rice out on a warmed serving dish and sprinkle the nuts and raisins on top.

Menu

*Tandoori Murgh
with
Kachumbar
Parathas*

Suji Barfi

Sharbat Gulab or lager

Quantities given serve 4

Kachumbar (Onion Salad)

Slice 2 onions, 1 red pepper and 1 green pepper. Put them in a salad bowl with a dressing made from 2 tablespoons of lemon juice, seasoned to taste with sugar and salt. Toss the salad well, garnish with chopped coriander leaves, then chill thoroughly before serving.

An unusual summer menu for 4– Tandoori Murgh served with Kachumbar and Parathas, followed by Suji Barfi. Sharbat Gulab, a rose-flavoured cordial, makes a cooling drink.

Tandoori Murgh

Tandoori Chicken

Tandoori cooking is a speciality of what was the North West Frontier Province of British India, and is now a part of Pakistan. A tandoor is a special clay, jar-shaped oven which is charcoal-fired. A hot domestic oven or a charcoal barbecue are acceptable alternatives.

Serves 4 ☆☆
Preparation: 15 minutes plus 24 hours marinating
Cooking: 25-30 minutes

---

4 chicken breasts, skinned
1 teaspoon salt
1 teaspoon cayenne pepper
½ teaspoon ground black pepper
2 tablespoons lemon juice
1 medium onion, coarsely chopped
2 garlic cloves, peeled
2-in (5-cm) piece of fresh root ginger, peeled
1 teaspoon ground cumin
½ teaspoon ground turmeric
2 teaspoons ground coriander
½ teaspoon orange food colouring (optional)
5 tablespoons natural yogurt
2 tablespoons melted butter or ghee

Using a sharp knife, make 2 or 3 slashes in each chicken breast. Mix the salt, cayenne, black pepper and lemon juice together and rub into the flesh. Set aside for 20 minutes.

☐ Put all the other ingredients, except the butter or ghee, into a blender and process until smooth to make a marinade.

☐ Place the chicken pieces in a dish and pour the marinade over them. Ensure that the pieces are well coated, using your fingers to rub in the marinade. Cover and refrigerate for 24 hours, turning the pieces occasionally.

☐ Set the oven to 400F (200C) gas 6. Put the chicken pieces on a rack in a baking dish and cook, basting regularly with butter or ghee and the marinade, for 25-30 minutes. The chicken can also be cooked over a hot charcoal grill for 20 minutes.

☐ Serve with Kachumbar and Parathas.

Variation: Whole chicken can be cooked in this way too. Remove the skin and marinate as for chicken pieces. Allow the usual roasting time for a whole chicken.

Parathas

Fried unleavened bread

A North Indian speciality, parathas are unleavened, flaky fried bread made from wholemeal or a mixture of flours. Before being cooked they are sometimes stuffed with spicy vegetables or minced meat.

Serves 4 ☆☆☆
Preparation: 1 hour 10 minutes
Cooking: 15 minutes

4oz (125g) wholemeal flour
4oz (125g) plain flour
½ teaspoon salt
1oz (25g) butter
6-8 tablespoons water
6-8 tablespoons melted butter or ghee

Put both flours and salt into a bowl. Rub in the butter with your fingertips. Mix in the water to make a smooth and pliable dough, adding more water if necessary. Knead well for 5 minutes then cover the dough and leave for 1 hour.

☐ Knead the dough well again and divide into 8 pieces. Shape each piece into a ball. Flatten each ball and roll out on a floured surface into a thin round. Brush with melted butter and fold in half. Brush with butter again and fold in half. Roll the paratha into a round.

☐ Lightly grease a heavy-based frying-pan or griddle and heat until hot. Put in one paratha and cook for 1 minute. Brush the top with melted butter and turn it over. Cook for a further 1 minute, moving the paratha around in the pan. The bread should be lightly coloured with brown spots on both sides.

☐ Fry the other parathas in the same way, keeping them warm on a heated plate covered with foil.

Suji Barfi

Semolina sweets

Serves 4 ☆☆☆
Preparation: 5 minutes
Cooking: 15 minutes

4oz (125g) semolina
8oz (225g) sugar
1½ pints (900ml) milk
4oz (125g) butter, cut into pieces
4 tablespoons raisins
2 teaspoons cardamom seeds, crushed
4 tablespoons flaked almonds

Mix the semolina with the sugar in a saucepan. Pour in the milk slowly, stirring all the time, until the mixture is smooth. Bring to the boil and add the butter, raisins and cardamom seeds. Simmer for 10-15 minutes, stirring occasionally, until the mixture is thick. Be careful not to let it catch and burn.

☐ Butter a shallow dish or plate and pour in the mixture. Sprinkle the almonds on top, pressing them down lightly. Leave to get cold.

☐ When cold cut into diamonds.

Sharbat Gulab

Rose cordial

Makes 8 glasses ◯
Preparation: 2 minutes
Cooking: 5 minutes

1lb (500g) sugar
1 pint (600ml) water
24 drops rose essence or 2 tablespoons rosewater
3-5 drops red food colouring

Put the sugar in a saucepan with the water. Place over low heat and stir to dissolve the sugar. When dissolved, increase the heat and bring the syrup to the boil. Boil without stirring for 1 minute.

☐ Stir in the essence or rosewater and the colouring. Stir to mix and leave to get cold.

☐ To serve, spoon 3 to 4 tablespoons into a tall glass. Fill with ice cubes and top up with cold water or soda water and stir.

Kaju Murgh

Chicken with cashew nuts

Serves 4   ★★☆
Preparation: 10 minutes
Cooking: 40-45 minutes

2in (5cm) piece of fresh root ginger, peeled
4 garlic cloves
1 teaspoon cayenne pepper
1 tablespoon ground coriander
1 teaspoon ground cumin
6oz (175g) cashew nuts
4 tablespoons water
4 tablespoons oil
6 cardamom pods
6 cloves
2-in (5-cm) piece of cinnamon stick
2lb (1kg) chicken pieces, skinned
2 onions, finely chopped
½ pint (300ml) natural yogurt
salt
2 tablespoons chopped mint or coriander
    leaves

Grind the ginger, garlic, cayenne, coriander, cumin and 4oz (125g) of the cashew nuts in a blender then blend to a paste, with the water.

☐ Heat the oil in a large, deep frying-pan over a moderate heat. Add the cardamom, cloves and cinnamon and fry, stirring, for 30 seconds. Put in the chicken pieces and fry gently, turning them over to brown lightly on both sides. Remove the chicken pieces.

☐ Add the onions to the pan and fry, stirring, until lightly coloured. Put in the cashew nut paste and fry, stirring constantly, for 2-3 minutes, adding a little water if necessary to prevent it catching.

☐ Stir in the yogurt a spoonful at a time, allowing each addition to be absorbed before adding the next. Add salt to taste and put in the chicken pieces. Cover the pan and simmer very gently for 30-35 minutes or until tender. Stir occasionally.

☐ About 5 minutes before the end of the cooking time, stir in the remaining cashew nuts and the chopped mint or coriander leaves.

Kaju Murgh (bottom) and Kitchri.

China

Of all the exotic far-eastern styles, Chinese cuisine must easily rank as emperor. Certainly it is the most varied, with 80 different cookery methods which can be used to create some 400,000 dishes. Chinese cuisine follows four basic concepts: taste, texture, quality and beauty. Indeed these principles are in complete accord with the nouvelle cuisine style which now has such an enthusiastic following in Europe. Crisp vegetables and tender meats, stir-fried to perfection, epitomize our impression of Chinese cookery but there are a wealth of styles to explore and master. The varying cuisines from the Chinese provinces – Canton, Peking, Szechuan, Hunan, Fukien and Shantung – include styles which span the spectrum from the subtle delicacy of steamed dim sum to the fiery piquancy of Szechuan hot and sour soup.

In the north of China, the old Imperial City gives its name to one of the most famous of all Chinese dishes, Peking Duck. This is a delicious mixture of tastes and textures: tender flakes of duck meat and crunchy skin are seasoned with fruity hoisin sauce and rolled up in a delicate pancake with tiny strips of crisp, raw vegetables.

In this region, strong, rich sauces are flavoured with the liberal use of dark soy sauce, garlic, ginger and other spices and flavourings. Wheat is the basic cereal grown here and it is used to make pancakes, noodles and dumplings.

Peking cuisine still shows influence from the Mongol invaders of earlier eras, and lamb, a meat largely disliked elsewhere in China, is popular in this region. Mongolian hot pot is a winter favourite; its huge pot of bubbling broth is used, fondue-style, to cook tiny strips of lamb. These are eaten with spicy sauces and the savoury broth, enriched with the meat juices, is drunk as a soup.

The milder climate of Shantung in the south, provides a variety of rich produce: vegetables, fruits, nuts and poultry.

China, showing the different regions and their food specialities.

Szechuan province, a fertile basin to the west, is renowned for its hot, piquant dishes and superb fungi, particularly truffles. Chillies, hot pepper oil and peppercorns are used with fermented rice, wine vinegar and sugar to create a fascinating range of hot-sour, savoury-spiced and sweet-hot-piquant dishes. In this inland region, smoking and pickling in salt and vinegar are techniques frequently used for preserving many foods. Szechuan pickles give a characteristic 'bite' to many of their dishes.

Between Szechuan and Shantung lies Hunan, another province known for its hot-spicy-sweet-sour sauces. This central region also uses techniques such as salting and smoking to preserve food and their smoked meats are particularly favoured. Hunan cooks also created the dip-fry method of cooking where the food is repeatedly dipped into boiling fat and then removed.

Coastal Fukien, lying east of Hunan, produces a fascinating range of unusual seafood dishes and delicate soups. Fukien cooks also have the reputation for snack-making, particularly spring rolls with their savoury fillings wrapped, parcel-like, in crisp paper-thin bean curd sheets.

The largest and most varied selections of Chinese dishes are found in the southern coastal region of Canton where farm produce and seafood are available all year round.

The most famous technique of all, in Chinese cooking, stir-frying, is as much an art as a way of cooking. The wok, a round, sloping-sided pan is perfect for this fast cooking. The food is constantly kept on the move around the pan and it is cooked in just a few moments, ensuring that the ingredients remain crisp and tender, retaining the natural goodness.

Dim sum, now internationally popular, originated in Cantonese teahouses where tiers of bamboo steamers were kept bubbling away all day, each one containing deliciously different tit-bits.

Speciality

Spring Rolls

This popular snack can be produced at home now that frozen spring roll wrappers are available from Chinese grocery shops. Thaw the wrappers before use.

Makes 8 ☆☆

Preparation: 30 minutes

Cooking: 20 minutes

---

8 ready-made spring roll wrappers
3 tablespoons groundnut oil
8oz (225g) prawns, pork or chicken, finely chopped, or a mixture of all three
2oz (50g) bok choy or Chinese leaves, finely shredded
2oz (50g) canned bamboo shoots, cut into strips
2oz (50g) bean sprouts
1 tablespoon dark soy sauce
½ teaspoon salt
1 tablespoon cornflour
oil for deep-frying

The flour paste:
1 tablespoon plain flour mixed with 1 tablespoon cold water

Heat the groundnut oil in a large wok, add the prawns, pork or chicken or a mixture and stir-fry for 4 minutes. Add the vegetables, soy sauce and salt and stir-fry for a further 2 minutes.

☐ Mix the cornflour with 2 tablespoons water and stir into the wok. Cook for another 2 minutes until the mixture has thickened, then remove from the heat and let cool slightly.

☐ Lay the wrappers out flat and spread 2 tablespoons of the mixture on the bottom half of each one. Fold over the top of the wrapper, then fold over the two sides and tightly roll up the pancake. Seal the edges with a little flour paste.

☐ Heat a large pan one-third full of oil to 350F (180C), then carefully slide in 2 rolls. Deep fry for 4 minutes, until golden and crispy, then drain on kitchen paper. Cook the remaining rolls in the same way and serve immediately.

A crisp Spring Roll, filled with a selection of vegetables, prawns and chicken.

Speciality

Gwoo Lo Yook
Sweet-sour pork

Serves 4   ☆☆☆
Preparation: 1 hour
Cooking: 30 minutes

1lb (450g) pork fillet, cut into 1in
   (2.5cm) cubes
2 tablespoons rice wine or dry sherry
$\frac{1}{4}$ teaspoon salt
$\frac{1}{2}$ teaspoon coarsely ground black pepper

The batter:
2 tablespoons flour
2 tablespoons water
1 tablespoon sesame oil
2 egg whites
oil for deep-frying

The sauce:
3 tablespoons groundnut oil
1 teaspoon fresh ginger root, grated
1 garlic clove, finely chopped
2 tablespoons dark soy sauce
1 tablespoon tomato purée
2 tablespoons red wine vinegar
3 tablespoons soft brown sugar
2 small onions, coarsely chopped
2oz (50g) canned water chestnuts, halved
2 tablespoons frozen peas, thawed
4in (10cm) piece of cucumber or 1 slice
   of unripe melon, cut into fine strips
2 teaspoons cornflour

Sprinkle the meat with half the rice wine or sherry and the salt and pepper and marinate for 30 minutes.
☐ Make a smooth batter by mixing the flour with 2 tablespoons water, then stir in the oil.
☐ One-third fill a deep-frying pan with oil and heat to 350F (180C).
☐ Heat the groundnut oil in a large wok and add the grated ginger and garlic. Stir-fry for 1 minute, then add the remaining wine, soy sauce, tomato purée, vinegar and sugar. Stir-fry for a further minute, then add the onions, water chestnuts and peas. Stir-fry for 5 minutes, then add the cucumber or melon.
☐ Mix the cornflour with 1 tablespoon cold water and stir into the wok. Continue cooking for 3-4 minutes until the sauce is thick.
☐ Whisk the egg whites until stiff and fold them into the batter. Dip the meat in the batter, then deep-fry for 3-4 minutes until golden and crisp. Remove from the pan and drain on kitchen paper.
☐ Pour the sauce on to a serving dish and arrange the meat on top. Serve with boiled rice.

Gwoo Lo Yook (Sweet-sour pork) served with boiled rice.

Soy Sauce
Made from fermented soya beans, soy sauce is widely used all over China. It comes in several different grades, from light to very dark. The lighter soy sauces are best used for dips and white meats and fish, while the darker ones impart a richer flavour and are suitable for spicier dishes or those requiring slow cooking.

Gwoo Lo Yook
Prawns can be substituted for the pork in this recipe. Instead of dipping them in batter and deep-frying them, stir-fry the prawns for 5 minutes in the wok with $\frac{1}{2}$ teaspoon cayenne pepper and the sauce ingredients plus $\frac{1}{2}$ green pepper.

Menu

Lahng Poon

Hai Yook Dhan Gung

Hung Shiu Yue Har Guen

Buck Ging Ngap
with
Pok Pang

Doong Fong Sik Gow Lahm

China tea or rice wine

Quantities given serve 6

Marbled Eggs

Hard boil 6 eggs for 10 minutes, then gently tap the shells all over with the back of a spoon making a very fine network of cracks. Return to the pan with cold water and 1 tablespoon black China tea, 2 tablespoons soy sauce, 1 teaspoon salt and 1 whole star anise. Bring to the boil, simmer for 1 hour – check water intermittently and add more if necessary – then leave eggs to cool in the pan. Just before serving carefully peel the eggs to reveal the beautiful marbled pattern.

Lahng Poon
Cold appetizers

Serves 6   ☆☆☆
Preparation: 1 hour
Cooking: 45 minutes plus cooling

---

8 dried Chinese mushrooms
1 tablespoon dark soy sauce
1 tablespoon soft brown sugar
2 teaspoons sesame oil
1 tablespoon groundnut oil
14oz (400g) canned abalone
8oz (225g) lean pork, grilled
7oz (200g) chicken breast, skinned
 and poached
6 Marbled Eggs (see sidelines)
1 small cucumber, obliquely sliced
3 giant radishes (mooli), thinly sliced

The marinade:
3 tablespoons soy sauce
1 tablespoon soft brown sugar
1 tablespoon rice wine or dry sherry
2 teaspoons sesame oil
½ teaspoon grated fresh ginger root

The garnish (optional):
2 tomatoes, skinned and sliced
parsley
spring onion curls

Rinse the mushrooms thoroughly, then put in a bowl of hot water and soak for 30 minutes. Drain them,

keeping 7 fl oz (200ml) of the liquid, then rinse again, cut off the stalks and slice the caps into fine strips.

☐ Mix the reserved liquid with the soy sauce, sugar and sesame oil, then heat the mixture until the sugar has dissolved and keep warm over a low heat.

☐ Heat the groundnut oil in a wok, add the mushrooms and fry for 3 minutes. Pour in the soy sauce mixture, stir well then reduce the heat and simmer for about 30 minutes, stirring from time to time, until most of the liquid has been absorbed by the mushrooms. Remove from the heat and cool.

☐ Meanwhile, drain the abalone and cut into thin slices. Slice the pork and chicken breast finely and peel the marbled eggs.

☐ Mix together the marinade ingredients, whisking until amalgamated. Put the abalone in a shallow bowl and pour just under half the marinade over. Leave to stand for 10 minutes.

☐ Arrange the vegetables, eggs and other appetizers on separate plates, pour marinade over the chicken and

pork, and serve the remainder separately in a sauceboat.

Tip: Garnish the appetizers with slices of tomato, parsley or the green tops of spring onions.

Hai Yook Dhan Gung

Fish soup with crab and egg

Serves 6 ☆
Preparation: 15-20 minutes
Cooking: 20 minutes

12oz (350g) white crab meat, fresh, canned, or frozen and defrosted
2 pints (1.2 litres) Fish Stock
2 teaspoons cornflour
1 tablespoon water
1 teaspoon light soy sauce
3 eggs, whisked thoroughly
6 spring onions, finely chopped

Flake the crab meat if necessary and remove any pieces of shell.

☐ Bring the stock to the boil over a high heat. Mix the cornflour with 1 tablespoon cold water and stir in the soy sauce. Add 2 tablespoons of the boiling stock, stir thoroughly then return to the pan and stir for 2-3 minutes, until slightly thickened.

☐ Add the crab meat to the pan, and then pour in the beaten eggs, whisking constantly so that the eggs form fine strands. Sprinkle over the spring onion and serve immediately.

Hung Shiu Yue Har Guen

Fish rolls with prawns

Serves 6 ☆
Preparation: 40 minutes
Cooking: 5 minutes

1¼lb (575g) filleted turbot, halibut or brill, cut into 18 thin equal slices
18 large prawns or crayfish tails, peeled, defrosted if frozen
   1 tablespoon lemon juice
   1 tablespoon groundnut oil
   1 tablespoon sesame oil
   7 fl oz (200ml) plus 1 tablespoon water
   1 teaspoon grated root ginger
   1 tablespoon light soy sauce
   1 tablespoon rice wine or dry sherry
1 teaspoon sugar
1 teaspoon cornflour
3 spring onions or 1 thin leek, finely chopped
1 stick of celery, finely sliced

Rinse the slices of fish under cold water, pat dry with kitchen paper and lay flat on a large plate. Sprinkle with lemon juice, then place one prawn or crayfish on each slice of fish. Roll up the slices and secure with cocktail sticks.

☐ Heat the oils in a wok and stir-fry the rolls for 2 minutes. Pour in 7 fl oz (200ml) boiling water, stirring all the time, then add the ginger, soy sauce, wine or sherry and sugar. Stir well then simmer for 1 minute.

☐ Mix the cornflour with 1 tablespoon of cold water, then push the ingredients in the wok to one

side. Stir the cornflour into the liquid, leave it to cook for 30 seconds, then return the rolls to the middle of the wok. Add the chopped spring onion or leek and the celery. Stir for a further minute, then serve immediately.

A Chinese menu for 6. From left to right Lahng Poon (Cold appetizers), Hai Yook Dhan Gung (Fish soup with crab and egg), Hung Shiu Yue Har Guen (Fish rolls with prawns), Buck Ging Ngap with Pok Pang (Peking roast duck with mandarin pancakes) and Doong Fong Sik Gow Lahm (Oriental fruit salad).

Buck Ging Ngap

Peking roast duck

A justly famous dish, the duck has a crisp, mahogany coloured skin which is traditionally eaten rolled in Mandarin pancakes with hoisin sauce, spring onions and cucumber. The real secret to achieving the crisp skin is to hang the duck up to dry in a breezy place, or in front of an electric fan, for 12 hours.

Serves 6   ☆ ☆

Preparation: 20 minutes plus
12 hours hanging
Cooking: about 1½ hours

4¼lb (2kg) duck
2 tablespoons dry sherry or rice wine
2 tablespoons dark honey or black treacle
1 tablespoon dark soy sauce
7 fl oz (200ml) hot water
18 Pok pang (Mandarin pancakes)
7 fl oz (200ml) hoisin sauce
5 spring onions, cut into 3in (7.5cm)
    long, ¼in (5mm) thick julienne strips
¼ cucumber, cut in julienne strips

Put the duck in a large bowl and slowly pour over 2 pints (1.2 litres) boiling water, making sure all the skin has some water poured over it. Pat dry with kitchen paper.

☐ Mix together the sherry or rice wine, honey or treacle, soy sauce and hot water, then brush this mixture all over the duck skin. Pull the wings away from the body and push a skewer through the bird behind the wings so that the wings are pinioned away from the body. Hang the duck up in a cool, draughty place for 12 hours to dry.

☐ Heat oven to 400F (200C) gas 6. Remove skewer and place the bird on a rack in a roasting pan and roast for 45 minutes.

☐ Reduce the heat to 375F (190C) gas 5, prick the duck all over with a fork, and roast for a further 40-50 minutes until very crisp and tender.

☐ To serve: Peel off the skin and cut into small pieces, then carve the flesh and cut into thin slices. Put on separate plates and serve with Mandarin pancakes, a bowl of hoisin sauce and plates of spring onions

and cucumber strips. To eat the duck, each person brushes a pancake with a little sauce, puts 2 or 3 pieces of spring onion and cucumber in the middle, then tops this with a piece of duck skin and flesh. Fold over the bottom of the pancake, and roll up.

Tip: Traditionally, this dish is served with spring onion brushes, one per person. To make the brushes, trim off the top 1in (2.5cm) of the green part, then make 2in (5cm) deep cuts, crossways, in the bulb of the onion up towards the stalk. Put the onions in a bowl of iced water until the 'brushes' open.

Pok Pang

Mandarin pancakes

Makes 18 pancakes   ☆

Preparation: 1 hour
Cooking: about 30 minutes

10oz (275g) flour
8 fl oz (250ml) boiling water
1-1½ tablespoons sesame oil

Sift the flour into a large bowl, add the water and stir thoroughly to form a dough (or put the sifted flour and water into a food processor and process until a ball of dough is formed).

☐ Flour a board and your hands and knead the dough until spongy and elastic, about 3-4 minutes. Cover with a damp cloth and leave for 30 minutes.

☐ Roll out the dough into a long cylinder 1in (2.5cm) in diameter. Cut the cylinder into 18 pieces – each about 1in (2.5cm) thick, and roll each piece into a very thin pancake 5in (13cm) in diameter.

☐ Brush each pancake with a little sesame oil, then sandwich two together, oiled side inwards.

☐ Put a frying-pan over a moderate heat for 30 seconds (do not oil the pan), then add a pair of pancakes. Cook for 1½ minutes until the pancake begins to bulge then flip over and cook the other side for 1½

minutes. Slide on to a plate, gently pull the pancakes apart, and then cook the remaining pancakes.

☐ Just before serving, place the pancakes in a steamer or colander over a pan of boiling water and steam them for 5-6 minutes.

Doong Fong Sik Gow Lahm

Oriental fruit salad

Serves 6   ○

Preparation: 40 minutes
Cooking: 5 minutes plus chilling

---

1 medium-sized watermelon
1 large ripe mango
4 mandarins
12 lychees, fresh or canned
2 tablespoons sugar
3 fl oz (75ml) water
1 tablespoon lemon juice, strained

Cut a large cap off the top of the watermelon and, using a melon baller, cut balls out of the flesh, including the cap, avoiding the seeds which should be discarded. Hollow out the melon completely, pat dry and put in the freezer for 30 minutes.

☐ Put the melon balls in a bowl in the refrigerator. Peel the mango, cut the fruit in 2 lengthways and remove the stone. Cut the flesh into small dice and refrigerate.

☐ Peel the mandarins and divide into segments, removing as many pips as possible. Refrigerate in another bowl.

☐ Peel the lychees if using fresh ones, or drain if canned, then slice the flesh off the stones. Refrigerate in a separate bowl.

☐ Make a sugar syrup by gently heating the sugar in 3 fl oz (75ml) water until the sugar has dissolved. Boil for 2 minutes, then remove from the heat and cool.

☐ Just before serving, mix all the fruits together, then spoon into the melon. Stir the lemon juice into the sugar syrup and pour over the fruit. Put on the melon cap and serve.

Japan

Although Japan has been subject to various foreign influences throughout history, it effectively remained a closed society, sealed off from the rest of the world, for an astonishing 200 years, until the middle of the 19th century. This partly explains why so much of Japanese culture and social life is veiled in mystery from the Western point of view – and the same is true of the Japanese style of cooking. Only recently has this fascinating cuisine become more familiar in the West: as increasing numbers of Japanese travel and go to work abroad, more Japanese food shops have opened in large cities, offering an intriguing glimpse into a way of life in which the rituals of eating and drinking play a fundamental part.

Although most Westerners are unfamiliar with the intricacies of Japanese culture, they will nevertheless be immediately struck by a number of features which characterize Japanese cooking: its essential simplicity; its use of absolutely fresh natural ingredients; and the elegance and artistry with which the food is garnished, presented and served.

As in Chinese cookery, Japanese food is usually cooked quickly, by a number of basically simple methods. Japanese dishes tend to be described collectively, according to the cooking method: 'teriyaki' describes foods that are marinated before grilling or frying; 'yakimono' is the collective term for grills; 'mushimono' means steamed foods. Some Japanese dishes require no cooking at all – 'shashimi', or raw fish, is probably the most famous example of this.

Other ingredients vital to Japanese cooking are 'tofu' (soy bean curd), 'shoyu' (soy sauce), 'mirin' (cooking wine) and 'miso' (bean paste). Rice is short grained, and there are a number of types of noodle including 'udon' made from white flour and 'soba' (buckwheat flour).

Japan was introduced to Zen Buddism, with its strong emphasis on vegetarianism, by the Chinese in the 13th century, and modern Japanese continue to eat very little meat; the best of their cooking is based on a wonderful range of vegetables and seafood, resulting in a very healthy diet.

A typical Japanese meal is not divided into courses. The food is presented all at once, and would almost certainly include a clear or thickened soup, a fish dish, a vegetable dish or a combination of both as in 'tempura', rice and pickles (tsukemono), of which the Japanese are particularly fond.

The meal would be served at a low table with the diners seated on low cushions.

In the old days, food used to be served at individual tables, and on formal occasions this custom is still sometimes followed today. The food is eaten with chopsticks (smaller and lighter than the Chinese variety), from the individual lacquer or china bowls.

Usually saké (rice wine) would be served in tiny cups as an aperitif or throughout the meal, or beef or ocha (unfermented green tea) might be drunk instead.

Although a dessert might be served for a special occasion, fresh fruit more commonly concludes a Japanese meal, and cakes, such as castera (a sponge cake) or omochi (rice cakes) tend to be eaten as snacks rather than as part of a meal.

Speciality

Tempura

Possibly the best known Japanese dish in the West, tempura consists of small pieces of fish and vegetables dipped in batter and deep-fried in oil. For perfect tempura, the batter should not be too thick so that the food fries really crisply, and the oil should be maintained at the correct temperature and skimmed frequently during frying.

Serves 4 ☆☆
Preparation: 20 minutes
Cooking: about 25 minutes

---

8 large prawns, peeled but with tails left on
8 mushrooms, stalks removed
1 large green pepper, cored, seeded and
    sliced into rings
1 small aubergine, sliced into ¼in (5mm) rings
1 onion, sliced into ¼in (5mm) rings
salt
600ml (1 pint) vegetable oil for frying

For the batter:
1 egg, size 2
¼ pint (150ml) water
3oz (75g) plain flour
1oz (25g) cornflour

For the sauce:
½ pint (300ml) Dashi (see page 273)
1 tablespoon mirin
1 tablespoon shoyu or soy sauce
2-3 tablespoons grated daikon

Sprinkle all the ingredients with salt. Heat the oil in a deep fat fryer to 180C (350F).

☐ Meanwhile, make the batter: Beat the egg with the water and sift in the flour and cornflour. Mix lightly and quickly, taking care not to over mix.

☐ Dip the prawns and vegetables into the batter, lower them into the hot oil in small batches and fry until light golden brown. Drain quickly on absorbent paper.

☐ Meanwhile make the sauce: Heat all the ingredients except the daikon to boiling point, then pour into individual small dishes and spoon a portion of grated daikon into the centre of each.

☐ Serve the tempura immediately, with sauce for dipping.

Suimono

Clear soup with prawns and chicken balls

―――――――

Serves 4 ☆
Preparation: 20 minutes
Cooking: 5 minutes

―――――――

4oz (100g) boneless chicken, minced
1½ tablespoons finely chopped ginger root
½ teaspoon shoyu or soy sauce
1 teaspoon egg white
salt
12 mangetout peas or French beans
1½ pints (900ml) Dashi (see sidelines)
  or Chicken Stock
½ teaspoon soy sauce or shoyu to finish
8 large prawns, cooked and peeled

―――――――

Place the chicken, ginger, soy sauce and egg white in a bowl and stir well to mix. Divide into 8 equal portions and shape into balls.

☐ Put the chicken balls in a pan of boiling salted water to cook for 3 minutes, then remove.

☐ Meanwhile cook the mangetout peas for 2 minutes, then rinse under cold running water and drain.

☐ Season the stock to taste with salt and stir in the soy sauce. Bring to the boil.

☐ Divide the chicken balls, mangetout and prawns between 4 heated individual soup bowls. Add the boiling stock and serve immediately.

Clockwise from the right: Suimono (Clear soup with prawns and chicken balls); Sunomono (Crab and cucumber salad); Tori No Teriyaki (Teriyaki chicken); Awajukikan (Snow jelly with strawberries).

Sunomono

Crab and cucumber salad

Serves 4   ☆

Preparation: 15 minutes

1 cucumber
salt
10oz (300g) cooked crab claws or crab meat,
    fresh, thawed if frozen, or canned
rice or prawn crackers to serve

The sauce:
1½ tablespoons white wine vinegar
1½ tablespoons shoyu or soy sauce
1½ tablespoons Dashi (see sidelines)
    or Chicken Stock
pinch of ajinomoto (monosodium glutamate)

Wash the cucumber and dry with kitchen paper. Trim off the ends and cut the cucumber in half lengthways. Remove the seeds from each half with a teaspoon. Cut each cucumber in half lengthways into 3 equal strips. Then cut each strip crossways into 2in (5cm) pieces.

☐ Place the cucumber in a colander set over a plate, sprinkle with salt and leave to drain for 10 minutes. Rinse under cold running water and dry with kitchen paper.

☐ Meanwhile remove the shell and cartilage from the crab claws, keeping the meat in one piece. Cut the crab meat into 2in (5cm) strips.

☐ Thoroughly combine all the sauce ingredients in a bowl, whisking with a fork to make sure they are well blended.

☐ Arrange the cucumber and crab meat strips upright to form a pyramid in each of 4 individual salad bowls.

☐ Just before serving, spoon the sauce over the salad.

☐ Serve with a bowl of rice or prawn crackers, which are widely available from supermarkets.

Variation: Omit the crab and marinate the salted and rinsed cucumber in the sauce for at least 1 hour. Serve small quantities as a side salad or relish. A little grated root ginger added to the sauce gives extra piquancy.

Tori No Teriyaki

Teriyaki chicken

Serves 4   ☆☆☆

Preparation: about 10 minutes
Cooking: about 15 minutes plus cooling

1½lb (750g) chicken leg pieces, boned
1½ teaspoons ground ginger
1½ tablespoons groundnut oil
1 teaspoon sesame seed oil
3 tablespoons shoyu or soy sauce
2 tablespoons mirin or dry sherry
2 teaspoons caster sugar
4oz (100g) lotus root
salt
3½ fl oz (100ml) white wine vinegar
¼ pint (150ml) Dashi (see sidelines or
    Chicken Stock
parsley sprigs to garnish

Dry the chicken meat with kitchen paper then rub the ginger into it.

☐ Heat the oils in a large frying-pan. Add the chicken and fry over a moderate heat for about 10 minutes until golden brown on all sides.

☐ Meanwhile stir the shoyu, mirin and sugar together until the sugar has dissolved. Pour over the chicken, cover and simmer gently for 5-6 minutes. Remove from the heat and leave to cool.

☐ Thinly peel and slice the lotus root (see right). Soak for 15 minutes in cold salted water to cover with a teaspoon of the vinegar.

☐ Put the dashi, the remaining vinegar and a pinch of salt in a saucepan and bring to the boil. Drain the lotus root slices and add to the pan. Cook for 2 minutes, then leave to cool in the liquid. Drain.

☐ Cut the chicken into finger-thick slices and arrange on a serving plate. Garnish with the lotus root slices and parsley sprigs and serve with boiled rice sprinkled with a little white wine vinegar and mirin.

Variations: Marinate the chicken in the remaining ingredients for several hours and grill, turning often, for about 20 minutes, brushing with the marinade from time to time.

● Roast the marinated chicken for about 30 minutes, basting often.

Dashi

Dashi stock, made from kombu (dried seaweed) and katsuobushi (dried bonito fish) is a basic ingredient in many Japanese dishes. Dashi powder, available from Japanese food shops, gives excellent results and is used as frequently by the Japanese as we in the West use stock cubes. To make homemade dashi, bring 2 pints (1.2 litres) water to the boil, add a 2in (5cm) piece of kombu and 2 tablespoons katsuobushi. Simmer, stirring, for 3 minutes, then remove from the heat, allow to stand for 5 minutes and strain.

Japanese-style Chicken Stock

If the ingredients for dashi are not available, make a chicken stock instead. Simmer 2 chicken joints and chicken bones in 2 pints (1.2 litres) water flavoured with spring onions, salt and a few slices of root ginger.

Shoyu – Japanese soy sauce
Mirin – Japanese rice wine which is used only for cooking. Dry sherry can be used as a substitute.

Shaping lotus root flowers

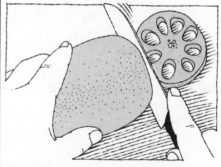

Cut the peeled lotus root crossways into thin slices.

Trim the outer edge of each slice to make a flower shape.

Beat the gelatine mixture until foamy.

Pour the foam mixture over the strawberries.

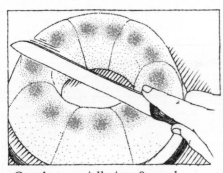
Cut the snow jelly into 8 equal portions.

Picture on opposite page—Sushi, from top to bottom: Norimaki-sushi, Inari-sushi, Nigiri-sushi, Fukusa-sushi. -

Awajukikan
Snow jelly with strawberries
An unusual, fresh looking dessert which is created by whisking the jelly when it is almost set, so that it forms a white foam.

Serves 4
Preparation: about 30 minutes, including standing, then 3-4 hours setting

---

3 teaspoons powdered gelatine
¾ pint (450ml) cold water
4oz (100g) caster sugar
16 fresh strawberries, hulled
extra strawberries to decorate
sponge fingers to serve

Place the gelatine in a large bowl and pour over ¼ pint (150ml) of the water. Stir well and leave to stand for 15 minutes, until spongy.
☐ Place the remaining water in a saucepan with the sugar and bring to the boil, stirring, until the sugar has dissolved.
☐ Remove the pan from the heat and set aside for 5 minutes.
☐ Pour the sugar syrup in a steady stream on to the gelatine, stirring all the time. Set aside until the mixture is on the point of setting, then beat with an electric or balloon whisk until the mixture is foamy.
☐ Chill for 5 minutes, then beat again until the mixture resembles snow.
☐ Rinse a 1 pint (600ml) ring mould with cold water. Arrange the strawberries in the base of the mould and pour the foam mixture over the top.
☐ Chill for 3-4 hours until set.
☐ To unmould, dip the mould in boiling water for a few seconds, then cover with an inverted plate and invert, giving the mould a sharp shake as you do so. Turn the jelly out on the plate.
☐ Cut into equal portions and serve decorated with extra strawberries.
☐ Accompany with sponge fingers, and small bowls or cups of Japanese green tea.

Sushi
Sushi are popular lunchtime snacks. They have one common feature in sushi rice, which is cooked with distinctive flavourings, then wrapped in seaweed, fried bean curd, wafer thin raw fish or omelette, or simply shaped into small cakes and topped with strips of raw fish.

Sushi Rice

Makes 24 Sushi
Preparation: 5 minutes
Cooking time: about 15 minutes

8oz (225g) short-grain rice
½ pint (300ml) cold water
salt
2-3 tablespoons Dashi (see sidelines page 273)
2-3 tablespoons white wine vinegar
2 tablespoons sugar
1 tablespoon mirin or dry sherry

Wash the rice thoroughly, drain and place in a saucepan with the water and a pinch of salt. Bring to the boil, then cover and boil gently for 15 minutes or until the rice is just tender and the liquid is absorbed.
☐ Remove from the heat, add the dashi and stir well. Combine the vinegar, sugar, 1½ teaspoons of salt and the mirin. Stir well. Pour over the hot rice and stir in quickly, then allow to cool before using. (The more quickly the sushi rice cools, the shinier the rice will be: the Japanese fan it to achieve the gloss much prized in sushi-making.)

Norimaki-sushi
Mix the cooked basic sushi rice with strips of omelette (see page 276) and 2 tablespoons finely chopped cucumber. Grill 6 sheets of nori (dried seaweed) until crispy, then lay flat on a board. Spoon the rice over the seaweed, roll up tightly and set aside for 10 minutes, then cut each roll into 4 pieces.

Inari-sushi

Place 12 sheets of aburage (fried bean curd), halved lengthways, in a colander and pour over boiling water. Drain, pat dry with kitchen paper and sprinkle with a little soy sauce and mirin. Divide the basic rice mixture between the bean curd sheets and roll up from one end. Slice.

Nigiri-sushi

Mix the basic rice with 5oz (150g) flaked crabmeat and divide between 24 thin slices (total weight $\frac{3}{4}$lb/ 350g) raw or smoked salmon. Roll up tightly.

Fukusa-sushi

Make 2 omelettes as described on page 276, spoon over the basic rice and roll up firmly. Set aside for 10 minutes, then cut the rolled omelettes into slices.

Dashimaki Tamago
Rolled omelette

Dashimaki Tamago – a rolled omelette flavoured with dashi and shoyu, which is served cold as a snack.

Serves 4 ☆☆
Preparation: 10 minutes
Cooking: 12-15 minutes plus cooling

6 eggs, beaten
pinch of salt
1½ teaspoons sugar
3½ fl oz (100ml) Dashi or Chicken Stock (see
    sidelines page 273)
2 teaspoons shoyu or soy sauce
1 tablespoon peanut oil

Beat together all the ingredients except the oil. Heat a large omelette pan (a special Japanese rectangular pan is ideal), brush with oil and pour in one-third of the egg mixture. Cook over moderate to low heat, turning once, until the omelette is light and golden on both sides, then roll up as illustrated.

☐ Brush the pan with more oil, and with the rolled omelette still in the pan, make another omelette in the same way with half the remaining egg. Unroll the first omelette over the second, then roll up again and push to the side of the pan.

☐ Repeat with the remaining egg, until you have 3 omelettes rolled up together. Allow to cool completely, then cut crossways into slices to serve.

Islamic Cooking

The Islamic religion arose in Arabia in the 7th century AD as a result of the teachings of the Prophet Muhammad, and spread rapidly to encompass the whole of the Middle East and Central Asia, from Spain to India and the islands of the Pacific. Islam is essentially a way of life, regulating social as well as spiritual existence. The Koran, its Holy Book, lays down detailed rules for everyday living, including a number on diet. Food is described as a gift from God, which perhaps explains the importance attached to cooking and eating as social activities, the essence of a way of life in which hospitality is of first importance, and where it is an equal honour to be a host or a guest.

Dishes tend to fall into two main categories: those that have origins in peasant cooking, and more sophisticated dishes dating back to the courts of the Caliphs. In both types the use of spices is of great importance, for Arab traders plied the spice routes from the Far East to Europe.

In the simpler, more rustic-type dishes, grains, nuts, pulses and fresh vegetables feature prominently: cracked wheat (also known as burghul or bulgur) combines with parsley in Tabbouleh, a very popular Lebanese salad, and with minced lamb in Kibbeh, a kind of meat paste that can be grilled or fried; couscous, a grain closely resembling semolina, is steamed over rich meat and vegetable stews; rice combines with meat, vegetables, fruit and nuts in pilafs. Pulses feature in stews, soups and side dishes such as Egyptian 'ful medames', and are used to make Ta'amia, savoury rissoles, and Hummus, a chick pea purée often combined with Tahina, a paste of roasted ground sesame seeds. Stuffed vegetables of all kinds are popular, onions being a Saudi favourite, and aubergines Turkish.

Dairy products have an important place in Islamic cooking; yogurt is used in soups, marinades, sauces and dressings, and to make a delicious cream cheese, Labna, often served for breakfast. Eggs are used to make Eggah, a thick, flat omelette.

Bread is a staple of the Islamic diet, and is usually flat, being unleavened or only slightly leavened. Pitta bread is perhaps the best-known type, but there are also sweet breads baked with dried fruit.

Other Islamic dishes that have been introduced to the West include charcoal-grilled and spit-roasted meat (usually lamb or poultry, for pork is prohibited by Islamic law), for example Doner kebab, Shish kebab and minced Kofta. Fruits such as apricots, apples, quinces, dates and currants combine with meat in Tagine, or stews, and are used in stuffings. Chicken stuffed with fruits is a speciality of Iran, and is representative of the more sophisticated Islamic cuisine, as is Faisinjan (duck with nuts and pomegranate sauce).

Pastries can be both savoury (Turkish Börek, for example), or sweet (like Baklava), and desserts include creamy milk puddings delicately flavoured with rose or orange blossom water, fruit compotes and Rahat Lokum—Turkish delight—perhaps the most famous of all.

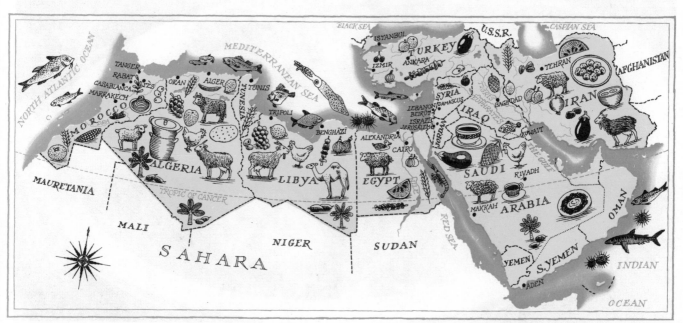

Menu

Imam Bayildi

Sayyadiyah

Baklava

White wine: Turkish Muscat

———————

*Quantities given serve 4
(except for the Baklava)*

Imam Bayildi literally means 'The priest fainted', probably at the delicious flavour of the dish, although it is sometimes said that the reason may have been the cost of the oil. However, good olive oil is absolutely essential to the flavour of the dish.
Serve Imam Bayildi as a substantial first course or light vegetarian main course, with hot pitta bread.

Imam Bayildi—stuffed and baked aubergines.

Turkey

Imam Bayildi

Stuffed aubergines

Serves 4 ☆☆☆
Preparation: about 45 minutes, including draining
Cooking: about 1 hour

2 medium aubergines
salt
¼ pint (150ml) olive oil
2 onions, roughly chopped
1 green pepper, cored, deseeded and
    chopped
1 garlic clove, very finely chopped
4 large tomatoes, skinned and chopped
freshly ground black pepper
1 teaspoon dried oregano
1 teaspoon caster sugar
3 tablespoons lemon juice
1oz (25g) pine kernels
1½ tablespoons chopped fresh parsley
¼ pint (150ml) boiling water
coriander leaves, to garnish

Cut the aubergines in half lengthways. Using a small sharp knife, cut out the flesh, leaving ½in (1cm) flesh inside the shells.

☐ Sprinkle the shells with salt. Chop the flesh into cubes and place in a colander set over a plate. Sprinkle with salt and leave for 30 minutes, then rinse flesh and shells under cold running water and pat dry.

☐ Heat oven to 325F (160C) gas 3. Heat 3 tablespoons of the oil in a large frying-pan with a lid, add the onion and fry gently for about 5 minutes, until soft.

☐ Add the green pepper, garlic, tomatoes and cubed aubergine. Mix well, cover the pan and fry gently for a further 3 minutes. Remove from the heat, season with salt and pepper and stir in the oregano, a pinch of sugar, 1 tablespoon of the lemon juice, the pine kernels and parsley.

☐ Pile the mixture into the aubergine shells. Place in a shallow ovenproof dish. Combine the remaining oil, lemon juice and sugar with the water, season with salt and pepper and pour around aubergines.

☐ Bake in the oven for 45-60 minutes, until tender, basting from time to time. Leave to cool.

☐ Serve garnished with coriander.

Sayyadiyah

Fish with rice

Serves 4 ☆☆☆
Preparation: 5 minutes
Cooking: about 1 hour

1½lb (750g) haddock fillets
3oz (75g) butter
8oz (225g) long-grain rice
salt and freshly ground black pepper
½ teaspoon powdered saffron
1 pint (600ml) boiling water
5 tablespoons lemon juice
4 tablespoons chopped parsley
3½ fl oz (100ml) olive oil
1 onion, finely chopped
4 tablespoons pine kernels
1 tablespoon raisins
1 teaspoon ground allspice
1 tablespoon dried mint
½ teaspoon ground cumin

Rinse the fish under cold running water and pat dry.

☐ Heat two-thirds of the butter in a large saucepan, add the rice and fry, stirring, for 2-3 minutes, until thoroughly coated. Season with salt and pepper and stir in the saffron, then pour in the water, boil, and cook, covered, for 15-20 minutes until the rice is just tender and the liquid is absorbed. Fork to separate the grains.

☐ Meanwhile, heat the oven to 325F (160C) gas 3. Melt half the remaining butter in a large shallow ovenproof dish. Add the fish, sprinkle with 2 tablespoons of the lemon juice and half the parsley and dot with the remaining butter. Season well and bake for 15-20 minutes or until the fish flakes easily.

☐ Remove the fish from the dish, flake coarsely, discarding any skin and bones, and set aside.

☐ Heat two-thirds of the oil in a large saucepan, add the onion and fry gently for 5 minutes. Add half the pine kernels, the raisins, allspice and rice, with 2 tablespoons of the lemon juice and the remaining parsley. Season and mix well.

☐ Spread half the rice over the base of the dish, top with half the fish,

then the remaining rice and the remaining fish.

☐ Heat the remaining oil in a small pan. Add the remaining pine kernels and lemon juice, with the mint and cumin, and fry, stirring, until the kernels are golden. Pour over the fish and cook for 10-15 minutes.

Baklava

Candied nuts in pastry

Makes about 24 ☆☆
Preparation: about 30 minutes
Cooking: about 1 hour

8oz (225g) unsalted butter, melted
1lb (500g) packet ready-made filo pastry
8oz (225g) pistachios or walnuts, shelled
  and chopped
2 tablespoons sugar

The syrup:
8oz (225g) sugar
¼ pint (150ml) water
1 tablespoon lemon juice
1 tablespoon orange blossom water

Make the syrup: Put the sugar into a saucepan with the water and lemon juice and bring to the boil. Stir until the sugar dissolves, then simmer for 10-15 minutes until syrupy. Add the orange blossom water and chill.

☐ Set oven to 350F (180C) gas 4.

☐ Brush a large deep ovenproof dish with butter. Arrange half the filo pastry sheets in the dish, brushing each with butter and trimming edges.

☐ Combine the nuts with the sugar and spread over the pastry. Cover with the remaining pastry sheets, brushing each sheet with butter and trimming the edges. Brush top with butter, then score diagonally into diamond shapes, cutting right through layers with a sharp knife.

☐ Bake the baklava for 30 minutes, then raise heat to 425F (220C) gas 7, and bake for a further 15 minutes, until puffed and light golden.

☐ Remove from the oven and immediately pour over the cold syrup. Leave to cool completely, then cut into pieces.

Baklava
The sugar syrup is ready when it will coat the back of a wooden spoon. It is important that it is of this correct consistency and that it is very cold when poured over the hot Baklava pastry.
Serve the Baklava as a dessert, with Turkish coffee to follow.

Börek
These small pastries, made with puff or filo pastry are filled with a savoury mixture and served as appetizers or snacks. To make your own, use frozen pastry and one of the fillings given below. Make small parcels – triangles, rounds, or 'half-moons'. Deep-fry, or bake in a moderate oven. Serve hot or cold.

Suggested fillings:
Meat
Fry a small, finely chopped onion in a little butter with 8oz (225g) minced lamb or beef until browned. Add 1 tablespoon chopped walnuts and season to taste with salt, pepper and allspice. Cook gently for 10 minutes, cool and use to fill the pastries.

Cheese
Crumble 8oz (225g) feta or halloumi cheese and mix it with a beaten egg, a little fresh chopped parsley, seasoning and crushed garlic to taste.

Spinach
Mix 8oz (225g) thawed frozen spinach with sultanas, 2 tablespoons lightly fried onions and 2 tablespoons toasted or fried almonds. Season with salt, pepper and nutmeg.

Kebabs
There are two distinct types of kebab: döner kebabs are made by winding and pressing long strips of lamb around a revolving spit. Slices of cooked meat are carved off, exposing the next layer to the heat.
Shish kebabs are made from cubes of meat threaded on skewers, grilled over charcoal.

Tabbouleh

Serve as part of a selection of salads with cold meats or buffet food.
Cracked wheat (burghul or bulgur) is available from better supermarkets and health food shops.

Faisinjan

Duck portions are available from the chilled cabinets of large supermarkets. Many supermarkets now stock a wide range of exotic fruit and vegetables, and pomegranates are often readily available. Chicken pieces may be substituted for duck.

Serve on a bed of plain boiled rice, or with steamed rice moistened with butter and a lightly beaten egg yolk.

Faisinjan is an ancient dish from the courts of the old Persian Empire and consists of duck, or chicken, simmered gently in a sauce flavoured with nuts and pomegranate juice.

Lebanon

Speciality

Tabbouleh

Cracked wheat and parsley salad

Serves 4
Preparation: 45 minutes, including soaking

8oz (225g) fine cracked wheat, soaked in cold water for 30 minutes
3 tablespoons finely chopped spring onions
3oz (75g) finely chopped fresh parsley
4 tablespoons chopped fresh mint or 2 tablespoons dried mint
4 tablespoons olive oil
4 tablespoons lemon juice
salt and freshly ground black pepper
crisp lettuce leaves, to serve

Drain the soaked cracked wheat very thoroughly, squeezing out the moisture with your hands.
☐ Place cracked wheat in a mixing bowl, add the spring onions and stir well to mix. Add the parsley, mint, oil and lemon juice and season to taste with salt and pepper. Stir well again.
☐ Pile the Tabbouleh into a salad bowl lined with lettuce leaves to serve.

Iran

Speciality

Faisinjan

Duck with nut and pomegranate sauce

Serves 4
Preparation: about 15 minutes
Cooking: about $1\frac{1}{2}$ hours

4 duck portions, each about 10oz (275g)
4 tablespoons olive oil
2 medium onions, chopped
1 teaspoon ground turmeric
12oz (350g) walnuts, finely ground
salt
$1\frac{3}{4}$ pints (1 litre) boiling water
juice of 2 pomegranates
juice of 2 lemons
3 tablespoons sugar
2 tablespoons chopped walnuts, to garnish

Pat the duck portions dry.
☐ Heat $1\frac{1}{2}$ tablespoons of the oil in a large saucepan, add the onion and fry gently for 5 minutes until soft and lightly coloured.
☐ Stir in the turmeric, then add the ground walnuts, a little salt and the water. Stir well to mix, bring to the boil, then lower the heat and simmer for 20 minutes, stirring from time to time.
☐ Heat the remaining oil in a frying-pan, add the duck portions and fry over a moderate heat, turning once or twice, until browned on all sides. Remove from the pan and drain on kitchen paper, then add to the nut sauce, turning to coat thoroughly. Cover and simmer for 40-50 minutes, stirring from time to time.
☐ Add the pomegranate and lemon juices with the sugar and mix well. Simmer for a further 20 minutes.
☐ Transfer the duck portions to a warmed serving dish and sprinkle with the chopped walnuts. Serve the sauce separately in a warmed bowl or jug.

Egypt

Speciality

Melokhia

Green leaf soup

Serves 4

Preparation: about 15 minutes

Cooking: about 15 minutes

1½lb (750g) lokhia or spinach

1¾ pints (1 litre) hot Chicken Stock

2 teaspoons olive oil

3 garlic cloves, finely chopped

2 teaspoons ground coriander

salt and freshly ground black pepper

Wash the lokhia or spinach very thoroughly in cold water and remove the stalks. Shred the leaves fairly finely.

☐ Put the leaves into a large saucepan with the stock and simmer very gently for 10 minutes.

☐ Meanwhile, heat the oil in a frying-pan, add the garlic and fry gently until soft and lightly coloured. Stir in the coriander.

☐ Add the garlic and coriander mixture to the soup, stir well and simmer for a further 5 minutes. Season to taste with salt and pepper and serve hot or cold.

Morocco

Speciality

Moroccan Couscous

Lamb and mixed vegetable stew

Serves 8   ☆☆

Preparation: about 15 minutes

Cooking: 2 hours

2lb (1kg) boneless lamb, trimmed and cut into 1½in (4cm) cubes

2 onions, chopped

2oz (50g) chick peas, soaked overnight, then drained

2 small turnips, peeled and quartered

2 carrots, sliced

2 tablespoons olive oil

¼ teaspoon ground ginger

¼ teaspoon powdered saffron

salt and freshly ground black pepper

1lb (500g) couscous

2oz (50g) raisins

2 large courgettes, sliced

4oz (100g) shelled broad beans

2 tomatoes, quartered

4 tablespoons chopped fresh parsley

1 teaspoon cayenne pepper

1 teaspoon sweet paprika

1oz (25g) butter

Put the lamb, onion, chick peas, turnip and carrot into the bottom section of a double steamer or a large saucepan with a tight-fitting lid. Pour in fresh cold water to cover, stir in the oil, ginger and saffron and season with salt and pepper. Bring to the boil, then lower the heat and simmer for 1 hour.

☐ Moisten the couscous with a little water, breaking it up with your fingers to prevent lumps from forming. Place the couscous in the top part of the steamer, or in a sieve placed over the saucepan, cover tightly with a lid or foil and cook for a further 30 minutes.

☐ Remove the couscous and moisten with a little more water, forking through the grains.

☐ Add the raisins, courgettes, beans, tomatoes and parsley to the stew, then return the couscous to the top of the steamer and simmer for a further 30 minutes.

☐ Ladle out a cupful of the sauce and pour into a warmed jug. Stir in the cayenne and paprika. Spoon the couscous on a warmed serving dish, fork in the butter and pile the meat and vegetables on top.

☐ Serve with the sauce handed separately.

Variations: Throughout the Islamic world the quantities and actual ingredients of couscous dishes vary widely, and they also change in the same district according to seasonal availability. Try using half lamb and half chicken as a base, or try adding peeled button onions, sliced red or green peppers and fresh peas to the stew.

Moroccan Couscous

Couscous is a very typically Arab dish in that the cooking time is relatively long compared to the preparation; the dish is cooked on top of the stove (ovens are comparatively rare in the Islamic countries for cooking food other than bread); and the utensils – in Morocco a special couscousière would be used – are very similar to those used in ancient times.

Melokhia

Lokhia, which closely resembles spring greens, is available from Asian food stores, but fresh spinach makes a good substitute. This soup would make a pleasant first course for a simple supper, perhaps followed by an Eggah made with courgettes or leeks.

Mint tea

Alcohol is forbidden by Islamic law, so a variety of other drinks is popular: there are thirst-quenching sherbets, creamy yogurt-based drinks and fragrant teas, including the favourite mint tea – which is especially popular in Morocco. To make mint tea, use 1 tablespoon of fresh or frozen mint or 1 tablespoon of dried mint leaves per cup. Add freshly boiled water and leave to infuse for 5 minutes. Sweeten to taste with honey or sugar. Serve garnished with a slice of lemon. Traditionally, mint tea is served very sweet.

Eggah

This is simply a firm egg 'cake' which can be served hot or cold as an hors d'oeuvre, as a side dish for grilled meats, or as a main course with a salad. To make a courgette Eggah, trim and slice 1lb (500g) courgettes. Boil them briefly in salted water until cooked but still crisp. Drain well then add 6 large beaten eggs. Melt a little butter in a frying-pan, pour in the mixture, season lightly and cook over low heat until eggs are set. Quickly brown the top under a pre-heated hot grill, then turn out on to a plate and cut in portions to serve.

Index